Yale French Studies

50 Years of *Yale French Studies:* A Commemorative Anthology Part 2: 1980–1998

Yale French Studies

Charles A. Porter and Alyson Waters, *Special editors for this issue*

Alyson Waters, *Managing editor*

Editorial board: Edwin Duval (Chair), Patricia Armstrong, Ora Avni, R. Howard Bloch, Peter Brooks, Susan Brubaker-Cole, Shoshana Felman, Françoise Jaouën, Christopher Miller, Charles A. Porter, Susan Weiner

Editorial assistant: Jeffery D. Boyd

Editorial office: 82-90 Wall Street, Room 308

Mailing address: P.O. Box 208251, New Haven, Connecticut 06520-8251

Sales and subscription office:

Yale University Press, P.O. Box 209040

New Haven, Connecticut 06520-9040

Published twice annually by Yale University Press

Designed by James J. Johnson and set in Trump Medieval Roman by The Composing Room of Michigan, Inc. Printed in the United States of America by the Vail-Ballou Press, Binghamton, N.Y.

ISSN 044-0078
ISBN for this issue 0-300-08324-6

ALYSON WATERS

Preface to Part 2

This second part of an anthology that commemorates the first 50 years of *Yale French Studies* (1948–1998) begins with the 1980s and takes us to today.

Now that readers can have both parts in hand, with their total of nineteen previously published articles, several short prefatory pieces, and the two indexes (volume and author) at the back of this volume, they can complete that "stroll through the archives" of *YFS* mentioned in the general introduction to the anthology included in Part 1.

The nineteen articles were selected out of a total of over 1,400 and should, we hope, serve to whet the reader's appetite, tempting him or her to take a more leisurely, less "directed" ramble through the pages of *Yale French Studies* that could not be included here.

The indexes are first of all meant to act as indicators of what we have had to exclude, but they are fascinating documents in themselves: they have much to teach us about the journal's evolution as it reflects both trends in French studies in general and the idiosyncrasies of the Yale French Department.

A perusal of the volume index reveals, in a new light, the sheer variety of topics featured in *YFS* over the years, and underscores the need for the continued existence of such a journal—that rare space where it is still possible to explore a single theme or author in depth.

This perusal also serves to point to several topics whose appearance or reappearance in our pages is long overdue. For example, the last *Yale French Studies* devoted to the visual arts was number 19–20 (*Contemporary Art*), published in Spring 1957–Winter 1958. While France may not be the mecca for painters that it was in the early days of *YFS*, it is safe to say that there has been sufficient activity—both critical and creative—to warrant another volume on the visual arts in

YFS 97, *50 Years of Yale French Studies, Part 2*, ed. Porter and Waters, © 2000 by Yale University.

France in the last forty years. Fortunately, some of the recent and up-coming volumes use an interdisciplinary approach, in which the visual arts indeed figure prominently.

And what of poetry? The last time a volume was devoted solely to poetry was also in 1958! An article from that volume, "On Bonnefoy's Poetry," by Mario Maurin, appears in the first part of this anthology. The diverse poetic activity of the past ten years in France—the poets of the "new lyricism," or those gathered around Editions P.O.L, to name only two of many possible examples—makes a volume on poetry long overdue.

"Feminism" has fared somewhat better. In 1961, *Women Writers* (27) appeared, with essays on Simone de Beauvoir, Elsa Triolet, Marguerite Duras, Nathalie Sarraute, and Marguerite Yourcenar, along with an opening essay by Edith Kern entitled "Author or Authoress?" In 1981, *Feminist Readings: French Texts/American Contexts* (62) appeared and, in the true feminist cooperative spirit of the time, it had *seven* special editors, all women, and all the articles were written by women. The year 1988 witnessed the birth of *The Politics of Tradition: Placing Women in French Literature* (75) and this time 2 men were included in the table of contents. In 1995, *Another Look, Another Woman: Retranslations of French Feminism* (87) appeared, again with an all female cast. Still, the first and only volume devoted to an authoress/*écrivaine* appeared in 1986, on Simone de Beauvoir, whereas I have counted nineteen volumes devoted to authors/*écrivains* from Gide (1951) to Blanchot (1998). Here again, then, there is room for improvement, especially considering the remarkable flowering of fiction by French and francophone women in the last two decades, not to mention women *cinéastes*.

And speaking of cinema: *The Art of Cinema* was published in 1956 (17), with essays on Ophuls, Clouzot, Cocteau, Renoir, Buñuel, among others, and a bibliography of books in French on the cinema. Twenty-four years later, *Cinema/Sound* was published (60), with articles that stressed the role of music and voice in the films of Bresson, Duras, and Renoir, among others. But this was already two decades ago. Has anything happened in French and francophone cinema since? The answer, emphatically, is yes.

Now, speaking of francophone. Unsurprisingly, very few articles on or by what today is called "francophone" writing appeared in the journal's pages before the 1970s. An essay on "French Negro Poetry" by François Hoffman appears in the 1958 *Poetry since the Liberation* and one on the *écrivaine québecoise* Anne Hébert, entitled "Anne Hébert: Rebirth in the Word" appears in the 1970 *Language in Action* (45). In 1976, a volume entitled *Traditional and Contemporary African Literature* appeared (53), edited by Hilary H. Okam, who wrote that the purpose of the volume was twofold: to "introduce the amateur of African literature to its myriad genres and broad scope" and to measure its literary creativity and esthetic achievement.[1] In 1983, *The Language of Difference: Writing in QUEBEC(ois)* (65) was published. And ten years later, the double volume *Post/Colonial Conditions: Exiles, Migrations, and Nomadisms* appeared. In the introduction to the first of those volumes, the editors Françoise Lionnet and Ronnie Scharfman sound a note very similar to Okam's above, and insist that the significance of their project "lies in its effort to rise above the particularist approaches of criticism which tend to compartmentalize literatures according to ethnogeographical categories."[2] A recent (November 1999) conference at Yale on the place of francophone studies in French departments and curricula demonstrated that these words are still topical.

But here I have been cheating, as I look at the volumes themselves rather than just the volume index. In any event, these are just a few of the topics that *YFS* will no doubt explore in the near future. Upcoming issues now include interdisciplinary approaches to "The French 50s" and "France/USA: The Cultural Wars," and a volume on "Belgian Memories," with essays by Belgian, American, French, and Dutch scholars, on everything from Belgian *bandes dessinées* to urban development. And so, scanning the volume index, each reader can play the game of weighing what has been sufficiently examined as opposed to what remains to be done.

Turning briefly now to the author index, we see it was in the early years, because of the then very "in-house" nature of the journal, that authors were inclined to "recidivate." The winner for most articles in *YFS* is Jacques Guicharnaud, who was recently made Chevalier des arts et des lettres (although probably not for winning this particular contest!), and who clocks in with sixteen (!) articles between 1951 and 1971. (One of those, "Existentialism: The Early Years," from *YFS* 16, is reprinted in the first volume of this anthology). Runners-up include

1. Hilary H. Okam, "Introduction." *Yale French Studies* 53, *Traditional and Contemporary African Literature*, 1976, 3.
2. Francoise Lionnet and Ronnie Scharfman, "Editors' Preface." *Yale French Studies* 82, *Post/Colonial Conditions: Exiles, Migrations, and Nomadisms*, 1993, 1.

Jacques Ehrmann (14 articles), Henri Peyre (also 14), and Victor Brombert (12). This index can be read as a kind of "who's who," with some no doubt surprising discoveries for all.

This anthology has been a cooperative effort from start to finish. As Managing Editor of the journal, and as co-special editor of this anthology, I would particularly like to thank Georges May for sharing his reminiscences, and for providing clarification of some of the mysterious pseudonyms that appeared in the early years; Charles Porter, who unselfishly agreed to co-special edit this volume, sharing thereby much drudgery (and, one hopes, some glory); Daryl Lee and James Austin, who worked countless hours in the preparation of the indexes; and those members of the *YFS* editorial board who collectively read through the fifty years of *Yale French Studies* to select and preface the articles that appear in both parts: Ora Avni, Howard Bloch, Françoise Jaouën, Charles Porter, and Susan Weiner.

I. 1980–1989

SUSAN WEINER

The 1980s

What has been the "lesson of Paul de Man" and the critical methodology of deconstruction that defined Yale from the mid-seventies
through the late eighties? When the commemorative *Yale French
Studies* volume appeared in 1985 less than a year after his death, the
lesson seemed clear: that ultimately nothing, in texts or in human experience, lies outside of language. Four years later, with the discovery
of his literary column for the Belgian collaborationist newspaper *Le
soir,* de Man's lesson turned on him as an accusation. In the American
media, his name became indelibly associated with a willful and suspect evasion of history, politics, and ethical reflection. The academic
response was divided: while there remained orthodox de Manians in
literature departments, by the end of the decade the dominance of de-
constructive close readings gave way to the latest variation of a brand
of scholarship where the referent had never lost its potency: historicism. De Man's lesson seemed no longer relevant. And yet, ironically,
it was. As we can see in "'Conclusions' on Walter Benjamin's 'The
Task of the Translator',," the allegedly ahistorical stance of deconstruction gestures toward the awareness that texts are cultural artifacts, and contains the possibility of reading historically.

"'Conclusions' " provides a good example of what history means
for deconstruction: it is a form of translation. Translation is the literal
example of what de Man calls "interlinguistic phenomena." Like critical philosophy, literary theory, and history, translation is a "secondary activity" in that it does not imitate or resemble the original,
but "relate[s] to what in the original belongs to language and not to
meaning." The secondary activity thus reveals that aspect of the original that is vacillating, mobile, and unreliable. Taking interlinguistic
phenomena together, as de Man does with Benjamin's text in the orig-

YFS 97, *50 Years of Yale French Studies, Part 2*, ed. Porter and Waters, © 2000
by Yale University.

inal German and the French and English translations, exposes both the necessary failure of the secondary activity to pin down in language what cannot be fixed—in the world, in the poetic text, in the past, in another language—and the essential failure of the original to communicate a definitive meaning. As a pithy example of this two-sided faltering, de Man notes that, while interlinguistic phenomena are not based on resemblance, the German word for translation also means metaphor: "The metaphor is not a metaphor," he writes, a sentence that comes as the dramatic and vertiginous culmination of a complex and careful argument. It is also a sentence that lends itself to the academy-bashing whose floodgates have remained open ever since the revelation of the *Le soir* writings.

But the unreliability of rhetoric was not an impediment to understanding for de Man; in deconstruction the workings of metonymy are inseparable from those of ideology. Both are movement that "never reaches its mark." Scholars working to historicize texts as cultural artifacts have renegotiated this relationship, putting the emphasis on ideology as a force that does indeed reach its mark as the capacity to shape historical understandings of texts and of the world. Joan DeJean's essay, "Classical Reeducation: Decanonizing the Feminine," examines the course by which literary history is actually constructed, taking as her test case the category of "classic" and its reconstitution from the late seventeenth to the mid-eighteenth centuries. This was a period of contest over the place of women writers, whose prominence and visibility on the literary scene of the time can be partially attributed to the cultural work of anthologies that then were arbiters of worldly adult tastes. The challenge to literary anthologies destined for adult readers took the form of the new pedagogical canon: tool of the developing national education program, which was seeking to instill a sense of citizenship in French youth through the space of the classroom. In this process culminating in the early nineteenth century, works of women writers deemed unsuitable for children of school age and unrepresentative of the dominant concept of a universal "human nature" passed to a position of marginality and negative exemplarity, anthologized only to explain why they should not be read.

DeJean points to a pivotal moment in modern French cultural history when "classic" came to mean "exemplary" for literary works, a signifier of greatness that carried with it an obligatory pedagogical suitability. Pedagogical choices also interest Kristin Ross, whose essay "Rimbaud and the Transformation of Social Space" goes against the grain of the long-standing "cult of the masterpiece" that is our traditional approach to the study of poetry. Ross convincingly demonstrates that Rimbaud's poetry demands a political reading alongside the Communards' acts in the streets of Paris: as a "site of interactions," a making do with everyday materials: "Trouve des Fleurs qui soient des chaises!" Poetic texts and social context collide on the same plane in Ross's examination of the revolutionary acts and dreams of exploding Haussmanized Paris in its ordered topography and accompanying social stratification. The resistance of Rimbaud's poetry to the sort of linguistic reading whose goal is to unveil the protean quality of language and experience brings Ross back to history, specifically literary history. She hypothesizes that the modernist canon has placed Rimbaud second to Mallarmé because it is Mallarmé's hermetic poetry that lends itself most readily to the close readings that establish masterpieces in academia. Just as DeJean does for women writers and the canon in modern France, Ross reveals and situates the role that ideology plays in shaping contemporary notions of literary greatness that are inherited unquestioningly. For DeJean that ideology is citizenship and universalism; for Ross, though not explicitly, it is deconstruction—for Mallarmé is one of deconstruction's favored poets. Both of these scholars take into consideration literary texts as they have been traditionally framed, stepping back in order to reframe them in the stakes of their particular historical moment: a critical move that has been the most durable of de Man's lessons.

PAUL DE MAN

"Conclusions" on Walter Benjamin's "The Task of the Translator" Messenger Lecture, Cornell University, March 4, 1983 *

Editorial Note

What appears here is an edited transcript of the last of six Messenger Lectures delivered at Cornell in February and March of 1983. The text is based on a collation of three sets of tape recordings, supplemented with eight pages of manuscript notes. Aside from differences in detail, formulation, and emphasis, the notes diverge significantly from the tapes only on the last sheet, where de Man wrote: "Im Anfang war das Wort und das Wort war bei Gott/Dasselbe war bei Gott/ohne Dasselbe" (the last two words lined out)—the beginning of Luther's translation of St. John's gospel, which Benjamin quotes in Greek and to which de Man made reference in the question session following the Cornell lecture. This text retains traces of the context in which the lecture was delivered, notably in references to the three preceding lectures. **

Though the task of the transcriber—to give to an unwritten text the afterlife of canonicity—may be undertaken only by suspending the ideal of fidelity that underwrites it, I have tried wherever possible to resist the necessity of fixing or immobilizing passages which appeared to be still underway toward formulation. De Man's sometimes unnaturalized English has been preserved, with the exception of a few modifications attempted for the sake of coherence. Some sentences, and a few paragraphs, had to be rearranged. Solecisms and redundan-

*From *Yale French Studies* 69 (1985): *The Lesson of Paul de Man*.

** Hegel on the Sublime" (in Mark Krupuick, ed., *Displacement: Derrida and After*, Bloomington: University of Indiana Press, 1983), "Phenomenality and Materiality in Kant" (in Shapiro and Sica, *Hermeneutics: Questions and Prospects*, Amherst: University of Massachusetts Press, 1983), añd "Kant and Schiller" (unpublished).

YFS 97, *50 Years of Yale French Studies, Part 2*, ed. Porter and Waters, © 2000 by Yale University.

cies have been retained, however, where the possibility of foregrounding a gap between oral performance and printed text seemed to outweigh the likelihood of inconvenience; in this way I have tried to transmit some of the burden and risk of reconstruction on to the reader. Omissions and emendations are intended to conform to this principle. I have punctuated less with an eye to correct usage than with the aim of remaining faithful to the tentative nature of the act of transcription. Here it was my intention to reproduce the pace of oral delivery and to close off as few readings as possible, even when leaving ambiguities open may have been less true to de Man's intent than to a certain reluctance to compromise the instability of this artifact. Paragraphing generally follows de Man's oral pauses and the repetitions of thesis statements with which he seemed to demarcate articulations in his argument; such breaks are to an extent reflected in the manuscript outline. Except for a few passages in which de Man adopts Harry Zohn's translation, quotations in this text reproduce de Man's own impromptu translations, which sometimes bear little resemblance to the available English translations cited in my notes.

The article is printed with the kind permission of the University of Minnesota Press to whom it had been promised.

—William D. Jewett

I at first thought of leaving this last session open for conclusions and discussion; I still hope for the discussion, but I have given up on the conclusions. It seemed to me best, rather than trying to conclude (which is always a terrible anticlimax), just to repeat once more what I have been saying since the beginning, using another text in order to have still another version, another formulation of some of the questions with which we have been concerned throughout this series. It seemed to me that this text by Benjamin on "The Task of the Translator" is a text that is very well known, both in the sense that it is very widely circulated, and in the sense that in the profession you are nobody unless you have said something about this text. Since probably most of us have tried to say something about it, let me see what I can do, and since some of you may be well ahead of me, I look forward to the questions or suggestions you may have. So, far from concluding or from making very general statements, I want to stay pretty close to this particular text, and see what comes out. If I say stay close to the text, since it is a text on translation, I will need (and that is why I have all these books) translations of this text; because if you have a text which says it is impossible to translate, it is very nice to see what happens when that text gets translated. And the translations confirm, brilliantly, beyond any expectations which I may have had, that it is impossible to translate, as you will see in a moment.

Nevertheless, I have placed this within a kind of framework, a framework which is historical. Since the problems of history have come up frequently, I thought it would be good to situate it within a historical or pseudohistorical framework, and then to move on from there. Therefore I start out with a recurrent problem in history and historiography, which is the problem of modernity. I use as an introduction into this a little essay by the German philosopher Gadamer, who in a collection called *Aspekte der Modernität* wrote, many years ago, interesting articles called "Die philosophischen Grundlagen des zwanzigsten Jahrhunderts" ["The Philosophical Foundations of the Twentieth Century"]. Gadamer asks the somewhat naive but certainly relevant question, whether what is being done in philosophy in the twentieth century differs essentially from what was being done before, and if it then makes sense to speak of a modernity in philosophical speculation in the twentieth century. He finds as the general theme, the general enterprise of contemporary philosophy, a critical concern with the concept of the subject. Perhaps one wouldn't say this now, which perhaps dates this piece a little, but it is still relevant. His question then is whether the way in which the critique of the concept of the subject is being addressed by present-day philosophy, differs essentially from the way it had been addressed by the predecessors of contemporary philosophy, in German Idealist philosophy—in some of the authors with whom we have been concerned, such as Kant, Hegel, and others. He writes the following sentence, which is our starting point:

> Is the critique of the concept of the subject which is being attempted in our century something else, something different from a mere repetition of what had been accomplished by German Idealist philosophy— and, must we not admit, with, in our case, incomparably less power of abstraction, and without the conceptual strength that characterized the earlier movement?[1]

1. The German text, which appeared in *Aspekte der Modernität* (Göttingen: Vanderhoeck & Ruprecht, 1965), 77–100, is most readily available in Gadamer's *Kleine Schriften* (Tübingen: J. C. B. Mohr, 1967), v. 1, 131–48. An English translation may be found in the collection *Philosophical Hermeneutics*, trans., David E. Linge, (Berkeley: University of California Press, 1976), 107–29. Cf. *Kleine Schriften*, v. 1, 141; *Philosophical Hermeneutics*, 119.

Is what we are doing just a repetition? And he answers, surprise: "There is not the case." What we are doing really is something new, something different, and we can lay claim to being modern philosophers. He finds three rubrics in which we—contemporary philosophers—he, Gadamer—is ahead of his predecessors, and he characterizes these three progressions in terms of a decreased naiveté. To us now it seems, if we look back on Hegel or Kant, that there is a certain naiveté there which we have now grown beyond. He distinguishes between three types of naiveté, which he calls *Naivität des Setzens* (naiveté of positing), *Naivität der Reflexion* (naiveté of reflection), and *Naivität des Begriffs* (naiveté of the concept).

Very briefly, what is meant by the first, by a certain naiveté of position, is a critique which we have been able to develop of pure perception and of pure declarative discourse, in relation to the problem of the subject. We are now ahead of Hegel in that we know better that the subject does not dominate its own utterances; we are more aware that it is naive to assume that the subject really controls its own discourse; we know this is not the case. Yet he qualifies this one bit: nevertheless, understanding is available to us to some extent, by a hermeneutic process in which understanding, by a historical process, can catch up with the presuppositions it had made about itself. We get a development of Gadamer, disciple of Heidegger, of the notion of a hermeneutic circle, where the subject is blind to its own utterance, but where nevertheless the reader who is aware of the historicity of that blindness can recover the meaning, can recover a certain amount of control over the text by means of this particular hermeneutic pattern. This model of understanding is ahead of the Hegelian model exactly to the same extent that one could say that the hermeneutics of Heidegger are ahead of the hermeneutics of Hegel, in Gadamer's sense.

He then speaks of the naiveté of reflection, and develops further what is already posited in the first; namely, he asserts the possibility now of a historicity of understanding, in a way that is not accessible to individual self-reflection. It is said that Hegel, in a sense, was not historical enough, that in Hegel it is still too much the subject itself which originates its own understanding, whereas now one is more aware of the difficulty of the relationship between the self and its discourse. Where in the first progression he refers to Heidegger's contribution, here he refers very much to his own contribution: historicizing the notion of understanding, by seeing understanding (as the later *Rezeptionsästhetik*, which comes from Gadamer to a large extent, will develop it) as a process between author and reader in which the reader acquires an understanding of the text by becoming aware of the historicity of the movement that occurs between the text and himself. Here Gadamer also makes a claim that something new is going on nowadays, and indeed, the stress on reception, the stress on reading, are characteristics of contemporary theory, and can be claimed to be new.

Finally, he speaks of the naiveté of the concept, in which the problem of the relationship between philosophical discourse and rhetorical and other devices which pertain more to the realm of ordinary discourse or common language were not, with Kant and Hegel, being examined critically. We alluded to an example of that yesterday when Kant raises the problem of *hypotyposis* and invites us to become aware of the use of metaphors in our own philosophical discourse. That type of question, which at least was mentioned by Kant, and was mentioned by Hegel much less, is now much more developed. Gadamer's allusion is to Wittgenstein, and also indirectly to Nietzsche. We no longer think, says Gadamer, that conceptual and ordinary language are separable; we now have a concept of the problematics of language which is less naive in that it sees to what extent conceptual philosophical language is still dependent on ordinary language, and how close it is to it. This is the modernity which he suggests, and which he details by these three indications.

Now although this is Kantian to some extent in its critical outlook, it is still very much a Hegelian model. The scheme or concept of modernity, as the overcoming of a certain nonawareness or naiveté by means of a critical negation, by means of a critical examination which implies the negation of certain positive relationships and the achieving of a new consciousness, allows for the establishment of a new discourse which claims to overcome or to renew a certain problematic. This pattern is very traditionally Hegelian, in the sense that the development of consciousness is always shown as a kind of overcoming of a certain naiveté and a rise of consciousness to another level. It is traditionally Hegelian, which does not mean that it is in Hegel, but it is in Hegel the way Hegel is being taught in the schools. Indeed, Gadamer ends his piece with a reference to Hegel:

> The concept of spirit, which Hegel borrowed from the Christian spiritual tradition, is still the ground of the critique of the subject and of the subjective spirit that appears as the main task of the post-Hegelian, that is to say modern, period. This concept of spirit (*Geist*), which transcends the subjectivity of the ego, finds its true abode in the phenome-

non of language, which stands more and more as the center of contemporary philosophy.[2]

Contemporary philosophy is a matter of getting beyond Hegel in Hegelian terms, by focusing the Hegelian *démarche*, the Hegelian dialectic more specifically on the question of language. That is how modernity is here defined, as a Hegelianism which has concentrated more on linguistic dimensions.

If we compare the critical, dialectical, nonessentialist (because pragmatic to some extent, since an allowance is made for common language) concept of modernity which Gadamer here advances, with Benjamin's text on language in "The Task of the Translator," then at first sight, Benjamin would appear as highly regressive. He would appear as messianic, prophetic, religiously messianic, in a way that may well appear to be a relapse into the naiveté denounced by Gadamer; indeed, he has been criticized for this. Such a relapse would actually return to a much earlier stage even than that of Kant, Hegel, and idealist philosophy. The first impression you receive of Benjamin's text is that of a messianic, prophetic pronouncement, which would be very remote from the cold critical spirit which, from Hegel to Gadamer, is held up as the spirit of modernity. Indeed, as you read this text, you will have been struck by the messianic tone, by a figure of the poet as an almost sacred figure, as a figure which echoes sacred language. All references to particular poets in the text put this much in evidence. The poets who are being mentioned are poets one associates with a sacerdotal, an almost priestlike, spiritual function of poetry: this is true of Hölderlin, of George, and of Mallarmé, all of whom are very much present in the essay.

(Since I mention George, one is aware of the presence of George—a name which has now lost much of its significance, but which at that time in Germany was still considered the most important, central poet, although in 1923 or 1924 when this was written this was already getting toward its end. For example, Benjamin quotes Pannwitz, a disciple of George, at the end of the text. And he refers to George in a relevant way; in George there was a claim made for the poet again as some kind of prophet, as a kind of messianic figure—George doesn't kid around with that, he sees himself at least as Virgil and Dante combined into one, with still quite a bit added to it if necessary—therefore he has a highly exalted notion of the role of the poet, and incidentally

2. Cf. *Kleine Schriften*, v. 1, p. 148; *Philosophical Hermeneutics*, p. 128.

of himself, and of the benefits that go with it. But this tone hangs over the German academic discourse, and over a certain concept of poetry, which were then current. There are many echoes of it in the way Benjamin approaches the problem, at least seen superficially. The same is true of references to Hölderlin, who at that time was a discovery of George and of his group, where you find a certain messianic, spiritual concept of Hölderlin. Many echoes of this are still to be found in Heidegger, who after all dedicated his commentaries on Hölderlin to Norbert von Hellingrath, who was a disciple of George and a member of the George circle, and who was, as you know, the first editor of Hölderlin. I sketch in this little piece of background—it may be familiar to you, it may be entirely redundant—to show that the mood, the atmosphere in which this essay was written is one in which the notion of the poetic as the sacred, as the language of the sacred, the figure of the poet as somehow a sacred figure, is common, and is frequent.)

It is not just in the form of echoes that this is present in Benjamin, it almost seems to have been part of the statement itself. This notion of poetry as the sacred, ineffable language finds perhaps its extreme form already from the beginning, in the categorical way in which Benjamin dismisses any notion of poetry as being oriented in any sense, toward an audience or a reader. This passage has provoked the ire of the defenders of *Rezeptionsästhetik*, who analyze the problem of poetic interpretation from the perspective of the reader—Stanley Fish or Riffaterre in this country follow that line to some extent, but it is of course Jauss and his disciples who do this the most. For them, a sentence like the one which begins this essay is absolutely scandalous. Benjamin begins the essay by saying:

> In the appreciation of a work of art or an art form, consideration of the receiver never proves fruitful. Not only is any reference to a certain public or its representatives misleading, but even the concept of an "ideal" receiver is detrimental in the theoretical consideration of art, since all it posits is the existence and nature of man as such. Art, in the same way, posits man's physical and spiritual existence, but in none of its works is it concerned with his response. No poem is intended for the reader, no picture for the beholder, no symphony for the listener.[3]

3. Walter Benjamin, "The Task of the Translator," in *Illuminations*, trans., Harry Zohn, (New York: Schocken Books, 1969), 69. Quotations from the French translation of Maurice de Gandillac are taken from Walter Benjamin, *Oeuvres* (Paris: Editions Denoël, 1971). Page numbers referring to either of these versions are given in parentheses; translations not identified with a page number are the author's. Page numbers supplied with quotations in German refer to the paperback *Illuminationen* (Frankfurt, Suhrkamp, 2d ed., 1980).

He couldn't be more categorical than in this assertion at the beginning of the essay. You can see how this would have thrown them into a slight panic in Konstanz, a panic with which they deal by saying that this is an essentialist theory of art, that this stress on the author at the expense of the reader is pre-Kantian, since already Kant had given the reader, the receptor, the beholder an important role, more important than the author's. This then is held up as an example of the regression to a messianic conception of poetry which would be religious in the wrong sense, and it is very much attacked for that reason.

But on the other hand, Benjamin is also frequently praised as the one who has returned the dimension of the sacred to literary language, and who has thus overcome, or at least considerably refined, the secular historicity of literature on which the notion of modernity depends. If one can think of modernity as it is described by Gadamer as a loss of the sacred, as a loss of a certain type of poetic experience, as its replacement by a secular historicism which loses contact with what was originally essential, then one can praise Benjamin for having re-established the contact with what had there been forgotten. Even in Habermas there are statements in that direction. But closer to home, an example of somebody who reads Benjamin with a great deal of subtlety, who is aware of the complications, and who praises him precisely for the way in which he combines a complex historical pattern with a sense of the sacred, is Geoffrey Hartman, who writes in one of his latest books as follows:

> This chiasmus of hope and catastrophe is what saves hope from being unmasked as only catastrophe: as an illusion or unsatisfied movement of desire that wrecks everything. The foundation of hope becomes remembrance; which confirms the function, even the duty of historian and critic. To recall the past is a political act: a "recherche" that involves us with images of peculiar power, images that may constrain us to identify with them, that claim the "*weak* Messianic power" in use (Thesis 2). These images, split off from their fixed location in history, undo concepts of homogeneous time, flash up into or reconstitute the present. "To Robespierre," Benjamin writes, continuing Marx's reflections in *The Eighteenth Brumaire*, "ancient Rome was a past charged with the time of now (*Jetztzeit*) which he blasted out of the continuum of history. The French revolution viewed itself as Rome incarnate" (Thesis 14).[4]

4. Geoffrey H. Hartman, *Criticism in the Wilderness: The Study of Literature Today* (New Haven: Yale University Press, 1980), 78.

The reference here is to historical remembrance, to a historical concept which then dovetails, which injects itself into an apocalyptic, religious, spiritual concept, thus marrying history with the sacred in a way which is highly seductive, highly attractive. It is certainly highly attractive to Hartman, and one can understand why, since it gives one both the language of despair, the language of nihilism, with the particular rigor that goes with that; but, at the same time, hope! So you have it all: you have the critical perception, you have the possibility of carrying on in apocalyptic tones, you have the particular eloquence that comes with that (because one can only really get excited if one writes in an apocalyptic mode); but you can still talk in terms of hope, and Benjamin would be an example of this combination of nihilistic rigor with sacred revelation. A man who likes a judicious, balanced perspective on those things, like Hartman, has reason to quote and to admire this possibility in Benjamin. The problem of the reception of Benjamin centers on this problem of the messianic and very frequently it is this text on "The Task of the Translator" that is quoted as one of the most characteristic indicators in that direction.

We now then ask the simplest, the most naive, the most literal of possible questions in relation to Benjamin's text, and we will not get beyond that: what does Benjamin say? What does he say, in the most immediate sense possible? It seems absurd to ask a question that is so simple, that seems to be so unnecessary, because we can certainly admit that among literate people we would at least have some minimal agreement about what is being said here, allowing us then to embroider upon this statement, to take positions, discuss, interpret, and so on. But it seems that, in the case of this text, this is very difficult to establish. Even the translators, who certainly are close to the text, who had to read it closely to some extent, don't seem to have the slightest idea of what Benjamin is saying; so much so that when Benjamin says certain things rather simply in one way—for example he says that something is *not*—the translators, who at least know German well enough to know the difference between something *is* and something *is not*, don't see it! and put absolutely and literally the opposite of what Benjamin has said. This is remarkable, because the two translators I have—Harry Zohn, who translated the text in English, and Maurice de Gandillac, who translated the text in French—are very good translators, and know German very well. Harry Zohn, you may know; Maurice de Gandillac is an eminent professor of philosophy at the University of Paris, a very learned man who knows German very well, and who should be able to tell the difference between, for example, "Ich gehe nach Paris" and "Ich gehe nicht nach Paris." It is not more difficult than that, but somehow he doesn't get it.

An example which has become famous and has an anecdote is the passage near the end of Benjamin's essay, where Benjamin says the following: "Wo der Text unmittelbar, ohne vermittelnden Sinn," and so on, "der Wahrheit oder der Lehre angehört, ist er übersetzbar schlechthin" (62). "Where the text pertains directly, without mediation, to the realm of the truth and of dogma, it is, without further ado, translatable"—the text can be translated, *schlechthin*, so there is no problem about translating it. Gandillac?—I won't comment on this— translates this relatively simple, enunciatory sentence: "Là où le texte, immédiatement, sans l'entremise d'un sens ... relève de la vérité ou de la doctrine, il est purement et simplement *in*traduisible" (275)—*un*translatable. What adds some comedy to this particular instance is that Jacques Derrida was doing a seminar with this particular text in Paris, using the French—Derrida's German is pretty good, but he prefers to use the French, and when you are a philosopher in France you take Gandillac more or less seriously. So Derrida was basing part of his reading on the "intraduisible," on the untranslatability, until somebody in his seminar (so I'm told) pointed out to him that the correct word was "translatable." I'm sure Derrida could explain that it was the same—and I mean that in a positive sense, it *is* the same, but still, it is not the same without some additional explanation. This is an example, and we will soon see some other examples which are more germane to the questions which we will bring up about this text.

Why, in this text, to begin with, is the translator the exemplary figure? Why is the translator held up in relation to the very general questions about the nature of poetic language which the text asks? The text is a poetics, a theory of poetic language, so why does Benjamin not go to the poets? or to the reader, possibly; or the pair poet-reader, as in the model of reception? And since his is so negative about the notion of reception anyway, what makes the essential difference between the pair author-reader and the pair author-translator—since one's first, simple impression would be that the translator is a reader of the original text? There are, to some extent, obvious empirical answers one can give. The essay was written, as you know, as an introduction to Benjamin's own translation of the *Tableaux parisiens* of Baudelaire; it might just be out of megalomania that he selects the figure of the translator. But this is not the case. One of the reasons why he takes the translator rather than the poet is that the translator, per definition, fails. The translator can never do what the original text did. Any translation is always second in relation to the original, and the translator as such is lost from the very beginning. He is per definition underpaid, he is per ,definition overworked, he is per definition the one history will not really retain as an equal, unless he also happens to be a poet, but that is not always the case. If the text is called "Die Aufgabe des Übersetzers," we have to read this title more or less as a tautology: *Aufgabe*, task, can also mean the one who has to give up. If you enter the Tour de France and you give up, that is the *Aufgabe*—"er hat aufgegeben," he doesn't continue in the race anymore. It is in that sense also the defeat, the giving up, of the translator. The translator has to give up in relation to the task of refinding what was there in the original.

The question then becomes why this failure with regard to an original text, to an original poet, is for Benjamin exemplary. The question also becomes how the translator differs from the poet; and here Benjamin is categorical in asserting that the translator is radically unlike, differs essentially from the poet and from the artist. This is a curious thing to say, a thing that goes against common sense, because one assumes (and obviously it is the case) that some of the qualities necessary for a good translator are similar to the qualities necessary for a good poet. This does not mean therefore that they are doing the same thing. The assertion is so striking, so shocking in a way, that here again the translator (Maurice de Gandillac) does not see it. Benjamin says (in Zohn's translation), "Although translation, *unlike* art, cannot claim permanence for its products . . ." (75); Gandillac, the same passage: "Ainsi la traduction, encore qu'elle ne puisse élever une prétention à la durée de ses ouvrages, et en cela elle *n'est pas sans ressemblance* avec l'art . . ." (267). The original is absolutely unambiguous "Übersetzung also, wiewohl sie auf Dauer ihrer Gebilde nicht Anspruch erheben kann und hierin *unähnlich der Kunst . . .*" (55). As you come upon it in a text, the statement is so surprising, goes so much against common sense, that an intelligent, learned, and careful translator cannot see it, cannot see what Benjamin says. It is remarkable. Zohn saw it—don't get the impression that Zohn gets it all right and Gandillac gets it all wrong—basically Gandillac is a little ahead of Zohn, I think, in the final analysis.

At any rate, for Benjamin there is a sharp distinction between them. It is not necessary for good translators to be good poets. Some of the best translators—he mentions Voss (translator of Homer), Luther, and Schlegel—are very poor poets. There are some poets who are also translators: he mentions Hölderlin, who translated Sophocles and others, and George, who translated Baudelaire—Dante also, but primarily Baudelaire, so Benjamin is close to George. But then, he says, it is not because they are great poets that they are great translators, they are great poets *and* they are great translators. They are not purely, as Heidegger will say of Hölderlin, *Dichter der Dichter*, but they are *Übersetzer der Dichter*, they are beyond the poets because they are also translators.

> A number of the most eminent ones, such as Luther, Voss, and Schlegel, are incomparably more important as translators than as creative writers; some of the great among them, such as Hölderlin and Stefan George, cannot be simply subsumed as poets, and quite particularly not if we consider them as translators. As translation is a mode of its own, the task of the translator, too, may be regarded as distinct and clearly differentiated from the task of the poet. (76)

Of the differences between the situation of the translator and that of the poet, the first that comes to mind is that the poet has some relationship to meaning, to a statement that is not purely within the realm of language. That is the naiveté of the poet, that he has to say something, that he has to convey a meaning which does not necessarily relate to language. The relationship of the translator to the original is the relationship between language and language, wherein the problem of meaning or the desire to say something, the need to make a statement, is entirely absent. Translation is a relation from language to language, not a relation to an extralinguistic meaning that could be copied, paraphrased, or imitated. That is not the case for the poet; poetry is certainly not paraphrase, clarification, or interpretation, a copy in that sense; and that is already the first difference.

If it is in some fundamental way unlike poetry, what, in Benjamin's text, does translation resemble? One of the things it resembles would be philosophy, in that it is critical, in the same way that philosophy is critical, of a simple notion of imitation, of philosophical discourse as an *Abbild* (imitation, paraphrase, reproduction) of the real situation. Philosophy is not an imitation of the world as we know it, but it has another relationship to that world. Critical philosophy, and the reference would be specifically to Kant again, will be critical in the same way of the notion of the imitative concept of the world.

Um das echte Verhältnis zwischen Original und Übersetzung zu er-
fassen, ist eine Erwägung anzustellen, deren Absicht durchaus den
Gedankengängen analog ist, in denen die Erkenntniskritik die Un-
möglichkeit einer Abbildstheorie zu erweisen hat. (53)

In order to seize upon the real relationship between the original and its
translation, we must start reflection of which the intent is in general
similar to the modes of thought by means of which a critical epistemology—there's Kant, *Erkenntniskritik*—demonstrates the impossibility of a theory or simple imitation.

Kant indeed would be critical of a notion of art as imitation; this
would be true of Hegel to some extent too, because there is precisely a
critical element that intervenes here and which takes this image, this
model, away, which destroys, undoes this concept of imitation.

Translation is also, says Benjamin, more like criticism or like the
theory of literature, than like poetry itself. It is by defining himself in
relation to Friedrich Schlegel and to German Romanticism in general
that Benjamin establishes this similarity between literary criticism
(in the sense of literary theory) and translation; and this historical reference to the Jena Romanticism here gives to the notion of criticism
and literary theory a dignity which it does not necessarily normally
have. Both criticism and translation are caught in the gesture which
Benjamin calls ironic, a gesture which undoes the stability of the original by giving it a definitive, canonical form in the translation or in the
theorization. In a curious way, translation canonizes its own version
more than the original was canonical. That the original was not purely
canonical is clear from the fact that it demands translation; it cannot
be definitive since it can be translated. But you cannot, says Benjamin,
translate the translation; once you have a translation you cannot
translate it any more. You can translate only an original. The translation canonizes, freezes, an original and shows in the original a mobility, an instability, which at first one did not notice. The act of critical,
theoretical reading performed by a critic like Friedrich Schlegel and
performed by literary theory in general—by means of which the original work is not imitated or reproduced but is to some extent put in motion, de-canonized, questioned in a way which undoes its claim to
canonical authority—is similar to what a translator performs.

Finally, translation is like history, and that will be the most difficult thing to understand. In what is the most difficult passage in this
text, Benjamin says that it is like history to the extent that history is

not to be understood by analogy with any kind of natural process. We are not supposed to think of history as ripening, as organic growth, or even as a dialectic, as anything that resembles a natural process of growth and of movement. We are to think of history rather in the reverse way; we are to understand natural changes from the perspective of history, rather than understand history from the perspective of natural changes. If we want to understand what ripening is, we should understand it from the perspective of historical change. In the same way, the relationship between the translation and the original is not to be understood by analogy with natural processes such as resemblance or derivation by formal analogy; rather we are to understand the original from the perspective of the translation. To understand this historical pattern would be the burden of any reading of this particular text.

All these activities that have been mentioned—philosophy as critical epistemology, criticism and literary theory (the way Friedrich Schlegel does it), or history understood as a nonorganic process—are themselves derived from original activities. Philosophy derives from perception, but it is unlike perception because it is the critical examination of the truth-claims of perception. Criticism derives from poetry because it is inconceivable without the poetry that precedes it. History derives from pure action, since it follows necessarily upon acts which have already taken place. Because all these activities are derived from original activities, they are singularly inconclusive, are failed, are aborted in a sense from the start because they are derived and secondary. Yet Benjamin insists that the model of their derivation is not that of resemblance or of imitation. It is not natural process: the translation does not resemble the original the way the child resembles the parent, nor is it an imitation, a copy, or a paraphrase of the original. In that sense, since they are not resemblances, since they are not imitations, one would be tempted to say they are not metaphors. The translation is not the metaphor of the original; nevertheless, the German word for translation, *übersetzen*, means metaphor. *Übersetzen* translates exactly the Greek *meta-phorein*, to move over, *übersetzen*, to put across. *Übersetzen*, I should say, *translates* metaphor—which, asserts Benjamin, is not at all the same. They are not metaphors, yet the word means metaphor. The metaphor is not a metaphor, Benjamin is saying. No wonder that translators have difficulty. It is a curious assumption to say *übersetzen* is not metaphorical, *übersetzen* is not based on resemblance, there is no resemblance between the translation and the original. Amazingly paradoxical statement, metaphor is not metaphor.

All these activities—critical philosophy, literary theory, history—resemble each other in the fact that they do not resemble that from which they derive. But they are all interlinguistic: they relate to what in the original belongs to language, and not to meaning as an extralinguistic correlate susceptible of paraphrase and imitation. They disarticulate, they undo the original, they reveal that the original was always already disarticulated. They reveal that their failure, which seems to be due to the fact that they are secondary in relation to the original, reveals an essential failure, an essential disarticulation which was already there in the original. They kill the original, by discovering that the original was already dead. They read the original from the perspective of a pure language (*reine Sprache*), a language that would be entirely freed of the illusion of meaning—pure form if you want; and in doing so they bring to light a dismembrance, a de-canonization which was already there in the original from the beginning. In the process of translation, as Benjamin understands it—which has little to do with the empirical act of translating, as all of us practice it on a daily basis—there is an inherent and particularly threatening danger. The emblem of that danger is Hölderlin's translations of Sophocles:

> Confirmation of this as well as of every other important aspect is supplied by Hölderlin's translations, particularly those of the two tragedies of Sophocles. In them the harmony of the languages is so profound that sense is touched by language only the way an aeolian harp is touched by the wind. . . . Hölderlin's translations in particular are subject to the enormous danger inherent in all translations: the gates of a language thus expanded and modified may slam shut and enclose the translator with silence. Hölderlin's translations from Sophocles were his last work, in them meaning plunges from abyss to abyss until it threatens to become lost in the bottomless depths of language. (81–82)

Translation, to the extent that it disarticulates the original, to the extent that it is pure language and is only concerned with language, gets drawn into what he calls the bottomless depth, something essentially destructive, which is in language itself.

What translation does, by reference to the fiction or hypothesis of a pure language devoid of the burden of meaning, is that it implies, in bringing to light what Benjamin calls "die Wehen des eignenen"—the suffering of what one thinks of as one's own—the suffering of the original language. We think we are at ease in our own language, we feel a coziness, a familiarity, a shelter in the language we call our own, in which we think that we are not alienated. What the translation reveals is that this alienation is at its strongest in our relation to our own original language, that the original language within which we are engaged is disarticulated in a way which imposes upon us a particular alienation, a particular suffering. Here too the translators, with considerable unanimity, cannot see this statement. Benjamin's text is, ". . . dass gerade unter allen Formen ihr als Eigenstes es zufällt, auf jene Nachreife des fremden Wortes, auf die Wehen des eigenen zu merken" (54). The two translators—I guess they didn't correspond with each other, they did this *d'un commun accord*—translate *Wehen*, pains, as "birth pangs," as being particularly the pains of childbirth. Gandillac is very explicit about it, he calls it "les douleurs obstétricales" (266) in the most literal, clinical way; Zohn says "birth pangs" (73). Why they do this is a mystery. *Wehen* can mean birth pangs, but it does mean any kind of suffering, without necessarily the connotation of birth and rebirth, of resurrection, which would be associated with the notion of birth pangs because you suffer in producing something—and this is a magnificent moment, you'd be willing to suffer (especially easy for us to say). Benjamin has just been speaking of the "*Nachreife* des fremden Wortes," translated by Zohn as "maturing process," which again is wrong. *Nachreife* is like the German word *Spätlese* (a particularly good wine made from the late, rotten grape), it is like Stifter's novel *Nachsommer* ("Indian Summer")—it has the melancholy, the feeling of slight exhaustion, of life to which you are not entitled, happiness to which you are not entitled, time has passed, and so on. It is associated with another word that Benjamin constantly uses, the word *über-leben*, to live beyond your own death in a sense. The translation belongs not to the life of the original, the original is already dead, but the translation belongs to the afterlife of the original, thus assuming and confirming the death of the original. *Nachreife* is of the same order, or has to do with the same; it is by no means a maturing process, it is a looking back on a process of maturity that is finished, and that is no longer taking place. So if you translate *Wehen* by "birth pangs," you would have to translate it by "death pangs" as much as by "birth pangs," and the stress is perhaps more on death than on life.

The process of translation, if we can call it a process, is one of change and of motion that has the appearance of life, but of life as an afterlife, because translation also reveals the death of the original. Why is this? What are those death pangs, possibly birth pangs, of the original? It is easy to say to some extent what this suffering is not. It is certainly not subjective pains, some kind of pathos of a self, a kind of manifestation of a self-pathos which the poet would have expressed as his sufferings. This is certainly not the case, because, says Benjamin, the sufferings that are here being mentioned are not in any sense human. They would certainly not be the sufferings of an individual, or of a subject. That also is very hard to see, for the translators. Zohn, confronted with that passage (I will stop this game of showing up the translators, but it is always of some interest), translates: "if they are referred *exclusively* to man" (70). Benjamin very clearly says, "wenn sie nicht . . . auf den Menschen bezogen werden" (51), if you *do not* relate them to man. The stress is precisely that the suffering that is mentioned, the failure, is not a human failure, it does not refer therefore to any subjective experience. The original is unambiguous in that respect. This suffering is also not a kind of historical pathos, the pathos that you heard in Hartman's reference to Benjamin as the one who had discovered the pathos of history; it is not this pathos of remembrance, or this pathetic mixture of hope and catastrophe and apocalypse which Hartman captures, which is present certainly in Benjamin's tone, but not so much in what he says. It is not the pathos of a history, it is not the pathos of what in Hölderlin is called the "dürftige Zeit" between the disappearance of the gods and the possible return of the gods. It is not this kind of sacrificial, dialectical, and elegiac gesture, by means of which one looks back on the past as a period that is lost, which then gives you the hope of another future that may occur.

The reasons for this pathos, for this *Wehen*, for this suffering, are specifically linguistic. They are stated by Benjamin with considerable linguistic structural precision; so much so that if you come to a word like "abyss" in the passage about Hölderlin, where it is said that Hölderlin tumbles in the abyss of language, you would understand the word "abyss" in the nonpathetic, technical sense in which we speak of a *mise en abyme* structure, the kind of structure by means of which it is clear that the text itself becomes an example of what it exemplifies. The text about translation is itself a translation, and the untranslatability which it mentions about itself inhabits its own texture and will inhabit anybody who in his turn will try to translate it, as I am now trying, and failing, to do. The text is untranslatable, it was untranslatable for the translators who tried to do it, it is untranslatable for the commentators who talk about it, it is an example of what it states, it is a *mise en abyme* in the technical sense, a story within the story of what is its own statement.

What are the linguistic reasons which allow Benjamin to speak of a suffering, of a disarticulation, of a falling apart of any original work, or of any work to the extent that that work is a work of language? On this Benjamin is very precise, and offers us what amounts in very few lines to an inclusive theory of language. The disjunction is first of all between what he calls "das Gemeinte," what is meant, and the "Art des Meinens," the way in which language means; between logos and lexis, if you want—what a certain statement means, and the way in which the statement is meant to mean. Here the difficulties of the translators are a little more interesting, because they involve philosophical concepts that are of some importance. Gandillac, a philosopher who knows phenomenology and who writes in a period when phenomenology is the overriding philosophical pressure in France, translates by "visée intentionelle" (272). The way we would now translate in French "das Gemeinte" and "Art des Meinens" would be by the distinctions between *vouloir dire* and *dire:* "to mean," "to say." Zohn translates by "the intended object" and the "mode of intention" (74). There is a phenomenological assumption here, and Gandillac has a footnote which refers to Husserl: both assume that the meaning and the way in which meaning is produced are intentional acts. But the problem is precisely that, whereas the meaning-function is certainly intentional, it is not a priori certain at all that the mode of meaning, the way in which I mean, is intentional in any way. The way in which I can try to mean is dependent upon linguistic properties that are not only [not] made by me, because I depend on the language as it exists for the devices which I will be using, it is as such not made by us as historical beings, it is perhaps not even made by humans at all. Benjamin says, from the beginning, that it is not at all certain that language is in any sense human. To equate language with humanity—as Schiller did, as we saw yesterday—is in question. If language is not necessarily human—if we obey the law, if we function within language, and purely in terms of language—there can be no intent; there may be an intent of meaning, but there is no intent in the purely formal way in which we will use language independently of the sense or the meaning. The translation, which puts intentionality on both sides, both in the act of meaning and in the way in which one means, misses a philosophically interesting point—for what is at stake is the possibility of a phenomenology of language, or of poetic language, the possibility of establishing a poetics which would in any sense be a phenomenology of language.

How are we to understand this discrepancy between "das

Gemeinte" and "Art des Meinens," between *dire* and *vouloir dire?*
Benjamin's example is the German word *Brot* and the French word
pain. To mean "bread," when I need to name bread, I have the word
Brot, so that the way in which I mean is by using the word *Brot*. The
translation will reveal a fundamental discrepancy between the intent
to name *Brot* and the word *Brot* itself, in its materiality, as a device of
meaning. If you hear *Brot* in this context of Hölderlin, who is so often
mentioned in this text, I hear *Brot und Wein* necessarily, which is the
great Hölderlin text that is very much present in this—which in
French becomes *Pain et vin*. "Pain et vin" is what you get for free in a
restaurant, in a cheap restaurant where it is still included, so *pain et
vin* has very different connotations than *Brot und Wein*. It brings to
mind the *pain français, baguette, ficelle, bâtard*, all those things—I
now hear in *Brot* "bastard." This upsets the stability of the quotidian.
I was very happy with the word *Brot*, which I hear as a native because
my native language is Flemish and we say *brood*, just as in German,
but if I have to think that *Brot [brood]* and *pain* are the same thing, I
get very upset. It is all right in English because "bread" is close enough
to *Brot [brood]*, despite the idiom "bread" for money, which has its
problems. But the stability of my quotidian, of my daily bread, the reassuring quotidian aspects of the word "bread," daily bread, is upset by
the French word *pain*. What I mean is upset by the way in which I
mean—the way in which it is *pain*, the phoneme, the term *pain*, which
has its set of connotations which take you in a completely different direction.

This disjunction is best understood (to take it to a more familiar
theoretical problem) in terms of the difficult relationship between the
hermeneutics and the poetics of literature. When you do hermeneutics, you are concerned with the meaning of the work; when you do poetics, you are concerned with the stylistics or with the description of
the way in which a work means. The question is whether these two
are complementary, whether you can cover the full work by doing
hermeneutics and poetics at the same time. The experience of trying
to do this shows that it is not the case. When one tries to achieve this
complementarity, the poetics always drops out, and what one always
does is hermeneutics. One is so attracted by problems of meaning that
it is impossible to do hermeneutics and poetics at the same time. From
the moment you start to get involved with problems of meaning, as I
unfortunately tend to do, forget about the poetics. The two are not
complementary, the two may be mutually exclusive in a certain way,

and that is part of the problem which Benjamin states, a purely linguistic problem.

He states a further version of this when he speaks of a disjunction
between the word and the sentence, *Wort* and *Satz*. *Satz* in German
means not just sentence, in the grammatical sense, it means statement—Heidegger will speak of *Der Satz vom Grund; Satz* is the statement, the most fundamental statement, meaning—the most mean-
ingful word—whereas word is associated by Benjamin with *Aussage*,
the way in which you state, as the apparent agent of the statement.
Wort means not only the agent of the statement as a lexical unit, but
also as syntax and as grammar. If you look at a sentence in terms of
words, you look at it not just in terms of particular words but also in
terms of the grammatical relationships between those words. So the
question of the relationship between word and sentence becomes, for
Benjamin, the question of the compatibility between grammar and
meaning. What is being put in question is precisely that compatibility,
which we take for granted in a whole series of linguistic investiga-
tions. Are grammar (word and syntax) on the one hand, and meaning
(as it culminates in the *Satz*) on the other hand—are they compatible
with each other? Does the one lead to the other, does the one support
the other? Benjamin tells us that translation put that conviction in
question because, he says, from the moment that a translation is really
literal, *wörtlich*, word by word, the meaning completely disappears.
The example is again Hölderlin's translations of Sophocles, which are
absolutely literal, word by word, and which are therefore totally unin-
telligible; what comes out is completely incomprehensible, completely undoes the sentence, the *Satz* of Sophocles, which is entirely
gone. The meaning of the word slips away (as we saw, a word like *Aufgabe*, which means task, also means something completely different,
so that the word escapes us), and there is no grammatical way to control this slippage. There is also a complete slippage of the meaning
when the translator follows the syntax, when he writes literally,
wörtlich. And to some extent, a translator has to be *wörtlich*, has to be
literal. The problem is best compared to the relationship between the
letter and the word; the relationship between the word and sentence is
like the relationship between letter and word, namely, the letter is
without meaning in relation to the word, it is *asēmos*, it is without
meaning. When you spell a word you say a certain number of meaningless letters, which then come together in the word, but in each of
the letters the word is not present. The two are absolutely indepen-

dent of each other. What is being named here as the disjunction between grammar and meaning, *Wort* and *Satz*, is the materiality of the
letter: the independence, or the way in which the letter can disrupt the
ostensibly stable meaning of a sentence and introduce in it a slippage
by means of which that meaning disappears, evanesces, and by means
of which all control over that meaning is lost.

So we have, first, a disjunction in language between the hermeneutic and the poetic, we have a second one between grammar and meaning, and finally, we will have a disjunction, says Benjamin, between the
symbol and what is being symbolized, a disjunction on the level of
tropes between the trope as such and meaning as a totalizing power of
tropological substitutions. There is a similar and equally radical disjunction, between what tropes (which always imply totalization) convey in terms of totalization and what the tropes accomplish taken by
themselves. That seems to be the main difficulty of this particular text,
because the text is full of tropes, and it selects tropes which convey the
illusion of totality. It seems to relapse into the tropological errors that
it denounces. The text constantly uses images of seed, of ripening, of
harmony, it uses the image of seed and rind (*l'écorce et le noyau*)—
which seem to be derived from analogies between nature and language,
whereas the constant claim is constantly being made that there are no
such analogies. In the same way that history is not to be understood in
terms of an analogy with nature, tropes should not be based on resemblances with nature. But that is precisely the difficulty, and the challenge of this particular text. Whenever Benjamin uses a trope which
seems to convey a picture of total meaning, of complete adequacy between figure and meaning, a figure of perfect synecdoche in which the
partial trope expresses the totality of a meaning, he manipulates the al-
lusive context within his work in such a way that the traditional symbol is displaced in a manner that acts out the discrepancy between symbol and meaning, rather than the acquiescence between both.

One striking example of that is the image of the amphora:

> Fragments of a vessel which are to be glued together must match one
> another in the smallest details, although they need not be like one an-
> other. In the same way, a translation, instead of resembling the mean-
> ing of the original, must lovingly and in detail incorporate the origi-
> nal's mode of signification, thus making both the original and the
> translation recognizable as fragments of a greater language, just as frag-
> ments are part of a vessel. For this very reason translation must in large
> measure refrain from wanting to communicate. . . . (78)

According to this image, there is an original, pure language, of which any particular work is only a fragment. That would be fine, provided we could, through that fragment, find access again to the original work. The image is that of a vessel, of which literary work would be a piece, and then the translation is a piece of that. It is admitted that the translation is a fragment, but if the translation relates to the original as a fragment relates, if the translation would reconstitute as such the original, then—although it does not resemble it, but matches it perfectly (as in the word *symbolon*, which states the matching of two pieces or two fragments)—then we can think of any particular work as being a fragment of the pure language, and then indeed Benjamin's statement would be a religious statement about the fundamental unity of language.

Benjamin has told us, however, that the symbol and what it symbolizes, the trope and what it seems to represent, do not correspond. How is this to be made compatible with a statement like the one made here? An article by Carol Jacobs called "The Monstrosity of Translation," which appeared in *Modern Language Notes*, treats this passage in a way which strikes me as exceedingly precise and correct. First, she is aware of the Kabbalistic meaning of the text, by referring to Gershom Scholem, who in writing about this text relates the figure of the angel to the history of the *Tikkun* of the Lurianic Kabbalah:

> Yet at the same time Benjamin has in mind the Kabbalistic concept of the *Tikkun*, the messianic restoration and mending which patches together and restores the original Being of things, shattered and corrupted in the "Breaking of Vessels," and also (the original being of) history.

Carol Jacobs comments,

> Scholem might have turned to "Die Aufgabe des Übersetzers," where the image of the broken vessel plays a more direct role. . . . Yet whereas Zohn suggests that a totality of fragments are brought together, Benjamin insists that the final outcome is still "a broken part."[5] (763, note 9)

All you have to do, to see that, is translate correctly, instead of translating like Zohn—who made this difficult passage very clear—but who in the process of making it clear made it say something com-

5. Carol Jacobs, "The Monstrosity of Translation," *Modern Language Notes*, v. 90 (1975), 763, note 9.

pletely different. Zohn said, "fragments of a vessel which are to be glued together must match one another in the smallest detail." Benjamin said, translated by Carol Jacobs word by word: "fragments of a vessel, in order to be *articulated* together"—which is much better than *glued* together, which has a totally irrelevant concreteness—"must *follow* one another in the smallest detail"—which is not at all the same as *match* one another. What is already present in this difference is that we have *folgen*, not *gleichen*, not to match. We have a metonymic, a successive pattern, in which things follow, rather than a metaphorical unifying pattern in which things become one by resemblance. They do not match each other, they follow each other; they are already metonyms and not metaphors; as such they are certainly less working toward a convincing tropological totalization than if we use the term "match."

But things get even more involved, or more distorted, in what follows.

> So, instead of making itself similar to the meaning, to the *Sinn* of the original, the translation must rather, lovingly and in detail, in its own language, form itself according to the manner of meaning (*Art des Meinens*) of the original, to make both recognizable as the broken parts of the greater language, just as fragments are the broken parts of a vessel.

That is entirely different from saying, as Zohn says:

> in the same way a translation, instead of resembling the meaning of the original, must lovingly and in detail incorporate the original's mode of signification, thus making both the original and the translation recognizable as fragments of a greater language, just as fragments are part of a vessel.

"Just as fragments are part of a vessel" is a synecdoche; "just as fragments," says Benjamin, "are the *broken* parts of a vessel": as such he is not saying that the fragments constitute a totality, he says the fragments are fragments, and that they remain essentially fragmentary. They follow each other up, metonymically, and they will never constitute a totality. I'm reminded of an example I heard given by the French philosopher Michel Serres—that you find out about fragments by doing the dishes: if you break a dish it breaks into fragments, but you can't break the fragments any more. That's an optimistic, a positive synecdochal view of the problem of fragments, because there the fragments can make up a whole, and you cannot break up the fragments. What we have here is an initial fragmentation; any work is to-tally fragmented in relation to this *reine Sprache,* with which it has nothing in common, and every translation is a fragment, is breaking the fragment—so the vessel keeps breaking, constantly—and never reconstitutes it; there was no vessel in the first place, or we have no knowledge of the vessel, or no awareness, no access to it, so for all intents and purposes there has never been one.

Therefore the distinction between symbol and symbolized, the nonadequation of symbol to a shattered symbolized, the nonsymbolic character of this adequation, is a version of the others, and indicates the unreliability of rhetoric as a system of tropes which would be productive of a meaning. Meaning is always displaced with regard to the meaning it ideally intended—that meaning is never reached. Benjamin approaches the question in terms of the aporia between freedom and faithfulness, the question which haunts the problem of translation. Does translation have to be faithful, or does it have to be free? For the sake of the idiomatic relevance of the target language, it has to be free; on the other hand, it has to be faithful to some extent to the original. The faithful translation, which is always literal, how can it also be free? It can only be free if it reveals the instability of the original, and if it reveals that instability as the linguistic tension between trope and meaning. Pure language is perhaps more present in the translation than in the original, but in the mode of trope. Benjamin, who is talking about the inability of trope to be adequate to meaning, constantly uses the very tropes which seem to postulate the adequation between meaning and trope; but he prevents them in a way, displaces them in such a way as to put the original in motion, to de-canonize the original, giving it a movement which is a movement of disintegration, of fragmentation. This movement of the original is a wandering, an *errance,* a kind of permanent exile if you wish, but it is not really an exile, for there is no homeland, nothing from which one has been exiled. Least of all is there something like a *reine Sprache,* a pure language, which does not exist except as a permanent disjunction which inhabits all languages as such, including and especially the language one calls one's own. What is to be one's own language is most displaced, the most alienated of all.

Now it is this motion, this errancy of language which never reaches the mark, which is always displaced in relation to what it meant to reach, it is this errancy of language, this illusion of a life that is only an afterlife, that Benjamin calls history. As such, history is not human, because it pertains strictly to the order of language; it is not natural, for the same reason; it is not phenomenal, in the sense that no cognition, no knowledge about man, can be deprived from a history which as such is purely a linguistic complication; and it is not really temporal either, because the structure that animates it is not a temporal structure. Those disjunctions in language do get expressed by temporal metaphors, but they are only metaphors. The dimension of futurity, for example, which is present in it, is not temporal, but is the correlative of the figural pattern and the disjunctive power which Benjamin locates in the structure of language. History, as Benjamin conceives it, is certainly not messianic, since it consists in the rigorous separation and the acting out of the separation of the sacred from the poetic, the separation of the *reine Sprache* from poetic language. *Reine Sprache*, the sacred language, has nothing in common with poetic language; poetic language does not resemble it, poetic language does not depend on it, poetic language has nothing to do with it. It is within this negative knowledge of its relation to the language of the sacred that poetic language initiates. It is, if you want, a necessarily nihilistic moment that is necessary in any understanding of history.

Benjamin said this in the clearest of terms, not in this essay but in another text called "Theological and Political Fragment,"[6] from which I will quote a short passage in conclusion. He said it with all possible clarity, it seemed to me, until I tried to translate that particular passage, and found that English happens to have a property which makes it impossible to translate. Here is the passage:

> Only the messiah himself puts an end to history, in the sense that it frees, completely fulfills the relationship of history to the messianic. Therefore, nothing that is truly historical can want to relate by its own volition to the messianic. Therefore the kingdom of God is not the *telos* of the dynamics of history, it cannot be posited as its aim; seen historically it is not its aim but its end.

That is where I have a great deal of trouble with English, because the English word for "aim" can also be "end." You say, "the end and the means," the aim and the means by which you achieve it. And the English word "end" can mean just as well *Ziel* as it can mean *Ende*. My end, my intention. So that if we want to use that idiom, the translation

---

6. Cf. *Illuminationen* op. cit., 262. An English translation of the "Theologico-Political Fragment" may be found in *Reflections*, Edmund Jephcott, trans., Peter Demetz, ed. (New York: Harcourt Brace Jovanovich, 1978), 312–13.

then becomes: "seen historically it is not its end but its end," its termination—it would be perfect English. But it would indicate that the separation which is here undertaken by Benjamin is hidden in this word "end" in English, which substitutes for "aim" the word "end," the two things which Benjamin asks us to keep rigorously apart.

> It cannot be posited as its aim; seen historically it is not its aim but its end, its termination; therefore the order of the profane cannot be constructed in terms of the idea of the sacred. Therefore theocracy does not have a political but only a religious meaning.

And Benjamin adds:

> To have denied the political significance of theocracy, to have denied the political significance of the religious, messianic view, to have denied this with all desirable intensity is the great merit of Bloch's book *The Spirit of Utopia*.

Since we saw that what is here called political and historical is due to purely linguistic reasons, we can in this passage replace "political" by "poetical," in the sense of a poetics. For we now see that the nonmessianic, nonsacred, that is the *political* aspect of history is the result of the *poetical* structure of language, so that political and poetical here are substituted, in opposition to the notion of the sacred. To the extent that such a poetics, such a history, is nonmessianic, not a theocracy but a rhetoric, it has no room for certain historical notions such as the notion of modernity, which is always a dialectical, that is to say an essentially theological notion. You will remember that we started out from Gadamer's claim to modernity, in terms of a dialectic which was explicitly associated with the word "Spirit," with the spirituality in the text of Hegel. We have seen, and it is for me gratifying to find, that Hegel himself—when, in the section of the *Aesthetics* on the sublime, he roots the sublime in this separation between sacred and profane—is actually much closer to Benjamin in "The Task of the Translator" than he is to Gadamer. I will end on that note, and I will be glad to answer questions if you want. Thank you very much.

KRISTIN ROSS

Rimbaud and the Transformation of Social Space*

To constitute "social space" as an object of analysis is to confront the difficulty of focusing on the ideological content of socially created space. Our tendency, that is, is to think of space as an abstract, metaphysical context, as the container for our lives rather than the structures we help create. The difficulty is also one of vocabulary, for while words like "historical" or "political" convey a dynamic of intentionality, vitality, and human motivation, "spatial," on the other hand, connotes stasis, neutrality and passivity. Space, as Feuerbach suggested, tolerates and coordinates, while time excludes and subordinates—and thus becomes the privileged category for the dialectician.

It is perhaps not so surprising then to find Marxist theory, following the example of Marx himself, somewhat lax in developing a theory of space.[1] Analogously, the current generation of Marxist critics has, for the most part, neglected to concern itself with poetry and has reasserted the traditionally dominant Marxist concern with narrative, and especially with the novel. In this essay I want to explore the advantages of a spatial comprehension of cultural production and I want to do so by looking at lyric poetry—specifically the poetry of Rimbaud.

*From *Yale French Studies* 73 (1987): *Everyday Life*.

1. The work of Henri Lefebvre, particularly the important series of works on urbanism from the late 1960s and 1970s, *Le Droit à la ville* (1968), *La Révolution urbaine* (1970), and *La Production de l'espace* (1974) remains a notable exception to this, as does the work of geographers in France and America publishing in journals like *Antipode* and *Hérodote*. Lefebvre and anyone else who shows a preoccupation with spatial categories, has run the risk of being labeled within Marxism as a "spatial fetishist"—of conceptualizing space separately from the structure of social relations and class conflict. For a brief history of spatial theory within Marxism, see Edward Soja, "The Socio-Spatial Dialectic," *Annals of the Association of American Geographers*, 70: 207–25.

YFS 97, *50 Years of Yale French Studies, Part 2,* ed. Porter and Waters, © 2000 by Yale University.

One of the major reasons for the left's neglect of poetry has to do with the ideology of "poethood" itself, and perhaps no French poet so much as Rimbaud has suffered the effects of a massive critical mythification of that "poethood"—whether it be the boy genius, the mystical or hallucinogenic "voyant," or the solitary adventurer. Recent critical work which reacted against the biographical mythification, has produced a textual Rimbaud exemplary of the most progressive strains of a polysemic and counterdiscursive modernism. One of my tasks in this essay is to try to rescue the peculiar and repressed strain of Rimbaud's modernism from this generalized "politics" of the signifier—and this will entail a different perspective on both the biographical (historical) data and the information to be gleaned from textual interpretation. I want to show how the expansive, centrifugal energy of Rimbaud's brief production not only resists a purely linguistic analysis, but opens up onto a whole synchronic history of his particular moment. This task is made all the more necessary by Rimbaud's theoretical comprehension *of* that moment—one which marks two distinct spatial impulses or events. The first of these, which will concern us here, is the Paris Commune, the construction of the revolutionary city, or what the Situationists were to single out in the 1950s as "the only realization of a revolutionary urbanism to date." And the second, on a global scale, is the passage from market capitalism into a farflung and geographic world system, the "spatialization of history" into what would become the Imperialist heyday of the late nineteenth century.[2]

Certainly the renewed fascination with the Paris Commune on the part of the Situationists, Henri Lefebvre, and other participants in proto- and post- May '68 culture, has something to do with the Commune as spatial "event"—its privileged status as a utopian moment of spatial transformation and reorganization.[3] To mention just a few of the spatial problems posed by the Commune, consider, for example, the relationship of Paris to the provinces, the post-Haussman social division of the city and the question of who, among its citizens, has a

2. This essay forms part of a forthcoming book on Rimbaud and the political language of the 1870s. There I treat the question of Rimbaud and geography; see also Fredric Jameson, "Rimbaud and the Spatial Text," in *Re-writing Literary History,* ed. Tak-Wai Wong and M. A. Abbas (Hong Kong: Hong Kong University Press, 1984), 66–93.

3. See Lefebvre, *La Proclamation de la Commune* (Paris: Gallimard, 1965); and the Situationist theses on the Commune in *Internationale Situationniste 1958–69* (Paris: Editions Champ-Libre, 1975), 109–12: English version, *Situationist International Anthology,* ed. and trans. Ken Knabb (Berkeley: Bureau of Public Secrets, 1981), 314–16.

"right to the city," the military and tactical use of city space during the fighting. But it is important to avoid granting either the Commune or Rimbaud the status of privileged object for theoretical analysis. Space, in other words, as a social fact, and as an instance of society, is always political and strategic. (And because it is characterized, among other things, by the difference in age of the elements which form it— the sum of the action of successive modernizations—spatial structure cannot be understood according to an old "history vs. structure or logic" opposition). But one of the particularities of social relations within capitalist culture is its ability to persuade us that space is not a dimension of the mechanisms of transformation but is instead natural, physical—our unchanged and unchanging surroundings. While people's experience of their bodies in space, their physical perceptions, their entrances and exits, their minds' attention, are all *social* facts, the particular way in which social relations are reproduced and organized through repeated daily practices dulls the perception of that social aspect, and subsumes it into a biological or natural given.

I hope then to suggest larger methodological advantages for the critical concept of social space beyond its particular efficacy for writing about the 1870s in France. Social space can help us avoid the pitfalls of so much of the social or "contextual" analysis of art—the kind of analysis which would attempt, say, to decode a single "masterwork" by Rimbaud, for example, in such a way that it reveals all of the social relations of the 1870s. The restrictions and political drawbacks of such analyses are numerous—not the least of which is their leaving unquestioned the cult of the masterpiece in a way that is singularly not in keeping with either Rimbaud or the people who pulled down the Vendôme Column. Secondly, the "social history" which emerges full blown from such interpretations of the masterwork tends itself to be left unanalyzed—as if the deconstruction of a text offered up a social context which did not in turn have to be deconstructed! My aim, rather, is something like "synchronic history": considering cultural production, in this case Rimbaud, as one "phoneme," so to speak, among many in the political language of the 1870s.

I.

Attempts to discuss Rimbaud in terms of the events of 1871 have for the most part been limited to frenzied interrogations by literary historians and biographers anxious to ascertain the precise physical whereabouts of Rimbaud during the months of March to May 1871.[4] The actual, complex links binding Rimbaud to the events in Paris are not to be established by measuring geographic distance. Or, if they are, it is perhaps by considering Rimbaud's poetry, produced at least in part within the rarified situation of his isolation in Charleville, as one creative response to the same objective situation to which the insurrection in Paris was another. In what way does Rimbaud figure or prefigure an adjacent—side-by-side rather than analogous—social space to the one activated by the insurgents in the heart of Paris?

To begin to answer this question I propose bypassing Rimbaud's most explicitly "political" poems—poems like "Les Mains de Jeanne-Marie" which praises the revolutionary actions of women during the Commune, or like "Chant de guerre parisien"—this latter announced by Rimbaud under the rubric of a "psaume d'actualité" and featuring verbal caricatures of Favre and Thiers lifted straight from the political cartoons and *gravures* of the early months of 1871. Such overtly political verse is important for an ideological reading of Rimbaud, but no more so, I hope to show, than the early Charleville erotic verse (or, for that matter, than the late "hermetic" prose poems): in Rimbaud there is little distance between political economy and libidinal economy. And the significance of the Commune is most evident in what Marx called its "working existence": in its *displacement* of the political onto seemingly peripheral areas of everyday life—the organization of space and time, changes in lived rhythms and social ambiances. The insurgents' brief mastery of their own history is perceptible, in other words, not so much on the level of governmental politics as on the level of their daily life. Taking seriously such a "displacement of the political" points us in the direction of certain of Rimbaud's poems thematically at a distance from the turbulence in Paris: the early ironic and erotic everyday Rimbaud of kisses, beer, and country walks.

Like much of Rimbaud's early lyric poetry, "Rêvé pour l'hiver" (1870) puts forth a particular imagination of the nineteenth-century

4. The one notable exception is Steve Murphy, in his "Rimbaud et la Commune?", *Rimbaud Multiple*, ed. Bedou and Touzot (Gourdon: Dominique Bedou, 1985), 50–65. Murphy addresses the biographical question intelligently and with much relevant erudition, situating Rimbaud in terms of Communard culture: Vermersch, Vallès, Rochefort, political journals of the time, political and sexual slang—establishing, in other words, a sphere of influence and interaction distinct from the Parnassian, or Symbolist context with which Rimbaud's production is usually placed in dialogue.

commonplace of "the voyage." The poem opens with the dream of an enclosed, infantile universe:

> L'hiver, nous irons dans un petit wagon rose
>   Avec des coussins bleus.
> Nous serons bien. Un nid de baisers fous repose
>   Dans chaque coin moelleux.

> In winter we shall travel in a little pink railway carriage
>   With blue cushions.
> We'll be comfortable. A nest of mad kisses lies in wait
>   In each soft corner.[5]

The interior of the carriage is created oppositionally to the winter outside; inside is warmth, well-being and comfort—the simplicity of "Nous serons bien"—repose and restfulness. The muted pastel colors suggest a child's nursery; the carriage is a nest where the violence and jolts of the voyage are cushioned and where all sensation or sound of moving through space is dulled. The passage will not be noticed.

But if the carriage is a nest, it is also the container of nests—a potential disturbance in the nursery is suggested by the adjective "mad," whose threat is for the moment attenuated by the verb "repose." Madness is there, a violence oddly separated and detached from the actors and seemingly part of the environment, but it is, at least at present, a sleeping *folie*.

> Tu fermeras l'oeil, pour ne point voir, par la glace,
>   Grimacer les ombres des soirs,
> Ces monstruosités hargneuses, populace
>   De démons noirs et de loups noirs.

> You will close your eyes, so as not to see through the window
>   The evening shadows grimacing,
> Those snarling monsters, a swarm
>   Of black devils and black wolves.

The second stanza opens out onto the landscape, continuing the childlike tone whereby shadows are frozen into grimaces not unlike the anthropomorphized nature illustrations in the popular children's books ("petits livres d'enfance") Rimbaud mentions in "Alchimie du verbe." Still, it is the gesture of cushioning, or refusing the experience

5. Arthur Rimbaud, *Oeuvres complètes*, ed. de Renéville and Mouquet (Paris: Gallimard, Pléiade, 1967), 65. All future references to Rimbaud will be to this edition; translations from the French, here and elsewhere, are mine.

of voyaging, which appears to hold sway. You will close your eyes to the outside, shutting off vision—that which continually makes and undoes relations between the voyager and the outer world. You will believe yourself intact because surrounded by the walls of the carriage. But the refusal of vision is double-edged: it is also a relinquishing of the mastery involved in any viewer/viewed relation: the domination of the look. To stop seeing the horrifying exterior through the window is, by the same token, to shut off the possibility of defining the interior by its contrary. Gone then is the protection of being distanced from the outside world which would remain there, detached, frozen into an illustration. The closing of the eyes makes the illustration come alive and awakens the sleeping madness:

> Puis tu te sentiras la joue égratignée . . .
> Un petit baiser, comme une folle araignée,
>   Te courra par le cou . . .
>
> Et tu me diras: "Cherche!" en inclinant la tête,
> —Et nous prendrons du temps à trouver cette bête
>   —Qui voyage beaucoup . . .
>
> Then you will feel your cheek scratched . . .
> A little kiss, like a mad spider
>   Will run about your neck . . .
>
> And you'll say to me "Find it!" bending your head,
> —And we'll take a long time to find that creature
>   —Who travels far . . .

A kiss begins its journey; as a spider, it shares with the outer world the quality of darkness; its threatening aspect is underlined by the repetition of the adjective "mad." The outside invades the inside, the nursery is threatened by erotic madness. Closing the eyes awakens the possibility of haptic perception—touch rather than an abstracted and distanced mastery of the scenery. The word "égratignée" signals the movement from *voir* to *faire*; the violence of contact is reminiscent of key moments in many of the poems of *opening*, moments when seams are exposed, the instant of scratching the surface: the fingernails on the child's scalp in "Les Chercheuses de poux," the "picotement" of "Sensation," the holes in the pockets and trousers in "Ma Bohème"; "A blast of air pierces gaps in the partitions, . . . blows away the limits of homes" ("Nocturne vulgaire"). Rimbaud's poetry as a poetry of transformation is crystallized in this moment: the phenomenon of an absolutely commanding perception of the transformation brought on in us by the event of "contact," "opening," "rupture." Thus the importance of the reflexive form in many of these movements: "Puis tu *te* sentiras . . .".

The adjective "petit" used to describe the carriage in the first verse is repeated apropos of the kiss; the kiss shares with the carriage the properties of motion and time as well. The movement of the poem follows the invisible silent machine, the carriage, tracing its passage through space, and the spider/kiss, tracing its passage along the microgeography of the woman's body. These two transgressive movements become one, and what has initially functioned as a mode of separation, an enclosed module transporting its passengers through space, becomes in the intruding spider/kiss what articulates or breaks down the division between interior and exterior. Roland Barthes, speaking of the more extensive and dramatic play with the boundary between inner and outer space that occurs in Rimbaud's "Bateau ivre," calls this the move beyond a psychoanalysis of the cavern to a true poetics of exploration. And indeed, the lover's exclamation, "Cherche!," the only sound in the poem, becomes a true "invitation au voyage"—the invitation to conceive of space *not* as a static reality, but as active, generative; to experience space as created by an interaction, as something which our bodies reactivate, and which through this reactivation, in turn modifies and transforms us. The space of the voyage, whose unmapped itinerary lies in the dashes and ellipses which crowd the end of the poem, merges with a temporal passage ("And we'll take a long time . . .") which guarantees that the voyagers will not be the same individuals at the end of the trip that they were at the beginning.

The poem, as such, constitutes a movement and not a tableau, a *récit* rather than a map. Instead of the abstract visual constructions proper to the stasis of a geographic notion of space, the poem creates a "nonpassive" spatiality—space as a specific form of operations and interactions. In the late 1860s the expression "chercher la petite bête" was a prevalent popular slang expression for wanting to know the inner workings of a thing, the hidden reasons of an affair—like a child wanting to know what lies beneath a watch face. But it was also a slang expression popular among literati, who used it to signify amusing oneself on the level of stylistics instead of bearing down on serious matters of content.[6] The turns and detours of the spider—ruse, mad-

6. Alfred Delvau, *Dictionnaire de la langue verte* (Paris: C. Marpon and E. Flammarion, 1883), 87.

ness, desire, passage—are at once the turns and detours of figures of style, an erotics, and a manner of moving through the world. It is this prefiguration of a reactivated space that in turn becomes transformative which we will take as our point of access to the event or "working existence" of the Commune.

II.

In his *Mémoires*, Gustave-Paul Cluseret, the Commune's first Delegate of War, reflects on the lessons to be learned from the street fighting at the end of the Commune, and, in the process, details the philosophy and strategic use of that topographically persistent insurgent construction, the barricade. The building of barricades was, first of all, to be carried out as quickly as possible; in contrast to the unique, well-situated and centralized civic monument, whose aura derives from its isolation and stability, barricades were not designed around the notion of a unique "proper place": street platoons were to set up as many barricades as they could as quickly as possible. Their construction was, consequently, haphazard and makeshift:

> It is therefore not necessary for these barricades to be perfectly constructed; they can very well be made of overturned carriages, doors torn off their hinges, furniture thrown out of windows, cobble-stones where these are available, beams, barrels, etc.[7]

Monumental ideals of formal perfection, duration or immortality, quality of material and integrity of design are replaced by a special kind of *bricolage*—the wrenching of everyday objects from their habitual context to be used in a radically different way. A similar awareness of the tactical mission of the commonplace can be found in Rimbaud's parodic "Ce qu'on dit au poète à propos de fleurs" where standard Parnassian "tools" are rendered *truly* utilitarian: "Trouve, ô Chasseur, nous le voulons, / Quelques garances parfumées / Que la Nature en pantalons / Fasse éclore!—pour nos Armées! . . . Trouve des Fleurs qui soient des chaises!" (Find, O Hunter, we desire it, / One or two scented madder plants / Which Nature may cause to bloom into trousers / —For our Armies! . . . Find Flowers which are chairs!). In this poem and elsewhere Rimbaud's paradoxical solution to the sterility of Parnassian imagery is, on the one hand, an unqualified return to the full range of ordinary experience—everyday life—at its most banal and, on the other hand, a breakthrough to a distinctly utopian space.

7. Gustave-Paul Cluseret, *Mémoires* (Paris: Jules Levy, 1887), vol. 2: 274–87.

Similarly, anything, writes Cluseret, can serve as building material, anything can be a weapon—"explosives, furniture, and in general, anything that can be used as a projectile"—and any person can be a soldier:

> Passers-by were stopped to help construct the barricades. A battalion of National Guards occupied the area, and the sentries called on everyone passing to contribute their cobble-stone willy-nilly to the defense effort.[8]

But perhaps the most crucial point to emphasize concerning the barricades was their strategic use: they were *not*, as Auguste Blanqui also makes clear in his *Instructions pour une prise d'armes*, to be used as shelter. Barricades, writes Cluseret, "are not intended to shelter their defenders, since these people will be inside the houses, but to prevent enemy forces from circulating, to bring them to a halt and to enable the insurrectionists to pelt them with . . . anything that can be used as a projectile." The immediate function of the barricades, then, was to prevent the free circulation of the enemy through the city—to "halt" them or immobilize them so that they, the enemy, could become targets. The insurgents, meanwhile, who have mobility on their side, offer no targets: "offering them no targets. . . . No one is in sight. This is the crucial point." To this end Blanqui outlines the strategy known as "le percement des maisons":

> When, on the line of defense, a house is particularly threatened, we demolish the staircase from the ground floor, and open up holes in the floorboards of the next floor, in order to be able to fire on the soldiers invading the ground floor.[9]

Cluseret writes of a "lateral piercing" of the houses: "Troops guard the ground floor while others climb quickly to the next floor and immediately break through the wall to the adjoining house and so on and so forth as far as possible." Houses are gutted in such a way that the insurgents can move freely in all directions through passageways and networks of communication joining houses together; the enemy on the street is rendered frozen and stationary. "Street fighting does not take place in the streets but in the houses, not in the open but undercover." Street fighting depends on a practice of mobility or permanent

    8. L.-N. Rossel, *Mémoires, procès et correspondance* (Paris: J. J. Pauvert, 1960), 276.
    9. Auguste Blanqui, *Instructions pour une prise d'armes* (Paris: Editions de la tête de feuilles, 1972), 61.

displacement. It depends on changing houses into passageways—reversing or suspending the division between public and private space. Walter Benjamin writes that for the *flâneur*, the city is metamorphosed into an interior; for the Communards the reverse is true: the interior becomes a street.

III.

Commentators on the Commune from Marx and Engels on have singled out the failure on the part of the Communards to attack that most obvious of monumental targets, the Bank of France:

> The hardest thing to understand is certainly the holy awe with which they remained outside the gates of the Bank of France. This was also a serious political mistake. The Bank in the hands of the Commune— this would have been worth more than 10,000 hostages.[10]

Engels evaluates the "serious political mistake" by calculating a rate of exchange between bank and hostages. Not surprisingly, his analysis is situated soundly in the realm of political economy. In the early 1960s the Situationists—a group whose project lay at the intersection of the revolutionary workers' movement and the artistic "avant-garde"— proposed another sort of analysis: one which altered the sphere of political economy by bringing transformations on the level of everyday life from the peripheries of its analysis to the center. To the extent that the Situationist critique of everyday life was inseparable from the project of intervening in, transforming lived experience, the activities of the group can be seen to fall under the dual banner of Engels's "making conscious the unconscious tendencies of the Commune" and Rimbaud's "changer la vie." In the failure of the Commune—its failure, that is, in the classical terms of the workers' movement, to produce what the more "successful" revolutions succeeding it produced, namely a state bureaucracy—in that failure the Situationists saw its success. To view the Commune from the perspective of the transformation of everyday life would demand, then, that we juxtapose the Communards' political failure or mistake—the leaving intact of the Bank of France—with one of their (what we really oughtn't to call) "monumental" achievements: the pulling down of the Vendôme Column, built by Napoleon to glorify the victories of the Grand Army. On

---

10. Friedrich Engels, introduction, Karl Marx and V. I. Lenin, *The Civil War in France: The Paris Commune* (New York: International Publishers, 1940), 18.

the one hand, a reticence, a refusal to act; on the other, violence and destruction as complete reappropriation: the creation, through destruction, of a positive social void, the refusal of the dominant organization of social space and the supposed neutrality of monuments. The failure of the Communards in the "mature" realm of military and politicoeconomic efficacy is balanced by their accomplishments in the Imaginary or preconscious space which lies outside specific and directly representable class functions—the space that could be said to constitute the realm of political desire rather than need.

What monuments are to the Communards—petrified signs of the dominant social order—the cannon is to Rimbaud:

> Les blancs débarquent. Le canon! Il faut se
> soumettre au baptême, s'habiller, travailler.
>   J'ai reçu au coeur le coup de grâce. Ah! je ne
> l'avais pas prévu!

> The whites are landing. The cannon! We will have
> to submit to baptism, get dressed, and work.
>   I have received in my heart the *coup de grâce*.
> Ah! I had not foreseen it!

This imaginary historical reconstruction, which occurs near the middle of the "Mauvais Sang" section of *Une Saison en enfer*, depicts a scene in the colonization of everyday life. The narrator, in his attempt to rewrite his genealogy, to find another history, another language, has adopted the persona of a black African. Precisely at that moment, the colonists arrive. The "coup de grâce" is also the shot of the cannon: in this context, the word "canon" should be taken, as Rimbaud said elsewhere, "littéralement et dans tous les sens"—not only as a piece of artillery or as a law of the Church, but as the group of books admitted as being divinely inspired. The cannon is also an arm which implies an economic investment that only a State apparatus can make.

(The issue of canonization should play an important role in any discussion of Rimbaud *today*, given the ideologically significant modification of the "place" of Rimbaud in the literary canon which has occurred over the last twenty years. Dominant methodological or theoretical concerns have always generated a list of chosen texts which best suit their mode of analysis. Literary theory of the last twenty years—from structuralism to deconstruction—is no exception. It has, to a certain extent, brought about a rewriting of the canon which has elevated Mallarmé while visibly neglecting Rimbaud; this rewriting in and of itself attests to Rimbaud's resistance to a purely linguistic or "textual" reading.)

It is, however, the most extended sense of the word "canon"—the set of rules or norms used to determine an ideal of beauty in the Beaux Arts—which dominates *Une Saison en enfer*. Beauty appears in the opening lines of the poem, capitalized and personified, seated on the knees of the narrator and cursed by him: "Un soir, j'ai assis la Beauté sur mes genoux.—Et je l'ai trouvée amère.—Et je l'ai injuriée." [One evening I sat Beauty on my knees. And I found her bitter. And I cursed her.] It is the transformation of this idealized beauty into a "decanonized," lower case form by the end of the narrative—"Je sais aujourd'hui saluer la beauté—which constitutes, along with the gradual construction of a plural subject, the primary direction and movement of the poem. But the decanonization of beauty is not just a change in the object; it is a transformation in the relation of the narrator to the object—a transformation signaled by the verb "saluer" (a greeting which is both a hello and a farewell): thus, a relation to beauty which is no longer timeless or immortal, but transitory, acknowledging change and death.

The verb "saluer" appears again near the conclusion in one of the poem's most celebrated passages:

> Quand irons-nous, par delà les grèves et les monts, saluer la naissance du travail nouveau, la sagesse nouvelle, la fuite des tyrans et des démons, la fin de la superstition, adorer—les premiers!—Noël sur la terre!

> When will we journey beyond the beaches and the mountains, to hail the birth of new work, new wisdom, the flight of tyrants and demons, the end of superstition; to adore—the first!—Christmas on earth!

Here "saluer" is unambiguous and the poem concludes with the anticipation of, the unmitigated yearning for the birth of new social relations figured in properly spatial terms: the as yet to emerge revolutionary space of "Noël sur la terre." The various geographical synonyms to "Noël sur la terre" which spring up at the end of the poem, the "splendides villes," the "plages sans fin," are all situated in a future time which suggests that "Noël sur la terre" is not to be construed as the founding of a new "proper place," but rather that which, in its instability, in its displacement or deferment, exists as the breakdown of the notion of proper place: be it heaven or hell, Orient or Occident, winter or summer. The dizzying religious or vertical topography of the poem, with its meteoric descents and ascensions ("I believe myself to be in hell, so I am"; "hell is certainly *below*—and heaven above"; "Ah! to climb back up into life"; "It's the flames which rise up with their damned one") is resolved in the narrative's final sections by a horizontal and social topography ("I, who called myself magus or angel, exempt from all morality, I am given back to the earth, with a task to pursue"), a kind of lateral vision, which is not so much a vision as a movement ("The song of the heavens, the march of peoples!"), and not so much a movement as a future movement: "Let us receive all the influx of vigor and real tenderness. And, at dawn, armed with an ardent patience, we will enter into splendid cities."

To the extent that the particular revolutionary realization of the Commune can be seen in its political understanding of social space, we can speak here of an analogous breakdown of the notion of "proper place." Class division is also the division of the city into active and passive zones, into privileged places where decisions are made in secret, and places where these decisions are executed afterwards. The rise of the bourgeoisie throughout the nineteenth century was inscribed on the city of Paris in the form of the Baron Haussman's architectural and social reorganization which gradually removed workers from the center of the city to its northeast peripheries, Belleville and Ménilmontant. An examination of the voting records in the municipal elections organized by the Commune shows this social division clearly: less than twenty-five percent of the inhabitants of the bourgeois *arrondissements*, the seventh and eighth, voted in the election; only the tenth, eleventh, twelfth and eighteenth workers' *arrondissements*, and the fifth, the university district, voted at more than half.[11] The workers' redescent into the center of Paris follows in part from the political significance of the city center within a tradition of popular insurgency, and in part from their desire to reclaim the public space from which they had been expelled, to occupy streets which were no longer their own.

If workers are those who are not allowed to transform the space/time allotted them, then the lesson of the Commune can be found in its recognition that revolution does not consist in changing the juridi-

11. Pierre Gascar, *Rimbaud et la Commune* (Paris: Gallimard, 1971), 66.

cal form which allots space/time (for example, allowing a party to appropriate bureaucratic organization) but rather by completely transforming the nature of space/time. It is here that Marx's "transform the world" and Rimbaud's "changer la vie" become, as the Surrealists proclaimed, the same slogan. The working existence of the Commune constituted a critique pronounced against geographical zoning whereby diverse forms of socioeconomic power are installed: a breakdown of a privileged place or places in favor of a permanent exchange between distinct places—thus, the importance of the *quartier*. Lefebvre's work is especially important in emphasizing the disintegration of the practical, material foundations and habits which organized daily life during the hardships of the Siege of Paris in the fall and winter of 1870. In the midst of this disintegration sprang up new networks and systems of communication solidifying small groups: local neighborhood associations, women's clubs, legions of the National Guard, and, above all, the social life of the *quartier:* new ambiances, new manners of looking at one another or of meeting which are both the product and instrument of transformed behavior.[12]

The breakdown of spatial hierarchy in the Commune, one aspect of which was the establishment of places of political deliberation and decision making which were no longer secret but open and accessible, brought about a breakdown in temporal division as well. The publicity of political life, the immediate publication of all the Commune's decisions and proclamations, largely in the form of *affiches*, resulted in a "spontaneous" temporality whereby citizens were no longer informed of their history after the fact but were in fact occupying the moment of its realization. Writing in his journal, E. de Goncourt complains about this on 17 April 1871: "Des affiches, toujours des affiches et encore des affiches!" On the same day Rimbaud writes a letter to Paul Demeny reporting on the proliferation of verbal and visual material in the

12. Manuel Castells, a student of Lefebvre, has substantially developed Lefebvre's hypothesis of the Commune as a specifically urban revolution in his chapter on the Commune in *City and the Grassroots* (Berkeley: University of California Press, 1983), 15–26. The Communards, while primarily manual workers, were not the industrialized proletariat evoked by Marx. Their self-definition, if not their origins, was decidedly Parisian, and their immediate concerns had less to do with gaining control over the means of production than with avoiding eviction. Thus the enemy and obvious target of the Communards was not the industrial capitalist, but rather those three nightmare figures known for their policing of everyday life: the *curé*, the *gendarme*, and the *concierge*.

streets of Paris; his tone is decidedly more celebratory than that of Goncourt:

> On s'arrêtait aux gravures de A. Marie, les *Vengeurs*, les *Faucheurs de la mort;* surtout aux dessins comiques de Draner et de Faustin. . . . Les choses du jour étaient le *Mot d'ordre* et les fantaisies, admirables, de Vallès et de Vermersch au *Cri du peuple.*
> Telle était la littérature—du 25 Février au 10 Mars.

> We stopped in front of engravings by A. Marie, *les Vengeurs, les Faucheurs de la mort;* and especially the cartoons by Draner and Faustin. . . . The items for the day were le *Mot d'Ordre* and the admirable fantasies by Vallès and Vermersch in the *Cri du peuple.*
> Such was literature—from 25 February to 10 March.[13]

The workers who occupied the Hôtel de Ville or who tore down the Vendôme Column were not "at home" in the center of Paris; they were occupying enemy territory, the circumscribed proper place of the dominant social order. Such an occupation, however brief, provides an example of what the Situationists have called a *détournement*—using the elements or terrain of the dominant social order to one's own ends, for a transformed purpose; integrating actual or past productions into a superior construction of milieu. *Détournement* has no other place but the place of the other; it plays on imposed terrain and its tactics are determined by the absence of a "proper place." Thus, the *détournement* of churches: using them to hold the meetings of women's clubs or other worker organizations. *Détournement* is no mere Surrealist or arbitrary juxtaposition of conflicting codes; its aim, at once serious and ludic, is to strip false meaning or value from the original. Such an aim is apparent in Rimbaud's "Ce qu'on dit au poète à propos de fleurs," where the literary code of Parnassian estheticism is *détourné* by a jarring influx of social, utilitarian vocabulary:

> Ainsi, toujours vers l'azur noir
> Où tremble la mer des topazes,
> Fonctionneront dans ton soir
> Les Lys, ces clystères d'extases!

> Thus, continually towards the dark azure
> Where the sea of topazes shimmers,
> Will function in your evening
> Lilies, those enemas of ecstasy!

13. Rimbaud, *Oeuvres complètes*, 266. The *Mot d'ordre* was Rochefort's journal which appeared from 1 February to 20 May 1871.

Here the echo to Lamartine at his most elegiac ("Ainsi toujours poussés vers de nouveaux rivages . . .") coexists with the most mechanistic and technical of jargons: "fonctionneront" and "clystères." Elsewhere in Rimbaud's work, a similar subversion is carried out by the trivial, commonplace nature of the represented object, the introduction of the detail which is neither distinguished nor abject, the detail which has no higher significance than itself: the clove of garlic in "Au Cabaret-vert."

Rimbaud's poetry constitutes a genuine "lieu mixte": a half real, half fantastic libidinal geography of class exchange. It assembles formal elements from the realm of high culture—the alexandrine, the sonnet form—with Ardennais slang, scatological invective, and political diatribe. Nevertheless, it would be difficult to call this verse "counter-cultural" in relation to the philosophy, art, or poetry of the dominant high culture of Rimbaud's time. Such a rigid system of cultural purification or hierarchy was characteristic *of* that high culture—of Leconte de Lisle and others of the most conservative representatives of the Parnassian school. Rimbaud's work resonates instead with all the anxieties of the real and imaginary displacements authorized by a cultural place which enables passages, meeting places, contagion *between* one class and another, or even between one species and another:

> Chinois, Hottentots, bohémiens, niais, hyènes, Molochs, vieilles démences, démons sinistres, ils mêlent les tours populaires, maternels, avec les poses et les tendresses bestiales. [Parade]

> Chinese, Hottentots, gypsies, simpletons, hyenas, Molochs, old insanities, sinister demons, they mingle popular, homespun turns with bestial poses and caresses.

> J'aimais les peintures idiotes, dessus de portes, décors, toiles de saltimbanques, enseignes, enluminures populaires; la littérature démodée, latin d'église, livres érotiques sans orthographe, romans de nos aïeules, contes de fées, petits livres d'enfance, opéras vieux, refrains niais, rhythmes naïfs. [Alchimie du verbe]

> I liked absurd paintings, pictures over doorways, stage sets, carnival backdrops, billboards, colored prints, old-fashioned literature, Church Latin, erotic books badly spelled, the kind of novels our grandmothers read, fairy tales, little children's books, old operas, silly refrains, naive rhythms.

The point to emphasize about this famous heap is not so much the collective or popular "authorship" of most of its elements, but rather the latent political effect of the juxtaposition of badly spelled erotic books with Church Latin—all under the affirmation ("J'aimais") which renders them at once specific and equivalent. In Rimbaud there is no isolation of the popular into a regional preserve, into some ritualized carnivalesque space of pure *dépense*.[14] He is not a regionalist—his interest, rather, lies in promoting the danger and utopian fantasy which, both, result from contagion. The disorder of his poetry, in other words, is less about his having created a savage, adolescent, or Communard culture, than it is about his having articulated a savage, adolescent, or Communard relationship *to* culture.

IV.

Accounts of the Commune and accounts of the "phenomenon" of Rimbaud rely on a shared vocabulary:

> Rimbaud erupts into literature, throws a few lightning bolts and disappears, abandoning us from then on to what looks like twilight. We had hardly time to see him. . . . This is enough for the legend to be born and develop. . . .[15]

> The seventy-two days from 18 March to 28 May 1871, the length of time Paris was able to hold out against the National Government at Versailles and its army, though too short to carry out any permanent measures of social reform, were long enough to create the myth, the legend of the Commune as the first great workers' revolt.[16]

Brevity, eruption, lightning flash, myth, legend—these are the words which recur.[17] Neither Rimbaud, "the first poet of a civilization that has not yet appeared" (Char), nor the Commune, that "unplanned, unguided, formless revolution" (Edwards), reached maturity, and their lingering in the liminal zone of adolescence—"a perverse and superb puberty" (Mallarmé)—tends to create anxiety. It is striking to see the way in which narratives of both subjects follow a traditional developmental model, concluding almost invariably with a consideration of

---

14. "There is a zoo of pleasures to Rabelais. To Rimbaud. . . . It would be wrong to say that the zoo was a jungle, but the animals did not seem to have cages." Jack Spicer, "A Fake Novel About the Life of Arthur Rimbaud" in *The Collected Books* (Los Angeles: Black Sparrow Press, 1975), 154.

15. Gascar, 9.

16. Stewart Edwards, ed., *The Communards of Paris, 1871* (Ithaca: Cornell University Press, 1973), 9–10.

17. Mallarmé, for instance, uses the metaphor of a meteor when speaking of Rimbaud; René Char writes of his "sudden evaporation."

the reasons for the failure of the Commune to become stabilized, of Rimbaud to remain loyal to literature, and ensuing motifs: the silence of Rimbaud, the demise of the Commune. Speculations abound as to what "fulfillment" or "adulthood" *might have* looked like: the poems Rimbaud would have written in Africa, the social reforms the Commune would have put through had it been given the time to stabilize.

But such an omniscient theoretical viewpoint gives way to easy proofs that the Commune was objectively doomed to failure and could not have been fulfilled. This viewpoint, as the Situationists point out, forgets that for those who really lived it, the fulfillment was *already there*. And as Mallarmé said of Rimbaud, "I think that prolonging the hope for a work of maturity would harm, in this case, the exact interpretation of a unique adventure in the history of art."[18] It is in this sense that Marx should be understood when he says that the most important social measure of the Commune was its own working existence.

The Commune, wrote Marx, was to be a working, not a parliamentary body. Its destruction of hierarchic investiture involved the displacement (revocability) of authority along a chain or series of "places" without any sovereign term. Each representative, subject to immediate recall, becomes interchangeable with, and thus equal to, its represented.

The direct result of this kind of distributional and revocable authority is the withering away of the political function as a specialized function. Rimbaud's move beyond the idea of a specialized domain of poetic language or even of poetry—the fetishization of writing as a privileged practice—does not begin in 1875 with his "silence," but rather as early as 1871 with the "Lettres du voyant." In these letters writing poetry is acknowledged as one means of expression, action, and above all of *work* among others:

> I shall be a worker: that is the idea that holds me back when mad rage drives me towards the battle of Paris—where so many workers are dying as I write to you!

The *voyant*, as has been frequently pointed out, "*se fait* voyant": "I *work* at making myself a *voyant.*" The emphasis is on the work of self-transformation as opposed to predestination. The *voyant* project emerges in the letters as the will to combat not merely specific past or

18. Stéphane Mallarmé, *Oeuvres complètes*, ed. Mondor and Jean-Aubry (Paris: Gallimard, Pléiade, 1945), 518.

contemporary poetry practices, but the will to overcome eventually and supersede "poetry" altogether. Like the "abolition of the State," the process outlined by Rimbaud is a long and arduous revolutionary process which unfolds through diverse phases. The work is not solitary but social and collective: "other horrible workers will come: they will begin at the horizons where the first one has fallen!"; and its progress is to be measured, Rimbaud implies, by the degree to which "the infinite servitude of women" is broken: "When the unending servitude of woman is broken, when she lives by and for herself, when man—until now abominable—has given her her freedom, she too will be a poet!" An exclamation from the letters like "Ces poètes seront!" must be placed in the context of the emergence, particularly in Rimbaud's later work, of a collective subject: the "nous" of the concluding moments of *Une Saison* ("Quand irons-nous . . . ," of "A une Raison," of "Après le déluge"). Masses in movement—the human geography of uprisings, migrations, and massive displacements—dominate the later prose works: "the song of the heavens, the march of peoples" (*"Une Saison"*); "migrations more enormous than the ancient invasions" ("Génie"); "the uprising of new men and their march forward" ("A une Raison"); "companies have sung out the joy of new work" ("Villes"). The utopian resonance of "travail nouveau"—"saluer la naissance du travail nouveau"—can be found even in the project of *voyance:* an enterprise of self and social transformation which implies that poets themselves accept their own uninterrupted transformation—even when this means ceasing to be a poet.

JOAN DEJEAN

Classical Reeducation: Decanonizing the Feminine*

Each age has its canon, its own peculiarly idiosyncratic vision of the literature of preceding centuries. One way of approaching the study of canons is palimpsest-style, by peeling back superimposed layers of critical judgment in search of the hierarchies and the process of inclusion-exclusion that commentators of a given period developed to package contemporary literary production and that of earlier ages for pedagogical dissemination and consumption. In the case of seventeenth-century literature, the stripping away of canonical layers would take us back to the period from the end of the seventeenth century to the middle of the eighteenth century during which two related developments transformed the meaning of "classic" in French. In the first place, modern (French) authors were placed on an equal footing with their ancient precursors as models for pedagogical instruction, thus becoming "classic" according to the most standard usage, the primary sense of the term attested in seventeenth-century dictionaries ("author who is taught in classes, in the schools"). In the second place, selected authors of the second half of the seventeenth century (the period that baptized itself France's Golden Age) gradually became accepted as "classic" in another sense of the word, this time one particular to the French language and one included only in modern dictionaries: "that which pertains to the great authors of the seventeenth century and their period, considered as expressing an ideal" (Robert dictionary).[1]

*From *Yale French Studies* 75 (1988): *The Politics of Tradition: Placing Women in French Literature.* For references in this article to "this volume" or "this issue," see *YFS* 75.

1. There is considerable confusion about the origin of this usage. To date, I have not been able to reach a satisfactory conclusion. However, I do not accept the attribution of this sense of "classic" to Voltaire. The Robert dictionary states that this usage was only

YFS 97, *50 Years of Yale French Studies, Part 2*, ed. Porter and Waters, © 2000 by Yale University.

In the course of this semantic drift, these two meanings of classic are often considered synonymous; in many periods it is almost universally understood that "the great authors of the seventeenth century" are alone worthy to be taught in the schools. At the same time and as part of the same evolution of linguistic usage and pedagogical practice, the most influential women writers of the Golden Age are pronounced unworthy of membership in the class of "great authors of the seventeenth century" because the "ideal" their works express is deemed unfit to be proposed to schoolchildren as a model. However, these women writers are still proposed as models as long as the original canon of French literature, a canon, as we will see, for adult readers rather than schoolchildren, still survives (roughly until the beginning of the nineteenth century). In search of an explanation for the exclusion of women writers from classic status, I will contrast the two types of pedagogical programs available in France from the late seventeenth century until shortly after the Revolution, what I have just referred to as the canon for adults and the first canon for schoolchildren to include modern authors.

In the closing decades of the seventeenth century, French writers began to draw up lists of their precursors and then to edit anthologies of their representative works. The best known of these is the *Recueil des plus belles pièces des poètes français*, published anonymously in 1692 and considered the work of either Fontenelle, a man of letters sympathetic to women writers, or a noted woman writer of the day, Marie-Catherine d'Aulnoy.[2] This compilation is in many ways a model for the most central early tradition of anthologizing. It is devoted exclusively to French authors and almost exclusively to seventeenth-century writers. Its editor makes no claim to be a literary arbiter: all authors are included who have acquired a certain "reputa-

---

introduced at the turn of the nineteenth century by Staël. If this is true, we have still another indication of Staël's sensitivity to semantic innovation. (Time and again, I have traced the origin of terms crucial for the history of women's writing to her works.)

2. *Recueil des plus belles pièces des poètes français depuis Villon jusqu'à M. de Benserade*, 5 vols. (Paris: Barbin, 1692). Initially, the anthology was generally accepted as d'Aulnoy's. Only later is Fontenelle's name attached to it and, even though no convincing reason for the change in attribution has ever been offered, it has gained wide acceptance. (G. Reed, *Claude Barbin* [Geneva: Droz, 1974], 40, n. 1). Today, the compilation is most often referred to as the Recueil Barbin, after the publisher who signs its dedicatory preface. (He was the publisher of many early women writers.)

tion," whether or not they can be considered "great" authors. The editor makes no attempt to dictate literary taste but tries simply to give a sense of the field.

Today's readers familiar with the French pedagogical tradition probably think of anthologies exclusively as works intended to introduce literature into the classroom in order to mold the taste of schoolchildren. However, in France for over a century until just after the Revolution, almost all these volumes were compiled for adults who wished to keep abreast of the literary scene. The principle of inclusion on which the Fontenelle/d'Aulnoy anthology is based makes it clear that this anthology, like the dozens that imitated it throughout the eighteenth century, was destined for a precise public, the adults who frequented milieux like the salons, in which literature was a major topic of discussion and who wished to have a sense of the range of modern literature, a subject not yet part of the curriculum at the time of their official education. These early anthologies are therefore pedagogical in a sense of the term perhaps closest to the recent usage "continuing education." In the vision of literary production they propose, the canon is made up of works read by an adult public active in the world rather than a public isolated in an educational establishment, a pedagogical role for literature promoted actively at least until the early nineteenth century. Indeed, prior to the mid-eighteenth century, the only canonical status to which *French* authors could aspire was inclusion in worldly anthologies compiled for adults, a canonical status that was never officially legitimated. Only under the most exceptional circumstances did a new work become canonical in the original French sense of the term, that which is introduced into the classroom as a model for students. Prior to the mid-eighteenth century, the classics, the works taught in the *collèges*, were all Greek and Latin, whereas modern works could become influential only by appealing to the worldly adult public.

The view of the literary scene found in the continuing education anthologies of the late seventeenth and early eighteenth centuries is remarkably different from the vision of that era presented in today's manuals. Perhaps the most striking difference concerns the presence of women writers. In anthologies devoted to writers in general, women writers are admitted in numbers far more important than at any time since. In addition, between the late seventeenth and the late eighteenth century, at least a dozen literary anthologies devoted exclusively to women writers were published. Before presenting the canonical revision that was the end result of the new literary pedagogy of the Enlightenment, I will consider very briefly two of these continuing education anthologies, one near the beginning of the tradition and one at its end, in order at least to suggest the magnitude of the options eventually sacrificed to the remodeled classical ideology.

Marguerite Buffet's *Nouvelles observations sur la langue française, avec l'éloge des illustres savantes tant anciennes que modernes* (1668), one of the first such anthologies, is a fascinating critical hybrid. Buffet's volume is the clearest demonstration of the genre's goal of contributing to the continuing education of an adult public: its first half is a French grammar and a treatise on correct usage and orthography destined for a general audience and in particular female readers who had been denied formal linguistic training. These grammatical considerations are joined to a portrait gallery of literary women in which Buffet, alone among the representatives of this worldly tradition, broadens the definition of the literary to include demonstrations of the linguistic excellence she defines in her grammatical treatise, oral as well as written. She is thereby able to record accomplishments, such as conversational brilliance, otherwise excluded from the domain of literary criticism, and to privilege the particular artistic manifestations then being developed in the salons. Volumes like Buffet's— as well as those of her contemporaries Jean de La Forge, Jacquette Guillaume, and Claude de Vertron—provide information on numbers of influential seventeenth-century literary women who have been virtually lost to readers since the demise of the worldly canon after the Revolution.[3]

Early anthologies like Buffet's have none of the pedagogical qualities of the eighteenth-century compilations whose techniques we will analyze. They are often closer to collections of eulogies than to literary manuals from which a potential student of any age could obtain information on what an individual author actually wrote, much less on what that literary production was like. By the end of the worldly anthology tradition, however, editors had made great progress in the ped-

3. Buffet, *Nouvelles observations sur la langue française, avec l'éloge des illustres savantes tant anciennes que modernes* (Paris: Jean Cusson, 1668); La Forge, *Le Cercle des femmes savantes* (Paris: Loyson, 1663); Guillaume, *Les Dames illustres* (Paris: Thomas Jolly, 1665); Claude Charles Guionet, seigneur de Vertron, *La Nouvelle Pandore ou les Femmes illustres du siècle de Louis le Grand,* 2 vols. (Paris: Veuve Mazuel, 1698).

agogical presentation of material, clearly having learned from their predecessors (almost every such compilation contains references to precursor volumes) as much as from the rival tradition of manuals for classroom instruction. Both the most eloquent and the most pedagogical of the worldly anthologies is one of the final examples of the tradition, an enterprise that would clearly have realized the genre's potential, had it not become still another victim of the events of 1789.

The fourteen existing volumes of Louise Keralio Robert's *Collection des meilleurs ouvrages français composés par des femmes* (1786–1789) stand as a monument to the tradition's potential for growth. Furthermore, as she makes clear in the preface to volume one, Keralio had initially planned a venture far more vast, "about 36 volumes" that would have presented a panorama of French literary history from the Middle Ages through the end of the eighteenth century, with the lion's share devoted to the "classical age" of French women's writing, the seventeenth century.[4] Had Keralio completed her anthology, she would have provided an alternative history of French literature until the Revolution, a narrative demonstrating the deficiency of any French literary history that omits the contributions of women to every period, a history challenging the adequacy of the notions of periodization then commonly accepted—many of which are still accepted today—to account for the production of women writers. But Keralio did not come close to finishing her history. After the initial five volumes devoted to the Middle Ages and the Renaissance (Christine de Pisan alone is allotted two volumes), she jumps ahead to Scudéry. She then skips over volumes 7 and 8, which she leaves blank, as she explains, in the hope of returning some day to fill in the gaps, and proceeds directly to Sévigné. It is easy to offer a historical explanation for Keralio's failure to complete the ambitious contract she initially offered her readers: the last volumes of her collection appeared in 1789, surely an inauspicious date, as Germaine de Staël would soon observe, both for feminist writing in general and for the until then largely aristocratic tradition of French women's literature in particular. No one would ever fill in the gaps in Keralio's history, although the tradition she represents was killed off by a movement that began long before 1789, and one that was hardly revolutionary in its politics.

The volumes Keralio did manage to complete are astonishingly

---

4. Louise Félicité Guinemet de Keralio Robert, *Collection des meilleurs ouvrages français composés par des femmes*, 14 vols. (Paris: Lagrange, 1786–89), 1: i–ii.

well-researched and put together and could easily be used today as the basis for a curriculum in French women's writing. Her format is highly pedagogical: biography followed by selections from major works, with an important innovation found in no other early anthology. Keralio understands that the best literary history presents an overview, a framework in which individual pieces can be situated. Thus she alternates her treatment of women authors from a given period with a history of French literature, presented in segments, from its origins (defined as the time of the Gauls), always integrating the women writers she is about to discuss in the general literary context of their day. And Keralio's volumes are the logical summation of the movement that begins with Buffet and her contemporaries. An examination of early French literary histories shows that, until the dawn of the nineteenth century, women writers were just about as likely as their male counterparts to be included in canonical compilations. However, at the same time as the editors of worldly anthologies were learning to make their case more forcefully, the countertradition was developing that would in the long run become so influential that it would succeed in establishing its program of French literary classics as the only vision possible of the early history of French literature.

No sooner had the first anthologists established the existence of a French tradition (by the early eighteenth century) than the power of the pedagogical canon began to be recognized. Historians have traced the movement whereby, from the sixteenth to the eighteenth century, the family gradually turned over to the *collège* the boy's preparation for professional life. Yet, despite the fact that the student was supposed to enter a profession directly upon leaving the *collège*, schools continued throughout the eighteenth century to rely almost exclusively on literary texts to teach all subjects. In the course of the eighteenth century, theorists began increasingly to call for a "national" education, a "uniform" education that would replace "provincial prejudices" with "homogeneous ideas of civic and religious virtue."[5] Contemporaneous with the development of the desire to standardize the teaching of Frenchness is the movement to give French authors at least equal importance in the curriculum that was to perform this new pedagogical mission. In a standardized, national educational program

5. Roger Chartier, M.-M. Compère, and D. Julia, *L'Education en France au XVIIe et XVIIIe siècles* (Paris: PUF, 1964), 209. Subsequent references to this work will be included in parentheses in the text, a practice I follow with all works I cite more than once. All translations from the French are my own.

whose primary goal was to use the teaching of literature to form model Frenchmen, educators realized that the newly recognized French literary tradition should play a major role. Under these circumstances, pedagogical authorities initiated the process of teaching teachers how the works of literary moderns could be held up as models of Frenchness.

This project for the ideological packaging of literature took shape over the first half of the eighteenth century. Scholars gradually developed the anthology into a full-scale literary program: in 1740, for example, Goujet produced an eighteen-volume *Histoire de la littérature française* still directed at a post*collège* public, no longer governed by the principle of the worldly anthologies—that is, an author should be included if he or she is being talked about. On the contrary, Goujet's aim was strictly judgmental: "I want to lead my readers by the hand through our literary riches, to teach them what we have in each literary domain, to show them what they should choose and reject."[6] Goujet transforms the worldly anthology into the arm by which critics could police the reading habits of the "honnête homme" and could thereby shape both his taste and his national prejudices. Such a project would in effect be a form of reeducation, an undoing of the vision of the contemporary literary scene spread by the worldly anthologies. He concludes his "preliminary discourse" with a call for a similar effort on the part of pedagogues, who should be adapting the texts of literary moderns the better to accomplish their task of making their young charges into "good Christians" "useful to civil society" (xli).

Pedagogues quickly heeded his call to arms. The ancestor of the modern system of national exams, the *concours général des collèges parisiens*, at its inception in 1747 had a double prize, *amplification française* side by side with *amplification latine*. From this point on, Parisian professors of rhetoric "categorically" demanded that French poets and orators be introduced into the curriculum and that students begin to write *in* French about French authors (Chartier et al., 199). At the very same time that the system of *concours* was being founded, the pedagogical philosophy and even the pedagogical tools that are still used today to prepare students for the national exams were given their original formulation. L'abbé Batteux's companion volumes *Les Beaux arts réduits à un seul principe* of 1746 and his *Cours de belles-lettres*

6. *Bibliothèque française; ou Histoire de la littérature française*, 18 vols. (Paris: Mariette, 1740–56), ii.

of 1747 were designed to provide teachers with both what we know from Lagarde and Michard as a *"program of great* French authors" and the techniques for using these authors to teach Frenchness, most notably the reduction of works deemed masterpieces to *morceaux choisis* made pedagogical through an *explication de texte.* The canon that can be assembled on the basis of the worldly anthologies is quite different from the program for the study of seventeenth-century French literature generally proposed today. The ancestor of the manuals in which those of us currently teaching received our first ideas of the period is Batteux: the "reduced" canon he proposes is remarkably close to what, for better or for worse, we think of as the classic French canon. Batteux throws his considerable authority as holder of the Chair of Greek and Latin philosophy at the Collège de France behind a program for the study of the French tradition that aims to eliminate all literature deemed dangerous to civic virtue, especially the women writers who figure so prominently in the nonpedagogical anthology tradition. Before taking up the question of women writers and the case Batteux builds against them, however, I will first discuss the strategy on which Batteux's pedagogy is founded.

For his reform, Batteux calls on pedagogues to follow the new scientific model, "to collect data as the basis for a system that reduces their findings to common principles."[7] In *Les Beaux arts réduits,* Batteux defines the nature and the origin of the unique artistic principle he claims to have unearthed, and he also demonstrates the ideological goal of this method of literary and critical reduction. Let me outline the reasoning on which Batteux's model pedagogical system is founded. Good taste is unique: "there is only one good taste, that of nature" (1: 127). There is, however, progress in the spread of good taste because the public "allows itself, without noticing it, to be taken in (*se laisser prendre*) by the examples [it encounters in literature]. . . . One shapes oneself unconsciously on that which one has seen." Since moderns have the advantage of access to a greater number of authors, it is logical that good taste has become more widespread and that modern taste provides the definitive guide to classical status. On the basis of these two rules, Batteux constructs the following scenario: there is only one "natural" taste. The great artists are those who have "exposed" the natural design in their works. An educated public is able

7. I cite Batteux in the four-volume 1774 reedition of his works, *Principes de la littérature* (Paris: Saillant), 1: 126.

immediately to appreciate and to "approve" this greatness and then, instinctively and without even realizing it, to form itself according to the standards proposed by the classic literary texts. Then, as a matter of course, the model esthete becomes a model citizen: "One wishes to seem good, simple, direct; in other words, the complete citizen will be revealed" (1: 145). The ideal citizen, furthermore, is also a perfect Christian, and the artistic manifestations of good taste inspire both civic virtue and Christian ideals (1: 146).

Batteux's logic, which he calls "simple, straightforward," is based on a premise never clearly exposed in his initial treatise: good taste may be unique and innate, but it must also be taught, for only an educated public immediately understands great literature. The implied conclusion of Batteux's theory of universal taste and esthetic progress is that the French educational system should use its power to create the ideals and the standards of Frenchness. This service Batteux himself provides in the companion volume to his reductionist theory, in which he selects the precise examples that should be imposed upon the minds of those to be made into model Christian citizens, to mold them, without their knowledge, into the recognition of socially correct greatness. In his *Cours de belles-lettres*, he provides the outline for the teaching of literature designed to produce educated French male Christians. He gives examples from Greek, Latin, and French literature, although "of course French letters will occupy the first rank" (2: 9). Both his volume's organization and his description of it are resolutely direct:

> We will cover all the genres in succession, beginning with the simplest. We will give a summary presentation of the nature, the parts, and the rules of each of them; we will briefly trace its history; after which we will apply the rules to the most famous works in each genre, which will be analyzed both in terms of their content and in terms of their form. [2: 9–10]

In the three volumes of his curriculum, Batteux proceeds genre by genre, giving first general history and principles, followed by a short biography of each author, and finally, selected passages from each author's work, passages which—and this is his work's major long-term innovation—he then analyzes. In the *Cours de belles-lettres*, anthologizing is always accompanied by a demonstration for teachers of how to use literature in the classroom. The *Cours de belles-lettres* is the first example in France of the pedagogical genre we now call a literary manual.

When Batteux begins the course itself, it quickly becomes apparent that "our" taste simply singles out again and again those works that conform to "our" preconceived notions of what a work on a specific subject should say. When he sets up his presentation of La Fontaine, Batteux lays out the foundation for his method for reading literary texts, a method with a prodigious future in the French pedagogical tradition. His technique—"which presupposes real genius"—"consists in the comparison of a work with nature itself or, *that which amounts to the same thing, with the ideas that we have about what one can, and what one must say about the chosen subject"* (2: 61, my emphasis). He illustrates his method with a reading of La Fontaine's "Le Chêne et le Roseau" that is a classical model for the critical/pedagogical genre today known as *explication de texte.*

Before examining the text, however, Batteux shows why it deserves to be singled out as an exemplary work: "Before reading it, let us try to see for ourselves what ideas nature would present us on this subject" (2: 61). He then shows how the major elements in La Fontaine's fable correspond to "our" preestablished ideas of what they should be. In his *explication de texte,* furthermore, Batteux goes on to demonstrate that "our" expectations, when properly fulfilled, produce a work that is the perfect embodiment of all the stylistic and formal qualities previously characterized as the highest literary values. The great work, the classic, is the work that contains no surprises for the educated critic/reader and the work that conforms perfectly to the French male Christian critic's ideas of (human) nature. All "we" have to do to explicate literature properly is to articulate "our" prejudices and proclaim as classics those works that best exemplify "our" vision of what the world should be.

Thus Batteux's program reveals that the teaching of literature in France has been founded from its origin on the phenomenon that Anne-Marie Thiesse and Hélène Mathieu, in an indispensable recent study of the evolution of the canon of French literature in the nineteenth century that has been expanded and translated for this volume, refer to as "l'histoire littéraire par les textes" [literary history through texts]. Just as in the nineteenth-century process whose unfolding Thiesse and Mathieu retrace, in Batteux's formulation of "l'histoire littéraire par les textes" works are initially singled out allegedly only because of their value as examples, that is, for the extent to which they lend themselves to the techniques of the *explication de texte.* Yet the overall implication of his work, and of the nineteenth-century programs that follow his example, is that literary history can be written solely on the basis of the works thus isolated.

Batteux's program is also a monument to the official exclusion of the novel from the pages of literary history, and therefore of the women writers who were until then its most illustrious practitioners. The self-styled Boileau of his age (his collected works appear in 1774 to coincide with the centenary of the publication of the *Art poétique*), Batteux continues his precursor's battle against prose fiction. Boileau, however, had at least discussed the novel, if only to dismiss it, in the *Art poétique* and in more detail in the *Dialogue des héros de roman*.[8] But even the scornful condemnations of the premier critic of the Golden Age had not succeeded in diminishing the genre's popularity in Batteux's day: seventeenth-century novels continued to be reedited throughout the eighteenth century and were given enormous coverage in the worldly anthologies, proof that they remained an essential part of the canon for adult readers that, at least until the Revolution, offered a challenge to the classic canon being developed by Goujet, Batteux, and their colleagues. Batteux's resolute avoidance of the novel could well have been a new tactic for eliminating the genre that for decades had proved stubbornly resistant to the decree denying it classic status. Since Batteux does not allude to the genre's existence, even in the volume he devotes to prose forms, it might be possible to explain his omission on the grounds that the novel was perhaps the mode least malleable to the demands of the *explication de texte*. However, this explanation is invalidated by the terms on which Batteux judges the only two women writers he chooses to include.

In the volume Batteux devotes to prose genres, he concludes with a discussion of the letter, for which his representative modern author is Sévigné. However, the goal of the *explications de texte* he performs on her epistles is to point out their defects, to prove that she is not a suitable pedagogical model. Her letters are so full of "dead time" (*longueurs*) that they frequently "languish" (355–56). Her arguments are "without body" (356). Her style, in short, is an appropriate model only for "overly tender mothers" (354), and it is unworthy of exem-

---

8. Lack of space prevents me from repeating any part of an argument I have already developed elsewhere: for Boileau, the novel is dangerous first and foremost because it is marked by the values of the women writers who dominated the genre's production in his day. See my "Sappho's Leap: Domesticating the Woman Writer," *L'Esprit créateur* 25, no. 2 (1985): 14–21.

plary status because it is too "risky (*hasardé*) for anyone but her, and *especially for a man of letters*" (354–55, my emphasis).

This reasoning becomes even clearer in Batteux's treatment of Deshoulières, the only other woman writer he includes. (She was, in 1671, the winner of the first prize for poetry awarded by the Académie Française, and she is the ideal example of the woman writer always part of the worldly adult canon, but since eliminated, following the judgment of Batteux's followers, from their canon for children.) Her pastoral poetry is judged "the most delicate," "the *softest* possible," but

> unfortunately, the doctrine—the "esprit de mollesse," the "essence of flabbiness or pliancy"—that her poetry fosters is conducive to a weakening of moral fiber, and turns it into a sort of epicurianism entirely opposed, not only to Christian morality, but also to that vigor of the soul, to that *male force*, that is the foundation and the support of true integrity. [2: 188, my emphasis]

Thus Deshoulières, like Sévigné, seems to have been included in the first pedagogical canon of French literature the better to justify the exclusion of women's writing in general. These token women achieve exemplary status above all as illustrations of the threat to "vigorous" male Christian standards represented by the "softening" and "languishing" tendencies of female literary models. Women writers, Batteux warns, had to be eliminated from the curriculum because they were a direct threat to church and state.

Classicists have long been sensitive to the central role in the preservation of Greek literary texts played by the anthologies edited for schoolboys in antiquity. For example, of the forty to forty-four comedies of Aristophanes known to the ancients, we know only the eleven edited by a grammarian as "selected theater" for classes. Similarly, all that has come down to us of the vast production of Aeschylus and Sophocles are the seven plays selected for the curriculum.[9] In the case of French literature, one cannot, of course, speak of a phenomenon as dramatic as the permanent destruction of works. Nevertheless, for nearly two centuries it has been as if the works of most of the French women writers included in the early canon for adults no longer existed. Once modern writers had entered the pedagogical curriculum, within decades the anthologies for a cultivated adult public ceased to

9. Henri Marrou, *Histoire de l'éducation dans l'antiquité* (Paris: Seuil, 1948), 225.

be compiled, and the other canon they had kept alive began to be forgotten. Increasingly, the modern writers who continued to be read were only those who could be promoted as French classics, that is, as part of a national, and a nationalistic, literary program. The educators entrusted with the creation of a literary model for the exclusively male public of the *collèges* followed Batteux's lead and excluded the "dangerous," the "inimitable" as Lafayette would have it, examples of virtue provided by women writers.[10]

The terms in which Batteux eliminated women writers were frequently repeated as the original French pedagogical canon was set in place. I will cite one example from another pedagogue-critic of the day because I believe that the importance of repetition in canon formation must never be underestimated. Critics-pedagogues most often just reiterate the judgments of others. "[Villedieu's] works are little read today, and I dare say that they are still read too much, considering the danger that young men above all cannot fail to run from their reading" (Goujet, 18: 138). When women writers are evoked by any of the eighteenth century's literary pedagogues, it is almost always simply to explain in summary fashion why their works should no longer be read. Often, Batteux's argument about their threat to the nation's male fiber is restated. Just as often, the pedagogue turns to the argument Boileau used, quite prematurely, about Scudéry (in his *Dialogue des héros de roman*): "she is no longer read." Their pronouncements are just as premature as their master's—Villedieu, for example, continued to be reedited throughout the eighteenth century; but that is not the point. Women writers were so threatening to the ideology of the developing pedagogical canon that their elimination had to be reimposed until the new curriculum was firmly established.

Thus, in the sixteen-volume compilation that may best represent the view of the canon that the nineteenth century inherited from the eighteenth, *Lycée ou cours de littérature ancienne et moderne* (1797–1803), the Voltaire disciple and long-time journalist La Harpe uses this argument, virtually without exception, whenever he evokes a woman writer. He mentions eleven seventeenth-century women, not an

---

10. There were occasional attempts to found a pedagogical canon for schoolgirls, the most celebrated of which was drawn up at Saint-Cyr for and by the Marquise de Maintenon. These curricula always make frequent use of women's writing—witness the impressive role played by Scudéry at Saint-Cyr. However, given the tiny percentage of girls among the school children of the day, it is obvious that these alternative pedagogical curricula are largely merely utopian artifacts.

unimpressive list, but for all but Lafayette and Sévigné, the entry is limited to: "her boring novels, plays, etc., have been forgotten," or "her works are no longer read." La Harpe devotes fully half of the *Lycée*'s volumes to the literature of his own, not quite finished, century. In these eight volumes, however, he includes only four women writers: Tencin, de Beaumont, Riccoboni, Graffigny. La Harpe's compilation demonstrates that the flowering of the pedagogical tradition brought about the termination of the worldly tradition. Contrary to what you probably imagine, his *Lycée* is intended not for the formation of schoolchildren but as "a supplement to [the studies they've already done] for people of the world who don't have the time to begin new studies."[11] (The *Lycée* is, in fact, the record of La Harpe's lectures at what has been described as a worldly Sorbonne with an elegant public.) This is the first work of adult education to be a work of *reeducation:* La Harpe is trying to destroy the influence of the tradition of worldly anthologies, to make over the vision of the canon proposed for adult readers in the image of the pedagogical canon drawn up for schoolchildren. In the worldly anthology thus brought into the nationalistic line, women writers were virtual nonentities. This new pedagogical nationalism arrived just in time for its message to be heard by those who were involved in the canonical revision of the 1820s, whose influence on the image of sixteenth-century French literature still projected by today's manuals is demonstrated by Ann Jones and Nancy Vickers in this issue.[12]

Such consideration of canonical genealogies seems naturally to call for reflection on the process of canon formation taking place today. The critics who seem most inclined to consider the type of question—if not pronouncing on the value of a literary text, at least championing a text for inclusion in a curriculum—that was the exclusive concern of their classical precursors are for the most part those, whether feminists of the so-called American persuasion or supporters of other minority traditions, who ask that the canon be revised in order to include voices that have traditionally been excluded. The most visible contemporary canonical gestures have taken the form either of the critique of existing curricula and other pedagogical tools, or the promotion of parallel canons to which students are to be exposed at the same time as more traditional programs. Not since the turn of the

11. *Lycée ou cours de littérature ancienne et moderne,* 16 vols. (Paris: Lefèvre, 1816), vi.

12. La Harpe's compilation is reprinted four times between 1813 and 1816 alone.

eighteenth century have pedagogues been faced with the choice between two opposing plans for the programmatic packaging of French
literature, one of which would systematically grant a place to women
writers. It is hard to predict the ideological grounds on which a decision will be made this time.

It is, of course, possible that there is now room for more than one
canon of French literature. Certainly the dissemination of French culture is no longer the relatively manageable phenomenon that it was
the last time this canonical option was available: various centers,
more or less distant from the source of French nationalism and with
more or less regular transfusions of native blood (presumably, those
trained at the source are more likely to share received ideas of Frenchness) now promote visions of the canon that may well become gradually more irreconcilable with that formulated by and for the French
national educational system. Finally, it is even possible that new technologies might inadvertently generate a challenge to received ideas of
the canonical.[13]

Consider the example of the ARTFL (*CNRS*/University of Chicago
Trésor de la langue française) data base. Many American universities
now subscribe to this program that allows users, for an hourly fee, to
have access on their computers to a long list of works of French literature from the Middle Ages to the twentieth century. (A new list is due
soon; the one I consulted includes some seventy texts from the seventeenth century alone.) The data base was constituted by the Institut
National de la Langue Française rather than one of the branches of the
CNRS more directly entrusted with a pedagogical mission. Texts were
selected for the ARTFL data base solely on the basis of their linguistic
richness (the project's long-range goal is a new dictionary of the French
language).[14] In the meantime, anyone at a subscribing institution has
access to what looks for all intents and purposes like a computerized
canon of French literature with nothing to indicate its lexicographic
mission. For some time, I derived great satisfaction from the list,
which I imagined to be some sort of subversive canon of French literature, generated in the bosom of the CNRS: the data base includes,
among other texts that are since the Revolution no longer part of liter-

13. In an interview for this volume, Julia Kristeva expresses the belief that there will
no longer be canons because of the influence of the media. I think rather that mass communication will revise traditional methods of canon transmission.

14. I would like to thank Bernard Quemada and Evelyne Martin for this information.

ary programs, a good selection of the poetry of Deshoulières (the very verse Batteux castigates as a danger to "Christian morality" and "male force"), as well as no fewer than seven works, both fairy tales and travel literature, by d'Aulnoy, the possible editor of the original worldly anthology. My satisfaction continues even now that I know that the French intend to propose these women writers as models only of linguistic variety. After all, no one will be around to instruct the evergrowing ranks of American students who, far from the Hexagon, rely increasingly on computers rather than any printed source of information, that the works so readily available on their screen (when they may have been out-of-print for decades, if not centuries) are valuable solely for their word-count. Without a critical apparatus to direct their judgment, students might even take Deshoulières for the classic author she was for generations of adult French readers. The first canon of classic French literature just may be due for a revival.

II. 1990–1998

R. HOWARD BLOCH

Fin de Siècle Nuclear Sublime

In a stunningly brilliant article published in 1990, Richard Klein lays out the relationship between theory and the world historical positioning of the superpowers on the brink of nuclear disaster. Klein articulates the unthinkable event in terms of *when* and not *if*. For the Cold War, defined by the arms race as the "dominant mechanism of capitalization in the world," entails the capacity—yea, the necessity—to think the future as a "nuclear fable." To think a future without history, oblivious to memory or archive, a future without "narrative configuration," without literature, a future seen from a godlike perspective, a future beyond time, a "negative future anterior" projecting into an unredeemed end without witness and thus without tragedy.

In the perception of the ways in which the radical global polarization of the Cold War is linked to the suspension of the binary synonymous with theory (and the word has gained of late just a slight archeological ring), Klein has hit a rich vein of truth. Indeed, once upon a time, one way of tolerating the totalizing balance of the superpowers on the brink of world destruction was to refuse narration and the referent, a privileging of one side that would have been the equivalent of a preemptive first strike provoking a reactive launch, to reason in terms of an unresolvable paradox like the Class-A Blackout that usurps Klein's argument, which is never fully articulated in terms of specific cultural effects. The balance of the antimony, possible or impossible (and here the hesitation is a performance of the thing itself), is the guarantee of a future, the maintenance, deep in the zone where words veer toward ideas and ideas verge on the perceptions that are the stuff of events and things, of linguistic and logical equilibrium as a caution against a loosening of "launch on warning strategies." The nuclear age is the age of theory, its geopolitical balance a factor in the

YFS 97, *50 Years of Yale French Studies, Part 2*, ed. Porter and Waters, © 2000 by Yale University.

urge toward an allegorization of the world, the interpretative instance that was nowhere more fully articulated than in the French world systems of the late 1960s through the 80s. For as long as the world was double it was hermeneutically charged in terms of a present reality and its implicit other, the literal, philological sense of literary language and its displaced meanings and intention, language and its difference from itself. In the logic of the nuclear sublime, nothing could be what it seemed, the foreclosure of binarism in the privileging of one or the other of its terms held in abeyance as a pledge to the future. Which was not, of course, without its utopic temptations, the positing of a social space whose idealization gave the lie to the dangerous monocracy of the West.

In this Y2K-ready essay Klein inaugurates what has become a decade of millenial thinking, intensified toward the end by the apocalyptic specter of planes falling from the sky, the collapse of financial markets, the breakdown of failsafe military systems, and the disappearance of the (electronic) archives as a result, in a shift in the metaphorics of the end from the explosion of atoms to electronic implosion, of a failure of the chip literally to think its own future as an extra zero at the end of the date. The "zeroless date" is a ruse of history, which is never quite where one expects it and which has taken its own back in the crumbling of the suspended antinomy of the nuclear fable, in the erosion of utopias, and in the shrinking of allegorized space beginning with Czechoslovakia and leaving, finally, toward the end, only Cuba and Albania. (A colleague at the University of California once suggested that Berkeley may be all that's left.)

Between the time Klein's article was written and its publication the world did not end, but history as we knew it collapsed along with the Eastern Bloc, leaving in the place of the arms race to feed capital a retrofitting of the military synonymous with the Internet, globalization, and the spectacular disappearance of theory whose own nuclear winter consists of a return of the past—history, the referent, memory, the body, biography, narrative, the archive; a wallowing in ethics and the disappearance of universal theoretical man (logic, after all, is, by definition, one); and, along with the advent of identity politics and the fission of its ethnically and sexually discrete subjects, a recentering of postnuclear critical space along the lines of multicultural, gender, francophone, and cultural studies, all of which are represented in the pages of *Yale French Studies* reproduced from the 1990s.

In "In an Era of Testimony: Claude Lanzmann's *Shoah*," which appeared in the volume on "Literature and the ethical question," Shoshana Felman reorients Richard Klein's thinking of a hypothetical future in the direction of a real past in order to treat the questions of individual responsibility, the truth-value of historical witnessing, moral commitment and narrative, narrative and community, community and the unspeakable events of the Holocaust. Felman revives the concept of the person along with a personality of every individual's attachment to history. She posits a return—via art—of the referent and, through the film's signature, the song of one of Lanzmann's interviewees, Srebnik, shot at age thirteen and left to die, a relationship of the voice to the materiality of the body—a resurrection of the bodies raised by the singing witness to speak.

Laurent Jenny's "Genetic Criticism and its Myths" focuses upon the materiality of the text in relation to the biographical recuperation of an imaginary, originary, pre-textual event. Nourished by the technological models of the information age, the electronic archive and hypertext, genetic criticism is, Jenny asserts, rooted in nineteenth-century psychology and in a superannuated literary positivism that has always mistaken origin for meaning, both of which we had imagined to have been surpassed by the structuralist poetics of the 1970s. Jenny demonstrates convincingly how resolutely the literary texts most susceptible to the search for a "pre-textual, eternally anterior, minor, primitive, raw, illogical . . . and fecund Other" that would "re-dynamize the trace so as to relive the event"—that is, the works of Hugo and Flaubert—resist the genetic method. Despite the mass of pre-textual documentation surrounding great literary works and because of the lack of closure that such a mass implies, genetic criticism not only cannot produce a reading, but participates profoundly in what appears as an end-of-the-century, antitheoretical, phantasmatic longing for the real.

One direction this longing has taken is that of francophone studies here represented by Maryse Condé's essay "Order, Disorder, Freedom, and the West Indian Writer." Defying expectations as she loves to do, Condé locates a founding malaise in West Indian literature in a series of explicit and implicit commands issued by predominantly male African and Caribbean writers and having to do with the social and sexual limits of suitable subject matter, with canonical modes of description, character, and plot, and, finally, with the restrictive invitation issued in Jean Bernabé, Patrick Chamoiseau, and Raphaël Confiant's *Eloge de la Créolité*, "to give a name to everything and true to *créolité* say that it is beautiful." The women writers of the West Indies, on the other hand, have broken the taboos laid down by their male counterparts. In portraying black-on-black racism, madness and suicide, the pleasures of female sexuality, by transgressing the traditional image of Africa, but, most of all, by offering a more realistic portrayal of irresponsible males and fathers in the place of "triumphant . . . messianic heroes coming back home to revolutionize their societies," writers such as Suzanne Lacascade, Mayotte Capécia, Michèle Lacrosi, Simone Schwarz-Bart, Myriam Warner-Vieyra, and Maryse Condé herself have placed women at the "forefront of the daily battle for survival" and have thus, as is obvious in the final quotation from Maurice Blanchot, rendered literature true to itself.

Condé's introduction of gender into the francophone mix stands in curious resonance with a more general turning in the late 1980s from feminism *strictu sensu* toward gender studies, given a transnational twist in Christine Delphy's "The Invention of French Feminism: An Essential Move" (*YFS* 87, 1995). Here Delphy makes the not wholly original claim that the term "French Feminism" is an invention of British and American feminists based upon a conflation of women writers with the women's movement and upon a misperception of the "Holy Trinity" of "household names"—Cixous, Kristeva, Irigaray— who are increasingly divorced from social debate. Further, the very term "French Feminism" is, according to Delphy, an imperialistic appropriation rooted in a refusal among American feminists to take responsibility for their own race and class prejudice, a projection whose real target is the French, which has had noxious effects upon the French women's movement. As another of the productive transatlantic misunderstandings that over the years have filled the pages of *Yale French Studies*, Delphy articulates the difference between French and Anglo-American feminism in terms of conflicting ideologies of sexual difference, the one essentialist and additive, but neglectful of "the different things to which sexual difference refers," the other constructivist and voluntarist in the assumption that one is able to escape centuries of social conditioning.

In Delphy's recognition of the distinction between sex or anatomical difference, sexuation, sex roles, sexual activity, and sexual preference she opens a space for gay and lesbian studies represented in *Yale*

French Studies in "Same Sex/Different Text" (*YFS* 90), a volume that appeared the following year. And, in avoiding the pitfalls of binarism itself, Delphy affords just a glimpse of the logical rigor of the nuclear fable for whose intellectual moxie this critic—in what Eliot calls "these my middle years"—is nostalgic.

RICHARD KLEIN

The Future of Nuclear Criticism *

If the institution of Nuclear Criticism has a future, which is by no means certain, for the moment only a hypothesis, it would depend on its capacity to give us to think the future differently. The future of Nuclear Criticism, objective genitive, depends on the future of Nuclear Criticism, subjective genitive, its ability to produce a new concept, hence an altered model of anticipation, perhaps a new, nonnarrative future tense. Nuclear Criticism seeks to differentiate itself from abundant past efforts to imagine narrative scenarios, fictional or pseudo-documentary, that aim to represent or pretend to document a war without precedent, perhaps without model. That sort of mimetic imagining and its criticism, in the genres of fiction, of history, of political science, of journalism, has been productively going on for decades without need of a new concept of the future, without benefit of Nuclear Criticism—if there is such a thing and if it has a future. Indeed, the bibliography of those narrative representations is now enormous, in itself a vast archive remembering what until now has never occurred. From the englobing perspective of the archive, what is called Nuclear Criticism, despite its overweening ambition to think a new new, or new anew, is no news. Despite its ambition to institute a new concept of the future, another model of anticipation, Nuclear Criticism can only with difficulty avoid the claims of narrative—above all, the assumption that the future has a future, that there is, potentially, a story in the future of everything that has a future. Nevertheless, it aims to generate a concept, and institute a discourse that does not lend itself readily to narrative configurations—a discourse whose possibility has been created by the paradoxes of the nuclear condition, with

*From *Yale French Studies* 77 (1990): *Reading the Archive: On Texts and Institutions.*

YFS 97, *50 Years of Yale French Studies, Part 2,* ed. Porter and Waters, © 2000 by Yale University.

consequences for the production of culture that have only begun to be drawn.

It must not be assumed that thinking the future differently means anticipating anew the unthinkable prospect of total nuclear war; it has already been amply demonstrated that that task, thinking the unthinkable, is probably unavoidable, since it is not only the explicit aim of the project associated with eighteenth-century reflection on the sublime,* but, more permanently perhaps, the ambition of philosophical interpretation of future time since Plato. The nuclear sublime is that all too familiar aesthetic position from which one anticipatorily contemplates the end, utter nuclear devastation, from a standpoint beyond the end, from a posthumous, apocalyptic perspective of future mourning, which, however appalling, adorably presupposes some ghostly survival, and some retrospective illumination [apo-calypto: the emergence of what is hidden (in the secret cave of Calypso) out of the darkness into the light—the end as revelation of some essential truth: "Tel qu'en lui-même l'éternité le change." (Mallarmé)]. From a godlike perspective, beyond time and finitude, in the infinity of a pious fiction, future total nuclear war is contemplated; the paradigm of that perspective is Carl Sagan beyond the Earth, alight in his spaceship, intoning the end while the planet darkens under the inexorable progression of a cruel nuclear winter. The time or tense of the nuclear sublime is the already of a not yet, the mimetic reassurance of a future anterior: as when Plato, in the Philebus,[1] solves the problem of thought representing the future (since imitation, mimesthai, in a second time always follows what it re-presents, doubles the first) by treating the future as having a past. Seen from the perspective of the present, in the precipitation of anticipation, headlong, ahead of its head, the future is envisaged as if it were the past. Nuclear Criticism denies itself that posthumous, apocalyptic perspective, with its pathos, its revelations, and its implicit reassurances; it supposes that the only future may be the one we project forward from the time when total nuclear war, for the time being, has not taken place. Nuclear Criticism

*See Frances Ferguson, "The Nuclear Sublime," Diacritics 14, no. 2 (Summer 1984): 4–10.

1. Cf., Plato's Philebus (38e–39e), and Derrida's discussion in "The Double Session": "Socrates: We said previously, did we not, that pleasures and pains felt in the soul alone might precede those that come through the body? That must mean that we have anticipatory pleasures and anticipatory pains in regard to the future." In Dissemination, Trans., Barbara Johnson. (Chicago: Chicago University Press, 1981), 175. Page numbers will henceforth be cited in the text.

may even risk a jocular tone in order to signal its resistance to assuming the implications of the doleful language of anticipatory mourning, whose account of some total, unthinkable future loss inevitably presupposes that it is less than total, that the narrator, if only in imagination, survives. The lugubrious tone of the nuclear sublime conceals the interest that may be derived from evoking, in the present, the future possibility of total nuclear war; beneath its grim prospect, it masks some pleasure being taken or some profit being made—here and now.

Of course, historians may justifiably suspect the precipitation with which we leap to assume that the nuclear age is without precedent, that there is something new in the nuclear predicate. Is the magnitude or the nature of the horror, after all, incomparable? "What might prove," asks Derrida in "No Apocalypse, Not Now,"

> that a European in the period following the war of 1870 might not have been more terrified by the "technological" image of the bombings and exterminations of the Second World War (even supposing he had been able to form such an image) than we are by the image we can construct for ourselves of a nuclear war? [23]

The question forces us to wonder whether the haste with which we anticipate unprecedented destruction may be only the sign of an ideologically motivated ego's wish to be historically undetermined, narcissistically unique in history, and thus relieved of its burdens. For neither should we forget that there are those who never forget the holocaust and without hesitation assimilate its horror to the prospect of total nuclear war. For them, the first holocaust is a model, we might better say, a referential analogue for what then would be a second, nuclear one. But Nuclear Criticism determines the specificity of what it calls total nuclear war in so far as it is, potentially, a burning of practically everything, including memory. The difference is one between destruction on a vast scale that is collectively survived, archivally remembered, and politically mourned, and a total burning—a true *holos-kaustos*—in which no public survival, no collective recollection, no institutional mourning, remains.

Against the risk that the notion may acquire merely metaphorical significance, we will consider to be total any nuclear war which results in the exchange of at least one half of the strategic arsenal of both superpowers. It represents the exchange of not more than 5000 of the more than 12,000 strategic weapons each side possesses—that number only a fraction of the 50,000 weapons in toto, of which the majority are designed for so-called tactical deployment (the distinction at those levels of magnitude may in reality be difficult to maintain). Imagine the effect on our society if one bomb, at very least twenty to forty times the power of the one that fell on Hiroshima, were to strike each one of the 197 cities in the United States with populations above 120,000. But then, instead of 197 bombs, imagine that 5000 fell, twenty-five for each such city—less than one half, I repeat, of the Soviet strategic weapons armed and pointed at this moment in our direction. Let that far from total engagement of the strategic nuclear arsenal, less than one-fifth of the total number of weapons, constitute what we are calling total nuclear war.

Total nuclear war does not refer to anything that is or ever has been, so far; its real referent is in some still hypothetical future. Until the mirror is broken, we are suspended in this hypothetical phantasm, what Derrida with some qualification, has called "a fable—a pure invention: in the sense in which it is said that a myth, an image, a fiction, a utopia, a rhetorical figure, a fantasy, a phantasm, are inventions" (22). "We are suspended in this fabulous condition in which all our plans, and all our strategies, personal and public, are conditioned by a non-real referent, one which until today exists only as a thing without a model, about which we can only talk, and opine, and hope. If the mirror breaks into total nuclear war, if we were to escape the condition of the phantasm or fable, and enter the so-called real, the entry of the real of total nuclear war is expected to coincide, according to the fable, with the exit from all textuality, fabulous or otherwise. On that day, the fable has it, there may be no discourse left, no memory and no work of mourning capable of registering the then real referent; there will have been no more letters to take the news that there were no more letters. The conditions for any cultural record of the mirror having been broken will by virtue of its shattering cease to exist; the escape out of this imaginary relation to the nuclear phenomenon will have coincided with the end of the archive."[2]

Of course to call total nuclear war a kind of fable does not mean it could not occur; we are constantly preparing for it or against it, and it is already producing massive effects in the present, here and now, insofar as the arms race, its corollary, may indeed have become the dominant mechanism of capitalization in the world, the motive and motor

2. Richard Klein and William Warner, "Nuclear Coincidence and the Korean Airline Disaster," *Diacritics* 16, no. 1 (Spring 1986): 3. Page numbers will be cited in the text.

of capital formation itself. Nuclear Criticism is interested not only in the fable of total nuclear war, but in the difference between the fable of total nuclear war in the future and the reality, here and now, of the arms race. It is the relation between that fable and that reality that already constitutes what we might venture to call, at the risk of not being seriously understood, a literary problem for Nuclear Criticism.

But what we call literature may be precisely what is most at stake in the fable of total nuclear war. Being most at stake does not mean that we are more concerned with the survival of literature than with the loss of lives or the destruction of the ecological system. For indeed, it is not impossible to imagine, it is even likely perhaps, that human beings will survive, that the human habitat could regenerate, that even literature, epic poetry for example or lyric song, might revive in some form. But if total nuclear war meant the end of the archive, the destruction without a trace of the institutions of collective memory, then what is most absolutely vulnerable in the nuclear age is the institution of literature, and everything like literature which, at least since the eighteenth century, utterly depends on the archive's existence. Nuclear Criticism is an attempt to reflect on the peculiar vulnerability of literature in light of the prospect of total nuclear war. The repository of the archive, the institutions of public memory, not only insure the literal preservation of this text and that, fragments of which could of course survive total war. The institution of the archive not only makes possible positive remembering; it also permits systematic forgetting—all the possibilities for wandering, for error and discovery, for allusion and influence, for censorship and its undoing, that arise from the intertextual organization of the archive. That organization of course includes as well all the rhetorical and generic conventions, the protocols of commentary and criticism, canons and resistance to the canon, all the laws of copyright, and principles of authorship, all the technologies of publication and dissemination, all the systems of retrieval, cataloguing, bibliography, which have made access to the archive possible, at least since the eighteenth century. It is that institutional organization and that access, which is most utterly vulnerable in the prospect of total nuclear war; that, at least, is the hypothesis of Nuclear Criticism. If it were the case that what is for the moment a fable were to acquire a real referent, what conclusions then could one draw now, in advance, about the nature and the conditions of our contemporary cultural production? What effect does that fabulous possibility exercise here and now on the forms and themes, the substance and the shadows of our cultural products? Nuclear Criticism seeks to discover signs of that fabled future at work in the present and to determine how they may be read, with implications not only for the cultural critic, but perhaps as well for the historian, the political scientist, the nuclear strategist.

What may be most vulnerable is the collective memory of our culture, not merely its existence but the persistence of the memory of its loss. Its loss may be lost, with no trace of survival—a possibility that literary fiction has always claimed the prerogative of proposing: the fiction or fable of the loss of the trace of the loss of the trace. If the memory of the destruction of collective memory is lost there will be no one to mourn, no mourning that will internalize and preserve the memory of what will have vanished—destruction on a scale incomparable with the burning of the library at Alexandria. Our culture, such is the hypothesis, is facing the possibility of a futureless future, a time in which it may no longer be possible collectively to mourn the past, a future in which there will not have been a posthumous perspective. It is this altered relation to mourning in a future without future, this negative future anterior, that differentiates what the nuclear fable allows us to imagine from the Nazi holocaust in Europe, whatever its hideous magnitude, which will still have permitted the consolation, the interiorization, the working through of memory, in order to preserve the future from repetition.

"The practical or pragmatic implications of this nuclear perspective, the standpoint of temporal narrativity which it imposes, have already begun to affect our culture, massively, and to determine our cultural productions in ways we are only beginning to discover. The dilemma is that we are obliged to become the cultural historians of a time without a model, anticipating in the tense of the future anterior a decisive historical possibility which, if it occurs, our culture might never view historically. We are left to become the historians of the future, to invent its history before it happens, because if it happens, it may never have a history—if the fable means the end of discipline, organized memory. If it will have been the case that there was no future, then the only existence the future may have for us is behind us, in the present imagined from the anticipatory standpoint of its having already occurred" (Klein, 3).

The nuclear age under the shadow of the nuclear fable implies a different relation to the future of mourning; it obliges us to think the possibility of another concept of the future, which the nuclear condition has fabulously erected alongside and in the interstices of the Platonic one with which we are accustomed, in our culture, to think. If it could grasp the structure and the implications of this new future, Nuclear Criticism might perhaps begin to operate, not only rhetorically with a new style of argument, but grammatically in a new future tense, perhaps under a new logical model of a hypothetical future, one whose concept may be readable in certain paradoxical logical formulations concerning the way we can anticipate future certainty from within the horizon of the nuclear condition. If the institution of Nuclear Criticism has a future, which is by no means certain, for the moment only a hypothesis, it would depend on its capacity to determine the existence of an alternate concept of the future whose logical consequences for the possibility of anticipated certainty might, in certain crucial circumstances, alter the calculations of our strategies, and effect the very conditions of strategic thinking itself. Its effects might erupt in discrete and punctual forms at certain moments of strategic consideration, not only with fearful implications for our military and diplomatic calculations but with intimate consequences for the conditions of our experience. It would be the future task of Nuclear Criticism, if it has a future, to uncover the work and display the effects of this revised concept or altered tense, in places where, unobserved, that concept is already decisively affecting our cultural productions.

As a contribution to formulating the concept and extending the implications of the nuclear future, I would like to turn your attention to a well-known paradox which broke into print for the first time in 1948 in *Mind*, the British philosophical journal, in the course of an ar ticle by the famous Scottish logician, Donald John O'Connor.[3] Known in its first incarnation as the Class-A Blackout paradox, it has had a remarkable history. For, despite having been considered by O'Connor himself to be "a frivolous example" of those his article entitled "Pragmatic Paradoxes," it prompted more than thirty responses over the next twenty years. Quine's decisive intervention in the debate is republished from *Mind* as the first article in a book entitled *The Ways of Paradox*.[4] His brief piece, only two pages long, is called "On a So-called Antinomy," because it seeks to demonstrate the fallacy in the

3. Donald J. O'Connor, "Pragmatic Paradoxes," *Mind* 57 (July 1948): 358–59.
4. W. V. Quine, "On a Supposed Antinomy," *The Ways of Paradox, and Other Essays* (Cambridge, Massachusetts: Harvard University Press, 1979), 19–21. Page numbers will be cited in the text.

Class-A Blackout paradox that disqualifies it as an authentic anti-nomy—one which might bring on a genuine crisis in thought by pro-ducing a self-contradiction arrived at by accepted ways of reasoning. As Quine writes: "[An antinomy] establishes that some tacit and trusted pattern of reasoning must be made explicit and henceforward be avoided or revised" (Quine, 5). Authentic antinomies have been the basis for important technical progress in the history of logic, and have produced earthquakes in the discipline, as when Bertrand Russell sent a letter to Frege containing his discoveries on the self-membership of classes whose self-referential logic derived from his meditation on the pre-Socratic paradox of Epimenides the Cretan, commonly known as the *pseudomenon*, or liar paradox. It was the ground-shaking discov-ery contained in that letter that caused Gottlob Frege, in shock, to write, in 1902, an appendix to his just-finished *Grundegesetze des Arithmetik*, which began: "Arithmetic totters. . . . A scientist can hardly encounter anything more undesirable than to have the founda-tion collapse just as the work is finished. I was put in that position by a letter from Bertrand Russell."[5]

Quine's article seeks to demonstrate that the Class-A Blackout is merely a puzzle, a so-called antinomy, whose appearance of paradox, depending on a fallacious assumption at a decisive moment in its ar-gument, may hence be dismissed as an illusory threat to the integrity of logical procedures, with no power to deconstruct the unshaken foundations of logic. But I particularly wish to draw your attention to the title of another paper, by Richard Montague, "A Paradox Re-gained."[6] Montague counters what he considers to be Quine's evasion of the paradox by proposing a logical formulation that reinstates the antinomy. The Miltonic allusion in Montague's title suggests that for a logician, paradise is an authentic antinomy, and to regain one that had been considered lost is the most blessed culmination of a logi-cian's thorny path.

The following abbreviated history of the Class-A Blackout paradox aims to demonstrate the way its capacity to be a true antinomy has been repeatedly lost and regained. There are those in the tradition whose whole aim is critical, and consists in discrediting the paradox, revealing the fallacies in the presentation of its premises and argu-ments that disqualify it, and reducing it to a "frivolous example." Oth-

5. Quoted by Quine, 11.
6. Richard Montague and David Kaplan, "A Paradox Regained," *Notre Dame Jour-nal of Formal Logic* 1 (1960): 79–90. Page numbers will be cited in the text.

ers like Michael Scriven[7] and Richard Montague have worked, as the latter writes, "to discover an exact formulation of the puzzle which is genuinely paradoxical" (79). There are those who seek to interpret the paradox with the view of mitigating the disruptive negativity it seems to propose; others have sought to exacerbate its negativity by discovering an authentically paradoxical formulation. For the latter, the paradox is not a menace to be overcome but an invitation to be taken up, one that solicits them to think anew about possibilities of anticipated certainty.

The alternating history of paradox lost, paradox regained signals the difficulty, in certain instances, of deciding whether we are speaking rhetorically or analytically, poetically or logically, about future possibilities of knowing the future. This narrative aims not only to repeat the logical arguments which have been advanced, but to analyze the rhetorical terms and the narrative frame, what Quine calls "the embodiments of its plot" (20), into which the logical argument has been cast—in order to justify the perhaps abusive extension of its implications for the possibility of Nuclear Criticism. But this history of the paradox wishes also to point to the punctual nature of its appearance, as if its emergence in the philosophical literature after the war signaled some deeper crisis in logical thought of which the debate surrounding this paradox may be a historically determined index—or perhaps only a rhetorical phantasm, whose philosophical seduction an analyst might wish to explore, but whose logical terms remain entirely within the capacious confines of millennial Western conceptions. If the paradox proves to be only a puzzle, the fiction of a true antinomy, it may nevertheless betray, beneath its apparent frivolity, a heightened anxiety of anticipation prompted by the nuclear condition; if no puzzle, but an authentic paradox, its punctual eruption after the war may signal a crisis in the logic of the future inaugurated by the prospect of total nuclear war.

In *The Unexpected Hanging and Other Mathematical Diversions*, Martin Gardner reports that Lennart Ekbom, who taught mathematics at Ostermalms College, in Stockholm, may have pinned down the apocryphal origin of the paradox that first appeared in print in O'Connor's published version. Gardner writes:

> In 1943 or 1944, the Swedish Broadcasting Company announced that a civil-defense exercise would be held the following week, and to test the

7. Michael Scriven, "Paradoxical Announcements," *Mind* 60 (July 1951): 403–07.

efficiency of civil-defense units, no one would be able to predict, even
on the morning of the day of the exercise, when it would take place.
Ekbom realized that this involved a logical paradox, which he discussed with some students of mathematics and philosophy at Stockholm University. In 1947 one of those students visited Princeton,
where he heard Kurt Gödel, the famous mathematician, mention a
variation of the paradox. [21][8]

It does seem plausible to imagine that the origin would lie with
Swedish philosophers, suspended in precarious neutrality, anxiously
anticipating a blackout, while all around Europe was in flames; in the
pleasant groves of their academy they had ample incentive to demonstrate with anticipated certainty that the worst is never sure—a conclusion at which the sage of Princeton had presumably, in other terms,
arrived. It is not, however, until 1948 that O'Connor gives the world
this inaugural formulation of the problem:

> Consider the following case: The military commander of a certain
> camp announces on a Saturday evening that during the following week
> there will be a "Class A blackout." The date and the time of the exer-
> cise are not prescribed because a "Class A blackout" is defined in the
> announcement as an exercise which the participants cannot know is
> going to take place prior to 6:00 p.m. on the evening in which it occurs.
> It is easy to see that it follows from the announcement of this defini-
> tion that the exercise cannot take place at all. It cannot take place on
> Saturday because if it has not occurred on one of the first six days of the
> week it must occur on the last. And the fact that the participants can
> know this violates the condition which defines it. Similarly, because it
> cannot take place on Saturday, it cannot take place on Friday either, be-
> cause when Saturday is eliminated Friday is the last available day and
> is, therefore, invalidated for the same reason as Saturday. And by simi-
> lar arguments, Thursday, Wednesday, etc., back to Sunday are elimi-
> nated in turn, so that the exercise cannot take place at all. [358]

Before considering the history of the interpretation of this puzzle, I
wish to make two parenthetical remarks. The expression, "anticipated certainty," with which this history characterizes the object of
the dilemma, does not belong in the first place to the Anglo-American
tradition, but comes from the treatment of its logic in another puzzle,
the "Three prisoner problem," a version of which Jacques Lacan dis-

8. Martin Gardner, "The Paradox of the Unexpected Hanging," *The Unexpected
Hanging, and Other Mathematical Diversions* (New York: Simon and Schuster, 1969),
11–23, 21.

cusses in a brief, but crucial article entitled "Le Temps logique et l'assertion de certitude anticipée."[9] Lacan's treatment of that puzzle, or sophism, as he called it, appeared only a few years before O'Connor's Class-A blackout paradox, at the end of the Second World War. It would require another essay to demonstrate the remarkable similarities between these two puzzles, whose almost simultaneous appearance in two independent traditions, at the dawn of the Nuclear Era, could be taken to constitute the emergence of something like a new episteme—an index of a crisis in our conception of the future whose implications we are only beginning to gauge.

The second parenthesis concerns the anecdote. The puzzle over the years has been variously known as the Hangman, the Unexpected Egg, the Surprise Quiz, the Senior Sneak Week, the Prediction Paradox, and the Unexpected Examination. In principle, of course, the anecdotal form has no bearing on the logical dilemma that the puzzle advances. Still, it cannot be uninteresting to a literary mind, to one that wishes to discover here a decisive adumbration of a new nuclear temporality, that in the earliest and most common forms of the puzzle, the theme of a fateful blackout at the end persists, even in its domesticated version of a surprise examination—which for students, and the academic philosophers who invented that anecdotal variant, is the functional equivalent in terms of absolute anxiety to programmed certain death. What one hears in the anecdote, mostly repressed in the logical discussions, is the anxiety of anticipation, what the paradox engenders and risks exacerbating by converting it into a permanent, unavoidable antinomy, the anxiety of anxiety. It risks, for example, deconstructing the distinction, which Freud requires as a condition for therapy (in *The Problem of Anxiety*) between normal anxiety that inoculates us against real potential threats and neurotic anxiety that endlessly reproduces itself.

Before we begin to examine the earliest treatments of the paradox, which dismissed it, let us dispense with one of the most general, metaphysical objections to it, advanced by Paul Weiss in a subsequent discussion, in a famous article entitled, "The Prediction Paradox."[10] Put simply it is this. The Class-A blackout is no paradox because it illegitimately presumes a predictive, logical certainty (as distinct from prob-

9. Jacques Lacan, "Le Temps logique et l'assertion de certitude anticipée," *Ecrits* (Paris: Seuil, 1966), 197–213. This article was not included in the two-volume Livres de Poche, nor to my knowledge was it ever translated.

10. Paul Weiss, "The Prediction Paradox," *Mind* 61 (April 1952): 265–69. Page references will be made in the text.

abilistic or empirical certainty) that one of a collection of future possibilities will actually occur. Operating with distinctions he borrows from Aristotle's *De Interpretatione*,[11] Weiss discovers an ontological gap between knowing a range or tissue of possibilities and knowing in advance that one or the other of those possibilities will actually fall out. In metaphysical terms, one must distinguish between "the realm of possibility" and "the realm of time, history, becoming" (267). Weiss disputes the premise of the paradox that on the first day of the week, faced with a range of possible days, one may be permitted to leap ahead in thought to the penultimate sixth day, Friday, and know for certain that on that day one will know for certain when the blackout must occur. Leaping ahead in imagination, says Weiss, presupposes that we have left the realm of possibility for the realm of time, history, becoming. The power of imagination introduces the factor of history; its anticipatory leap is logically equivalent to time having already eliminated the alternative possibilities which the commander had announced. What allows us in leaping ahead to be certain, on the basis of the decree, that the event will occur on Saturday, the last day, is that we have already eliminated in imagination all the other days of the week, all the other possibilities which on the first day remained open. Eliminating them, "there will be no uncertainty regarding the remaining alternatives" (269); after Friday, faced with no other possibilities, only a necessity, Saturday, remains open. But that condition cannot be predicted with logical certainty from the perspective of the beginning of the week when all the possibilities still obtain. On Friday, we are treating the last day as "distinct from all the rest": at that time there is no longer a collection of alternatives, only a single distributive one. Weiss writes:

> I can say that I will positively do 'something or other' tomorrow and yet not know positively what it will be. I can be positive that 'this or that will be,' i.e., of a range of possible occurrences connected by a collective 'or,' which allows no one of these occurrences to stand apart or be distinct from the others. This does not make it possible for me to know that just this will be done, or that something other than this will be done. There is a great difference between 'It is true that either x or non-x is the case' and 'it is true that x is the case or it is true that non-x is the case,' between f(x v non-x) and f(x) v f(non-x). The former is a necessary truth, the latter is true only when one has isolated the x and the

11. Aristotle, "De Interpretatione," *The Complete Works of Aristotle*, ed., Jonathan Barnes (Princeton: Princeton University Press, 1948), 30; 18b ff.

non-x, an act which requires that one leave the realm of possibility for the realm of time, history, becoming. To become is to convert the collective into the distributive 'or.' [267]

For Weiss, the conversion of a range of collective possibilities into a single distributive alternative formally marks the passage, in the metaphysics of Aristotle, between *dunamis* and *energeia*, between what is only a possible world and what becomes effectively real. The Class-A blackout results from the confusion of those two realms; it depends on the power of imagination to substitute surreptitiously for the calculations of logical time, the stark necessity of history. Given a range of possibilities, one can never predict, with logical certainty, that this or that will really occur; not even the commander, when he makes his decree, can know for sure what will actually happen to his decree until the day he proceeds to fulfill it. For Weiss, it is only an illusion to think that the blackout, whenever it occurs, even on the last day, will not be Class-A, one whose precise occurrence cannot be predicted at the beginning of the week.

W. V. Quine locates an even more fundamental error in Weiss's willingness to credit "a false notion abroad that actual paradox is involved" (19). For indeed Weiss does argue as if the paradox might be logically sustained, if only one overlooked the confusion it promotes between possible being and actual becoming. But it is that initially false notion, says Quine (with a logician's ill-disguised contempt for metaphysics), that "has even brought Professor Weiss to the desperate extremity of entertaining Aristotle's fantasy that 'It is true that p or q' is an insufficient condition for 'It is true that p or it is true that q' " (19).[12] Quine, himself disputing the paradox, will have no recourse to that fantasy; he argues, as most logicians have, that it is plausible to assume, under some circumstances, that certain propositions about the future can be known analytically, and that it would be absurd and dangerous to assume that the time series, Sunday to Saturday, cannot be treated like a logical sequence of distributive alternatives. Without benefit of metaphysics, Quine's argument, we will see, claims to locate the strictly logical fallacy the paradox conceals.

12. "And the same account holds for contradictories: everything necessarily is or is not, and will be or will not be; but one cannot divide and say that one or the other is necessary. I mean, for example: it is necessary for there to be or not to be a sea-battle tomorrow; but it is not necessary for a sea-battle to take place tomorrow, nor for one not to take place—though it is necessary for one to take place or not to take place," (Aristotle, 30; 19a).

D. J. O'Connor, L. Jonathan Cohen, and Peter Alexander, the first logicians who treated the paradox, dismissed it, not because of its faulty metaphysical assumptions, nor on strictly logical grounds, but because they considered its argument to be pragmatically, not formally, contradictory. Since a Class-A blackout is defined as one whose occurrence cannot be known in advance of the evening on which it is ordained, the order both decrees its occurrence within a specific time period and decrees that it will be a surprise. Such an announcement, writes O'Connor, "is merely pragmatically self-refuting. The condition of the actions are defined in such a way that their publication entails that the action can never be carried out" (358). The performance of the constative announcement, "There will be a Class-A blackout during the following week," itself precludes the possibility of ever verifying the truth of its performative accomplishment. The public enunciation of the decree disrupts the contextual condition for enacting its fulfillment: if the commander had merely whispered to himself that the Class-A blackout will take place during the week, there would have been no contradiction involved in its occurring and in its being a surprise. According to L. Jonathan Cohen, the decree, although not a statement involving self-referential, ego-centric particulars (of the sort, "I am speaking French now") resembles them insofar as its truth "can be falsified by its own utterance."[13] Peter Alexander went even further in contemptuously dismissing the decree, "There will be a Class-A blackout during the following week," by comparing it to a conditional statement whose condition is empirically, not even pragmatically unrealizable—of the species, "If I can be without air, I will not breathe all day tomorrow."[14] "Of course," he says, "I might be able to live without air tomorrow but, similarly, men might cease next week to be able to realize that if the blackout had not occurred by Friday it must occur on Saturday and then the condition would be realizable" (539). For Alexander, the decree amounts to saying, "There will be a surprise blackout next week" if a surprise blackout next week were possible, which it is not, if the surprise is announced in advance. For these first analysts, there is no authentic paradox, no true antinomy; the decree itself conceals a contradiction that the argument, leaping forward and devolving backward, serves only to display.

Consider the fate of K, as he is called by Quine and others, in the

13. Jonathan L. Cohen, "Mr. O'Connor's 'Pragmatic Paradoxes'," *Mind* 59 (January 1950): 85–87.
14. Peter Alexander, "Pragmatic Paradoxes," *Mind* 58 (October 1950): 536–38.

Hangman anecdote, who sits in his cell on Sunday with his lawyer reflecting on the judge's decree that some day during the following week he will be hanged at noon and will not know until a few minutes before noon, what day that will be. Having arrived at the conclusion of O'Connor, Cohen, and Alexander, he begins to smile, because he realizes that the judge's decree is contradictory and therefore he cannot be hanged as promised. Anxiously anticipating the end of the week, in an imaginative gesture of anticipated certainty, he logically determines what conditions will prevail, on the basis of the decree, on the penultimate day before the last day of the week, and knows that if he survives until then, he will know when he must be hanged. But knowing that he must be hanged on Saturday contradicts the definition of a Class-A blackout, so on that day, the last possible day, there can be no blackout for K. Having eliminated the last day, by the same argument he retrospectively eliminates the rest of the days of the week. Concluding that there is no day of the week on which the hanging can be performed by surprise, K concludes that the decree cannot be fulfilled, and he has every reason to smile.

K would take less consolation if he knew the argument of Judith Schoenberg who asserts, also in *Mind*, that K's initial hypothesis that if he survives until Friday contradicts the judge's decree. It is not, as Weiss has claimed, that leaping ahead in imagination puts history in the place of possibility. The assumption of K's being unhanged on Friday requires the conclusion, based on the judge's specifications, that he cannot be hanged on Saturday and thus cannot be hanged at all under the prescribed conditions, which include a specified time interval. "But this conclusion is in plain contradiction with the [judge's] order, which states that the [hanging] is going to occur during the specified interval. Therefore, the proposition cannot be considered to be an inference from the defined conditions. On the contrary, its conclusion contradicts the [judge's] order, and it follows that the assumption of [K being unhanged] on Friday is incompatible with the order."[15] Skipping over the week, the argument thus *begins* with the premise that the hanging has not occurred under the prescribed conditions. "It is not so much that the argument reverses the temporal order as that its premise skips over the week, while the argument itself is a kind of smokescreen that conceals the implications of the premise" (126).

15. Judith Schoenberg, "A Note on the Logical Fallacy in the Paradox of the Unexpected Examination," *Mind* 75 (January 1966): 125–27. Page numbers will be cited in the text.

K, continuing to hope, might have countered the charge (that his premise, the assumption that he is unhanged on Friday contradicts the judge's specifications) by appealing to the judgment of Quine, who defends his argument on this point—and whose objections to it lie elsewhere. Quine finds nothing wrong in K's assuming, for the space of a recursive argument, that he is unhanged on Friday, in order to prove that the decree will not be fulfilled: "This," he says, "would be good *reductio ad absurdum*" (20):

> Suppose that a mathematician at work on the Fermat problem assumes temporarily, for the sake of exploring the consequences, that Fermat's proposition is true. He is not thereby assuming, even as a hypothesis for the sake of argument, that he knows Fermat's proposition to be true. The difference can be sensed by reflecting that the latter would actually be a contrary-to-fact hypothesis, whereas the former may or may not be. [21]

By leaping ahead to Friday, K assumes he is unhanged, for the sake of the argument, whereas in fact he may or may not be. He does not assume, even as a hypothesis for the sake of argument, that he *knows* he will be unhanged, which would contradict the specification of the judge's decree.

But the happiness of K turns to despair when, having decided on Sunday that he cannot be hanged at all because the decree is contradictory, the hangman walks in at 11:55 A.M. on Thursday and the hanging occurs at noon exactly as the judge has specified, i.e., during the week and by surprise.

Michael Scriven, who was the first to regain the paradox, writes as follows:

> I think this flavour of logic refuted by the world makes the paradox rather fascinating. The logician (namely K) goes pathetically through the motions that have always worked the spell before [i.e., the spell of contradicting the judge's decree], but somehow the monster, Reality, has missed the point and advances still. [403]

K is hanged on Thursday and it is a surprise, just as the judge decreed.

Scriven regains the paradox, if not K, by adopting K's assumption that he survives until Friday, embracing his perspective on the penultimate day, and concluding as follows. Either K will be hanged on Saturday, and it will not be a surprise—which would falsify the judge's decree; or he will not be hanged on that day, which would also falsify the decree. Either way, hanged or unhanged, K knows on Friday that the decree will be self-refuting. Arguing in the same way, K regressively eliminates the other days. Thus, he realizes in advance that, since he cannot draw any proper conclusion concerning the occurrence of the blackout relative to the governing announcement, if the hanging does occur on any day of the week, if the monster reality enters the cell on Thursday just before noon, it will be a surprise; and since the definition of a Class-A blackout is framed in such a way that the precise date of its occurrence cannot be deducible from the announcement made, the decree will have been fulfilled: "Now if the governing announcement . . . is self-refuting and a blackout occurs on any night of the week, the statement, 'There will be a Class-A blackout next week' will be verified. And if it was publicly stated, it would still be correct" (Scriven, 407). Exit K; the logician goes refuted to the gallows. For Michael Scriven, the paradox regained consists in this: since all the days have been negated as possible days, any day is possible; since the decree is self-refuting, cannot be logically fulfilled, it will in all instances, pragmatically, be fulfilled. Its "suicide," he says, "is accompanied by its salvation" (407). Of course, for K, sitting in his cell, the death and life of the paradox is a matter of life and death. What must be his state of mind when at the beginning of the week he concludes, on the basis of the decree, that his hanging is impossible, and because it is impossible, that the hangman may appear on any morning before noon? It must seem to him as if the anticipated certainty with which he concluded his calculations was itself responsible for confounding the possibility that his calculations might prove to be true.[16]

16. Judith Schoenberg, following G. C. Nerlich's treatment of the paradox in 1961 (which cites Scriven), locates the turning point which "transforms" the paradox and negates its initial negation. She then regains it at another level, when a valid inference from its defined conditions allows her to conclude that what at first was paradoxically impossible proves by that very result to be both impossible and possible. "He points out that if all the days are negated as possible days for the event, then there are no grounds for assuming that it will occur, so that whenever it does occur it comes as a complete surprise. It might also be argued, perhaps, that if all the days are negated, then all the days are the same insofar as their probability of being the day of the (hanging). But a difficulty appears here, for this turning of the argument makes the possibility of the event follow from the previously established negation. The result is that Saturday becomes a possible day, and this would seem to be a fatal result. Because the impossibility of Saturday was accepted at the beginning as being a valid inference from the defined conditions of the event, and as such was accepted as the original premise upon which the whole argument rests. To negate it, is to negate the point of departure of the argument. So that this constitutes a *reductio ad absurdum*, and if the reasoning leading to it were valid, this could only prove that the defined conditions lead to a contradiction. That is, Saturday would both be impossible and possible. Thus the original paradox is transformed, but not resolved" (127).

At the very moment in the history of the paradox when it was thought to have been regained, W. V. Quine, the astringent Boston logician, shattered its pretensions to be an authentic antimony, by proposing an interpretation of the paradox that seemed definitively to reveal its fallacy.[17] He attacks it at the point where K, leaping ahead to Friday, concludes, on the basis of the governing decree, that a Class-A blackout, an unexpected hanging, cannot occur on Saturday, the last possible day of the week. K at that moment seems to be making what all previous commentators had taken to be an unimpeachable valid inference from the defined conditions of the event, "and as such [it] was accepted as the original premise upon which the whole argument rests" (Schoenberg, 127). Even Scriven and Nerlich, whose hyperparadox requires the elimination of Saturday as a possible day, make an argument that begins by first assuming the validity of the premise: on Friday K knows that he must be hanged on Saturday. According to Quine, the fallacy arises at the moment K leaps to the penultimate moment and concludes either (a) the event will have occurred at or before that time; or (b) the event will (in keeping with the decree) occur on the last day and K will (in violation of the decree) be aware promptly after noon on Friday that the event will occur on Saturday. Rejecting (b) because it violates the decree, K elects (a) and turns to considering earlier days. Actually, says Quine, K should have envisaged four possibilities instead of merely two. On Friday, he should consider the possibility that (c) the event will not occur on Saturday, in violation of the decree, or (d) the event will (in keeping with the decree) occur on Saturday and K will (in keeping with the decree) remain ignorant meanwhile of that eventuality (not knowing whether the decree will be fulfilled or not). "He erred in not recognizing that either (a) or (d) could be true even compatibly with the decree. The same fault recurred in each of his succeeding steps" (20). K cannot assume at the beginning of the week, even as a hypothesis for the sake of argument, that on Friday he will know that he must be hanged on Saturday; he might legitimately suppose that he will be hanged, but not that he will know it, with anticipated certainty, even a day in advance. "It is notable," Quine adds,

> that K acquiesces in the conclusion (wrongly according to the fable of the Thursday hanging) that the decree will not be fulfilled. If this is a conclusion which he is prepared to accept (though wrongly) in the end

17. W. V. Quine, "On a So-called Paradox," *Mind* 54 (July 1953): 65–67.

as a certainty, it is an alternative which he should have been prepared
to take into consideration from the beginning as a possibility. [20]

That K accepts the (erroneous) conclusion that he will not be hanged
points up the fallacy of his embracing the premise that on Friday he
will know that he must be hanged. His conclusion should have led
him to realize from the first that one can never know analytically
what will happen on the morrow. With the pious realism of a Boston
Puritan submitting to the uncertainty attending predestined grace,
Quine admonishes the victim: "If K had reasoned correctly, Sunday af-
ternoon, he would have reasoned as follows: 'Rather than charging the
judge with self-contradiction, therefore, let me suspend judgment and
hope for the best' " (20).

In a final turn, in an article to which we have already alluded,
Richard Montague disputes Quine's judgment that the unexpected
Class-A hanging is merely a "so-called paradox," "a supposed antinomy." Montague's solution not only achieves the salvation of K but
brings us the blessing of a "A Paradox Regained." I may perhaps be allowed merely to indicate the direction of the solution he proposes, for
to follow the steps of the demonstration in all its complexity would
require having recourse to the symbolic language with which he formally represents both the logic of elementary syntax and intuitive
epistemological principles.

"Treatments of the paradox," writes Montague,

> have for the most part proceeded by explaining it away, that is, by of-
> fering formulations which can be shown not to be paradoxical. We feel,
> with Shaw, the interesting problem in this domain is of a quite differ-
> ent character; it is to discover an exact formulation of the puzzle which
> is genuinely paradoxical. The Hangman might then take a place beside
> the Liar and the Richard paradox, and, not unthinkably, lead like them
> to important technical progress. [79]

For Montague as well as for Shaw, Quine is guilty of evading the paradox rather than resolving it: "To see that this is the case, it is only necessary to state explicitly and unambiguously what is meant by 'knowing' that the examination will take place on the morrow."[18] Neither
Quine nor Montague dispute Quine's diagnosis of the fallacy in K's argument; he is right to say that K cannot know, simply on the basis of
his not having been hanged before Friday, that he will be hanged on

18. R. Shaw, "The Paradox of the Unexpected Examination," *Mind* 67 (July 1958):
382–84. Page numbers will be cited in the text.

Saturday; to the extent such knowledge cannot be logically deduced from the conditions of the decree, it is not analytical knowledge, and as Montague says, "one cannot know a non-analytic sentence about the future."[19] Knowing nothing for certain, K can only hope for the best. It might seem plausible to suppose that K draws the conclusion that he must be hanged from the assumption that the decree will be fulfilled; for on that assumption K could indeed deduce on Friday that he must be hanged. "But it is unreasonable to suppose that K knows the decree will be fulfilled, especially in view of his attempt to prove the contrary" (Montague, 82).

But whereas Quine adopts a vague common sense notion of knowing, Montague proposes to make the meaning of the decree depend explicitly, unambiguously, on K's "knowing" in the sense of being able to predict *on the basis of the decree* (80). "As Shaw has remarked, the paradoxical flavor of the hangman decree derives from a self-referential element in the decree which was not incorporated in Quine's formulation" (80). Montague permits K to propose a version of the decree which warrants his arriving at the conclusion that he will not be hanged; he is allowed to assume that the judge's decree may be expressed as follows: K will be hanged at noon on one of the days of the following week, and he will not be able to know, on the basis of the present decree, what day it will be. What distinguishes this formulation of the decree from the one that Quine proposes is that it restores a self-referential element to the decree. Leaping ahead to Friday, K is not now obliged to assume, as Quine has him doing, that the decree must be fulfilled on Saturday (a hypothesis contrary to the fact he wishes to prove), or that having eliminated the other alternatives, on the last day he will know he must be hanged (a nonanalytic statement about the future). In the self-referential version of the decree that K advances, he needs only to be able to claim that on Friday he will know, *on the basis of the decree*, that the decree itself logically implies that he will be hanged on Saturday. But since knowing that, and knowing that he will know it, contradicts the ordained surprise, the decree will be seen to be contradictory and K has nothing to fear. His argument is closely analogous to the earlier fallacious argument with which he had illegit-

19. Knowing here is used in the sense of being able logically to be deduced from pre-existing conditions assumed to maintain. That is not at all to deny that we can have nonanalytic, empirical certainty concerning possible future events: we know the sun will rise. By inference it does however reject Weiss's claim, following Aristotle, that no statements concerning future possibilities can ever be known analytically in advance.

imately concluded his salvation, but whereas in Quine's version he is obliged to assume, as a condition of his argument, that the decree will be fulfilled, in the self-reflexive version he concludes only that the decree itself logically implies that on Saturday he must be hanged, if the alternatives are eliminated. Arguing *on the basis of the decree* means that he takes its requirements not as conditions which must be fulfilled but as rules acting like axioms that lead to a logically contradictory conclusion.

Montague, following Shaw, has produced a plausible version of the decree that proves to be self-contradictory; K may be spared, but the logician has not yet regained the paradox, an authentic antinomy— one that would allow K to conclude analytically that he cannot be hanged while at the same time permitting the judge to prove that the conclusion is a nonanalytic statement about the future. To do that requires a final step, a last desperate attempt on the part of the judge to "avoid official embarrassment by reformulating his decree with an added stipulation" (84). The judge stipulates that K will be hanged unexpectedly during the following week, *unless he knows at the beginning of the week that the present decree is false.* Deviously, the judge seems to have confounded K's triumphant demonstration by making its conclusion an integral part of the decree: if K wins, he loses. If he proves that the unexpected hanging entails a contradiction, he knows that he knows that the decree cannot be fulfilled which fulfills the decree. "But in avoiding official embarrassment the judge has plunged himself into contradiction. Now we have a genuinely paradoxical decree" (84–85). Reduced to its simplest form, the stipulation comes down to the judge's ordaining that the following condition will be fulfilled: K knows at the beginning of the week that the present decree is false. It is short work to demonstrate that if the judge's decree is false and if K knows it at the beginning of the week, then he has fulfilled the condition of the judge's decree which ordained that K would know that the present decree is false, with the result that the decree is fulfilled. Montague writes: "In view of certain obvious analogies with the well-known paradox of the Liar, we call the paradox connected with [the judge's decree] the Knower" (88). Its assumptions lead to the genuinely paradoxical consequences that the decree cannot be fulfilled and that the decree necessarily will be fulfilled. Thus if the judge's formulation of the decree is adopted, Montague exclaims, "Both K and the hangman are correct!" (87). K knows, with analytical anticipated certainty, that the trap must fall and cannot fall on the appointed future date. Neither hopeful nor anxious, free of any uncertainty, he faces the future prospect of this decreed blackout with absolute terror as to its necessity and absolute confidence in its impossibility.

I fear I may have strayed so far into the history of the institution of this paradox, within the institution of logic, that I have long ago lost your willingness to hear this story in light of the question of the nuclear fable. And I fear even more that I will not be able to persuade you that the exacerbation of the negativity of the Class-A blackout paradox points to logical problems concerning the anticipation of the future in a nuclear condition. Let me invite you to reflect, briefly, on the implications of the Class-A blackout for the condition of launch on warning strategies that could be devised by our leaders. Consider the consequences of one of the prominent features of the Class-A blackout paradox, the way it seems to be pragmatically self-refuting—the way the publication of an order appears to make the order self-refuting. And yet, as we have seen, that appearance is itself the result of a perhaps fallacious interpretation of the decree that overlooks the way the order can seem, at another level of interpretation, to be perfectly capable of being fulfilled. Consider generally how this paradox reveals, in certain circumstances, that timing is decisive not merely for survival, but for the production of logical truth. If K waits too long before leaping ahead in thought to formulate the argument which saves him from the hangman, even though he might have proved that the decree was logically contradictory, having procrastinated, the decree is pragmatically fulfilled and he is hanged during the week and by surprise. Although the time of a logical syllogism is said to be the time of eternal truth, we seem to have here an instance in which the timing of the enunciation of a proposition determines its truth. Speed of utterance has become a crucial issue in the moment of firing, when one has to decide to make a response, before the enemy missiles have detonated, to what has not yet occurred. And this response may then in turn become an inaugurating moment in the production of the anticipated event—a future that has become the determining past of an event, total nuclear war, that if it occurs will never have a future, will never be said to have occurred. At that moment there is something like the reversibility of the times series; at that moment one may simultaneously know, as K knows with anticipated certainty, that a Class-A blackout, which must occur, can never occur, if leaping ahead in anxious anticipation produces the very consequences it forestalls. In those scenarios of total nuclear war, in the systems of what is called deterrence, lie possibilities for hallucinatory coincidence to arise of the sort William Warner and I undertook to analyze in our "Nuclear Coincidence and the Korean Airline Disaster."

All strategy depends on anticipated certainty, the confidence that, under certain conditions, a statement concerning the future may be performatively enacted, that an announcement projected in the future (say, knight takes rook) will be capable, under the right circumstances, of ordaining an anticipated result. It requires being able, on the basis of plausible assumptions, to draw logically impeccable conclusions concerning the possibility of future enactments. The gravest consequences may follow from the failure to understand in what way statements about the future can be analytic or nonanalytic, entailing contradictions, with the result that what is ordained may not be fulfilled as anticipated—or fulfilled for the wrong reason, or, paradoxically, despite reason. These possibilities for error are not of a statistical variety, inevitable margins of error that attend most announcements about the future, which disrupt the context a command may require in order to be carried out; rather they reside in the very logic of anticipated certainty whose paradoxical implications have been aggravated by the nuclear condition, perhaps even engendered by it. Whether the nuclear condition may be thought to have given rise to a new concept, or to have exacerbated logical implications of the future hitherto unobserved, strategic calculations are menaced by the existence of paradoxes of command lurking in the logic of our strategic calculations. All our strategies, private as well as public, are affected by the existence of a nuclear future, alongside or within the Platonic one, with which our thinking traditionally negotiates. Not a critique or a deconstruction, but a new version of the future, having become literalized in the nuclear fable, it risks giving rise to unexpected effects, strange encounters, phantasms, hallucinations, significant coincidences. Nuclear Criticism aims to uncover the ways in which the nuclear future may already be effecting our strategic decisions by observing its obscure influence, not only in the realm of military, diplomatic strategy, but in the production of cultural artifacts. Where its effects are produced cannot be determined in advance; Nuclear Criticism cannot be supposed even to know where to look for the intrusion of its uncanny power to disrupt our strategic considerations. Evidence of nuclear thinking may emerge, will emerge in the most unexpected and provocative ways; it carries risks which we cannot afford to ignore.

But let me insist, Nuclear Criticism is not an answer, it is a question—
a way of asking how to ask the question of whether the production of
culture in our society is being shaped and determined, mediated down
to the smallest details, by the implications engendered by the nuclear
fable for the way we think about the future. Not only for our thoughts,
I would add, but also for our dreams.

Nuclear Criticism considers it essential to our understanding of
the current cultural moment to explore literature insofar as it can be
seen anachronistically to have always enacted in the mode of fiction
what the nuclear era has made terrifyingly literal—the perspective future of memory disappearing without a trace, without leaving a trace.
Its capacity to represent that possibility in fiction is linked to what
makes it, in the nuclear age, the most fragile of all institutions, since,
being without a real referent, its survival absolutely depends on the
survival of the organized archive, on institutions of collective memory. Its acute vulnerability allows us to measure the vulnerability of
all other institutions which, like it, depend on the archive for their
perdurance. Its existence has become synonymous with the existence
of our culture itself at the historical time of the nuclear condition; it is
to it that we must turn to find anticipated figures of an altered future,
representations of anticipation that the nuclear era allows us retrospectively to uncover.

Consider, for example, more or less than an example, the possibility of the future summoned by these lines from Mallarmé's sonnet:
"Ses purs ongles." They invite you to observe, there on sideboards or
altars, the manifestation of the absence of anything where a ptyxis
[Ptyxis, from the Greek, *folding* is used as a general term for the folding of a single part, of an individual leaf, or page] had been, after the
Master, at his death, had taken it with him, this voluminous, bookish
shell,[20] in order to dip for the water of forgetfulness in the river Styx.
And I ask that you consider, narratologically as it were, the posthumous perspective of a narrator of this poem speaking about the loss of
loss in a future, in the tense, in the time of a negative future anterior,
from which all mourning is absent.

Sur les crédences, au salon vide: nul ptyx
Aboli bibelot d'inanité sonore

20. Cf., E. S. Burt, "Mallarmé's 'Sonnet en yx': The Ambiguities of Speculation,"
Yale French Studies 54 (1977).

(Car le Maître est allé puiser des pleurs au Styx
Avec ce seul objet dont le Néant s'honore).

　On the credenzas, in the empty salon: no ptyxis
Abolished bibelot of sonorous inanity
(For the Master has gone dipping for tears in the Styx
With only this object with which Nothingness is honored).

SHOSHANA FELMAN

In an Era of Testimony: Claude Lanzmann's *Shoah*[*][1]

I

History and Witness, or the Story of an Oath

"If someone else could have written my stories," writes Elie Wiesel, "I would not have written them. I have written them in order to testify. My role is the role of the witness. . . . Not to tell, or to tell another story, is . . . to commit perjury."[2]

To bear witness is to take responsibility for truth: to speak, implicitly, from within the legal pledge and the juridical imperative of the witness's oath.[3] To testify—before a court of Law or before the court of history and of the future; to testify, likewise, before an audience of readers or spectators— is more than simply to report a fact or an event or to relate what has been lived, recorded and remembered. Memory is conjured here essentially in order to *address* another, to impress upon a listener, to *appeal* to a community. To testify is always, metaphorically, to take the witness's stand, or to take the position of the witness insofar as the narrative account of the witness is at once engaged in an appeal and bound by an oath. To testify is thus not merely to narrate but to commit oneself, and to commit the narrative, to others: to *take*

[*]From *Yale French Studies* 79 (1991): *Literature and The Ethical Question.* © 1991 by Shoshana Felman.

1. The present essay is part of a more extensive study, constituting the chapter on *Shoah* in my forthcoming book: *In an Era of Testimony: Crises of Witnessing in Literature, Psychoanalysis and History* (London: Routledge, 1991; volume coauthored with Dori Laub, M.D.)

2. "The Loneliness of God," published in the journal *Dvar Hashavu'a* (magazine of the newspaper *Davar*): Tel-Aviv (1984). My translation from the Hebrew.

3. "To tell the truth, the whole truth, and nothing but the truth"; an oath, however, which is always, by its nature, susceptible to perjury.

YFS 97, *50 Years of Yale French Studies, Part 2,* ed. Porter and Waters, © 2000 by Yale University.

responsibility—in speech—for history or for the truth of an occurrence, for something which, by definition, goes beyond the personal, in having general (nonpersonal) validity and consequences.

But if the essence of the testimony is impersonal (to enable a decision by a judge or jury—metaphorical or literal—about the true nature of the facts of an occurrence; to enable an objective reconstruction of what history was like, irrespective of the witness), why is it that the witness's speech is so uniquely, literally irreplaceable? "If someone else could have written my stories, I would not have written them." What does it mean that the testimony cannot be simply reported, or narrated by another in its role as testimony? What does it mean that a story—or a history—cannot be told by someone else?

It is this question, I would suggest, that guides the ground-breaking work of Claude Lanzmann in his film *Shoah* (1985), and constitutes at once the profound subject and the shocking power of originality of the film.

A Vision of Reality

Shoah is a film made exclusively of testimonies: first-hand testimonies of participants in the historical experience of the Holocaust, interviewed and filmed by Lanzmann during the eleven years which preceded the production of the film (1974–1985). In effect, *Shoah* revives the Holocaust with such a power (a power that no previous film on the subject could attain) that it radically displaces and shakes up not only any common notion we might have entertained about it, but our very vision of reality as such, our very sense of what the world, culture, history, and our life within it, are all about.

But the film is not simply, nor is it primarily, a historical document on the Holocaust. That is why, in contrast to its cinematic predecessors on the subject, it refuses systematically to use any historical, archival footage. It conducts its interviews, and takes its pictures, in the present. Rather than a simple view about the past, the film offers a disorienting vision of the present, a compellingly profound and surprising insight into the complexity of the *relation between history and witnessing*.

It is a film about witnessing: about the witnessing of a catastrophe. What is testified to is limit-experiences whose overwhelming impact constantly puts to the test the limits of the witnesses and of the witnessing, at the same time that it constantly unsettles and puts into question the very limits of reality.

Art as Witness

Secondly, *Shoah* is a film about the *relation between art and witnessing*, about film as a medium which *expands* the capacity for witnessing. To understand *Shoah*, we must explore the question: what are *we* as spectators made to witness? This expansion of what we in turn can witness is, however, due not simply to the reproduction of events, but to the power of the film as a work of art, to the subtlety of its philosophical and artistic structure and to the complexity of the creative process it engages. "The truth kills the possibility of fiction," said Lanzmann in a journalistic interview.[4] But the truth does not kill the possibility of art—on the contrary, it requires it for its transmission, for its realization in our consciousness as witnesses.

Finally, *Shoah* embodies the capacity of art not simply to witness, but to *take the witness's stand:* the film takes responsibility for its times by enacting the significance of our era as an *age of testimony*, an age in which witnessing itself has undergone a major trauma. *Shoah* gives us to witness a *historical crisis of witnessing*, and shows us how, out of this crisis, witnessing becomes, in all the senses of the word, a *critical* activity.

On all these different levels, Claude Lanzmann persistently asks the same relentless question: what does it mean to be a witness? What does it mean to be a witness to the Holocaust? What does it mean to be a witness to the process of the film? What does testimony mean, if it is not simply (as we commonly perceive it) the observing, the recording, the remembering of an event, but an utterly unique and irreplaceable topographical *position* with respect to an occurrence? What does testimony mean, if it is the uniqueness of the *performance of a story* which is constituted by the fact that, like the oath, it cannot be carried out by anybody else?

The Western Law of Evidence

The uniqueness of the narrative performance of the testimony in effect proceeds from the witness's irreplaceable performance of the act of seeing—from the uniqueness of the witness's "seeing with his/her own eyes." "Mr. Vitold," says the Jewish Bund leader to the Polish

4. An interview with Deborah Jerome ("Resurrecting Horror: The Man behind *Shoah*"), *The Record*, 25 October 1985.

Courrier Jan Karski, who reports it in his cinematic testimony thirty-five years later, in narrating how the Jewish leader urged him—and persuaded him—to become a crucial visual witness: "I know the Western world. You will be speaking to the English. . . . It will strengthen your report if you will be able to say: *'I saw it myself.'*"[5]

In the legal, philosophical, and epistemological tradition of the Western world, witnessing is based on, and is formally defined by, first-hand seeing. "Eyewitness testimony" is what constitutes the most decisive law of evidence in courtrooms. "Lawyers have innumerable rules involving hearsay, the character of the defendant or of the witness, opinions given by the witness, and the like, which are in one way or another meant to improve the fact-finding process. But more crucial than any one of these—and possibly more crucial than all put together—is the evidence of eyewitness testimony."[6]

Film, on the other hand, is the art par excellence which, like the courtroom (although for different purposes), calls upon a *witnessing* by *seeing*. How does the film use its visual medium to reflect upon eyewitness testimony, both as the law of evidence of its own art and as the law of evidence of history?

Victims, Perpetrators, and Bystanders: About Seeing

Because the testimony is unique and irreplaceable, the film is an exploration of the *differences* between heterogeneous points of view, between testimonial stances which can neither be assimilated into, nor subsumed by, one another. There is, first of all, the difference of perspective between three groups of witnesses, or three series of interviewees; the real characters of history who, in response to Lanzmann's inquiry, play their own role as the singularly real actors of the movie, fall into three basic categories:[7] those who witnessed the disaster as its *victims* (the surviving Jews); those who witnessed the disaster as its *perpetrators* (the ex-Nazis); those who witnessed the disaster as *bystanders* (the Poles). What is at stake in this division is not simply a di-

---

5. *Shoah*, the complete text of the film by Claude Lanzmann (New York: Pantheon Books, 1985), 171. Quotations from the text of the film will refer to this edition, and will be indicated henceforth only by page number (in the parentheses following the citation).

6. John Kaplan, "Foreword" to Elizabeth R. Loftus: *Eyewitness Testimony* (Cambridge, Mass. and London, England: Harvard University Press: 1979), vii.

7. Categories which Lanzmann borrows from Hilberg's historical analysis, but which the film strikingly *embodies* and rethinks. Cf., Raul Hilberg, *The Destruction of the European Jews* (New York: Holmse and Meier, 1985).

versity of points of view or of degrees of implication and emotional involvement, but the *incommensurability* of different topographical and cognitive positions, between which the discrepancy cannot be breached. More concretely, what the categories in the film give to see is *three different performances of the act of seeing.*

In effect, the victims, the bystanders, and the perpetrators are here differentiated not so much by what they actually see (what they all see, although discontinuous, does in fact follow a logic of corroboration), as by what and how they *do not see*, by what and how they *fail to witness.* The Jews see, but they do not understand the purpose and the destination of what they see; overwhelmed by loss and by deception, they are blind to the significance of what they witness. Richard Glazar strikingly narrates a moment of perception coupled with incomprehension, an exemplary moment in which the Jews fail to read, or to decipher, the visual signs and the visible significance they nonetheless see with their own eyes:

> Then very slowly, the train turned off of the main track and rolled . . . through a wood. While he looked out—we'd been able to open a window—the old man in our compartment saw a boy . . . and he asked the boy in signs, "Where are we?" And the kid made a funny gesture. This: (draws a finger across his throat) . . .

> *And one of you questioned him?*

> Not in words, but in signs, we asked: "what's going on here? And he made that gesture. Like this. We didn't really pay much attention to him. We couldn't figure out what he meant. [34]

The Poles, unlike the Jews, *do* see but, as bystanders, they do not quite *look*, they avoid looking directly, and thus they *overlook* at once their responsibility and their complicity as witnesses:

> You couldn't look there. You couldn't talk to a Jew. Even going by on the road, you couldn't look there.

> *—Did they look anyway?*

> Yes, vans came and the Jews were moved farther off. You could see them, but on the sly. In sidelong glances. [97–98]

The Nazis, on the other hand, see to it that both the Jews and the extermination will remain unseen, invisible; the death camps are surrounded, for that purpose, with a screen of trees. Franz Suchomel, an ex-guard of Treblinka, testifies:

Woven into the barbed wire were branches of pine trees. . . . It was known as "camouflage". . . . So everything was screened. People couldn't see anything to the left or right. Nothing. You couldn't see through it. Impossible. [110]

It is not a coincidence that as this testimony is unfolding it is hard for us as viewers of the film to see the witness, who is filmed secretly: as is the case for most of the ex-Nazis, Franz Suchomel agreed to answer Lanzmann's questions, but not to be filmed; he agreed, in other words, to give a testimony, but on the condition that, as witness, *he* should not be seen:

> *Mr. Suchomel, we're not discussing you, only Treblinka. You are a very important eyewitness, and you can explain what Treblinka was.*
>
> But don't use my name.
>
> *No, I promised . . .* [54]

In the blurry images of faces taken by a secret camera that has to shoot through a variety of walls and screens, the film makes us see concretely, by the compromise it unavoidably inflicts upon *our* act of seeing (which, of necessity, becomes materially an act of *seeing through*), how the Holocaust was a historical assault on seeing and how, even today, the perpetrators are still by and large invisible: "everything was screened. You couldn't see anything to the left or right. You couldn't see through it."

Figuren

The essence of the Nazi scheme is to make itself—and to make the Jews—essentially invisible. To make the Jews invisible not merely by killing them, not merely by confining them to "camouflaged," invisible death camps, but by reducing even the materiality of the dead bodies to smoke and ashes, and by reducing, furthermore, the radical opacity of the *sight* of the dead bodies, as well as the linguistic referentiality and literality of the *word* "corpse," to the transparency of a pure form and to the pure rhetorical metaphoricity of a mere *figure:* a disembodied verbal substitute which signified abstractly the linguistic law of infinite exchangeability and substitutability. The dead bodies are thus verbally rendered invisible, and voided both of substance and of specificity, by being treated, in the Nazi jargon, as *Figuren:* that which, all at once, *cannot be seen* and can be *seen through*.

The Germans even forbade us to use the words "corpse" or "victim." The dead were blocks of wood, shit. The Germans made us refer to the bodies as *Figuren*, that is, as puppets, as dolls, or as *Schmattes*, which means "rags." [13]

But it is not only the dead bodies of the Jews which the Nazis, paradoxically, do not "see." It is also, in some striking cases, the living Jews transported to their death that remain invisible to the chief architects of their final transportation. Walter Stier, head of Reich Railways Department 33 of the Nazi party, chief traffic planner of the death-trains ("special trains," in Nazi euphemism), testifies:

> But you knew that the trains to Treblinka or Auschwitz were—

> Of course we knew. I was the last district. Without me the trains couldn't reach their destination . . .

> Did you know that Treblinka meant extermination?

> Of course not. . . . How could we know? I never went to Treblinka. [135]
> . . . .

> You never saw a train?

> No, never. . . . I never left my desk. We worked day and night. [132]

In the same way, Mrs. Michelshon, wife of a Nazi schoolteacher in Chelmno, answers Lanzmann's questions:

> Did you see the gas vans?

> No. . . . Yes, from the outside. They shuttled back and forth. I never looked inside; I didn't see Jews in them. I only saw things from outside. [82]

The Occurrence as Unwitnessed

Thus, the diversity of the testimonial stances of the victims, the bystanders, and the perpetrators have in common, paradoxically, the incommensurability of their different and particular positions of not seeing, the radical divergence of their topographical, emotional, and epistemological positions not simply as witnesses, but as witnesses who *do not witness*, who let the Holocaust occur as an event essentially unwitnessed. Through the testimonies of its visual witnesses the film makes us *see* concretely—makes us *witness*—how the

Holocaust occurs as the unprecedented, inconceivable historical advent of *an event without a witness*, an event which historically consists in the scheme of the literal *erasure of its witnesses* but which, moreover, philosophically consists in an accidenting of perception, in a *splitting of eyewitnessing* as such; an event, thus, not empirically, but cognitively and perceptually without a witness both because it precludes seeing and because it precludes the possibility of a *community of seeing*; an event which radically annihilates the recourse (the appeal) to visual corroboration (to the commensurability between two different seeings) and thus dissolves the possibility of any *community of witnessing*.

Shoah enables us to see—and gives us insight into—the occurrence of the Holocaust as an absolute historical event whose literally *overwhelming evidence* makes it, paradoxically, into an *utterly proofless event*; the age of testimony is the age of prooflessness, the age of an event whose magnitude of reference is at once below and beyond proof.

The Multiplicity of Languages

The incommensurability between different testimonial stances, and the heterogeneous multiplicity of specific cognitive positions of seeing and not seeing, is amplified and duplicated in the film by the multiplicity of languages in which the testimonies are delivered (French, German, Sicilian, English, Hebrew, Yiddish, Polish), a multiplicity which necessarily encompasses some foreign tongues and which necessitates the presence of a professional translator as an intermediary between the witnesses and Lanzmann as their interviewer. The technique of dubbing is not used, and the character of the translator is deliberately not edited out of the film—on the contrary, she is quite often present on the screen, at the side of Lanzmann, as another one of the real actors of the film, because the process of translation is itself an integral part of the process of the film, partaking both of its scenario and of its own performance of *its* cinematic testimony. Through the multiplicity of foreign tongues and the prolonged *delay* incurred by the translation, the splitting of eyewitnessing which the historical event seems to consist of, the incapacity of seeing to translate itself spontaneously and simultaneously into a meaning, is recapitulated on the level of the viewers of the film. The film places us in the position of the witness who *sees* and *hears*, but *cannot understand* the significance of what is going on until the later intervention, the delayed processing and rendering of the significance of the visual/acoustic information by the translator, who also in some ways distorts and screens it, because (as is testified to by those viewers who are native speakers of the foreign tongues which the translator is translating, and as the film itself points out by some of Lanzmann's interventions and corrections) the translation is not always absolutely accurate.

The palpable foreignness of the film's tongues is emblematic of the radical foreignness of the experience of the Holocaust, not merely to us, but even to its own participants. Asked whether he had invited the participants to see the film, Lanzmann answered in the negative: "in what language would the participants have seen the film?" The original was a French print: "They don't speak French."[8] French, the native language of the filmmaker, the common denominator into which the testimonies (and the original subtitles) are translated and in which the film is thought out and gives, in turn, its own testimony happens (not by chance, I would suggest) not to be the language of any of the witnesses. It is a metaphor of the film that its language is a language of translation, and, as such, is doubly foreign: that the occurrence, on the one hand, happens in a language foreign to the language of the film, but also, that the significance of the occurrence can only be articulated in a language foreign to the language(s) of the occurrence.

The title of the film is, however, not in French and embodies thus, once more, a linguistic strangeness, an estrangement, whose significance is enigmatic and whose meaning cannot be immediately accessible even to the native audience of the original French print: *Shoah*, the Hebrew word which, with the definite article (here missing), designates "The Holocaust" but which, without the article, enigmatically and indefinitely means "catastrophe," here names the very foreignness of languages, the very namelessness of a catastrophe which cannot be possessed by any native tongue and which, within the language of translation, can only be named as the *untranslatable:* that which language cannot witness; that which cannot be articulated in *one* language; that which language, in its turn, cannot witness without *splitting.*

8. Interview given by Lanzmann on the occasion of his visit to Yale University, and filmed at the Video Archive for Holocaust Testimonies at Yale (Interviewers: Dr. Dori Laub and Laurel Vloch), on 5 May 1986. Transcript, 24–25. Hereafter, citations from this videotape will be referred to by the abbreviation "interview," followed by an indication of the page number in its (unpublished) transcript.

The Historian as a Witness

The task of the deciphering of signs and of the processing of intelligi-
bility—what might be called *the task of the translator*[9]—is, however,
carried out within the film not merely by the character of the professional interpreter, but also by two other real actors—the historian
(Raul Hilberg) and the filmmaker (Claude Lanzmann)—who, like the
witnesses, in turn *play themselves* and who, unlike the witnesses and
like the translator, constitute *second-degree witnesses* (witnesses of
witnesses, witnesses of the testimonies). Like the professional interpreter, although in very different ways, the filmmaker in the film and
the historian on the screen are in turn catalysts—or agents—of the
process of *reception*, agents whose reflective witnessing and whose
testimonial stances aid our own reception and assist us both in the effort toward comprehension and in the unending struggle with the foreignness of signs, in processing not merely (as does the professional
interpreter) the literal meaning of the testimonies, but also some perspectives on their philosophical and historical significance.

The historian is, thus, in the film, neither the last word of knowledge nor the ultimate authority on history, but rather, one more topographical and cognitive position of *yet another witness*. The statement of the filmmaker—and the testimony of the film—is by no
means *subsumed* by the statement (or the testimony) of the historian.
Though the filmmaker does embrace the historical insights of Hilberg,
which he obviously holds in utter respect and from which he gets both
inspiration and instruction, the film also places in perspective—and
puts in context—the discipline of history as such, in stumbling on
(and giving us to see) the very limits of historiography. "*Shoah*," said
Claude Lanzmann at Yale, "is certainly not a historical film. . . . The
purpose of *Shoah* is not to transmit knowledge, in spite of the fact that
there is knowledge in the film. . . . Hilberg's book, *The Destruction of
the European Jews*, was really my Bible for many years. . . . But in spite
of this, *Shoah* is not a historical film, it is something else. . . . To con-
dense in one word what the film is for me, I would say that the film is
an *incarnation*, a *resurrection*, and that the whole process of the film
is a philosophical one."[10] Hilberg is the spokesman for a unique and

9. Cf., Walter Benjamin, "The Task of the Translator," in *Illuminations*, trans.
Harry Zohn, ed. Hannah Arendt (New York: Schocken Books: 1969), 69–82.
10. "An Evening with Claude Lanzmann," 4 May 1986, first part of Lanzmann's

impressive knowledge of the Holocaust. Knowledge is shown by the film to be absolutely necessary in the ongoing struggle to resist the blinding impact of the event, to counteract the splitting of eyewitnessing. But knowledge is not, in and of itself, a sufficiently active and sufficiently effective act of seeing. The newness of the film's vision, on the other hand, consists precisely in the surprising insight it conveys into the radical ignorance in which we are unknowingly all plunged with respect to the actual historical occurrence. This ignorance is not simply dispelled by history—on the contrary, it *encompasses* history as such. The film shows how history is used for the purpose of a historical (ongoing) *process of forgetting* which, ironically enough, *includes* the gestures of historiography. Historiography is as much the product of the passion of forgetting as it is the product of the passion of remembering.

Walter Stier, former head of Reich railways and chief planner of the transports of the Jews to death camps, can thus testify:

What was Treblinka for you? . . . A destination?

Yes, that's all.

But not death.

No, no . . .

Extermination came to you as a big surprise?

Completely . . .

You had no idea.

Not the slightest. Like that camp—what was its name? It was in the Oppeln district. . . . I've got it: Auschwitz.

Yes, Auschwitz was in the Oppeln district. . . . Auschwitz to Krakow is forty miles.

That's not very far. And we knew nothing. Not a clue.

But you knew that the Nazis—that Hitler didn't like the Jews?

That we did. It was well known. . . . But as to their extermination, that was news to us. I mean, even today people deny it. They say there

visit to Yale, videotaped and copyrighted by Yale University. Transcript of the first videotape (hereafter referred to as "Evening"), 2.

couldn't have been so many Jews. Is it true? I don't know. That's what they say. [136–38]

To substantiate his own amnesia (of the name of Auschwitz) and his own claim of essentially *not knowing*, Stier implicitly refers here to the *claim of knowledge*—the historical authority—of "revisionist historiographies," recent works published in a variety of countries by historians who prefer to argue that the *number* of the dead cannot be *proven* and that, since there is no scientific, scholarly hard evidence of the *exact extent* of the mass murder, the genocide is merely an invention, an exaggeration of the Jews and the Holocaust, in fact, never existed.[11] "But as to their extermination, that was news to us. I mean, even today, people deny it. They say there could not have been so many Jews. Is it true? I don't know. That's what they say." 'I am not the one who knows, but there are those who know who say that what I did not know did not exist.' "Is it true? I don't know."

Dr. Franz Grassler, on the other hand (formerly Nazi commissioner of the Warsaw Ghetto), comes himself to mimic, in front of the camera, the very gesture of historiography as an alibi to *his* forgetting.

> *You don't remember those days?*
>
> Not much. . . . It's a fact: we tend to forget, thank God, the bad times . . .
>
> *I'll help you to remember. In Warsaw you were Dr. Auerswald's deputy.*
>
> Yes . . .
>
> *Dr. Grassler, this is Czerniakow's diary. You're mentioned in it.*
>
> It's been printed. It exists?
>
> *He kept a diary that was recently published. He wrote on 7 July 1941 . . .*

11. Cf., for instance, Robert Raurisson: "I have analyzed thousands of documents. I have tirelessly pursued specialists and historians with my questions. I have in vain tried to find a single former deportee capable of proving to me that he had really seen, with his own eyes, a gas chamber." (*Le Monde*, 16 January 1979.) We have "a selective view of history," comments Bill Moyers. "We live within a mythology of benign and benevolent experience. . . . It is hard to believe that there exist about a hundred books all devoted to teaching the idea that the Holocaust was a fiction, that it did not happen, that it has been made up by Jews for a lot of diverse reasons . . ." Interview with Margot Strom, in *Facing History and Ourselves* (Fall 1986), 6 and 7.

7 July 1941? That's the first time I've relearned a date. May I take notes? After all, it interests me too. So in July I was already there! [175–76]

In line with the denial of responsibility and memory, the very gesture of historiography comes to embody nothing other than the blankness of the page on which the "notes" are taken.

The next section of the film focuses on the historian Hilberg holding, and discussing, Czerniakow's diary. The cinematic editing that follows shifts back and forth, in a sort of shuttle movement, between the face of Grassler (who continues to articulate his own view of the ghetto) and the face of Hilberg (who continues to articulate the content of the diary and the perspective that the author of the diary—Czerniakow—gives of the ghetto). The Nazi commissioner of the ghetto is thus confronted structurally, not so much with the counterstatement of the historian, but with the firsthand witness of the (now dead) author of the diary, the Jewish leader of the ghetto whom the ineluctability of the ghetto's destiny led to end his leadership—and sign his diary—with suicide.

The main role of the historian is, thus, less to narrate history than to *reverse the suicide*, to take part in a cinematic vision which Lanzmann has defined as crucially an "incarnation" and a "resurrection." "I have taken a historian," Lanzmann enigmatically remarked, "so that he will incarnate a dead man, even though I had someone alive who had been a director of the ghetto."[12] The historian is there to embody, to give flesh and blood to, the dead author of the diary. Unlike the Christian resurrection, though, the vision of the film is to make Czerniakow *come alive precisely as a dead man*. His "resurrection" does not cancel out his death. The vision of the film is at once to make the dead writer come alive as a historian, and to make, in turn, history and the historian come alive in the uniqueness of the living voice of a dead man, and in the silence of his suicide.

The Filmmaker as a Witness

At the side of the historian, *Shoah* finally includes among its list of characters (its list of witnesses) the very figure of the filmmaker in the process of the making—or of the creation—of the film. Travelling be-

12. Statement made in a private conversation that took place in Paris, on 18 January 1987: *"J'ai pris un historien pour qu'il incarne un mort, alors que j'avais un vivant qui était directeur du ghetto."*

tween the living and the dead and moving to and fro between the different places and the different voices in the film, the filmmaker is continuously—though discreetly—present in the margin of the screen, perhaps as the most silently articulate and as the most articulately silent witness. The creator of the film speaks and testifies, however, in his own voice, in his triple role as the *narrator* of the film (and the signatory—the first person—of the script), as the *interviewer* of the witnesses (the solicitor and the receiver of the testimonies), and as the *inquirer* (the artist as the subject of a quest concerning what the testimonies testify to; the figure of the witness as a questioner, and of the asker not merely as the factual investigator but as the bearer of the film's philosophical address and inquiry).

The three roles of the filmmaker intermix and in effect exist only in their relation to each other. Since the narrator is, as such, strictly a witness, his story is restricted to the story of the interviewing: the narrative consists of what the interviewer hears. Lanzmann's rigor as narrator is precisely to speak strictly as an interviewer (and as an inquirer), to abstain, that is, from narrating anything directly in his own voice, except for the beginning—the only moment which refers the film explicitly to the first person of the filmmaker as narrator:

> The story begins in the present at Chelmno. . . . Chelmno was the place in Poland where Jews were first exterminated by gas. . . . Of the four hundred thousand men, women, and children who went there, only two came out alive. . . . Srebnik, survivor of the last period, was a boy of thirteen when he was sent to Chelmno. . . . I found him in Israel and persuaded that one-time boy singer to return with me to Chelmno. [3–4]

The opening, narrated in the filmmaker's own voice, at once situates the story in the present and sums up a past which is presented not yet as the story but rather as a pre-history, or a pre-story: the story proper is contemporaneous with the film's speech, which begins, in fact, subsequent to the narrator's written preface, by the actual song of Srebnik re-sung (reenacted) in the present. The narrator is the "I" who "found" Srebnik and "persuaded" him to "return with me to Chelmno." The narrator, therefore, is the one who *opens*, or re-opens, the story of the past in the present of the telling. But the "I" of the narrator, of the signatory of the film, has no voice; the opening is projected on the screen as the silent text of a mute script, as the narrative voice-over of a *writing* with no voice.

On the one hand, then, the narrator has no voice. On the other hand, the continuity of the narrative is ensured by nothing other than Lanzmann's voice, which runs through the film and whose sound constitutes the continuous, connective thread between the different voices and the different testimonial episodes. But Lanzmann's voice—the active voice in which we hear the filmmaker speak—is strictly, once again, the voice of the inquirer and of the interviewer, not of the narrator. As narrator, Lanzmann does not speak but rather vocally recites the words of others, *lends his voice* (on two occasions) to read aloud two written documents whose authors cannot speak in their own voice: the letter of the Rabbi of Grabow, warning the Jews of Lodz of the extermination taking place at Chelmno, a letter whose signatory was himself consequently gassed at Chelmno with his whole community ("Do not think"—Lanzmann recites—"that this is written by a madman. Alas, it is the horrible, tragic truth," [83–84]), and the Nazi document entitled "Secret Reich Business" and concerning technical improvements of the gas vans ("Changes to special vehicles . . . shown by use and experience to be necessary," [103–05]), an extraordinary document which might be said to formalize Nazism as such (the way in which the most perverse and most concrete extermination is abstracted into a pure question of technique and function). We witness Lanzmann's voice modulating evenly—with no emotion and no comment—the perverse diction of this document punctuated by the unintentional, coincidental irony embodied by the signatory's name: "signed: Just."

Besides this recitation of the written documents, and besides his own mute reference to his own voice on the written cinematic preface of the silent opening, Lanzmann speaks as interviewer and as inquirer, but as narrator, he keeps silent. The narrator lets the narrative be carried on by others—by the live voices of the various witnesses he interviews, whose stories must be able to *speak for themselves,* if they are to testify, that is, to perform their unique and irreplaceable firsthand witness. It is only in this way, by this abstinence of the narrator, that the film can in fact be a narrative of testimony, a narrative of that, precisely, which can neither be reported, nor narrated, by another. The narrative is thus essentially a narrative of silence, the story of the filmmaker's *listening;* the narrator is the teller of the film only insofar as he is the bearer of the film's silence.

In his other roles, however, that of interviewer and of inquirer, the filmmaker, on the contrary, is by definition a transgressor, and a breaker, of the silence. Of his own transgression of the silence, the interviewer says to the interviewee whose voice cannot be given up and whose silence must be broken: "I know it's very hard. I know and I apologize" (117).

As an interviewer, Lanzmann asks not for great explanations of the Holocaust, but for concrete descriptions of minute particular details and of apparently trivial specifics. "Was the weather very cold?" (11). "From the station to the unloading ramp in the camp is how many miles? . . . How long did the trip last?" (33). "Exactly where did the camp begin?" (34). "It was the silence that tipped them off? . . . Can he describe that silence?" (67). "What were the [gas] vans like? . . . What color?" (80). It is not the big generalizations but the concrete particulars which translate into a vision and thus help both to dispel the blinding impact of the event and to transgress the silence to which the splitting of eyewitnessing reduced the witness. It is only through the trivial, by small steps—and not by huge strides or big leaps—that the barrier of silence can be in effect displaced, and somewhat lifted. The pointed and specific questioning resists, above all, any possible canonization of the experience of the Holocaust. Insofar as the interviewer challenges at once the sacredness (the unspeakability) of death and the sacredness of the deadness (of the silence) of the witness, Lanzmann's questions are essentially desacralizing.

> *How did it happen when the women came into the gas chamber? . . .*
> *What did you feel the first time you saw all these naked women? . . .*
>
> . . . .
>
> *But I asked and you didn't answer: What was your impression the first time you saw these naked women arriving with children? How did you feel?*
>
> I tell you something. To have a feeling about that . . . it was very hard to feel anything, because working there day and night between dead people, between bodies, your feeling disappeared, you were dead. You had no feeling at all. [114–16]

Shoah is the story of the liberation of the testimony through its desacralization; the story of the decanonization of the Holocaust for the sake of its previously impossible historicization. What the interviewer above all avoids is an alliance with the silence of the witness, the kind of empathic and benevolent alliance through which interviewer and interviewee often implicitly concur, and work together, for the mutual comfort of an avoidance of the truth.

It is the silence of the witness's death which Lanzmann must historically challenge here, in order to revive the Holocaust and to rewrite the *event-without-a-witness* into witnessing, and into history. It is the silence of the witness's death and of the witness's deadness which precisely must be broken and transgressed.

We have to do it. You know it.

I won't be able to do it.

You have to do it. I know it's very hard. I know and I apologize.

Don't make me go on please.

Please. We must go on. [117]

What does *going on* mean? The predicament of having to continue to bear witness at all costs parallels, for Abraham Bomba, the predicament faced in the past of having to continue to *live on*, to survive in spite of the gas chambers, in the face of the surrounding death. But to have to *go on* now, to have to keep on bearing witness, is more than simply to be faced with the imperative to replicate the past and thus to replicate his own *survival*. Lanzmann paradoxically now urges Bomba to break out of the very deadness that enabled the survival. The narrator calls the witness to come back from the mere mode of surviving into that of living—and of living pain. If the interviewer's role is thus to break the silence, the narrator's role is to ensure that the story (be it that of silence) will go on.

But it is the inquirer whose philosophical interrogation and interpellation constantly reopen what might otherwise be seen as the story's closure.

Mrs. Pietrya, you live in Auschwitz?

Yes, I was born there . . .

Were there Jews in Auschwitz before the war?

They made up eighty percent of the population. They even had a synagogue here . . .

Was there a Jewish cemetery in Auschwitz?

It still exists. It's closed now.

Closed? What does that mean?

They don't bury there now. [17–18]

The inquirer thus inquires into the very meaning of *closure* and of narrative, political, and philosophical *enclosure*. Of Dr. Grassler, the exassistant to the Nazi "commissar" of the Jewish ghetto, Lanzmann asks:

> *My question is philosophical. What does a ghetto mean, in your opinion?* [182]

Differences

Grassler of course evades the question. "History is full of ghettos," he replies, once more using erudition, "knowledge," and the very discipline of history, to avoid the cutting edge of the interpellation: "Persecution of the Jews wasn't a German invention, and didn't start with World War II" (182). Everybody knows, in other words, what a ghetto is, and the meaning of the ghetto does not warrant a specifically *philosophical* attention: "history is full of ghettos." Because "history" knows only too well what a ghetto is, this knowledge might as well be left to history, and does not need in turn to be probed by us. "History" is thus used both to deny the *philosophical* thrust of the question and to forget the specificity—the *difference*—of the Nazi past. Insofar as the reply denies precisely the inquirer's refusal to *take for granted* the conception—let alone the preconception—of the ghetto, the stereotypical, preconceived answer in effect *forgets* the asking power of the question. Grassler essentially forgets the difference, forgets the *meaning* of the ghetto as the first step in the Nazi overall design precisely of the framing—and of the enclosure—of a difference, a difference that will consequently be assigned to the ultimate enclosure of the death camp and to the "final solution" of eradication. Grassler's answer *does not meet* the question and attempts, moreover, to *reduce* the question's difference. But the question of the ghetto—that of the attempt at the containment (the reduction) of a difference—perseveres both in the speech and in the silence of the inquirer-narrator. The narrator is precisely there to insure that the question, in its turn, will *go on* (will continue in the viewer). The inquirer, in other words, is not merely the agency which asks the questions, but the force which takes apart all previous answers. Throughout the interviewing process the inquirer-narrator, at the side of Grassler as of others, is at once the witness of the question and the witness of the gap—or of the difference—between the question and the answer.

Often, the inquirer bears witness to the question (and the narrator silently bears witness to the story) by merely recapitulating word by word a fragment of the answer, by literally repeating—like an echo—the last sentence, the last words just uttered by the interlocutor. But the function of the echo—in the very resonance of its amplification—is itself inquisitive, and not simply repetitive. "The gas vans came in here," Srebnik narrates: "there were two huge ovens, and afterwards the bodies were thrown into these ovens, and the flames reached to the sky" (6). "To the sky [zum Himmel]," mutters silently the interviewer, opening at once a philosophical abyss in the simple words of the narrative description and a black hole in the very blueness of the image of the sky. When later on, the Poles around the church narrate how they listened to the gassed Jews' screams, Lanzmann's repetitious echoes register the unintended irony of the narration:

> *They heard the screams at night?*
>
> The Jews moaned. . . . They were hungry. They were shut in and starved.
>
> *What kinds of cries and moans were heard at night?*
>
> They called on Jesus and Mary and God, sometimes in German . . .
>
> *The Jews called on Jesus, Mary, and God!* [97–98]

Lanzmann's function as an echo is another means by which the voicelessness of the narrator and the voice of the inquirer produce a *question* in the very answer, and enact a *difference* through the very verbal repetition. In the narrator as the bearer of the film's silence, the *question* of the screams persists. And so does the *difference* of what the screams in fact call out to. Here as elsewhere in the film, the narrator is, as such, both the guardian of the question and the guardian of the difference.

The inquirer's investigation is precisely into (both the philosophical and the concrete) particularity of difference. "*What's the difference between a special and a regular train?*," the inquirer asks of the Nazi traffic planner Walter Stier (133). And to the Nazi teacher's wife, who in a Freudian slip confuses Jews and Poles (both "the others" or "the foreigners" in relation to the Germans), Lanzmann addresses the following meticulous query:

Since World War I the castle had been in ruins. . . . That's where the Jews were taken. This ruined castle was used for housing and delousing the Poles, and so on.

The Jews!

Yes, the Jews.

Why do you call them Poles and not Jews!

Sometimes I get them mixed up.

There's a difference between Poles and Jews!

Oh yes!

What difference!

The Poles weren't exterminated, and the Jews were. That's the difference. An external difference.

And the inner difference!

I can't assess that. I don't know enough about psychology and anthropology. The difference between the Poles and the Jews? Anyway, they couldn't stand each other. [82–83]

As a philosophical inquiry into the ungraspability of difference and as a narrative of the specific differences between the various witnesses, *Shoah* implies a fragmentation of the testimonies—a fragmentation both of tongues and of perspectives—that cannot ultimately be surpassed. It is because the film goes from singular to singular, because there is no possible *representation* of one witness by another, that Lanzmann needs us to sit through ten hours of the film to begin to witness—to begin to have a concrete sense—both of our own ignorance and of the incommensurability of the occurrence. The occurrence is conveyed precisely by this fragmentation of the testimonies, which enacts the fragmentation of the witnessing. The film is a gathering of the fragments of the witnessing. But the collection of the fragments does not yield, even after ten hours of the movie, any possible totality or any possible totalization; the gathering of testimonial incommensurates does not amount either to a generalizable theoretical statement or to a narrative monologic sum. Asked what was his concept of the Holocaust, Lanzmann answered: "I had no concept; I had obsessions, which is different. . . . The obsession of the cold. . . . The obsession of the first time. The first shock. The first hour of the Jews in the camp, in Treblinka, the first minutes. I will always ask the question of the first time. . . . The obsession of the last moments, the waiting, the fear. *Shoah* is a film full of fear, and of energy too. You cannot do such a film theoretically. Every theoretical attempt I tried was a failure, but these failures were necessary. . . . You build such a film in your head, in your heart, in your belly, in your guts, everywhere" (*Interview*, 22–23). This "everywhere" which, paradoxically, cannot be totalized and which resists theory as such, this corporeal fragmentation and enumeration which describes the "building"—or the process of the generation—of the film while it resists any attempt at conceptualization, is itself an emblem of the specificity—of the uniqueness—of the mode of testimony of the film. The film testifies not merely by collecting and by gathering fragments of witnessing, but by actively exploding any possible enclosure—any conceptual frame—that might claim to *contain* the fragments and to fit them into one coherent whole. *Shoah* bears witness to the fragmentation of the testimonies as the radical invalidation of all definitions, of all parameters of reference, of all known answers, in the very midst of its relentless affirmation—of its materially creative validation—of the absolute necessity of speaking. The film puts in motion its surprising testimony by performing the historical and contradictory double task of the breaking of the silence and of the simultaneous shattering of any given discourse, of the breaking—or the bursting open—of all frames.

II

A Point of Arrival

The film opens in the filmmaker's own mute voice, which addresses the spectator from within the very writing on the screen that constitutes the film's silent opening.

> Of the four hundred thousand men, women, and children who went there, only two came out alive: Mordechaï Podchlebnik and Simon Srebnik. Srebnik, survivor of the last period, was a boy of thirteen when he went to Chelmno . . .
> I found him in Israel and persuaded that one-time boy singer to return with me to Chelmno. [3–4]

Something is found, here, in Israel, which embodies in effect a point of arrival in Lanzmann's journey, as well as the beginning—or the starting point—of the journey of the film. "*I found him in Israel*" (My emphasis). I would suggest that the artistic power of the film proceeds, precisely, from this *finding:* the *event* of *Shoah* is an event of finding.

What is it exactly that Lanzmann, at the outset of the film, *finds?* The inaugural event of finding is itself already constituted by a number of implied—and incommensurable—discoveries, which the film sets out to explore on different levels.

1) The *finding,* first and foremost, is the finding of Simon Srebnik, the astonishing winning survivor, "that one-time boy singer" who was literally executed (shot in the head) and yet miraculously, more than once, fooled death and survived:

> With his ankles in chains, like all his companions, the boy shuffled through the village of Chelmno each day. That he was kept alive longer than the others he owed to his extreme agility, which made him the winner of jumping contests and speed races that the SS organized for their chained prisoners. And also to his melodious voice; several times a week . . . young Srebnik rowed up the Narew, under guard, in a flat-bottomed boat. . . . He sang Polish folk tunes, and in return the guard taught him Prussian military songs . . .
>
> During the night of 18 January 1945, two days before Soviet troops arrived, the Nazis killed all the remaining Jews in the "work details" with a bullet in the head. Simon Srebnik was among those executed. But the bullet missed his vital brain centers. When he came to, he crawled into a pigsty. A Polish farmer found him there. The boy was treated and healed by a Soviet Army doctor. A few months later Simon left for Tel-Aviv along with other survivors of the death camps.
>
> I found him in Israel and persuaded that one-time boy singer to return with me to Chelmno. [3–4]

2) The *finding* is thus also, at the same time, the finding of a site of entering: the discovery of Israel is the finding of a place which enables Lanzmann, for the first time, to *inhabit* his own implication in the story of the Other (Srebnik's story).

3) The finding is the *finding of the testimony*—of its singular significance and functioning as the story of an *irreplaceable historical performance,* a narrative performance which no statement (no report and no description) can replace and whose unique enactment by the living witness is itself part of a *process of realization* of historic truth. Insofar as this realization is, by definition, what cannot simply be reported, or narrated, by another, Lanzmann finds in Israel, precisely, that which cannot be reported, both the general significance and the material, singular concretizations of the testimony (Srebnik's testimony, as well as others').

4) Finally, the finding is *the finding of the film* itself: *Shoah* rethinks, as well, the meaning and the implications of the advent (of the event) of its own finding. To find the film is to find a new possibility of sight, a possibility not just of vision—but of re-vision. Lanzmann finds precisely in the film the material possibility and the particular potential of *seeing again* someone like Srebnik whom, after his shooting, no one was likely or supposed to see ever again. Even more astonishingly, the finding of the film provides in general, in history, the possibility of *seeing again* what in fact was never seen the first time, what remained *originally unseen* due to the inherent blinding nature of the occurrence.

The Return

The film does not stop, however, at the site of its own finding(s), does not settle at its initial point of arrival, but rather, uses the arrival as a point of departure for another *kind* of journey, a *return trip* which, going back to the originally unperceived historical scene, takes place as a journey to another frame of reference, entering into what Freud calls *eine andere Lokalität*—into another scale of space and time: "I found him in Israel and persuaded that one-time boy singer to *return with me to Chelmno*."

Why is it necessary to return to Chelmno? What is the return about? Who, or what, returns?

> We are, I am, you are
> by cowardice or courage
> the ones who find our way
> back to this scene[13]
> carrying a knife, a camera
> a book of myths
> in which our names do not appear.[14]

The return in *Shoah* from Israel to Europe (Poland, *Chelmno*), from the place of the regeneration and the locus of the gathering of Holo-

13. "The film," Lanzmann says, "is at moments a crime film . . . , [on the mode of] a criminal investigation. . . . But it is a Western too. When I returned to the small village of Grabow, or even in Chelmno. . . . Okay. I arrive here with a camera, with a crew, but forty years after. . . . This creates an incredible . . . event, you know? Well . . . I am the first man to come back to the scene of the crime, where the crime has been committed . . ." (*Panel Discussion*), 53.

14. Adrienne Rich, *Diving into the Wreck* (New York and London: W. W. Norton, 1973), 22.

caust survivors back to the prehistory of their oppression and suppression, back to the primal scene of their annihilation, is at once a spatial and a temporal return, a movement back in space and time which, in attempting to revisit and to repossess the past is also, simultaneously, a movement forward toward the future.

The return to Chelmno by the boy singer for whom the Chelmno period ended with a bullet in the head concretizes at the same time, allegorically, a historical return of the dead. In a way, the returning forty-seven-year-old Srebnik ("He was then forty-seven years old," [4]), reappearing on the screen at the site of the annihilation, the improbable survivor who returns from Israel to the European scene of the crime against him, is himself rather a ghost of his own youthful performance, a returning, reappearing ghost of the one-time winner of chained races and of the boy singer who moved the Poles and charmed the SS, and who, like Scheherazade, succeeded in postponing his own death indefinitely by telling (singing) songs. Thus, if Srebnik on the screen at forty-seven, in the scene of Chelmno of today, embodies a return of the dead, his improbable survival and his even more improbable return (his ghostly reappearance) concretizes allegorically, in history, a return of the (missing, dead) witness on the scene of the event-without-a-witness.

Srebnik had, during the Holocaust, witnessed in effect himself, in Chelmno, a return of the dead—a return to life of the half-asphyxiated bodies tumbling out of the gas vans. But he witnessed this revival, this return of the dead, only so as to become a witness to their second murder, to an even more infernal killing (or re-killing) of the living dead, by a burning of their bodies while those are still alive and conscious of their burning, conscious of their own encounter with the flames by which they are engulfed, devoured:

> When [the gas vans] arrived, the SS said: "Open the doors!" . . . . The bodies tumbled right out. . . . We worked until the whole shipment was burned.
>
> I remember that once they were still alive. The ovens were full, and the people lay on the ground. They were all moving, they were coming back to life, and when they were thrown into the ovens, they were all conscious. Alive. They could feel the fire burn them. [101–02]

Srebnik's witness dramatizes both a burning consciousness of death, and a crossing (and recrossing) of the boundary line which separates the living from the dead, and death from life. But when Srebnik saw all

that, he was not really a [living] witness since, like Bomba,[15] like Podchlebnik,[16] he too was already *deadened*.

> When I saw all this, it didn't affect me. . . . I was only thirteen, and all
> I'd ever seen until then were dead bodies. Maybe I didn't understand,
> maybe if I'd been older, but the fact is, I didn't. I'd never seen anything
> else. In the ghetto in Lodz I saw that as soon as anyone took a step, he
> fell dead. I thought that's the way things had to be, that it was normal.
> I'd walk the streets of Lodz, maybe one hundred yards, and there'd be
> two hundred bodies. They went into the street and they fell, they fell
> . . .
>
> So when I came . . . to Chelmno, I was already . . . I didn't care about
> anything. [102–03]

Therefore, it is only now, today that Srebnik can become a witness to
the *impact* of the falling (and the burning) bodies,[17] only today that he
can situate his witnessing in a frame of reference that is not sub-
merged by death and informed solely by *Figuren*, by dead bodies. It is
therefore only now, in returning with Lanzmann to Chelmno, that
Srebnik in effect is returning from the dead (from his own deadness)
and can become, for the first time, a witness to himself, as well as an
articulate and for the first time fully *conscious* witness of what he had
been witnessing during the War.

The Return of the Witness

Urged by Lanzmann, Srebnik's return from the dead personifies, in
this way, a historically performative and retroactive *return of witnessing* to the witnessless historical primal scene.
Srebnik recognizes Chelmno.

> It's hard to recognize, but it was here. They burned people here. . . .
> Yes, this is the place. No one ever left here again. . . . It was terrible. No
> one can describe it. . . . And no one can understand it. Even I, here,
> now . . . . I can't believe I'm here. No, I just can't believe it. It was al-
> ways this peaceful here. Always. When they burned two thousand peo-

15. Bomba: "I tell you something. To have a feeling about that . . . it was very hard to
feel anything, because working there day and night between dead people, between bodies, your feeling disappeared, you were dead. You had no feeling at all." (116).

16. Podchlebnik: "*What died in him in Chelmno?* Everything died" (6).

17. On the impact of the falling body, in conjunction with an innovative theory of
reference, cf., Cathy Caruth, "The Claims of Reference," in *Yale Journal of Criticism*
(Fall 1990), vol. 4, No. 1.

ple—Jews—every day, it was just as peaceful. No one shouted. Everyone went about his work. It was silent. Peaceful. Just as it is now. [6]

Chelmno recognizes Srebnik. The Polish villagers remember well
the child entertainer who "had to . . . [sing when] his heart wept" (6),
and they identify and recognize the pathos and the resonance, the
lyrics and the melody of his repeated singing:

> He was thirteen and a half years old. He had a lovely singing voice, and
> we heard him.
>
> > A little white house
> > lingers in my memory
> > Of that little white house
> > I dream each night. [4]

"When I heard him again," one of the Polish villagers remarks, "my
heart beat faster, because what happened here . . . was a murder. I really relived what happened" (4).
    Lanzmann places Srebnik in the center of a group of villagers before
the church in Chelmno, which, at the time, served as a prison-house for
the deported Jews and as the ultimate waystation on their journey—via
gas vans—to the forest, where the (dead or living) bodies were being
burned away in so-called ovens. The villagers at first seem truly happy
to see Srebnik, whom they welcome cheerfully and warmly.

> *Are they glad to see Srebnik again?*
>
> Very. It's a great pleasure. They're glad to see him again because they
> know all he's lived through. Seeing him as he is now, they are very
> pleased. [95]

Why does memory linger?, the inquirer would like to know. What mo-
tivates this livelihood of the remembrance?

> *Why does the whole village remember him?*
>
> They remember him well because he walked with chains on his an-
> kles, and he sang on the river. He was young, he was skinny, he looked
> ready for the coffin. . . . Even the [Polish] lady, when she saw that child,
> she told the German: "Let that child go!" He asked her: "Where to?"
> "To his father and mother." Looking at the sky, [the German] said:
> "He'll soon go to them." [95–96]

When Lanzmann gets, however, to the specific subject of the role of
the Church in the past massacre of the Jews, the Polish testimony be-

comes somewhat confused. The evocation of the memories becomes itself unknowingly tainted with fantasies.

They remember when the Jews were locked in this church?

Yes, they do . . .

The vans came to the church door! They all knew these were gas vans, to gas people?

Yes, they couldn't help knowing.

They heard screams at night?

The Jews moaned, they were hungry . . .

What kind of cries and moans were heard at night?

They called on Jesus and Mary and God, sometimes in German . . .

The Jews called on Jesus, Mary and God!

The presbytery was full of suitcases.

The Jews' suitcases?

Yes, and there was gold.

How does she know there was gold? The procession! We'll stop now.
[97–98]

Like the Nazi teacher's wife (who only "sees things from outside," [82]), the Poles embody outside witness—present an outside view of the Jewish destiny, but an outside view which nonetheless believes it can account for the inside: in trying to account for the inner meaning of the Jewish outcry from inside the Church, and in accounting for the inner, unseen content of the robbed possessions of the Jews inside the confiscated suitcases, the Poles bear in effect *false witness*. Out of empathy in the first case, with respect to the imagined moaning of the Jewish prisoners of the Church, out of hostile jealousy and of competitive aggression in the second case, with respect to the imaginary hidden treasures and envied possessions, the Poles distort the facts and *dream their memory*, in exemplifying both their utter failure to imagine Otherness and their simplified negotiation of the inside and the outside, by merely projecting their inside on the outside. It is to their own fantasy, to their own (self-) mystification that the Poles bear witness, in attempting to account for historical reality. Their false witness is itself, however, an objective illustration and concretization of the radically delusional quality of the event.

The scene is interrupted by the silence—and the sound of bells—of the procession, a church ritual executed by young girls dressed in white, which celebrates the birth of the Virgin Mary.

This ritual celebration of the images of youth and the predominance of white in the religious ceremony connote the innocence of childhood, the pure integrity and the intactness of virginity, which the ritual is evoking as the attributes of the Holy Virgin. And yet, the presence of Srebnik at the scene reminds us of another kind of childhood, and the contiguity of this rather unvirginal and violated childhood (of the child who had to sing when his heart wept) with the immaculate virginity here enacted, of itself creates an almost sacrilegious, and desacralizing resonance, in an astounding, vertiginous, and breathtaking cinematic condensation and juxtaposition of different dimensions, of different registers of space and time, of different levels of existence and experience. The sudden, unexpected superimposition of the Holocaust in which the church served as a death enclosure (as the antechamber to the gas vans) and of the present Christian celebration of the birth of the Virgin Mary, brings out a terrible and silent irony, of a church that in effect embodies a mass tomb, at the same time that it celebrates a birth, of a site whose history is stained with blood, at the same time that it is the stage of an oblivious celebration of an ethical virginity and of an intactly white immaculateness. Very like the whiteness of the snow covering the forests of Sobibor, Auschwitz, and Treblinka, the whiteness of the ritual itself turns out to be an image which, quite literally, covers up history, as the embodiment (and as the disembodiment) of a *white silence*.

Viewing the procession, one recalls Benjamin's discussion of contemporary art and, particularly, of photography and film as vehicles, specifically, of desacralization, as accelerating agents in the modern cultural process of the "shattering"—and of the "liquidation"—of the *cult-values* of tradition:

> We know that the earliest art works originate in the service of a ritual—first the magical, then the religious kind. . . . [Now] for the first time in world history, mechanical reproduction [photography and film] emancipates the work of art from its parasitical dependence on ritual. . . . The total function of art is reversed. Instead of being based on ritual, [art] begins to be based on another practice—politics.[18]

18. Walter Benjamin, "The Work of Art in the Age of Mechanical Reproduction," op.cit., 223–24.

In a surprise translation, Lanzmann's camera converts, in the church scene, the religious and the artistic into the political. The church scene thus becomes the unexpected, sudden cinematographic exhibition of uncanny depths of political significance within the very ritual of the procession.

The Return of History

After the procession, Lanzmann—who does not forget—returns to the interrupted subject of the inside of the Jewish suitcases.

> *The lady said before that the Jews' suitcases were dumped in the house opposite [the church]. What was in this baggage?*
>
> Pots with false bottoms.
>
> *What was in the false bottoms?*
>
> Valuables, objects of value. They also had gold in their clothes . . .
>
> *Why do they think all this happened to the Jews?*
>
> Because they were the richest! Many Poles were also exterminated. Even Priests. [99]

Lanzmann's tour de force as interviewer is to elicit from the witness, as in this case, a testimony which is inadvertently no longer in the control or the possession of its speaker. As a solicitor and an assembler of the testimonies, in his function as a questioner but mainly, in his function as a listener (as the bearer of a narrative of listening), Lanzmann's performance is to elicit testimony which exceeds the testifier's own awareness, to bring forth a complexity of truth which, paradoxically, is *not available as such* to the very speaker who pronounces it. As a listener, Lanzmann endows the interlocutor with speech. It is in this way that he helps both the survivors and the perpetrators to overcome their (very different kind of) silence. Facing Lanzmann, the Polish villagers, in turn, exhibit feelings that would normally be hidden. But the silent interviewer and the silent camera urge us not simply to see the testimony, but to see *through* it: to see—throughout the testimony—the deception and the self-deception which it unwittingly displays, and to which it unintentionally testifies.

> *Why do they think all this happened to the Jews?*
>
> Because they were the richest! Many Poles were also exterminated. Even Priests.

In response to Lanzmann's question, Mr. Kantorowski, the player of the organ and the singer of the church, finds his way out of the crowd which surrounds Srebnik and, pushing himself in front of the camera, overshadows Srebnik and eclipses him:

> Mr. Kantorowski will tell us what a friend told him. It happened in Myndjewyce, near Warsaw.
>
> *Go on.*
>
> The Jews there were gathered in a square. The rabbi asked an SS man: "Can I talk to them?" The SS man said yes. So the rabbi said that around two thousand years ago the Jews condemned the innocent Christ to death. And when they did that, they cried out: "Let his blood fall on our heads and on our sons' heads." Then the rabbi told them: "Perhaps the time has come for that, so let us do nothing, let us go, let us do as we're asked."
>
> *He thinks the Jews expiated the death of Christ?*
>
> *He* doesn't think so, or even that Christ sought revenge. The rabbi said it. It was God's will, that's all.[19] [99–100]

Through the voice of the church singer which seems to take on the authority to speak for the whole group, and through the mythic mediation both of archetypal stereotypes of anti-Semitism and of the Chris-

---

19. On the generalizable historical significance of this passage, cf., Peter Canning's remarkable analysis in "Jesus Christ, Holocaust: Fabulation of the Jews in Christian and Nazi History": "The compulsive ritual of accusing the Jews of murder (or betrayal, or well-poisoning, or desecration of the Host) and attacking them is inscribed with bodies in history; it is not prescribed but only implicitly suggested in the New Testament, which preaches love and forgiveness. In the Gospel it is 'the Jews' who call down the wrath of God on themselves: 'Let his blood be on us and on our children!' (*Mt.* 27:25) Reciting this text, the Polish villagers whom Claude Lanzmann interviewed . . . excuse themselves, the Germans and God—all are absolved of responsibility for the Holocaust. Once again, 'the Jews brought it on themselves.' The Crucifixion was their crime. The Holocaust was the punishment which they called down on their own heads, and on their children.

The biblical myth functions as an attractor, not only of other narratives but of ongoing events which it assimilates. What I must risk calling the Holo-myth of Christianity—divine incarnation, crucifixion, resurrection—is not the one source or cause of the Holocaust, it 'attracted' other causal factors to it (the war, inflation, political-ideological crisis, socioeconomic convulsions), absorbed them and overdetermined their resolution. . . . Those other critical factors, and their resolution in a fascist syncretism, were not alone capable of turning antisemitism into systematic mass murder. Nazism reactivated the cliché it had inherited from the Christian Holomyth and its reenactment in the event of ritual murder, but transformed it into a regular, mechanized destruction process. (171–72). In *Copyright* 1, *Fin de siècle 2000* (Fall 1987).

tian story of the Crucifixion, the Poles endow the Holocaust with a strange comprehensibility and with a facile and exhaustive compatibility with knowledge: "It was God's will, that's all. . . . That's all. *Now you know!*" (100). It is by dehistoricizing the events of recent history, and by subsuming them under the prophetic knowledge of the Scriptures, that the Poles are literally washing their hands of the historical extermination of the Jews:

> So Pilate washed his hands and said: "Christ is innocent," and he sent Barabas. But the Jews cried out: "Let his blood fall on our heads!"
>
> That's all. Now you know. [100]

Thus the Poles misrepresent, once more, the Jews from the inside, and the objective nature of the Jewish destiny and slip, once more, across the boundary line between reality and fantasy; they unwittingly begin to dream reality and to hallucinate their memory. In testifying to a murder which they go so far as to call suicide, the Poles bear once again false witness both to the history of Nazism and to the history of the Jews.

But once again, this misrepresentation (this false witness) is itself attributed precisely to the Jews and represented as *their* inside story. Like the Nazis, who make the Jews *pay* for their own death traffic and participate—through "work details"—in the management of their own slaughter, the Poles pretend to have the Jews provide their own interpretation of their history and their own explanation of their murder. Kantorowski thus claims that his own mythic account is in fact the Jews' own version of the Holocaust.

> *He thinks the Jews expiated the death of Christ?*
>
> *He* doesn't think so, or even that Christ sought revenge. The rabbi said it. It was God's will, that's all. [100]

In forging, so to speak, the rabbi's signature so as to punctuate his own false witness and to authorize his own false testimony, Kantorowski disavows responsibility for his own discourse. In opposition to the act of signing and of saying "I" by which the authentic witnesses assume at once their discourse, their speech act and their responsibility toward history ("I found him in Israel and persuaded him to return . . . ," says Lanzmann; "I understand your role, I am here," says Karski; "I can't believe I'm here," says Srebnik), Kantorowski's testimony is destined to remain unsigned.

Mr. Kantorowski, after all, does indeed in some ways remain silent. Not only because, as he claims, it is the words of the dead rabbi that *speak for him.* But because what *speaks through him* (in such a way as to account for his role during the Holocaust) is, on the one hand, the (historic) silence of the Church and, on the other hand, the silence of all given frames of explanation, the non-speech of all preconceived interpretive schemes, which dispose of the event—and of the bodies— by reference to some other frame. The collapse of the materiality of history and the seduction of a fable, the reduction of a threatening and incomprehensible event to a reassuring mythic, totalizing unity of explanation, is in effect what all interpretive schemes tend to do. Mr. Kantorowski's satisfied and vacuous interpretation stands, however, for the failure of all ready-made cultural discourses both to account for—and to bear witness to—the Holocaust.

The film's strategy is not to challenge the false witness, but to *make the silence speak* from within and from around the false witness: the silence within each of the testimonies; the silence *between* various silences and various testimonies; the irremediable silence of the dead; the irremediable silence of the natural landscapes; the silence of the church procession; the silence of the ready-made cultural discourses pretending to account for the Holocaust; and above all, in the center of the film, Srebnik's silence in front of the church, in the middle of the talkative, delirious, self-complacent Polish crowd. The church scene is an astonishing emblem of the multiplicity and the complexity of layers which unfold between this central silence and the various speeches which proceed from it and encroach upon it. Like a hall of mirrors, the church scene is a hall of silences infinitely resonant with one another. "There are many harmonies," says Lanzmann, "many concordances in the film. I knew very quickly that the film would be built in a circular way, with a stillness at the center, like the eye of a hurricane."[20]

The silence reenacts the event of silence. "It was always this peaceful here," Srebnik had said, "Always. When they burned two thousand people—Jews—every day, it was just as peaceful. No one shouted. Everyone went about his work. It was silent. Peaceful. Just as it is now" (6).

20. Quoted in "A Monument Against Forgetting," *The Boston Globe*, 3 November 1985, 3. Cf., Lanzmann's remarks in his interview with Roger Rosenblatt, for channel 13 (Public Television WNET, USA 1987): "When one deals with the destruction of the Jews, one has to talk and to be silent at the same moment. . . . I think there is more silence in *Shoah* than words."

Indeed, the church scene is not just a hall (a mirroring) of silences, but the very stage of the performance—of the execution and the repetition—of an *act of silencing*. Although Srebnik here personifies the return of the witness—the return of witnessing into the very scene of the event-without-a-witness, what the church scene puts into effect and plays out, not in memory but in actual fact (and act), is how the real witness, in returning back to history and life, is once again *reduced to silence*, struck *dead* by the crowd. The scene is even more complex, since what the crowd points out as the Jews' crime and as the reason for the Holocaust is the Crucifixion, or the Jews' murder of Christ. But the Polish villagers are not aware that they themselves are in turn acting out precisely such a *ritual murder story*;[21] they are unaware of the precise ways in which they themselves are actually *enacting* both the Crucifixion and the Holocaust in *annihilating Srebnik*, in *killing once again the witness* whom they totally dispose of, and *forget*.

What Kantorowski's testimony chooses to deny—*his* signature, *his* voice, the Poles' responsibility—it thus performs, reenacts before our eyes. What is not available in words, what is denied, what cannot and what will not be remembered or articulated, nonetheless gets realized. What takes place in the film, what materially and unexpectedly *occurs* and what returns like a ghost, is *reference itself*, the very object—and the very content—of historical erasure.

I would suggest that what the film shows us here, in action, is the very process of the *re-forgetting of the Holocaust*, in the repeated murder of the witness and in the renewed reduction of the witnessing to silence. The film makes the testimony *happen*—happen inadvertently as a second Holocaust. The silent Srebnik in the middle of this picture—with his beautifully dignified and tragic mute smile, and with his mutely speaking face (a face signed by his silence) is in effect a ghost: a ghost which, as such, is essentially *not contemporaneous*; contemporaneous, in reality, neither with the voices of the crowd which surrounds him, nor even with himself—with his own muted voice. What the church scene dramatizes is the only possible encounter with the Holocaust, in the only possible form of a *missed encounter*.[22]

---

21. For an acute description of the functioning of the "ritual murder story" in history, cf., again, Peter Canning, "Jesus Christ, Holocaust: Fabulation of the Jews in Christian and Nazi History" (op.cit., 170–73).

22. Cf., Lacan's conception of "the Real" as a "missed encounter" and as "what re-

I would suggest precisely that the film is about the essence of this *missed contemporaneity* between Srebnik and the semicircle which surrounds him, between Srebnik's voice and his own silence, and fundamentally, between the Holocaust experience and the witness of the Holocaust experience.

Shoah addresses the spectator with a challenge. When we are made to witness this reenactment of the murder of the witness, this second Holocaust that appears spontaneously before the camera and on the screen, can we in our turn become *contemporaneous* with the meaning and with the significance of that enactment? Can we become contemporaneous with the shock, with the displacement, with the disorientation process that is triggered by such testimonial reenactment? Can we, in other words, assume in earnest, not the finite task of making sense out of the Holocaust, but the infinite task of encountering *Shoah?*

III

The Return of the Song

If the church scene is thus punctuated, signed by Srebnik's silence, where is Srebnik's testimony, here lost, to be found? The film includes, indeed, an element through which the very silencing of Srebnik's voice can be somehow reversed, through which the very loss of Srebnik's testimony can be somehow recovered, or at least resist its own forgetting and itself by reencountered, in the repetition of the melody and in the return of Srebnik's "melodious voice" in his reiterated singing. In spite of his own silencing and of his silence, the return of the witness undertaken by the film nonetheless persists, takes over, and survives in the return of the song. In the absence—and the failure—of the contemporaneity between the Holocaust and its own witness, the song nevertheless creates a different kind of contemporaneity between the *voice* and the historical (revisited) *site* of the voice, between the song and the place at which the song is (and was) heard, between the *voice* and the *place* to which, at the beginning of the film, the song in fact *gives voice:*

_____
. . . it was here. . . . Yes, this is the place. [5]

_____
turns to the same place." *Le Séminaire, livre XI, Les Quatre concepts fondamentaux de la psychoanalyse* (Paris: Seuil: 1973); trans. Alan Sheridan, *The Four Fundamental Concepts of Psychoanalysis* (New York: W. W. Norton: 1978) chapters 3–5.

The song creates, indeed, an unexpected contemporaneity between its reiterated resonance and the very silence of the place.

> It was always this peaceful here. Always. . . . It was silent. Peaceful. Just as it is now. [6]

At the same time, this contemporaneity between present and past, between the singing voice and the silent place, remains entirely incomprehensible to, and thus noncontemporaneous with, the witness.

> No one can understand it. Even I, here, now. . . . I can't believe I'm here. No, I just can't believe it. [6]

It is in hovering between the ways in which it is at once contemporaneous with the place and noncontemporaneous with the witness (with the singer), that the song returns to the inconceivable historical site of its own singing, and that the harmonies and the disharmonies of this return of the song provide an entrance, or a threshold, to the film. It is the song which is the first to testify, the first to speak after the voiceless opening of the narrator. The song encroaches on—and breaks—at once the silence of the landscape and the muteness of the writing on the screen. Through Srebnik's voice, the film introduces us into the soothing notes and the nostalgic lyrics of a Polish folk tune which itself, however, dreams about, and yearns for, another place.

> A little white house
> lingers in my memory
> Of that little white house
> each night I dream. [4]

The White House

Srebnik's voice inhabits his own song. But does anyone inhabit the "white house" of which he sings? Who can enter the white house? Does the "I" of Srebnik (the "I" who "can't believe he's here") inhabit what his voice is so dreamily and yearningly evoking? What in fact is there inside the "little white house"? What is there beyond the threshold, behind the whiteness of the house?

The longing for the white house recalls the white virginity of the procession. The white house seems as safe, as wholesome, as immaculate in its invitation and its promise, as the white procession of the youthful virgins. And yet, we know that it is not only virginity, but an aberrant violation of lives and of the innocence of childhood, that is implied ironically and silently by the juxtaposition of the church scene, and by the whiteness of the ritual ceremony.

Virginity is what is not written upon. The white is, on the one hand, the color of the virgin page before the writing—the white house sung before the writing of the film—but also, on the other hand, the very color of erasure.[23] For the viewer who has seen the film, and who has come full circle—like the film, like the song—to start again at the beginning, the "white house" brings to mind not just the snow that, whitely covering the peaceful meadows, covers up the emptied graves from which the dead bodies were disinterred so as to be reduced to ashes, burned away, but similarly in a different sense, the later image of white houses in the Polish village of Wladowa, a village once inhabited by Jews but whose Jewish houses have been since vacated (like the graves under the snow) by their original inhabitants (obliterated in extermination camps) and are now occupied, owned and inhabited by Poles. The little white house yearned for thus turns out to be itself, ironically enough, a ghost house; a ghost house that belongs at once to dreaming ("Of that little white house / Each night I dream") and to memory ("A little white house / lingers in my memory").

Calling us into a dream, the white house, paradoxically, will also force us to wake up. Plunged into the dreamy beauty of the landscape and into the dreamy yearning of the melody of the white house, the spectator as a witness—like the witness of history—has literally to *wake up* to a reality that is undreamt of, wake up, that is, into the unthinkable realization that what he is witnessing is not simply a dream. We will be called upon to see the film—and to view perception—critically, to discriminate reality from dream, in spite of the confusing mingling of memory and dream, in spite of the deceptive quality of what is given to direct perception. On the borderline between dreaming and memory, the song—as a concrete, material residue of history—is that "small element of reality that is evidence that we are not dreaming."[24] The residue of an implicit violence (the unquantifiable ransom with which Srebnik has to keep buying his life) which at the same time is luringly soothing, the song incorporates the real both in its literal, and yet also, in its deceptive quality. As a purveyor of the

23. White is thus, for instance, the color of the blank page of forgetfulness on which the ex-Nazi commissioner of the Warsaw ghetto, Dr. Grassler, claims to "take notes" to "refresh" the total blankness of his memory about his Nazi past.

24. As Lacan puts it in an altogether different context. Cf., "Tuché and Automaton" (Chapter 5:2), in *The Four Fundamental Concepts of Psychoanalysis*, op.cit., 60.

real, the song invites us, at the threshold of the film, to cross over from the landscape and the white house into an encounter (a collision) with the actuality of history. It melodiously invites us to a crossing of the distance between art and reference. And no one can suspect that this melodious invitation was in history, and is now in the film, an invitation to the shock of an awakening; of an awakening to a reality whose scrutiny requires a degree of vigilance, of wakefulness and of alertness such that it exceeds perhaps human capacity. No one can suspect that what awaits us from behind the white house is not simply a nightmare, but the urgency of waking up into a history and a reality with respect to which we are not, and perhaps cannot be, fully and sufficiently awake.

The place from which the song invokes us at the threshold of the film and to which it points, at the same time as the locus of the real and as the origin of singing, designates, I would suggest, the place of art within the film: the song becomes itself a metaphor for the whole film which is inaugurated by its melody, and which registers the impact and the resonance of its returns. Opened by the song, the film does not simply show itself, it calls us. It calls us through the singing it enacts. It is asking us to listen to, and hear, not just the meaning of the words but the complex significance of their return, and the clashing echoes of their melody and of their context. The film calls us into hearing both this clash and its own silence. It calls us into what it cannot show, but what it nonetheless can point to. The song inaugurates this calling and this act of pointing.

Yes, this is the place . . .

Shoah begins with the apparent innocence of singing, only to thrust us more profoundly and astonishingly into the discrepancy between the lyrics and their context, only to point us more sharply toward the ambiguity that lies behind that innocence.

A little white house
lingers in my memory . . . [4]

repeats sweetly the song. But another voice proceeds to speak over the resonance of the song:

When I heard him again, my heart beat faster, because what happened here . . . was a murder. [5]

Thus testifies, in Polish, the first voice-over—whose origin is not immediately identifiable, locatable—in the words of one of the bystanders, one of the Polish witnesses of history.

Then Srebnik's face in a close-up—the face that carries both the lightness, the enticing sweetness of the song and the weight, the outrage and the cruelty, of history—twists the silence of its pain into a smile and gazes vacantly, incredibly, incredulously through survival, death, and time, through piles of vanished burned bodies into the green trees, the brown earth, and the perspective of the blue horizon:

Yes, this is the place. . . . No one ever left here again. [5]

Darum, Warum

The contradictions riddling the very beauty of the first song are aggravated, underscored, and sharpened by the appearance of the second song which, narratively, is a singing replica—or a melodious counterpart—to the first song but which, rhetorically and musically, sets up a dissonance and a sharp contrast with the harmonies and with the innocence of the initial singing invitation.

He sang Polish folk tunes, and in return *the guard taught him Prussian military songs.* [3]

You, girls, don't you cry,
don't be so sad, for the dear summer is nearing . . .
and with it I'll return.
A mug of red wine, a piece of roast
is what the girls give their soldiers.

Therefore.—Why? Therefore.—Why?
  [*Darum.—Warum?, Darum.—Warum?*]
  [*Therefore—Wherefore?, Therefore—Wherefore?*]

When the soldiers march through the town,
the girls open their doors and windows.

Therefore. Why? Therefore. Why?
Only because of this [sound]
Tschindarrassa: Bum! [Cymbals, Drum]. [6][25]

The two songs sung by Srebnik are contrasted and opposed in many ways. Although they are both folk tunes and are both—by implication or explicitly—about returns, the dialogue between the tune in Polish and its counterpart in German is more than a mere dialogue of foreign

25. Translation modified and expanded, transcribing all the German lyrics that are clearly audible in the film.

tongues. Whereas the song about the white house concretizes a dream of arrival—an implicit dream of reaching—the Prussian military song is marked by a departure and a passage and is a ritual, not of arriving or of coming to inhabit, but of leaving. The act of leaving, at the same time, is disguised, denied, and masked by a discursive rhetoric of coming back and by a promise of returning. Apparently, the Prussian song is as sweet in its yearning and as harmless as the Polish song. And yet, the elements of lure on the one hand, and on the other hand of a subordinating force become (almost) apparent. By virtue of its function as a military march, and through the forceful beats of its percussions ("Tschindarrassa, Bum!"; "Darum, Warum"), the Prussian song[26] incorporates the latent rhythms of artillery and bombs. Hinting at both the malignancy of the deception and the violence to come, the song implicitly includes the military connotations—and the metaphoric, tactile contiguity—of war, of bloodshed ("a mug of red wine"), of brutality ("a piece of roast"), and of physical invasion ("the girls open their doors and windows"). The whole song, with the beats of its repeated rhymes between its questions and its answers ("Darum, Warum"), and with its metaphoric female gifts of drinking, eating, and of opening ("the girls open their doors and windows"), is a figure for a sexual interplay; but the interplay is one of conquest and of transitory military and sexual occupation. It is as though the enigma of the white house—the enigma of a space that is inviolate and intimate, sung in the first song—were, so to speak, invaded, cancelled out, forced open by the second. No wonder that, behind the lure of its enticing surface, the charm of the German song (which primarily plays out a sexual tease) turns out to be itself a sadistic tool by which the singing child becomes a hostage to the Germans, an instrument of torment and abuse through which young Srebnik is reduced by his adult spectators to a chained, dancing marionette transformed—playfully and cruelly—into a singing toy.

The Word of Our Commander

It is in this way that the shift between the Polish song and its German reply ("and in return, the guard taught him Prussian military songs") is accomplished at the threshold of the film, as a subtle—and yet ominous—transaction, an invisible—yet audible—exchange between the

26. In my analysis of the Prussian song, I owe both gratitude and inspiration to Dr. Ernst Prelinger, who has provided me with a sophisticated explanation of the original German lyrics of the song, an explanation which informs my discussion of it here.

music of the victim and the music of (and from the point of view of)
the perverse oppressor.

Another song which, later in the film, will mark Nazi perversity
and Nazi violence much more explicitly and in which the victim,
equally, will have to sing the point of view of the oppressor, is the song
whose singers are today entirely extinguished and to which only the
ex-Nazi Suchomel is able to bear witness, by singing it to Lanzmann.
In much the same way as the singers of the song sang it in a voice that
was not theirs—the voice of the oppressor—Suchomel, inversely, now
reproduces the forced singing of the victims in the alien and jaunty
voice of the ex-Nazi. It is thus that Suchomel repeats to Lanzmann the
Treblinka hymn that the camp prisoners were forced to sing, for the
guard's pleasure:

> Looking squarely ahead, brave and joyous, at the world,
> the squads march to work.
> All that matters to us now is Treblinka.
> It is our destiny.
> That's why we've become one with Treblinka
> in no time at all.
> We know only the word of our Commander,
> we know only obedience and duty,
> we want to serve, to go on serving,
> until a little luck ends it all. Hurray!

"Once more, but louder," Lanzmann requests, in response to Suchomel's completed singing. Suchomel obliges Lanzmann. "We're
laughing about it," he says with a mixture of complicity and condescension, "but it's so sad."

> *No one is laughing.*
>
> Don't be sore at me. You want history—I'm giving you history. Franz
> wrote the words. The melody comes from Buchenwald. Camp Buchen-
> wald, where Franz was a guard. New Jews who arrived in the morning,
> new "worker Jews," were taught the song. And by evening they had to
> be able to sing along with it.
>
> *Sing it again.*
>
> All right.
>
> *It's very important. But loud!*
>
> Looking squarely ahead, brave and joyous, at the world,
> the squads march to work.

All that matters to us now is Treblinka.
It is our destiny.
That's why we've become one with Treblinka
in no time at all.
We know only the word of our Commander,
we know only obedience and duty,
we want to serve, to go on serving,
until a little luck ends it all. Hurray! [105–06]

Having thus repeated once again the song, Suchomel, proud and bemused at his own memory, concludes:

Satisfied? That's unique. No Jew knows that today! [106]

The self-complacency, the eagerness of Suchomel in obliging Lanzmann suggest that he, too, in effect enjoys and takes implicitly sadistic pleasure in the act of his own singing, in his own staged, imitative musical performance and in the inconceivable discrepancy of his own representation of the victims. "You want history—I'm giving you history." Can history be *given?* How does Suchomel *give* history, and what does the act of "giving"—the gift of reality—here mean? Ironically enough, the song is literally history insofar as it conveys this historical discrepancy and this sadistic pleasure, at the same time that it speaks through the historical *extinction* of the message and the *objectification* of the voice. As a literal residue of the real, the song is history to the extent that it inscribes within itself, precisely, this historical discrepancy, this incommensurability between the voice of its sadistic author and the voice of its tormented singers. What is historically "unique" about the song is the fact that it is a Nazi-authored Jewish song that "no Jew knows today." "You want history—I'm giving you history." In the very outrage of its singing doubly, at two different moments (in the camp and in the film, by the victims and by Suchomel) in a voice that is not, and cannot become, its own, the song is, so to speak, the opposite of a signed testimony, an *antitestimony* that consists, once more, in the absence and in the very forging of its Jewish signature. Like Mr. Kantorowski's mythical account of the Holocaust, the Nazi narrative of the Jews' victimization (both in the camp song and in Suchomel's revoicing of it) is a speech act that can neither own its meaning nor possess itself as testimony. "You want history— I'm giving you history." As the extinction of the subject of the signature and as the objectification of the victim's voice, "history" presents itself as antitestimony. But the film restitutes to history—and to the song—its testimonial function. Paradoxically enough, it is from the very evidence of its enactment as an antitestimony that the song derives the testimonial power of its repetition and the historic eloquence of its unlikely and ghostly return: *"Sing it again. . . . It's very important. But loud!"*

The Quest of the Refrain, or the Imperative to Sing

I would suggest that the imperative, "Sing it again," is the performative imperative that artistically creates the film and that governs both its structure and its ethical and epistemological endeavor: to make truth happen as a testimony through the haunting repetition of an ill-understood melody; to make the referent come back, paradoxically, as something heretofore unseen by history; to reveal the real as the impact of a literality that history cannot assimilate or integrate as knowledge, but that it keeps encountering in the return of the song.

"Our memory," writes Valéry, "repeats to us what we haven't understood. Repetition is addressed to incomprehension."[27] We *"sing again"* what we cannot know, what we have not integrated and what, consequently, we can neither fully master nor completely understand. In *Shoah*, the song stands for the activation of the memory of the whole film, a memory that no one can possess, and whose process of collecting and of recollecting is constantly torn apart between the pull, the pressure and the will of the words and the different, independent pull of the melody, which has its own momentum and its own compulsion to repeat but which does not know what in fact it is repeating.

The whole film, which ends only to begin with the return of the song, testifies to history like a haunting and interminable refrain.[28] The function of the refrain—which is itself archaically referred to as "the burden of the song"—like the burden of the vocal echo which, as though mechanically, returns in the interviewer's voice the last words of the discourse of his interlocutors, is to create a difference through the repetition, to return a question out of something that appears to be

27. Valéry, "Commentaire de *Charmes*," in *Oeuvres* (Paris: Gallimard, bibliothèque de la Pléiade: 1957), vol. 1, 1510; my translation.

28. *"Shoah,"* says Lanzmann, "had to be built like a musical piece, where a theme appears at a lower level, disappears, comes back at a higher level or in full force, disappears, and so on. It was the only way to keep several parameters together" (*Panel Discussion*, 44).

an answer: *Darum, Warum* ("Therefore.—Why?") The echo does not simply reproduce what seems to be its motivation, but rather puts it into question. Where there had seemed to be a rationale, a closure and a limit, the refrainlike repetition opens up a vacuum, a crevice, and, through it, the undefined space of an open question.

> The flames reached to the sky.
> *To the sky* . . . [6]

The Singer's Voice

What gives this refrainlike structure of the film—the repetition of the song and of its burden, the return of the resonance of the refrain— the power not merely to move us but to strike and to surprise us, the power each time to astonish us and have an impact upon us as though for the first time? When Srebnik sings the two songs of the opening, and when the echo of the second song puts into question the apparent harmony and innocence of the first tune, what constitutes the power of the singing and the strength—the eloquence—of Srebnik's testimony through it, is neither the lyrics nor even the music (someone else's music), but the uniqueness of the singing voice. The uniqueness of the voice restores the signature to the repeated melody and to the cited lyrics, and transforms them from antitestimony into a compelling and unequalled testimony. What makes the power of the testimony in the film and what constitutes in general the impact of the film is not the words but the equivocal, puzzling relation between words and voice, the interaction, that is, between words, voice, rhythm, melody, images, writing, and silence. Each testimony speaks to us beyond its words, beyond its melody, like the unique performance of a singing, and each song, in its repetitions, participates in the searching refrain and recapitulates the musical quest of the whole film. Like Lanzmann, Srebnik facing an unspeakable event at thirteen and a half, and again at the beginning of the film—as a singer who remained alive because of his "melodious voice"—is in turn a sort of artist: an artist who has lost his words but who has not lost the uniqueness of the singing voice and its capacity for signature. What is otherwise untestifiable is thus transmitted by the signature of the voice. The film as a visual medium hinges, paradoxically, not so much on the self-evidence of sight as on the visibility it renders to the voice, and on the invisibility it renders tangible of silence. The film speaks in a multiplicity of voices that, like Srebnik's, all transmit beyond what they can say in words. In much the same way as the singing crematorium witnessed and evoked by Philip Müller, the film resonates like a whole chorus of testimonies and of voices that, within the framework of the film, sing together:

> The violence climaxed when they tried to force the people to undress. A few obeyed, only a handful. Most of them refused to follow the order. Suddenly, like a chorus, they all began to sing. The whole "undressing room" rang with the Czech national anthem, and the *Hatikvah*. That moved me terribly . . .
>
> That was happening to my countrymen, and I realized that my life had become meaningless. Why go on living? For what? So I went into the gas chamber with them, resolved to die. With them. Suddenly, some who recognized me came up to me. . . . A small group of women approached. They looked at me and said, right there in the gas chamber . . . "So you want to die. But that's senseless. Your death won't give us back our lives. That's no way. You must get out of here, alive, you must bear witness to . . . the injustice done to us." [164–65]

The singing of the anthem in the crematorium signifies a common recognition, by the singers, of the perversity of the deception to which they had been all along exposed, a recognition, therefore, and a facing, of the truth of their imminent death. The singing, in this way, conveys a repossession of their lost truth by the dying singers, an ultimate rejection of their Nazi-instigated self-deception and a deliberately chosen, conscious witnessing of their own death. It is noteworthy that this is the only moment in the film in which a community of witnessing is created physically and mentally, against all odds. Erasing its own witnesses and inhibiting its own eyewitnessing, the historical occurrence of the Holocaust, as we have seen, precluded by its very structure any such community of witnessing.[29] But this is what the film tries precisely to create in resonating with the singing chorus of the dying crematorium, whose many signatures and many voices are today extinguished and reduced to silence. The film, as a chorus of performances and testimonies, does create, within the framework of its structure, a communality of singing, an odd community of testimonial incommensurates which, held together, have an overwhelming testimonial impact.

29. See above, in part I, the section entitled "The Occurrence as Unwitnessed," 109–10.

The Disappearance of the Chorus

Müller wishes to die so as to belong, to be part of this community, to join the singing. But the dying singers have it as their last wish to exclude him from their common death, so that he can be not an extinguished witness like them, but a living witness to their dying and their singing. The singing challenges and dares the Nazis. The act of singing and of bearing witness embodies resistance. But for Müller, the resistance cannot mean giving up life; it has to mean giving up death. Resistance spells the abdication of suicidal death and the endurance of survival as itself a form of resistance and of testimony. Resistance signifies the price of the historical endurance—in oneself—of an actual return of the witness. As a returning delegate of the dead witnesses, Müller's act of testifying and his testimonial afterlife can no longer be, however, part of a living community. Facing his singing compatriots in the crematorium, Müller understands that the gift of witness they request from him, and his responsive, mute commitment to bear witness, leave him no choice but to stand alone, to step outside of the community[30] as well as of shared cultural frames of reference, outside of the support of any shared perception. The holding and the inner strength of the common singing empowers Müller and allows him to escape and to survive. But his survival cannot simply be encompassed by a common song, and his afterlife of bearing witness can no longer lose itself in a choral hymn. If his living voice is to speak for the dead, it has to carry through and to transmit, precisely, the cessation of the common singing, the signature of the endurance, the peculiarity and the uniqueness of a voice doomed to remain alone, a voice that has returned—and that speaks—from beyond the threshold of the crematorium.

Müller, Srebnik, and the others, spokesmen for the dead, living voices of returning witnesses that have seen their own death—and the

---

30. Cf., Rudolph Vrba's decision to escape, after the suicide of Freddy Hirsch that aborts the Resistance plan for the uprising of the Czech family camp: "It was quite clear to me then that the Resistance in the camp is not geared for an uprising but for survival of the members of the Resistance. I then decided to act . . . [by] leaving the community, for which I [was] coresponsible at the time. The decision to escape, in spite of the policy of the Resistance movement at the time, was formed immediately. . . . As far as I am concerned, I think that if I successfully manage to break out from the camp and bring the information to the right place at the right time, that this might be a help. . . . Not to delay anything but to escape as soon as possible to inform the world" (195–96).

death of their own people—face to face, address us in the film both from inside life and from beyond the grave and carry on, with the aloneness of the testifying voice, the mission of the singing from within the burning.

> Suddenly, from the part of the camp called the death camp, flames shot up. Very high. In a flash, the whole countryside, the whole camp, seemed ablaze. And suddenly one of us stood up. We knew . . . he'd been an opera singer in Warsaw. . . . His name was Salve, and facing that curtain of fire, he began chanting a song I didn't know:
>
> > My God, my God,
> > Why hast Thou forsaken us?
>
> > We have been thrust into the fire before
> > but we have never denied the Holy Law.
>
> He sang in Yiddish, while behind him blazed the pyres on which they had begun then, in November 1942, to burn the bodies in Treblinka. . . . We knew that night that the dead would no longer be buried, they'd be burned. [14]

A Winning Song

The entire film is a singing from within the burning of a knowledge: "We knew that night . . .". The knowledge of the burning is the knowledge—and the burning—of the singing. At the beginning of the film, Srebnik's song incorporates the burned bodies with whose death and with whose burning it still resonates. In singing, on the one hand, as he has been taught, about the girls "opening their doors" to soldiers who pass by, in the very way that he himself, uncannily, is commanded by the SS to "open the doors" of the arriving gas vans so as to receive—and to unload—the bodies to be burned, in singing also, on the other hand, his original melodious yearning for the sweetness of the white house, Srebnik's singing and his singular, compelling voice, is the bearer of a knowledge—and a vision—a vision of the half-asphyxiated bodies coming back to life only to feel the fire and to witness, conscious, their encounter with, and their consumption by, the flames:

> When [the gas vans] arrived, the SS said: "Open the doors!" We opened them. The bodies tumbled right out. . . . We worked until the whole shipment was burned . . .

> I remember that once they were still alive. The ovens were full, and the people lay on the ground. They were all moving, they were coming back to life, and when they were thrown into the ovens, they were all conscious. Alive. They could feel the fire burn them . . .
>
> When I saw all this, it didn't affect me. I was only thirteen, and all I'd ever seen until then were dead bodies. [101–02]

The deadening of the live witness, the burn of the silence of the thirteen-year-old child who is "not affected," passes on into his singing. The unique expression of the voice and of the singing both expresses and covers the silence, in much the same way as the unique expression of the face—of Srebnik's face at the opening of the film—both covers and expresses the deliberate and striking absence of dead bodies from *Shoah*'s screen. It is indeed the living body and the living face of the returning witness that, in *Shoah*, becomes a speaking figure for the stillness and the muteness of the bodies, a *figure* for, precisely, the *Figuren*. What the film does with the *Figuren* is to restore their muteness to the singing of the artist-child, to revitalize them by exploring death through life, and by endowing the invisibility of their abstraction with the uniqueness of a face, a voice, a melody, a song. The song is one that has won life for Srebnik, a life-winning song which, framed within the film and participating in the searching repetition of its refrain, wins for us a heightened consciousness and an increased awareness, by giving us a measure of an understanding that is not transmittable without it. As a fragment of reality and as a crossroad between art and history, the song—like the whole film—enfolds what is in history untestifiable and embodies, at the same time, what in art captures reality and *enables* witnessing. In much the same way as the testimony, the song exemplifies the power of the film to address, and hauntingly demands a hearing. Like Müller coming back to testify and speak—to claim an audience—from beyond the threshold of the crematorium, Srebnik, though traversed by a bullet that has missed his vital brain centers by pure chance, reappears from behind the threshold of the white house to sing again his winning song: a song that, once again, wins life and, like the film, leaves us—through the very way it wins us—both empowered, and condemned to *hearing*.

> *When I heard him again*, my heart beat faster, because what happened here . . . was a murder. [5]

He was thirteen and a half years old. He had a lovely singing voice, and *we heard him.* [4]

> A little white house
> lingers in my memory.
> Of that little white house
> each night I dream.

MARYSE CONDÉ

Order, Disorder, Freedom, and the West Indian Writer[*]

In a recent interview, the Martinican writer Edouard Glissant declared: "I don't believe that West Indian literature exists yet since literature supposes an action and a reaction between a public and an audience. I repeat that we West Indian writers, we are writing forewords to tomorrow's literature."[1] Last year when *Éloge de la Créolité* was published, two of his disciples, Raphaël Confiant and Patrick Chamoiseau, and the linguist Jean Bernabé repeated: "West Indian literature doesn't exist yet. We are in a state of pre-literature. Ours is a written production without an audience at home, deprived of the interaction between writers/readers which is necessary for any literature to exist."[2]

Although it seems difficult to state seriously that West Indian literature doesn't exist, we easily agree that there is a crisis, a malaise. But we don't blame it on the causes pointed out by Glissant, Confiant, and Chamoiseau. We attribute it to the very commands enumerated throughout the history of West Indian literature by the various generations of writers. For example, in *Éloge de la Créolité*, the authors state: "We must give a name to everything and true to *créolité* say that it is beautiful. Therefore we must see the human dignity of the "djobeurs," understand the life of the Morne Pichevin or of the vegetable markets of Fort-de-France, study how our storytellers operate . . . (*Éloge de la Créolité*, 40). Glissant, Chamoiseau, and Confiant are not the first ones to give commands to the future writers of our is-

[*]From *Yale French Studies* 83 (1993): *Post/Colonial Questions.*

1. Interview given to Priska Degras and Bernard Magniez in *Notre Librairie* 74 (1984).

2. Jean Bernabé, Patrick Chamoiseau, Raphaël Confiant, *Éloge de la Créolité* (Paris: Gallimard, 1989), 14.

YFS 97, *50 Years of Yale French Studies, Part 2,* ed. Porter and Waters, © 2000 by Yale University.

lands. West Indian literature born or not yet born has *always* been an object of deep concern.

We shall try to analyze the various commands decreed about West Indian literature, all of them contributing to the edification of an order very few writers have dared to transgress to introduce disorder. In conclusion, we shall try to see whether it is possible to hope for an era of freedom in West Indian writing.

ORDER

In 1927, in a journal called *La Trouée,* a group of young Haitian intellectuals declared: "Literature is the cry of a people who want to say what boils within them." 1927: the American Marines had invaded Haiti twelve years earlier because of political upheavals. The Haitian people, who already knew political oppression, were discovering racism. History repeats itself.

A few years later, with the Marines still present in Haiti, the mulatto and upper bourgeois writer Jacques Roumain declared in *La Revue indigène:* "Literature must be black and proletarian."[3]

In 1932, the manifesto called "Légitime Défense," signed by a group of Martinican and Guadeloupean intellectuals, was published in Paris. They had just discovered Marxism and in its name sentenced to death the bourgeois society to which they belonged. They also condemned its literature to death, stating "A foreigner would look in vain for any originality or depth, for the sensual and colorful imagination of the Black Man, or the echo of the aspirations of an oppressed people." On the eve of World War II, Suzanne Césaire, in the journal "Tropiques," uttered her famous command: "Martinican poetry shall be cannibalistic or shall not be."[4] As for Césaire himself, in *Cahier d'un retour au pays natal* [*Return to my Native Land*], speaking of the role of the poet, he summed up all these ideas saying "My mouth will be the mouth of those who have no mouth, my voice the voice of those who despair."[5] From that time on the foundations of order were laid. Even those who are not very familiar with West Indian literature know some of the basic rules, and we don't intend to repeat them again. One may simply say

3. Jacques Roumain in *La Revue indigène.*

4. Suzanne Césaire, *Misère d'une Poésie, Tropiques* (repr. Paris: Jean-Michel Place, 1978).

5. Aimé Césaire, *Return to my Native Land,* trans. Emile Snyder (Paris: Présence Africaine, 1968), 61. *The Collected Poetry,* translation with introduction and notes by Clayton Eshelman and Annette Smith (Berkeley: University of California Press, 1982).

that they were inspired by the theory of social realism which was sa-
vored in some quarters, since the victorious Soviet Revolution had her-
alded what seemed to be the dawn of a new era for the oppressed all over
the world. They were also influenced by Sartre who, in 1948, wrote the
foreword to the first anthology of French-speaking black poetry.

1. Individualism was chastised. Only the collectivity had the right to
express itself.
2. The masses were the sole producers of Beauty, and the poet had to
take inspiration from them.
3. The main, if not the sole, purpose of writing was to denounce one's
political and social conditions, and in so doing, to bring about one's liberation.
4. Poetic and political ambition were one and the same.

Therefore, pictures of individual love and psychological turmoil were
banished. Any description of nature was forbidden. Lyrical outbursts
about the mountains or the sea and the sky were left to the so-called
"exotic poets" writing at the beginning of the century, who had been
ridiculed and sentenced to literary death. The hills were the refuge
where the Maroons had escaped the sufferings of the plantation, the
trees the silent witnesses of an eternal exploitation. In the celebrated
opening lines of *Return to my Native Land*, Césaire gives an example
of this ideological description of nature. Looking at the magnificent
bay of Fort-de-France, he exclaims: "At the end of the dawn, flowered
with frail creeks, the hungry West Indies, pitted with smallpox, dyna-
mited with alcohol, stranded in the mud of this bay, in the dirt of this
city sinisterly stranded" (Césaire, *Return to my Native Land*, 40). Is it
not time to somehow rehabilitate the so-called exotic poets?

Victor Segalen has shown that exoticism can be considered the first
perception of difference: "The knowledge that something is not yourself."[6] In the case of the exotic poets of the West Indies, one could say
that to celebrate their land was the first, timid appropriation of their
own world. They were celebrating their land *before* celebrating their
peoples. Not *instead* of doing so. Their poetic abilities were ridiculed.
"Not art," said Césaire contemptuously, "not poetry. Only the ugly
leprosy of imitation."[7] He was forgetting that in those days, to imitate
to perfection was already a transgression. The black man was not

6. Victor Segalen, *Essai sur l'exotisme: une esthétique du divers* (Montpellier: Fata
Morgana, 1978).
7. Aimé Césaire, "Présentation" du no. 1 de la revue *Tropiques* (repr. Fort-de-
France, 1941).

entitled to have any talent, and during slavery to be caught reading a book meant death.

The new order didn't affect only poetry. It also affected history, sociology, and philosophy. West Indian society was not studied *per se*, as an autonomous object. It was always seen as a result of the slave-trade, slavery, and colonial oppression. This past was the cause of every social and cultural feature and thus explained everything: the relationships between men and women, the family system, as well as oral traditions or popular music. It is impossible to deny that the West Indian past weighs heavily on the present. Nevertheless, the plantation system in which this society evolved, the promiscuity of the white master, the arrival of new ethnic groups such as the Indians, are factors responsible for its characteristics as well. Not everything can be explained through slavery. West Indian society came to be considered as a Paradise perverted by Europe. Everything prior to colonization was idealized. Consequently, from the image of Africa, the motherland, were carefully eradicated any blemishes such as domestic slavery, or tribal warfare, and the subjugation of women.

In *The Wretched of the Earth*, Frantz Fanon was the first to realize the dangers of such idealization. But in turn, he blames it on Europe, stating: "Colonialism . . . never ceased to assert that the Negro was a savage and by Negro was meant not the Angolan or the Nigerian, but the Negro. . . . Therefore the efforts of the colonized to rehabilitate himself and escape the attacks of colonialism are to be logically understood on the same level."[8]

At the end of the Second World War, communications were resumed. The intellectuals from the West Indies and Africa were able to meet again and plan for the future. The *Société Africaine de Culture* was created in Paris, a few years after *Présence Africaine*. What was the purpose of this *Société*? Once again, let's consult Frantz Fanon: "This society . . . will limit its activity to a few exhibitions: it will try to prove to Europe that African culture does exist" (*The Wretched of the Earth*, 148). Among these exhibitions:

In 1956 in Paris, the First Congress of Writers and Artists of the Black World.
In 1959 in Rome, the Second Congress.

8. Frantz Fanon, *Les Damnés de la terre*, préface de Jean-Paul Sartre (Paris: Maspéro, 1961 [1967]), 145; *The Wretched of the Earth*, preface by Jean-Paul Sartre, trans. Constance Farrington (New York: Grove Press, 1963 [1977]).

It was during this Second Congress that Sekou Touré, the late president of Guinea, delivered his speech on "The political leader as the representative of a Culture" and declared: "There is no place for the artist or for the intellectual who is not totally mobilized with the people in the great struggle of Africa and suffering mankind."[9] Such sentences become very ironical when one knows of Touré's ulterior active imposition of suffering on the Guinean people. However, despite these reservations there was a wonderful, generous dream in those days. The dream of a black world which would not be broken up into distinct nations by the colonial languages and the various colonial systems of governments. A black world which would speak through one voice, through the univocal voice of its poets and writers. A black world which would recover its dignity and pride.

All that was soon to disappear. The end of World War II marked the beginnings of decolonization in Africa. Year after year, through a series of reforms and conflicts, the African countries arrived at political independence. The African poets and writers who had been close to the *Société Africaine de Culture* and to *Présence Africaine* became heads of state, prime ministers, ministers, thus completing the collusion between politics and literature. The islands of the West Indies, however, became and remained "French Overseas Departments." The black Americans went to fight racism at home. Thus the dream of a united black world was shattered.

Just before the end of the war the posthumous novel of the Haitian writer Jacques Roumain, *Gouverneurs de la rosée* [*Masters of the Dew*], was published.[10] If one compares this novel to *Return to my Native Land* by Césaire, one cannot help being struck by the structural similarities. In both cases, we have two messianic male heroes (Manuel and the Poet) whose ambition is to change their societies and thus rehabilitate the exploited Black Man. On the literary scene, these two works were to have the same effect: obliterate for years to come any literary production prior to themselves. Like *Return to my Native Land, Masters of the Dew* became a sacred text, a fundamental text. According to a Guadeloupean critic, every West Indian novel is noth-

9. Sekou Touré, *The Political Leader as the Representative of a Culture*, 2d Congress of Black Writers and Artists (Rome: 1959); *The Political Leader Considered* (Newark, N.J.: Jihad Productions, 1975).

10. Jacques Roumain, *Gouverneurs de la rosée* (Paris: Editeurs français réunis, 1946); *Masters of the Dew*, trans. Langston Hughes and Mercer Cook (London: Heinemann, 1982).

ing but the rewriting of *Masters of the Dew* and *Return to my Native Land*. The reason for the critical acclaim of *Masters of the Dew* cannot be purely aesthetic. As Alain Robbe-Grillet puts it: "There are no masterpieces for eternity; merely works marked by their time."[11]

With less obscurity and incandescence than Césaire, with a lesser concern for the black world, now limited to the islands, *Masters of the Dew* provides the West Indians with a perfect image of themselves and their islands. Freud said that the finality of art is to reconcile the people with a reality which they don't like. If this is true, in this extraordinary poetic novel the West Indians have everything they can dream of. *Master of the Dew* established a model which is still largely undisputed to this day.

1. The framework should be the native land.
2. The hero should be male, of peasant origin.
3. The brave and hardworking woman should be the auxiliary in his struggle for his community.
4. Although they produce children, no reference should be made to sex. If any, it will be to male sexuality.

I cannot resist the pleasure of quoting the passage in *Masters of the Dew* where Annaïse and Manuel make love for the first time:

> "Yes," she says, "I shall be the mistress of your house. I shall serve you at table and I shall stay standing while you eat and you will tell me 'I thank you, my woman' and I shall tell you 'As you like it, my master.' At night, I shall lie by your side. You will not say anything, but to your silence, to the touch of your hand, I shall reply 'Yes, my man,' because I shall be the servant of your desire." [131]

5. Of course, heterosexuality is the absolute rule.
6. Society should be pitied but never criticized. All its errors should be redeemed by the male hero. In *Masters of the Dew*, Manuel has been compared to a black Christ giving his life for the small community of "Fonds Rouges."

It is the privilege of Edouard Glissant to have united all these tendencies: the end of the Pan-African dream and the desire for a national literature to build a theory which slightly improved upon the existing order. It seems to me that the differences between Césaire and Glissant have been exaggerated. It is a fact that Glissant never really

11. Alain Robbe-Grillet, *Pour un nouveau roman* (Paris: Gallimard, 1946), 131.

adopted the Pan-African ideal. However, his close connections with *Présence Africaine* and the Société Africaine de Culture illustrate a definite concern for the future of the black world. He shares with Césaire the confusion between political and poetic ambitions and the belief in the importance of the community. (In *Le Discours antillais* he says: "The question any Martinican should ask himself is not: 'Who am I?' which is meaningless; but 'Who are we?'").[12]

Glissant's most important contribution to West Indian literature is the introduction of a new dimension, the one of language. Language is the cord which links the West Indian to his land, to his past, to his history. The cord which links the West Indian to the West Indian. "The Theory of *Antillanité*," he explains in *Le Discours antillais*, "aims at exploring all aspects of the African element, which is modified but always present in our societies, and the root of language, which is reinforced through multiplication. Derek Walcott perverts the English language in the same way that Nicolás Guillén perverts Spanish, in the same way that V. S. Naipaul asserts his origin while denying it. Maybe we don't all speak Creole. However, we speak variants of the same language" (Glissant, 182).

Glissant was certainly the first West Indian intellectual to stress the linguistic dimension of colonialism and the problem of diglossia in the islands. But more important than this analytical contribution is his stress on the relationship between the writer, his people, and language. The reproach of obscurity and obstruseness which is constantly hurled at him is but the consequence of his essential belief: language for the West Indian writer is the only way of shaping the future. Glissant is also responsible for the reintroduction of nature and the environment in the West Indian novel. But not nature *per se*. The description of nature remains symbolic if not ideological. In his own words, he associates the hills with the habitation where the white master used to live, and the plain with the daily life of the black man. Political consciousness is thus a symbolic journey through the island. That is the reason rivers play such a major role in Glissant's works. They flow across flat lands and highlands. Like language, they unite men to men, then ultimately merge with the sea which is the symbol of freedom, reconciliation with oneself, and political consciousness.

12. Edouard Glissant, *Le Discours antillais* (Paris: Seuil, 1981).

As I said earlier, Glissant tries to provide future writers with what he thinks will be a more elaborate model for fiction:

> 1. Characters should not be individuals, but the collective expression of the West Indian soul. In a recent discussion in an undergraduate class at Berkeley, he explained why in *Malemort* the characters are grouped by three (Dlan-Médellus-Silacier) and speak collectively.
> 2. Nature should be part of the story just like another character. This is particularly obvious in *Le Quatrième siècle*.
> 3. However, it is language itself which can be regarded as the main object of the novel. The cohabitation of Creole and French creates a new language, the adventures of which are the real subject of the novel. For Glissant, the question is not Creole *or* French, but Creole *and* French.

However elaborate and attractive this model may be, it has not been adopted by the majority of West Indian writers, who remain attached to such things as characters, plots, realistic descriptions of people and places, and who, above all, reject the very complexity of Glissant's language. Therefore, for many years, although "antillanité" has been accepted as a theory perfectly suited to the realities of the islands, the literary model it implies has not been able to impose itself.

Then came Raphaël Confiant and Patrick Chamoiseau, the two writers who, together with the linguist Jean Bernabé, call themselves "Le Groupe de la Créolité." Like their elders in "Légitime Défense," they signaled their entrance into the literary world with the publication of a manifesto called *Éloge de la Créolité*. Like Césaire in *Return to my Native Land*, the opening lines possess the violence of a declaration of war: "Neither Europeans, nor Africans, nor Asians, we proclaim ourselves to be Creoles. This will be a mental attitude. More, a watchfulness, a sort of mental envelope which will sustain our own world in the confrontation with other worlds" (*Éloge de la Créolité*, 13). In these first pages, too, although they state what they regard to be the limitations of "antillanité," they pay homage to Glissant, whom they consider to be their inspiration, their model and master. They inherit from Glissant the desire to make the inventory of their West Indian society, perceived as autonomous and complex, and, above all, a concern for language. However, whereas Glissant paid respect to Creole *and* French as the two languages the West Indian possesses, the new writers lay a heavy emphasis on *Créole*, considered to be the sole mother tongue. "Whenever a mother did everything she could to get her child to learn French and in doing so repressed his Creole tongue, what she did was to strike a mortal blow to his imagination and to exile his creativity forever" (ibid., 14).

However, it would be simplistic to believe that "créolité" is the mere rehabilitation of the Creole language. It is the reappropriation of oneself, of that "formidable migan" which created the West Indian personality. It is an aesthetic. Moreover, it is the future of the world. "The world is moving towards a state of *créolité*" (ibid., 52). In their novels, Raphaël Confiant and Patrick Chamoiseau give an illustration of their theory. There is no doubt that both writers produce very good fiction. But apart from the sumptuous invention of a language (especially in the case of Chamoiseau), we see only minor changes in the prevailing West Indian model, minor changes in the order. Here are the most striking innovations:

1. The characters are not confined to the usual trilogy: *béké* (white planter)/black man/mulatto. (For instance, Raphaël Confiant introduces an East Indian, up to now the forgotten soul of Guadeloupean and Martinican literature.)
2. Sexuality (especially in Confiant's novel)[13] is no longer absent, but is exclusively male sexuality.
3. The male characters (women remain confined to stereotypical or negative roles) don't have the messianic ambition to modify their world, like Manuel for instance. On the contrary, in *Chronique des sept misères*, Patrick Chamoiseau presents a deliberate satire of the "revolutionary behavior" of a *female* student:

It is around this time that a revolutionary student arrived who goaded us with her ideal as if it were a whip. Her voice covered the cries of the market women calling to customers and worrying about their breadfruits ripening or their "caimites" opening up in the heat. . . . She used to shout also: "You must organize yourselves, rationalize your production, gather your energies into a cooperative . . . '"[14]

Maybe it is too early to ask these writers to illustrate their theory fully. As a rule, theory comes before practice. Therefore, we have to refer ourselves to their manifesto *Éloge de la Créolité* in order to imagine fully the themes of the literature to come. In this respect, *Éloge de la Créolité* gives an impression of *déjà vu* or *déjà entendu*. Moreover, reading it, one seems to witness the emergence of a new order, even more restrictive than the existing one.

13. Raphaël Confiant, *Le Nègre et l'amiral* (Paris: Grasset, 1988).
14. Patrick Chamoiseau, *Chronique des sept misères* (Paris: Gallimard, 1986), 118.

The tedious enumeration of the elements of popular culture which is made in the first pages of the manifesto leaves very little freedom for creativity. Are we condemned *ad vitam aeternam* to speak of vegetable markets, story tellers, "dorlis," "koutem" . . . ? Are we condemned to explore to saturation the resources of our narrow islands? We live in a world where, already, frontiers have ceased to exist. Guadeloupe and Martinique, for better or for worse, have entered the European Common Market and welcome on their soil thousands of men and women from all sorts of countries. Half of the population of each island lives abroad. Part of it no longer speaks the Creole language, although they remain Creoles, since a damaging simplification, albeit made by a school of sociologists, equates identity with language. In new environments one faces new experiences which reshape the West Indian personality. For those who stay on the islands, changes occur also. As Glissant himself puts it, the Caribbean Sea, which he opposes to the Mediterranean, is not a closed area. On the contrary, it opens onto the world and its varied energetic influences.

West Indians should be as changing and evolving as the islands themselves. Above all, creativity is a complex process which obeys no rules. A writer confined to a small and isolated village of the West Indies is free to dream of "Another Land" and make of it the subject of his/her fiction. Creative imagination goes beyond the limits of reality and soars to areas of its own choice. In fact, dream is a factor which has always been neglected in West Indian literature. It constitutes the object of some of the most magnificent writings of the world.

Does its power frighten the West Indian writer?

DISORDER

In a Bambara myth of origin, after the creation of the earth, and the organization of everything on its surface, disorder was introduced by a woman. Disorder meant the power to create new objects and to modify the existing ones. In a word, disorder meant creativity.

Apart from one or two names, the female writers of the West Indies are little known. Their works are forgotten, out of print, misunderstood. The best example of incomprehension remains the criticism of Mayotte Capécia's *Je suis martiniquaise*[15] by Frantz Fanon. In *Black*

---

15. Mayotte Capécia, *Je suis martiniquaise* (Paris: Cornéa, 1948).

Skin, White Masks,[16] he singled her out to illustrate what he calls "le complexe de la lactification," the desire to be white and thereby to go down in history. First of all, Frantz Fanon takes a very dangerous stand. He deliberately confuses the *author* and the *object of her fiction.* Although Mayotte says *Je,* nothing proves that she was writing about herself. And even if she were! Let us recall that this novel was written in 1948. At that time, all the societies which had suffered from the wrongs of slavery and colonial exploitation were alienated in the same way. In *Masters and Slaves,* Gilberto Freyre explains the desire to "wash one's blood" which affected the blacks as well as the mulattoes in multiracial Brazil.[17] Mayotte Capécia was simply no exception to the rule. This unjust criticism has forever cast a slur on the book and overshadowed its other interesting aspects. For instance, it contains a deep and penetrating picture of Mayotte's father, whose irresponsibility and mistreatment of her mother might well be partially responsible for Mayotte's hatred of the black man. Contrary to what Frantz Fanon thinks and says, *Je suis martiniquaise* is a precious written testimony, the only one that we possess, of the mentality of a West Indian girl in those days, of the impossibility for her to build up an aesthetics which would enable her to come to terms with the color of her skin.

At the beginning of the century, long before Césaire desperately tried to redeem the black man's image, Suzanne Lacascade in her only novel, *Claire-Solange, âme africaine,* constructed a theory of the climates in order to prove the superiority of the colored woman over the white one.[18] It is obvious that neither Suzanne Lacascade nor Mayotte Capécia had a particular gift for writing, but the oblivion to which they have unfortunately been relegated is not due to their lack of literary skills.

Whenever women speak out, they displease, shock, or disturb. Their writings imply that before thinking of a political revolution, West Indian society needs a psychological one. What they hope for and desire conflicts with men's ambitions and dreams. Why, they ask, fight against racism in the world when it exists at home, among our-

16. Frantz Fanon, *Black Skin, White Masks,* trans. Charles Lam Harkmann (New York: Grove Press, 1982 [1967]).

17. Gilberto Freyre, *Masters and Slaves* (Berkeley: University of California Press, 1986).

18. Suzanne Lacascade, *Claire-Solange, âme africaine* (Paris: E. Figuière, 1924).

selves? There is nothing West Indian society hates more than facing the reality of color prejudice which reminds it of the days of slavery, of the time when to be black was a curse and to possess a fair skin was regarded as a blessing. Color prejudice is precisely the exclusive theme of Michèle Lacrosil's novels. Her first novel, *Sapotille et le serin d'argile*, portrays a girl's internalization of the inferiority complex during her childhood. Her second one, *Cajou*,[19] reads like the diary of a mental patient who cannot come to terms with life and takes refuge in death. It would be too easy to dismiss Michèle Lacrosil, as it is often done, by saying that she portrays a time gone by. West Indian society is not sure it is cured from the alienation Michèle Lacrosil portrays so vividly. Therefore it is forced to question itself. Is today really different from yesterday? Have we really changed? Aren't we at heart still the same people?

At the conclusion of *La Vie scélérate*,[20] the young narrator Coco expresses the literary viewpoint of the author when she states:

> Maybe I shall have to write this story? Maybe I shall have to pay my debt and so doing displease and shock everybody? Mine will be the story of very ordinary people who in their very ordinary ways had nevertheless shed the blood of others. I must write my own story and this will be my own personal homage to those who are no more. My book will be very different from the ambitious ones that my mother had dreamt of: 'Essay on the Revolutionary Movements of the Black World' and the like. . . . It will be a book without either great torturers or dignified martyrs. But it will, however, be loaded with flesh and blood. The story of my people. [*La Vie scélérate*, 340]

Mental breakdown, madness, and eventually suicide, are common themes among women writers. As I indicated earlier, Cajou commits suicide. Because of the difficulties of their sentimental lives, Télumée in *Pluie et vent sur Télumée Miracle* by Simone Schwarz-Bart,[21] as well as Thécla in *La Vie scélérate*, temporarily lose their minds. The heroines of *Le Quimboiseur l'avait dit* and *Juletane* by Myriam Warner-Vieyra are both mentally disturbed.[22]

19. Michèle Lacrosil, *Sapotille et le serin d'argile* (Paris: Gallimard, 1960); *Cajou* (Paris: Gallimard, 1961).

20. Maryse Condé, *La Vie scélérate*, (Paris: Le Livre de Poche, 1987).

21. Simone Schwarz-Bart, *Pluie et vent sur Télumée Miracle* (Paris: Éditions du Seuil, 1972).

22. Myriam Warner-Vieyra, *Le Quimboiseur l'avait dit* (Paris: Présence africaine, 1980); *Juletane* (Paris: Présence africaine, 1982).

Sexuality is another taboo in West Indian literature, and when reference is made to sexuality, it is to male sexuality. We have already discussed the portrayal of Annaïse, the servant of Manuel's desire in *Masters of the Dew*. The uproar about my novel *Heremakhonon*[23] was largely caused by Veronica, the heroine, expressing her own sexuality. For the first time a woman had the right to enjoy sex and to say it. But the most striking transgressions of the order imposed by the male writers are related to the image of men and to the image of Africa.

The family system of the West Indies has been the object of intensive studies. In 1928, the Jamaican researcher Edith Clarke wrote an unsurpassed classic, *My Mother who Fathered Me*,[24] echoed a few years ago by *Sé kouto sèl*, an essay based upon over seventy interviews of Guadeloupean women conducted by France Alibar and Perrette Lambèye-Boye.[25] Although widely set apart in time, both books registered the same complaints. Due to the absenteeism and irresponsibility of the fathers, the victimized mothers are forced to be the breadwinners and to assume the education of the children. However, in spite of this sociological reality, we have been fed upon triumphant portrayals of messianic heroes coming back home to revolutionize their societies. . . .

In *Pluie et vent sur Télumée Miracle*, Simone Schwarz-Bart was the first to dare to shatter this myth and place West Indian women where they belong—at the forefront of the daily battle for survival. This novel is too well known and the Lougandor dynasty of women too famous to be presented again. We must, however, say that few critics have done justice to the disturbing quality of *Pluie et vent sur Télumée Miracle*. Apart from a rejection of motherhood in the novel, we find the portrayal of a "bad mother," Victoire, and of a "bad woman," "a witch," personified by Laetitia. While Télumée is compared to a heliconia of the mountains, Laetitia is compared to a water lily. Thus, Schwarz-Bart associates her with the great goddesses of the West Indian pantheon who derive their powers from water: *Maman dlo, Yamanya*. . . . Télumée, creature of the air, "négresse planeuse," "flèche de canne à sucre" fights in vain against her. Before being hailed

23. Maryse Condé, *Heremakhonon: a Novel*, trans. Richard Philcox (Washington, D.C.: Three Continents Press, 1982).

24. Edith Clarke, *My Mother Who Fathered Me*, preface by Sir Hugh Foot, introduction by M. G. Smith (London: Allen & Unwin, 1979 [1966]).

25. *Sé kouto sèl* (Paris: Editions Caribéennes: Agence de Coopération Culturelle et Technique, 1981).

by the critics abroad, *Pluie et vent sur Télumée Miracle* received a great many adverse comments at home. It was thought to be pessimistic, negative, and fatalistic since it contained no elements of the conventional revolutionary bric à brac. The only allusion to social turmoil ends abruptly with Amboise's death. Eventually *Pluie et vent sur Télumée Miracle* was recuperated by some West Indian university critics who turned it into a female version of *Gouverneurs de la rosée*. By so doing, they deprived it of all its irreverence and could therefore celebrate it as a feminine masterpiece.

However, transgressing the image of the male is nothing compared with transgressing the traditional image of Africa. We shall not recall the quarrel over *Heremakhonon, Ségou,* and other novels about Africa written by myself and Myriam Warner-Vieyra. Those who want to veil their faces before the harsh realities of Africa cannot accept *our* truth. Let us quote Julio Cortazar, a Third World novelist who has fought all his life for the freedom of creativity: "It is the destiny of literature to provide for beauty. It is its duty to provide for truth in this beauty."[26]

FREEDOM

As we can see, we are far from this permanent questioning of text and context which characterizes literature today. In *Le Livre à venir*, Maurice Blanchot declared:

> The essence of literature is to escape any fundamental determination, any assertion which could stabilize it or even fix it. It is never already there, it is always to be found or invented again.[27]

On the contrary, in the West Indies, literature seems to exist to provide the reader with a few reassuring images of himself and his land. Although West Indian literature proclaims to be revolutionary and to be able to change the world, on the contrary, writer and reader implicitly agree about respecting a stereotypical portrayal of themselves and their society. In reality, does the writer wish to protect the reader and himself against the ugliness of the past, the hardships of the present, and the uncertainty of the future? Can we expect the liberation of the West Indian writer in the years to come?

Éloge de la Créolité gives a negative answer. However, other forces

---

26. Julio Cortazar, Lecture given at the University of California, Berkeley (1977).
27. Maurice Blanchot, *Le Livre à venir* (Paris: Gallimard, Idées, 1971 [1959]), 293.

are at work, such as the new mentality of our youth and our increased contacts with the rest of the world, especially the Americas. Among the writers themselves, a few dissenting voices, not just female voices, although still covered by those of the majority, make themselves heard and give cause for hope.

CHRISTINE DELPHY

The Invention of French Feminism: An Essential Move[*][1]

"French Feminism" is a baffling topic for everybody, and it is no less so for feminists from France than for feminists from the United States or Britain. There are many aspects to this topic and first of all, of course: what is "French Feminism"?

"French Feminism" is not feminism in France; that must be said at the outset. Feminists in France don't need to call their feminism a particular name any more than American feminists call theirs "American Feminism."

Most feminists from France find it extraordinary to be presented, when abroad, with a version of their feminism and their country of which they had previously no idea. British and American feminists are either fascinated or irritated, but always intrigued, by what is presented to them in Women's Studies as "French Feminism" or "French Theory."

The very attempt to attribute a specific content to a feminist movement shows that we are dealing with an outsider's view. So, even before we start looking at this content, we know that it cannot be a self-definition. This raises the question of the relationship between the way feminists from France see themselves and the way outsiders see them. This relationship bears a resemblance to that between observers and observed, between subjects and objects, a problem often raised in feminist methodology. It raises the question of who has the power to define whom to start with, who calls the shots. This is an important question, because that is what most irritates feminists in

[*]From *Yale French Studies* 87 (1995): *Another Look, Another Woman.*

1. I would like to thank Françoise Armengaud, Laura Cottingham, Judith Ezekiel, and Ailbhe Smyth for their support, their suggestions, and their help in the writing of this paper.

YFS 97, *50 Years of Yale French Studies, Part 2,* ed. Porter and Waters, © 2000 by Yale University.

France: that a "French Feminism" has been created unbeknownst to them in English-speaking countries. The content given to the category "French Feminism" is important in that respect: for the fact that feminists from France cannot recognize themselves in the picture they are presented with is a source of deeply-felt irritation. But the sole fact of creating a category "French Feminism" with a specific content— whatever the content—deprives feminists from France of the right to name themselves French Feminists. An ideological content—never mind which at this stage—has been given to a geographical specification.

This in turn raises a related issue: why has it been deemed necessary by Anglo-American feminists to specify, in ideological terms, the actions and the writings of feminists from France? And, reciprocally, to give a *national* label to a particular set of ideas or brand of feminism? How relevant *are* national boundaries to feminism—or indeed to other social and ideological movements—and how relevant *should* they be? That question has never been asked, although I think it is central. And finally, how was what is now known as "French Feminism" constructed? Who decided what it was and what it was not? *What went into the bag and what did not?*

What is taught as "French Feminism" has in fact little to do with what is happening in France on the feminist scene, either from a theoretical or from an activist point of view. This has been pointed out several times over the years by French and American scholars and activists.[2] More and more protests are being heard about the voluntary or involuntary distortions and omissions of the Anglo-American version of "French Feminism." The aim of this paper is not, however, to set the record straight: that work is already under way, and although it will take as many years probably to set the record straight as it has taken to get it wrong, it is already off to a good start with Claire Moses's brilliant analysis.[3]

In constructing "French Feminism," Anglo-American authors favored a certain overtly antifeminist political trend called "Psych et po," to the detriment of what is considered, by Anglo-American as

2. See my "La passion selon Wittig," *Nouvelles Questions Féministes* 11–12 (Winter, 1985): 151–56. See also, Claire Moses, "French Feminism's Fortune," *The Women's Review of Books* 5/1 (October, 1987): 44.

3. See Moses, "'French Feminism' in U.S. Academic Discourse," a paper presented at the Berkshire Conference on Women's History, 12 June 1992 (hereafter referred to as Moses 1992a).

well as French feminist historians,[4] to be the core of the feminist movement; and their bias has contributed to weakening the French movement (see Moses 1992a).

Anglo-American proponents of "French Feminism" have also consistently conflated "women writers" with "women's movement" (see Moses 1992a), thus eliminating the activist dimension of that movement. They promoted as "major French feminist theorists"[5] a "Holy Trinity" made up of three women who have become household names in the Anglo-American world of Women's Studies, which itself is increasingly divorced from the social movement: Cixous, Kristeva, Irigaray. This was in spite of the fact, which was never revealed to the non-French public, that the first two are completely outside feminist debate in France—and, not being considered feminist theorists, can hardly be considered "*major* feminist theorists"; and in spite of the fact, which is well-known and has been dealt with diversely by Anglo-American exporters, that at least the first two not only do not call themselves feminists, but have been known to actually denounce feminism.

Although the facts are well known, they are not seen as a problem. Why? "Never would Americans proclaim nonfeminists to be the figureheads of their own movement."[6] What do you call doing to somebody else what you would not have done unto you? The term "imperialism" springs to the lips. And that is indeed the conclusion reached by both Moses and Ezekiel. They see imperialism at work in the Anglo-American construction of "French Feminism," and, moreover, they see that imperialism as related to domestic agendas: "Opponents have taken as their targets, not its American agents, but the French themselves" (Ezekiel); and "the French . . . are blamed for aspects of ourselves that we do not like but do not take responsibility for (like our racism and our classism)" (Moses 1992a). It is impossible to deny the charge of imperialism: imperialism indeed made the construction of "French Feminism" possible. It is equally impossible to deny that the wish to evade responsibility for one's theories is at work here. I think that the "agents," as Ezekiel calls them, of "French Feminism"

4. See Françoise Picq, *Libération des femmes. Les Années-Mouvement* (Paris: Seuil, 1993).
5. Toril Moi, "Introduction" to *French Feminist Thought* (Oxford: Blackwell, 1987), 5.
6. Judith Ezekiel, Comments on Claire Moses's paper, Berkshire History of Women Conference, 12 June 1992.

wanted to present certain theories as "French" in order that the prestige accruing to what is foreign in intellectual circles, and especially to what is "French," would accrue to that position; and in order to be able to distance themselves from, and not take full responsibility for, the ideas they were defending, as they could always take the stand that they were merely introducing Anglo-Americans to foreign ideas. An added benefit they could expect was that their pretension that these ideas are "feminist" would not be questioned.

But although imperialism, and the motivations behind the imperialist stance, figure prominently in the construction of "French Feminism," they are not the whole story. They are important, even essential, but as a means rather than the ultimate ends. The ultimate ends are domestic, but I contend that the domestic agenda is more ambitious than just hiding behind the "French." Or, to put it differently, the real question is: why is it necessary to hide behind the "French"? I think one has to answer that question first, and to answer it, one has to define the ideological features that are being proposed and promoted under the guise of "French Feminism." What does it say about feminism, and about the central questions of oppression and liberation that feminism poses?

My contention is that the manner in which "French Feminism" addresses these questions—often in an obscure and pedantic style which would require an essay in its own right—is regressive and detrimental to feminism in general, and not only to feminism in France, as noted by Eléni Varikas:

> To reduce "French" feminism to a few particular theoretical positions is not only to obscure the fact that the majority of feminist struggles were fought without knowledge of and sometimes against these positions; it is not only to obscure the most influential theoretical positions of feminist thought in France; even more than that, it is to prevent further thought on the conditions in which these many positions emerged, on what makes them socially and academically acceptable, and on their subversive dynamic.[7]

But before I come to that, I submit that "French Feminism" is not so much a "construction"—a biased and imperfect version of the reality of feminism in France—as an invention: a theoretical statement or

7. Eléni Varikas, "Féminisme, modernité, post-modernisme. Pour un dialogue des deux côtés de l'océan," in *Féminismes au présent*, special issue of *Futur Antérieur* (Paris: L'Harmattan, 1993), 63.

series of statements that have only a spurious relation to any other "reality"; that these statements are highly contentious; and that this is the reason why they had to try and be passed off as French.

First I want to establish that the theses of "French Feminism," and therefore "French Feminism" itself, cannot be found in the body of works that its agents refer to, but in their own writings. In other words, I mean that "French Feminism" is not an Anglo-American construction solely, or even mainly, insofar as it selects, distorts, and decontextualizes French writings. That would imply that to find what "it" is, we would have to engage in more comments, distortions, and selections; in brief, we would have to play the game by their rules and chase our tails until doomsday. No, I mean that it is an Anglo-American invention quite literally: Anglo-American writings that are "about" it *are* it.

I will briefly try to characterize "French Feminism" as a political strand, from the point of view of its content, and expose why, on an analytical level, it is not compatible with feminist analysis. My contention is that the problems most apparent in that approach, such as the reclaiming of the "feminine" or a definition of sexuality that leaves no room for lesbianism, are not the *source* of its inadequacy. I propose instead that these claims, which are problematic for a feminist politics, are a consequence of adopting an outdated epistemological framework.

However, these problematic positions come back to the fore when one tries to understand why feminists—or anyone—would want to adopt such a framework. I contend that anxieties about one's sexual and personal identity, threatened by the development of feminism and the blurring of gender lines that it promises, explain the liking exhibited by some women for conceptual frameworks that renege on the approach in terms of gender. That leads me to examine how social constructionism—in particular in the United States—is today often equated with "social conditioning" or "discourse theory," and does not, therefore, present a real alternative to essentialism.

I move on to consider an alternative explanation of the popularity of "French Feminism," in which it is not seen as a response to a contemporary threat, but as a continuation of a "difference" school which has existed within feminism since the turn of the century.

In what may look at first like a conclusion (and indeed was for a time), I then suggest that the reason proponents of that position offered it as "French," and the reason therefore for the invention of "French Feminism," was to try and deflect the criticism its creators thought they would get—and that they got—from feminists, for offering an essentialist theory. And lastly, in my concluding remarks, I submit that the imperialism exhibited in the invention of "French Feminism" was necessary both to produce a particular brand of essentialism, and in order to pass off as feminist a "theory" in which feminism and feminists need not figure any longer.

FRENCH FEMINISM AS AN ANGLO-AMERICAN FABRICATION

To understand exactly what this "French Feminism" is in relation to feminism is the best way to understand why it was necessary to present it as "foreign." Once that is understood, the particular selection of authors and writings makes sense. And in turn, the distortions brought to the account of the feminist scene in France makes sense, once we understand that the particular selection of authors and writings was dictated by ideological choice.

If, on the other hand, we start with the distortions—that is, if we start by comparing the account given by "French Feminism" with the actual French scene—we are left with the realization that there is a huge gap between the two. But how are we to understand how that happened, if we take the proponents of "French Feminism" at their word, that their aim was indeed to give an account of the French feminist scene? We would have to assume that, over a period of fifteen years, scholar after scholar has "misunderstood" the French political or intellectual scene. Inasmuch as we can assume ignorance or misinformation on the part of one or several persons, we cannot assume that all have been blind, and indeed afflicted with the same selective blindness; we cannot assume moreover that no one tried at any time to correct the picture, or to question the dominant account. There were questions and corrections from Anglo-American scholars;[8] and there were protests from feminists from France.[9]

In the hypothesis that the misrepresentation of the French feminist scene was a bona fide mistake, these questions, protests, and cor-

8. See Dorothy Kauffman McCall, "Politics of Difference," *Signs* 9/21 (1983): 283–93.

9. See Delphy 1985, Moses 1987, and Eliane Viennot, "Review Article," *Études Féministes* 1 (1987): 40–47.

rections were treated with arrogance when mentioned at all.[10] So the hypothesis that the main protagonists of "French Feminism" wanted to give an account and that they were only "mistaken" is untenable. Only the hypothesis that these protagonists had an ideological and political agenda can explain the discrepancies between "French Feminism" and feminism in France, the fact that these discrepancies persisted over a period of years, and, finally, that these discrepancies are not random.

"French Feminism," a fabrication of American, and more widely, English-speaking scholars, was created by a series of distortions and voluntary or involuntary errors about what was happening in France from the mid-seventies on. These distortions have a pattern. We do not have several competing views or definitions which show that the distortions are not random. On the other hand, if we did have competing views, then we would not have "French Feminism." "French Feminism" is thus a highly consensual object in the sense that the only debates about it focus on its relevance to Anglo-American concerns. There are *no* debates about what it *is*. Everybody seems to know what "French Feminism" is. At the same time, it is never really defined and remains elusive. It is therefore impossible to give, in any objective way, an ideological definition to what is an ideological current, and is perceived as such, in feminism.

The only objective way to define it is to say that it is a body of comments by Anglo-American writers on a selection of French and non-French writers: Lacan, Freud, Kristeva, Cixous, Derrida, and Irigaray are the core groups. But there are others.

This presents us with two main questions: as I mentioned earlier, the question of the gap between this body of comments and feminism in France will not be addressed here, and I will concentrate instead on the theoretical and ideological pattern it presents. What are the substantive views these Anglo-American authors are promoting or attacking? What are they bringing to the debate on feminism in their respective countries?

But before tackling this, I want to look at its formal definition, that is, its definition as a body of Anglo-American writings. If we accept that "French Feminism" is an ideological and political trend in the countries where it exists as an object of debate, it follows that it has to

10. See, for example, Rosemary Tong's remarks about Viennot in her *Feminist Thought: A Comprehensive Introduction* (Boulder: Westview Press, 1989), 223, or Ezekiel.

be studied as such—and from then on, without quotation marks. It also follows that its message is contained in the sum of articles and books that purport to comment or build on French or other material. It *cannot* be said to consist of what its proponents claim: the complete works of the authors that they comment on, the authors listed above. These are the *referents* of "French Feminism," but they are not *it*. First, Anglo-American authors do not agree on the list of their referents—so that even if we accepted, as they would have us do, that the complete works of their referents is "French Feminism," as that list is infinite, we still would not have a finite and clearly delineated body of writings. Secondly, the supposedly original text of "French Feminism" is a series of bits and fragments taken from a heterogeneous universe. They do not make up an ensemble independent of the comments in which they are incorporated. That justifies seeing this body of comments as a separate entity from its referents, just as the Talmud is rightly seen as distinct from the Torah. We do not possess another text—an original homogeneous text, as in the case of the Torah.

But more importantly, a body of comments is really nothing more, nor less, than a theoretical statement or statements in the end. Or, put differently, there is no substantive difference between a theoretical work which is about something and a theoretical work which is about somebody. Whatever the detours, you end up saying something about the world, so that there is no legitimate difference of status between the text that presents itself as a "mere" comment, and the text it purports to comment on. These comments—including of course the bits and fragments, the quotes—therefore make up the only text we have of "French Feminism," and it is this body of work which constitutes "French Feminism."

For all these reasons, "French Feminism" is an Anglo-American strand of intellectual production within an Anglo-American context. From now on, when I speak of French Feminism and French Feminists without quotation marks, I am referring exclusively to this Anglo-American body of writings and its Anglo-American authors.

FRENCH FEMINISM AS AN IDEOLOGY OF DIFFERENCE: HOLISTIC VERSUS ADDITIVE EPISTEMOLOGIES

To study and to place this strand within each "national" feminism and feminism at large would require a study well outside the scope of this essay. However, if I tried, from my necessarily partial and impression-istic perspective, to give a description of it, I would say that the fea-tures that strike me most—apart from its pretension to be French—are the following:

—the conflation of "women" and "the feminine" and conversely, of "men" and "the masculine";

—the focus on the "feminine" and the "masculine," the belief that such things exist—or should exist—and that they provide or should provide a model for what actual women and men do and "are";

—the belief that "the feminine" and "the masculine" are a universal division of traits; that this division is found in all cultures because it is a trait of the universal psyche;

—the belief that the psyche is separate from and anterior to society and culture;

—the belief that the content of the psyche is both universal—not re-lated to culture—and based on a common condition shared by all hu-mans;

—the positing of a "sexual difference" between women and men which includes morphological differences, functional differences in reproduction, and psychological differences;

—the belief that sexual attraction between people is the desire for "difference";

—the belief that the only significant difference between people is "sexual difference";

—the belief that sexual difference is and should be the basis of psychic, emotional, cultural, and social organization, although the word "so-cial" only gets through the pens of French Feminists with some diffi-culty.[11]

11. See Carolyn Burke, "Report from Paris: Women's Writing and the Women's Movement," *Signs* 3/4 (1978): 843–55 and "Irigaray through the Looking Glass," *Feminist Studies* 7/2 (1981): 287–306; Claire Duchen, *Feminism in France* (London: Rout-ledge & Kegan Paul, 1986); Diana Fuss, *Essentially Speaking* (London: Routledge & Kegan Paul, 1989) and "'Essentially Speaking'/Luce Irigaray's Language of Essence," in Nancy Fraser and Sandra Lee Bartky, *Revaluing French Feminism* (Bloomington: Indi-ana University Press, 1992), 94–112; Jane Gallop, *The Daughter's Seduction* (Ithaca: Cornell University Press, 1982); Elizabeth Gross, "Philosophy, Subjectivity and the

One need not go on to stress the point that this approach to the problems raised by feminism is very problematic on analytical and political levels. On an analytical level, it turns its back on the main developments in feminist thinking; on a political level, it has implications that are unpalatable for many feminists.

Whereas some haggle over points of detail, or interpretation, I think it has to be recognized that *any* dealing with "human nature"— whatever form it takes, be it the "aggressiveness" of males, the "constraints of the symbolic order," or the "maternal-semiotic"—is bound to wield very disappointing results for any movement bent on changing the world or even simply on understanding it.

Now, the question is understanding why so many Anglo-American commentators have chosen the human nature approach. And in asking that question, we cannot simply talk about French Feminism anymore: we must include not only the people who write about it, but the people who listen to it, not only the Anglo-American participants, but the people—and in particular feminists—who all over the Western world find that kind of approach so enticing. I and others have tackled

Body: Kristeva and Irigaray," in *Feminist Challenges*, ed. Carol Pateman and Elizabeth Gross (Boston: Northeastern University Press, 1986), 125–43. Alice Jardine, "Pre-Texts for the Transatlantic Feminist," *Yale French Studies* 62 (1981): 220–36, "Introduction to Julia Kristeva's 'Women's Time,'" *Signs* 7/1 (1981): 7–35, *Gynesis* (Ithaca: Cornell University Press, 1985), and "Men in Feminism: Odor di Uomo or Compagnons de Route?" in *Men in Feminism*, a special issue of *Critical Exchange* 18 (1985): 23–31; Ann Rosalind Jones, "Assimilation with a Difference: Renaissance Women Poets and Literary Influence," *Yale French Studies* 62 (1981): 135–153, and "Writing the Body: Toward an Understanding of *l'écriture féminine*, *Feminist Studies* 7/2 (1981): 246–63; Peggy Kamuf, "Replacing Feminist Criticism," in *Conflicts in Feminism*, ed. Marianne Hirsch and Evelyn Fox Keller (London: Routledge & Kegan Paul, 1990), 104–11; Kamuf and Nancy K. Miller, "Parisian Letters: Between Feminism and Deconstruction," in Hirsch and Fox Keller, 120–33; Dorothy Leland, "Lacanian Psychoanalysis and French Feminism: Toward an Adequate Political Psychology," in Fraser and Bartky, 113–35; Miller, "The Text's Heroine: A Feminist Critic and Her Fictions," in Hirsch and Fox Keller, 11–120; Moi 1987 and Moi, *Sexual/Textual Politics* (London: Methuen, 1985), and *The Kristeva Reader* (Oxford: Blackwell, 1986); Ariel Salleh, "Contribution to the Critique of Political Epistemology," *Thesis Eleven* 8 (1984): 23–44; Naomi Schor, "This Essentialism Which Is Not One," *Differences* 1/2 (1989): 38–58; Paul Smith, *Discerning the Subject* (Minneapolis: University of Minnesota Press, 1988); Gayatri Chakravorty Spivak, "French Feminism in an International Frame," *Yale French Studies* 62 (1981): 154–84, and "French Feminism Revisited: Ethics and Politics," in *Feminists Theorize the Political*, ed. Judith Butler and Joan Scott (London: Routledge & Kegan Paul, 1992), 54–85; Domna Stanton, "The Fiction of *Préciosité* and the Fear of Women," *Yale French Studies* 61 (1981): 107–34, and "Language and Revolution: The Franco-American Dis-Connection," in *The Future of Difference*, ed. Hester Eisenstein and Alice Jardine (New Brunswick: Rutgers University Press), 52–87.

that issue many times over the years.[12] The appeal remains, and it is that of "difference" and, more precisely, of "*sexual* difference." The reasons for the theoretical and political flaws of this approach are also the reasons for its appeal.

The "sexual difference" approach is theoretically flawed on a basic level by the very premises it incorporates, and which are a throwback to epistemological postures that cannot be taken seriously today. I have listed some of them above, but there is a deeper level which makes that approach incompatible with the modern humanities and social sciences, including the so-called postmodern.

Briefly, one can trace back to the nineteenth century the development of a paradigm for understanding the world that I will call, for the time being, structural. This approach, to be found in the natural sciences as well as in the human sciences, considers the whole before it considers the parts. It is the whole, the configuration, that gives meaning to each of the parts. Indeed, it is the whole that gives rise to the parts. In other words, the whole precedes the parts.

This approach, in use in the natural sciences and in mathematics for more than a century, can be found in many models of the human sciences. For example, it is the still uncontested basis of Saussurian linguistics; even though later models have been developed, the basic Saussurian model remains: sounds do not pre-exist the total language, it is the total language which determines how the sound continuum will be cut up into discrete sounds. This model informs contemporary anthropology (not only that which calls itself structural, like the work of Lévi-Strauss), contemporary psychology, and sociology. This understanding of the world is already present in the work of Marx: the total society pre-exists each class, and it is the way it functions as a whole which creates the division principle; the division principle itself creates each class. Classes cannot be viewed independently of one another, as tribes having led their own lives and coming into contact almost by accident, no more than the "a" sound in a given language can be seen as existing independently of the next sound.

12. See my "Rethinking Sex and Gender," *Women's Studies International Forum* 16/1 (1993): 1–9 (hereafter referred to as Delphy 1993a) and "Proto-feminism and Anti-feminism," in my *Close to Home*, trans. Diana Leonard (London: Hutchinson Press, 1984), 182–211; see also Colette Guillaumin, *Sexe, race et pratique du pouvoir* (Paris: côté-femmes, 1992); Nicole-Claude Mathieu, *L'Anatomie politique* (Paris: côté-femmes, 1991); and Monique Wittig, *The Straight Mind* (Boston: Beacon Press, 1992).

For all these reasons, I think *holistic*[13] is the best adjective to characterize the structural approach. Needless to say, all modern and contemporary developments build on that approach. The structural or *holistic* approach is the matrix of all twentieth-century schools of thought, whether they call themselves materialist, social constructionist, or structuralist. The so-called "post" (as in "poststructuralist") trends are not contradictions but further developments of this more general approach.

The contemporary development of research on gender is part of that paradigm: it considers that gender, the dividing principle, is the constituting force behind the creation of genders. To put it simply, this means taking as a starting point that you cannot envision "men" and "women" separately, any more than "the feminine" and "the masculine"; that the two are created one by the other and at the same time. Now this stance has revolutionary implications; it implies that the one does not (indeed) move without the other; that the status of the category "women" cannot change without the status of the category "men" changing at the same time; it implies, moreover, that their respective status and their content are one and the same thing: that it is impossible to change the status of a category without changing its content and vice-versa (see Delphy 1993).

In contrast, French Feminism and the theories, such as psychoanalysis, on which it draws have remained immune to these developments. They go on considering the parts as independent of one another and pre-existing their coming into relation. It uses, from the point of view of the relationship of the parts to the whole, an *additive* approach.

Now such a view implies that the parts, which exist before the whole, have a meaning, and indeed a nature—an *essence*—of their own. It implies furthermore that the parts that make up any reality—the physical, social, or psychic world—are always the same, in number and in content, and are there to stay; therefore, that which we perceive is what *reality* is made up of: if we perceive two sexes for instance, it is because there *are* two sexes; that society or its instances—language for one instance—intervene only to rank these pre-existing realities; that these constituent parts can be shifted around without

13. I do not use the term "holistic" in the sense it was given by Quine, although the two are by no means contradictory.

changing the whole; and, conversely, that the only thing that can be done with them is to shift them around; that inasmuch as one wants to shift them around, one has to find their "real" meaning, their "real" essence. The *additive* approach is thus necessarily essentialist.

Only on that basis is it possible to imagine, as French Feminism does, that the only way to "up" the status of women is to up that of "the feminine"; and that, conversely, one of these statuses—that of the "feminine"—can be "revalued" without altering the status of "the masculine." More importantly, that alteration takes place without altering the whole and creating a new whole, and, therefore, new divisions of which "the feminine" and "the masculine" might not be a part (see Delphy 1984 and Delphy 1993).

This is where features of French Feminism which I earlier considered as secondary play a central role, especially the insistence on *not* defining the "sexual difference" it talks about, and leaving it as a mystical object whose mysteries must remain obscure. In order to do that, French feminists must ignore the now considerable work—empirical as well as theoretical—that has gone into cracking open that nut, and on studying the different things to which sexual difference refers. To speak today, without further ado, of undefined "sexual difference" amounts to eliding sex (anatomical), sexuation (gender identity and psychological sex-related differences), sex roles, sexual activity, and sexual preference. All these things are supposed, both in common-sense thinking and in French Feminism, to derive from one another or to be one and the same thing. This confusion is the basis of gender ideology. Psychoanalysis provided the "scientific" version of this common-sense ideology, putting sexual difference under one form or another—the penis, "castration," or the mother-child bond—in the place of the ultimate principle.

Feminism started—a long time ago—deconstructing all these links; extricating sex from sex role and sex identity; it has even forged whole new concepts, such as *gender*, to account for this deconstruction. From the early distinction between sex and sex roles, it has proceeded through the second half of the twentieth century to break down "sexual difference" into more and more component parts, only arbitrarily and socially related to one another, to the point where even sexual desires have been dissociated from the anatomical difference between females and males, and heterosexuality has lost its aura of naturalness and necessity.

GENDER THEORY AS A THREAT TO IDENTITY

This is all very threatening, not only to men, but to women as well, and the realm of sexuality—sexual practice and sexual preference—is particularly sensitive, invested as it is in contemporary society with the capacity to fill subjectivity: to provide a personal identity. Sexual activity both defines people as male or as female and defines them as *people*, in a society where you are *nobody* if you are not one or the other. At the same time, sexual activity is imbued with a strong sense of guilt and shame. People do not relish having to think that it is up to them—they don't readily let go of the idea that it has all been decided for them in some part of their hormone-influenced cortex. They do not like being, as they see it, "free-floating," with no sound "natural" basis for their tastes, which they experience, rightly, as irresistible impulses.

What has to be taken into account, too, or maybe first, is that gendered societies such as Western societies create their own subjectivities and in particular, as mentioned above, the inability to have an individual identity that is not a gendered identity. Our very languages preclude that possibility: how long can you talk about someone without saying "she" or "he"? (It's even worse in French, but only marginally.) What the language imposes has been confirmed by psychosocial studies: the notion of "human being" does not exist in our societies, or rather, there are two ideas of "human being." There is a "male human being" and a "female human being."[14]

This is our psychological make-up, what we've inherited not only from our childhood, but from every minute we've spent on this earth. This is being shattered by the findings of feminism about the social construction of gender. But how are we to integrate this newly acquired knowledge, which remains highly intellectual, with our "immediate" perceptions?

The two clash, and there's nothing we can do about it. We may know—or, rather, try to imagine—that gender is socially constructed, that is, arbitrary in its form and its very existence. But how are we to reconcile that with the evidence of our eyes which shows a very sturdy, all-pervasive, immovable gender on which all reality seems to be founded?

14. See Marie-Claude Hurtig and Marie-France Pichevin, "Masculine-Feminine: A New-Look Essentialism," a paper presented to the fifth Conference of the International Society for Theoretical Psychology, Bierville, France, April 1993.

IS SOCIAL CONSTRUCTION THE SAME THING
AS "SOCIAL CONDITIONING"?

One of the many shortcomings of contemporary theory, maybe particularly in the United States, is the false perception that what is socially constructed is somehow shallow, or superimposed, or easily overthrown.

This perception shows a naive contempt for the workings of society and is grounded in an implicit belief that somehow underlying social and cultural structures, there exists a "human nature" that could surface if given the chance. But there is no human nature, and we have no other perception or possibility of action than those given by society. There is no "beyond" (or indeed "before") social construction.

Only this kind of belief in an individual—or universal—nature, one that somehow pre-exists "social conditioning," can explain the belief that if we feel "male" or "female" it cannot be "all social," or the opposite but symmetrical belief that we can opt out of gender on an individual basis.[15] If there is something that is the most particularly American in French Feminism, it must be the belief that presumes, even when it does not say so, the existence of a primal individual, and reduces social construction to "social conditioning" or "socialization."

But social construction is not something that happens when you're not looking—it is what happens all the time, in all societies, and it started happening long before we were born. It is coterminous with being human, because this is the world that we find and there is no other: there is nothing else "underneath," contrary to what so many American writings, especially postmodern, seem to imply.

However, maintaining a belief in a "beyond" or "before" social and cultural organization together with an intellectual adherence to social constructionism, is not an American trait: it is a general inability to come to terms with the implications of social constructionism, an inability that is both an intellectual shortcoming and an emotional reluctance. Actually, it is remarkable that, gendered as we are in our psychological make-up, we (at least some of us) can even *envision* the non-necessity of gender.

The inability to correctly understand subjectivity as socially constructed, but *not* amenable to voluntaristic behavior, puts feminism

15. See Judith Butler, *Gender Trouble: Feminism and the Subversion of Identity* (London: Routledge & Kegan Paul, 1990).

between a rock and a hard place, and this is particularly visible in the American intellectual scene today. On the one hand, those who remain convinced that the category "women" exists feel that the only foundation for it must be essentialist—grounded in "Nature"—whereas those who supposedly take a social constructionist view argue that the implication is therefore that the category "women" does not really exist: "If gender is simply a social construct . . . what can we demand in the name of women if women do not exist?"[16]

I want to linger on this "simply social." This understanding of "social" amounts to equating social construction with what is called in everyday language "social conventions": something that you can take or leave—and if you leave it, at the worst you will be seen as impolite. Alcoff and Butler have different positions, the first wanting to stay with the category "women," the second not. But they share a philosophical "idealism" in their perception of human life and subjectivity. Either it is "real" and must be based in "Nature" (not "simply" social), or it is "social" and therefore "unreal" and can be undone by individual volition. Even though they differ in the outcome they favor, neither of them assumes a truly social constructionist view. Both Alcoff and Butler can envision the nonexistence or disappearance of the category "women" without at any time considering the implications of that for the category "men"—a category which therefore must be presumed to stay, and to be able to stay all by itself. In a social constructionist view, which is necessarily holistic, either the two categories exist, or neither. The fact that Alcoff and Butler can imagine one of them subsisting without the other reveals that they adhere to an *additive* world view, where the parts exist independently and can change or move independently of one another. What is still lacking is a notion that human arrangements are both social—arbitrary—and material: external to the action of any given individual.

It is difficult not to link this defect in social constructionist thinking in the United States to the way in which the only contesting of essentialism comes from women who are steeped in "French Theory." French Feminists and French Feminism are being "reprocessed" as "postmodern," and even though some, such as Linda Nicholson,[17] point out the incompatibility between the essentialism of classic

16. Linda Alcoff, "Cultural Feminism versus Post-Structuralism," *Signs* 13/31 (1988): 405–36.

17. Linda Nicholson, ed., *Feminism/Postmodernism* (London: Routledge & Kegan Paul, 1990).

French Feminism and the structuralism of "poststructuralism," the two are inextricably connected in the dozens of titles and mind-blowing new appellations that seem to crop up every day.

Inasmuch as one can make sense of the frenzy of incessant renaming that has seized Anglo-American academe, it appears that the heady mixture of Foucault and Derrida has given rise to something called "theory of discourse" or "deconstructionism." In this theory everything is a text, and the old contest between "reality" and discourse has been done away with: better, it has been won by discourse, of which "the text" is the best incarnation. All other things—such as social practices, institutions, belief systems, and subjectivities—are only bad approximations of the text.

Thus what seems to have happened is that as soon as it was rediscovered and used against essentialism,[18] social constructionism was watered down: it was conceptualized as constructionism without the power of society behind it; or, the power of society was reduced to that of an always interpretable and, moreover, multiple "discourse." Social constructionism is equated with male authors and with a nominalist version of itself which deprives it of any real content. Commenting on these developments as exemplified by Joan Scott's *Gender and the Politics of History*,[19] Joanna Russ writes:

> To say that language influences reality . . . is one thing. To say that nothing else exists . . . is another thing entirely. . . . One of the advantages of aging is that the second time you see the same damn nonsense coming around again you can spot it in one-tenth of the time it took you to recognize it the first time. The nineteen fifties' literary emphasis on the autonomy of texts was an escape into a realm divorced from the nasty world in which professors were being kicked out for being "subversive," and witch hunts against homosexuals were a regular feature of public life. Current reality is also mighty unpleasant; how nice it would be if it *were* only language and we could control it by controlling language, or if attempts to do anything else were impossible or useless. And look how important that would make us.[20]

---

18. See Alcoff; Butler; Fraser; Nicholson; Jane Flax, "Post-modernism and Gender Relations in Feminist Theory," *Signs* 12/4 (1987): 621–43; Joan W. Scott, "Deconstructing Equality Versus Difference," *Feminist Studies* 14/1 (1988): 33–50.

19. Joan Scott, *Gender and the Politics of History* (New York: Columbia, 1988).

20. Joanna Russ, Letter to the Editors of *The Women's Review of Books* 6/4 (1989): 4. This letter is about Claudia Koonz's review of Joan Wallach Scott's *Gender and the Politics of History*.

So the explanatory power of social constructionism, along with the fact that it was developed in feminism by feminists, and particularly by French, British, and Italian materialist feminists[21] is being ignored.[22]

Maybe some feminists do not want to accept the political implications of unadulterated social constructionism: that things can change, but that it will be long and arduous, and that we do not have an infinite power over our own individual lives, nor, to start with, over our own brains. Maybe they do not want to accept that even though things— including our own thoughts—present themselves to us qua individuals as external constraints, they are not imposed on us by God or Nature and that we, qua members of society, share in the responsibility for changing or not changing them.

DIFFERENCE AS A PERMANENT FEATURE OF TWENTIETH-CENTURY FEMINISM

In this attempt to explain the appeal of conceptual frameworks based on naturalistic premises, I have taken for granted that French Feminism is a contemporary reaction to a contemporary problem: that the progress of social constructionist views is, on a personal level, threatening to many people, because they let us envision a future where we might not have gender to rely on as a basis for our personal identity.

However, this emphasis on "difference" is not new. We find it throughout the history of feminism, which it has split since its very beginnings. The debate between these two currents of feminism is still alive and well, and its terms—"Difference" versus "Equality"—

21. See Delphy 1984 and 1993a; Delphy and Diana Leonard, *Familiar Exploitation: A New Analysis of Marriage in Contemporary Western Societies* (Cambridge: Polity Press, 1992); Guillaumin 1992; Guillaumin, "The Practice of Power and Belief in Nature," *Feminist Issues* 25 (1981): 25–31; Hurtig and Pichevin, "Masculine-Feminine"; Hurtig and Pichevin, "The Body as Support and Mediator of Sex Relations," in Lisa Adkins and Leonard, *The Other French Feminism*, forthcoming; Hurtig and Pichevin, "Salience of the Sex Category System in Personal Perception: Contextual Variations," *Sex Roles* 22/5–6 (1990): 369–95; Celia Kitzinger, *The Social Construction of Lesbianism* (London: Sage, 1987); Mathieu; Monique Plaza, "'Phallomorphic Power' and the Psychology of 'Woman,'" in Adkins and Leonard; Paola Tabet, "Les mains, les outils, les armes," *L'Homme* 19/3–4: 5–61, "Fertilité naturelle, reproduction forcée," in *L'arraisonnement des femmes*, ed. Mathieu (Paris: Editions E.H.E.S.S., 1985), 61–146, "Du don au tarif: les relations sexuelles impliquant compensation," *Les Temps Modernes* 490 (1987): 1–53, and "Imposed Reproduction: Maimed Sexuality," in Adkins and Leonard.

22. See Stevi Jackson, "The Amazing Deconstructing Woman," *Trouble and Strife* 25 (Winter 1992): 25–31, and Adkins and Leonard.

are still amazingly similar after a century and a half. There is a tendency to pretend that it is over or that one can go "beyond" it. But despite their promising titles,[23] articles that purport to "transcend" the debate always end up on one side or the other, and I see several reasons why this is so and, in fact, cannot be otherwise.

These two positions cannot be reconciled at an analytical level. One relies either on the conceptual framework I have tentatively described as holistic/social constructionist, or on an additive/essentialist framework. But positions are ultimately expressed by people, and although we often assume that people are coherent, they are not. They therefore come up with theoretical positions that mix elements resting on different and contradictory premises. So the fact that essentialism and social constructionism are combined in some, or even most positions, does not make them logically compatible. Furthermore, people's incoherence can extend to their endorsing positions which at the outset might seem at odds with what they think. This has led activists such as Carol Anne Douglas to wonder whether theory really mattered for feminism.[24]

In spite of all this, there *is* a logic to conceptual frameworks that makes eclecticism impossible to pursue beyond a certain point that is reached all too soon. Although social constructionism and essentialism are seldom presented in a pure form, for the reasons just outlined, they still are irreconcilable. Indeed, it is *because* they are seldom presented in a pure form that they can be seen as not completely antagonistic. However, that pure form exists and it consists of their intrinsic possibilities and limits—whether they are used or not at any given time. Some things are conceivable in social constructionism but not in essentialism and vice-versa. And the fact that we do not have to think them now does not mean that we will not need to think them tomorrow; on the analytical level as well, there are moments of reckoning. We have not yet thought through social constructionism, because it is emerging precisely *against* common-sense, essentialist thinking, and because it is resisted in the area of gender by those men who use it in every other area.

The impression that using one conceptual framework or the other does not make much difference is probably misleading. Dorothy Stet-

23. See Scott. Also, see Louise Toupin, "Une histoire du féminisme est-elle possible?" *Recherches féministes* 6/1 (1993): 25–53.

24. Carol Anne Douglas, Review of "Is the Future Female?" by Lynne Segal, *Off Our Backs* (January 1989): 16.

son has convincingly shown[25] that it was difference feminists in the Women's Bureau who defeated the passage of the E.R.A. Molly Ladd-Taylor makes the same point: "Maternalism and feminism coexisted and at times overlapped until the 1920s, when the bitter debate over the Equal Rights Amendment drove them apart."[26] In other words, there *are* different political agendas and times of reckoning when these differences can no longer be smoothed over.

Even though these different political agendas are not necessarily linked in a one-to-one way with different analyses, just as one cannot assume such coherence on the part of individuals, it is equally clear that there are correspondences between analytical frameworks and political agendas in general, whether in respect to feminism or in respect to other political questions.

The tendency to gloss over divergences is due to an unrealistic belief that basically we all want the same thing. It is, or should be, apparent by now that we do not all want the same thing, no more than "we" wanted the same thing during first-wave feminism or at any time between the two waves. We have to accept that not all women conceive of their interests in the same way, and that their different ways can be conflictual, as was strikingly demonstrated in the debate over the E.R.A.

I have for a long time (see Delphy 1984 and 1993a), like others, believed that only a faulty analysis, which could be sorted out by debate, led some Western women to argue that the way out of oppression lay in specific rights for women and the buttressing of gender identity, when so many women in other countries, especially in fundamentalist Muslim countries, are trying desperately to get rid of "codes of personal status" and other specific "rights" that are in reality a curtailing of citizenship for women.[27] But I believe now that we don't have the same vision of "liberation." Evidence of this is presented by the highly emotional rejection, by feminists I call "radical"—that is, looking for and wanting to eradicate the roots of patriarchy—of the group-identity sought by proponents of "difference"; and by the equally highly emotional disgust expressed by them at our vision of a world that would

25. Dorothy Stetson, *Women's Rights in the U.S.A.* (Belmont: Brooks/Cole, 1991).

26. Molly Ladd-Taylor, "Toward Defining Maternalism in U.S. History," *Journal of Women's History* 5/2 (1993): 110–14.

27. See A.E.L.F.H., "Les luttes de femmes en Algérie," and Marie-Aimée Hélie-Lucas, "Les stratégies des femmes à l'égard des fondamentalismes dans le monde musulman," *Nouvelles Questions Féministes* 16–18 (1991): 17–29 and 29–63.

make room for all individual differences, and also consider all differences as individual.[28]

To continue interpreting divergences within feminism as mere misunderstandings, or as different strategies, is to bury one's head in the sand: some divergences are not about different ways of achieving the same goals, *they are about different goals*. The most striking illustration of this proposition is found, I think, in the very terms of the debate about "Difference" versus "Equality." Among the oppressed groups of humankind, only women oppose "difference" to "equality," and that formulation alone is reflected in titles such as *Beyond Equality and Difference*. In the introduction to this paradigmatic book, "Contextualizing Equality and Difference," the only "contextualization" which would indeed make it possible to go "beyond" the question of "Difference" versus "Equality" is never once mentioned.[29] Such a contextualization would be the preliminary admission that "the opposite of 'equality' is 'inequality.'"[30]

DESTABILIZING FEMINISM

The main reason that its inventors invented their brand of feminism as "French" was that they did not want to take responsibility for what they were saying and, in particular, for their attempt to rescue psychoanalysis from the discredit it had incurred both in feminism and throughout the social sciences. They pretended that *another* feminist movement thought it was great—that in fact it was all the other, admittedly strange, movement was interested in.

That took some doing, a process which is excellently described and analyzed by Claire Moses (1992a). Moses points out that, at the time of the famous 1978 *Signs* issue, "the Prefaces always identified Cixous,

28. For the sake of being understood, I use the term "differences," although I think it is a loaded term in the context of the discussion of sex and gender, especially since "differences" are never referred explicitly to their implicit referent, be it the dominant category, or the realm of human action where they acquire, or do not acquire, relevance, and furthermore that "differences" are, at the most, opposed to "sameness" (see Scott). But levels of sameness—for example, belonging to the human species—are the unsaid but necessary context of finding differences within that level, in the same way as levels of differences—for example those between humans and other animals—are the unspoken basis for finding sameness.

29. "Contextualizing Equality and Difference," in *Beyond Equality and Difference*, ed. Gisela Bock and Susan James (London: Routledge & Kegan Paul, 1992), 1–13.

30. Christine Planté, in her "Questions de différences" in *Féminismes au présent*, wonders why Joan Scott, who makes this clear in her 1988 article, does not apply this insight to her analysis of the Sears Case.

Kristeva, and Irigaray as French 'writers' or 'intellectuals,' never as 'feminists.'" She goes on to note that the French movement was consistently presented by Elaine Marks and Isabelle de Courtivron as "in discontinuity with historical feminism"; that Domna Stanton (in the 1978 *Signs* issue) identifies language as the site of feminist struggle in France. Moses gives many examples of the way the French movement was misrepresented. The fact that it was a movement that shared many traits with other movements—in terms of preoccupations, analyses, campaigns, demands, activism—was not only ignored, but denied. It was said that there was a movement, but a movement of writers who "problematized the words 'feminist' and 'feminism'" (Marks and de Courtivron, cited in Moses 1992a).

One could go on, taking up factual errors in Anglo-American writings to this day and showing the distortions that the French movement suffered, and still suffers, at the hands of these writers. I want to focus here on one point in particular, and that is the personal and ideological closeness to psychoanalysis of the women selected by French Feminists, and their equal distance from feminism.

It has been noted by Moses that French Feminism was equated with "women writers," that two of the three writers in question are antifeminist and that only one—who has only recently started calling herself a feminist—has been read and commented upon by feminists from France. But if it has been mentioned that they are Lacanian, nowhere does it ever appear that two of them are practicing psychoanalysts: Irigaray and Kristeva. In the way that Cixous's and Kristeva's antifeminist declarations are, variously, treated as nonrelevant, the fact that they are not part of the feminist debate in France is considered as so irrelevant as to be not even worth mentioning. It is implied that actual feminists from France look up to these writers, which is necessary in order to make them look significant to the domestic reader. Their real importance in France is never evaluated—for instance, by the number of times they are quoted or appear in feminist discussions.

What is implied by portraying these women as important in feminism is that whether one calls oneself a feminist or not is not relevant; what is further implied by asserting that they are important for feminists in France is that feminists in France do not consider that relevant either. The message is that in order to speak in or of feminism, one does not need to be a self-defined feminist. The impact this had on domestic feminism was to blur the frontiers between feminists and nonfeminists.

However, this is not a consistent policy. At other times, Kristeva and Cixous are, on the contrary, reclaimed as feminists, in spite of themselves. This is a spectacular manifestation of imperialism. Kristeva's or Cixous's outspoken antifeminism can be dismissed in a way that no Anglo-American's opinion could be dismissed: "Despite their disclaimers, it is difficult not to classify Kristeva and Cixous as feminists" (Tong, 223).

It is suggested that they do not know their own minds. There is a level of contempt here that is truly unbearable. But if one manages to forget and forgive the condescension, what is the message to the Anglo-American reader? Again, it seems to be that writings meant as antifeminist are just as important to feminism as feminist writings. Again, the line is blurred, and the feminist debate opens up to welcome antifeminist opinions, which are to be treated *on a par* with feminist opinions.

That was opening the way for things yet to come: the introduction into feminism of Freud and Lacan, first as "French Feminists," then as feminists *tout court*, and finally as "Founding Fathers." The redeeming of psychoanalysis has now been achieved; and not only thanks to French Feminism, since Juliet Mitchell, Nancy Chodorow, and Carol Gilligan have paved the way for this development, albeit with a *soft* version of psychoanalytic essentialism. Proponents of French Feminism were able to use this opening to offer the real hard stuff: unreconstructed continental psychoanalysis. And the Anglo-American scene has been transformed to the extent that a book on psychoanalysis is seen as intrinsically part of feminist theory, in spite of the total absence of any discussion of feminism (see Gallop). That is something that could not have happened before the invention of French Feminism, and which could still not happen in France, whoever the author. (Marcelle Marini did write a book on Lacan, but that was not seen as part of her feminist writing; in fact it was actually seen as slightly odd.)

But the most interesting feature of French Feminism is the way it deals with essentialism. Most French Feminists do not hold up essentialism as a "Good Thing." But they often promote it by saying that it is not essentialism. A good deal of their time is taken up "defending" Irigaray against accusations of essentialism (see Schor 1989 and Fuss 1989, especially 55–83). But why exactly? Is it because they are convinced that Irigaray is not essentialist? They cannot be, as Irigaray makes no bones about it, and never tries to defend herself against something she does not see as an indictment. Anglo-American essentialists are in a more delicate position: they want the thing without the sting. And since of course this is not possible, what they are accomplishing on their domestic scene is a regression. Everybody talks about essentialism, but nobody knows what it is anymore, as essentialist theories are presented as nonessentialist. Even Freud and Lacan, whose essentialism was established a long time ago in *all* quarters, not only in feminist circles, are now being "revalued" and absolved.

Moreover, in an apparently contradictory, but really coherent movement, essentialism is increasingly presented as something which, although it cannot be endorsed outright, might not be "the damning criticism it is supposed to be" (Smith, 144). Paul Smith and Diana Fuss credit Irigaray with such sophistication that, it is implied, she can only "seem" essentialist; on the other hand, if she were found to be (and not just seem to be) essentialist, then, it is implied, might she not have a good reason? Although they cannot decide on the matter—Fuss even writes that "Irigaray both *is* and *is not* an essentialist" (Fuss 1989, 70)—they agree that if she is, it is a strategy, even "a key strategy . . . not an oversight" (Fuss 1989, 72). Thus, under the guise of trying to understand complex European thinking, Anglo-American authors are working their way toward a rehabilitation of essentialism.

CONCLUDING REMARKS: IMPERIALISM AS A TACTIC FOR ELIMINATING WITH ONE FELL SWOOP FEMINISM . . . AND WOMEN

The invention of French Feminism is contemporary with the invention of "French Theory." The two follow the same lines and indeed are, to some extent, the same thing. What is striking to the French reader, in the writings of the seventies as well as in more recent writings, is the manner in which all feminists from France are lumped together, regardless of their theoretical, esthetic, or political orientation. Wittig, for instance, is cited early on in the same breath as Cixous, and sometimes she is defined as belonging to the same strand, "écriture féminine." There is more than ignorance at work here. Even when it is recognized that Wittig cannot be in the same strand since she is very vocal about repudiating "écriture féminine" and all that it stands for, she is still always quoted in conjunction with the "Holy Three," very seldom by herself or in conjunction with Anglo-American feminists who are theoretically and politically close to her. The same of course holds true for Cixous: her plight is exactly symmetrical, although for reasons that should be clear by now, I feel for Wittig. Michèle Le Dœuff, who is not particularly bashful about her theoretical stand, is also lumped together with the essentialists, "despite her disclaimers," as Tong would put it (Tong, 223).

Do the stars of "French Theory"—who are also the masterminds behind the women, according to French Feminists (see infra)—fare better? No. Lacan, Derrida, Foucault, and Barthes are all one in the Anglo-American compulsion to unify and homogenize the "French," thus denying them any individuality. How is it possible to lump together in the same article, never mind in the same sentence, writers such as Foucault and Lacan, who come from totally opposite traditions, and who furthermore are very open about their disagreements?

Anglo-Americans have created whole new schools of thought—or at least academic trends—by comparing French writers who cannot be compared, by "putting in dialogue" people who have nothing to say to each other, and by giving this ready mix names like "poststructuralism" and "postmodernism." How will that improbable mixture withstand the test of time? Not very well: Foucault's social constructionism will *not*, even with the help of the Marines, ever blend with Lacan's essentialism.

And why are French authors—male or female, feminist or not—almost never compared to their Anglo-American counterparts, however similar, but only to other French writers, however different? Because that would show that there are differences among them, on the one hand, and similarities between them and their commentators or translators in the Anglo-American world, on the other. Internal homogenization and external differentiation: this is how groups—national, ethnic, sexual—are constituted. In exactly the same way, French authors are seen as a group which is defined by, and only by, its difference to the group which has the power to name; thus they are constituted as an Other.

If one has to admit that the work of writers can be interpreted, and that the word of the author on his or her own work need not be the last, or the only one, it is an entirely different kettle of fish to pretend that these works can be totally abstracted from their objective, historical contexts. And this is precisely what is being done, to female and male writers who were born in France. Moreover, if Anglo-Americans have the right to "take their good where they find it," as the French say, and to use quotations from France—or any other part of the world—to create their own theories, the line must be drawn at calling that creative endeavor "French Theory." Nobody owns their own writing; but everybody deserves a fair hearing, and that is what the French often do not get. They are entitled to be understood and appreciated, or dismissed, for what they did or said, not hailed or damned for what some other French person did or said: "It all happens as if the word French erased or diminished the serious tension between the works of Cixous and Irigaray (or those of Lyotard and Derrida)" (Varikas, 64). Interestingly, Anglo-American commentators who do try to put, say, Foucault or de Beauvoir in perspective, and to understand why they said what they said when they did, do *not* call that "French Theory."[31]

Claire Moses writes eloquently about this:

> We . . . in the role of imperial have expropriated some one aspect of French culture, used it for our purposes, with little regard for the French or the French context . . . with little interest for the people themselves. . . . The aspect that interests us is the least characteristic but the most different from our feminism; the more characteristic aspects bore us. We have exoticized French Feminism, decontextualized it, used it for our purposes, with little interest in French activists. In so doing, we have abused our power—involving ourselves, unwittingly, in a power struggle among French women and conferring prestige and status on one side—the psych et po group—which proved destructive to the interests of French women. [Moses 1992a]

When I read Claire Moses's paper, I had a flash of recognition—and, yes, gratitude—at seeing what I have been thinking for years so clearly and beautifully expressed. Then I had to write another paper, this time for *Nouvelles Questions Féministes*, on the Hill-Thomas hearings and its meaning for France and for feminism. I read Claire's paper again, and was struck this time by a sentence on the same page: "The French (and more generally 'Europeans') are blamed for aspects of ourselves that we do not like but do not take responsibility for (like our racism and classism); Europe or France is tainted; we are pure."

And I remembered having written exactly the same words just a few days before, but about the French caricature of the United States and Americans. The Hill-Thomas controversy was presented in

---

31. See Sonia Kruks, "Gender and Subjectivity: Simone de Beauvoir and Contemporary Feminism," *Signs* 18/1 (1992): 89–111.

France as a proof of American racism—to make their point, the media simply *overlooked* the fact that Hill, like Thomas, is African-American. There were headlines on "The New McCarthyism," on "sexual fundamentalism" and "the feminist lobby"; weeklies warned: "Puritanism, feminism and attacks on private life. . . . Is the American model threatening France?" (cited in Ezekiel 1992). The media use knee-jerk anti-Americanism, but fill it with a new content: it is everything that is progressive in the United States that they condemn. Kristeva's husband, Philippe Sollers, who has written a best-seller about his womanizing (*Femmes*), is in the forefront of the battle. There was, too, a domestic agenda: a year later when, forced by Europe, France had to legislate on sexual harassment, all the officials warned against "Americanization"; as a result we got the most restrictive law on the books to this day, a law that makes a mockery of sexual harassment.[32]

I have argued above that French Feminism was invented in order to legitimate the introduction on the Anglo-American feminist scene of a brand of essentialism, and in particular a rehabilitation of psychoanalysis, which goes further than the native kind expressed by Sara Ruddick, Chodorow, or Gilligan. The other feature of this intellectual current, which is definitely not exhibited by Ruddick, Chodorow, or Gilligan, is that it questions the very bases of what defines a feminist theoretical approach. In the usual definition, a feminist theoretical approach is tied to a political movement, a movement aimed at effecting actual change in actual society and in actual women's—and men's—lives; the main feature of this tie resides in the *questions* that are asked of the objects under study. That necessary tie does not mean that some abstract activist instance dictates the topics to be studied, but that any feminist—scholar or not—should be able to argue the relevance of the questions she raises to the feminist movement as a whole. In order to demonstrate that hypothesis, I will turn to a case study of one of the key moments of the whole operation: Alice Jardine's *Gynesis*.

In this work, "French Theory" is constituted as a "whole" by a series of rhetorical maneuvers that use distortion and generalization, imperialism and exoticism. First, the feminist movement in France is cast as D.O.A. in the "socialist" era, after a series of murderous struggles, from which it is supposed not to have recovered. So, *exit* French

---

32. See Delphy, "The Hill-Thomas Controversy and French National Identity," *Nouvelles Questions Féministes* 14/4 (1993): 3–13.

Feminism in the usual sense of "feminist." Feminists are still there, however. How is Jardine going to dispose of them? We have already been told that feminism, "that word," "poses some serious problems." It does, indeed, if, like Jardine, one can think of only one place to look for it: the dictionaries! She then dismisses the feminists "who qualify themselves as feminists in their life and work" (Jardine 1985, 20), because that would be too simple.

But here plain factual distortion gives way to imperialism: what counts is only what *I* say counts. It is not only because it would be too simple that actual feminists from France will not be discussed, but because: "When in the United States, one refers to . . . French feminisms, it is not those women one has in mind" (Jardine 1985, 20). There is something circular or tautological in the argument: "I will not interest myself in those women because they are not of interest to me." But circularity and tautology, as exemplary expressions of self-centeredness, are essential components of imperialist thinking.

In the next sentence, American interest is what constitutes feminists from France as important or not important in an objective, real way: these women are said to "have a major impact on theories of writing and reading" (Jardine 1985, 20). The place where that "major impact" is supposed to have happened is not specified: it may be the United States, it may be the whole world—isn't it the same thing? And Jardine lists: Cixous, Kofman, Kristeva, Lemoine-Luccioni, Montrelay.[33] Then she moves on to say that "the major new directions in

33. At the time Jardine's piece was published, and at the time it was written, Women's Studies and Feminist Studies were undergoing the only period of expansion they have ever known in France. A research program had been launched in the National Center for Scientific Research (CNRS) in 1983 which lasted until 1989. At the time Jardine was in France writing about the "Parisian scene," it was under way. It was extremely varied in its ideological and theoretical orientations, as it regrouped on its board the Who's Who of Women's Studies in France. Over a period of six years, it examined more than three hundred research projects and funded eighty, in all disciplines and on all topics, including, of course, literary criticism. Why is it that most of the names Jardine lists never appear in the bibliographies of any of these projects, even of the few that were psychoanalytically-oriented, if they made such a "major impact"? And why is it that Jardine does not mention this program, which was the talk of the—admittedly provincial—town of Paris and which she could not have helped hearing about?

Similar tactics are used by Moi: "The publishing history of French feminism in English-speaking countries confirms the overwhelming impact of the three names of Cixous, Irigaray and Kristeva" (Moi 1987, 5). A somewhat disingenuous and even perverse statement on two accounts: first, the publishing history of these three writers in English is supposed to prove their popularity *in France!* And secondly, that publishing history is not so external to Moi as she, pretending to "discover" it, would have us

French theory over the past two decades . . . have . . . posited themselves as profoundly . . . anti- and/or post-feminist" (Jardine 1985, 20).
This is a strategic move which overturns all previous understandings
about what kind of thinking is useful for feminism.

But the best is yet to come: this said, she proceeds to explain that
she will deal with the *men*, because "the women theorists in France
whose names have been mentioned here are . . . in the best French tradition . . . direct disciples of those men." And although she does "not
mean this as a criticism," she comments that these women's work
consists of "rewritings of the men . . . repetitions and dissidences from
those men" (Jardine 1985, 21).

We are given to understand that these women, who are antifeminist, are, however, the producers of the most important work for feminist thinking; that their thinking comes from men, to the extent that
they need not be considered themselves. The reader may be surprised.
But this is where the exoticism comes in to confuse and guilt-trip us:
that is the French brand of feminism, and even though it may seem
strange, what if feminists from France like it? As in all imperialist discourses, there's a mixture of fake respect for the culture and condescension. Enough respect to warrant the attention of the American
reader: "French Feminism" is important, we must listen to what it has
to say. But that respect is really condescension: for what sort of feminists can feminists from France be if they take as their major theorists
women who not only are antifeminists but who merely parrot men?
On what sort of clichés in the reader's mind is Jardine counting? What
sort of stereotypes are necessary to believe that of French feminists,
indeed of any *feminists*?

But she insists it is "in the best French tradition." So subservience
to the men is seen as both unique to the French[34] and not so damnable
as it might seem: from the moment it has been deemed "French," and
since the French are an interesting culture, it cannot be condemned as

---

think. By all accounts, her *Sexual/Textual Politics* was decisive in starting that trend.
And what was the thrust of that book? To pit "Anglo-American feminist criticism,"
which she finds disappointing, against what she calls—coining the phrase—"French
feminist theory." Its first chapter, entitled "From Simone de Beauvoir to Jacques Lacan," thus establishes Lacan as a "feminist theorist," a paradox not even the most psychoanalytically-oriented feminists in France would have dreamed of defending.

34. Again, Moi uses the same tactics: "French feminists on the whole have been ea-
ger to appropriate dominant intellectual trends for feminist purposes, as for instance in
the case of the theories of Jacques Derrida and Jacques Lacan" (Moi 1987, 1).

easily as all that. Jardine extends the cultural relativist wing to protect it. Could she have sent the same message using an American example? Could she have decided that So-and-so is an important writer for feminist issues even though that person does not address the topic, or worse, is against feminism? Could she say that today the most important American writers for feminism are Katie Roife or Camille Paglia? And if she did, where would it place her? But why could she not do so? After all, opponents are important. They do need to be discussed. But is it the same thing to say that Patrick Moynihan's theses must be discussed and to say that he is the main theorist of and for feminism?

There are three points that need to be made here. It is true that, since there exists a continuum of feminists and antifeminists, it creates particular problems, which have been noted by Judith Stacey,[35] for "drawing the line," especially when writers with clearly antifeminist views, such as Jean Elshtain or Paglia, call themselves feminist, as they increasingly do in the United States today. As mentioned earlier, the point has been raised regarding Irigaray by Maryse Guerlais and Eléni Varikas[36] in France, and it is a difficult one. Although Irigaray's work is not used in Women's Studies in France, her theses are very popular with important parts of the women's movement in Italy, and smaller but still significant audiences in France and Holland. However, inasmuch as there are, in feminism as elsewhere, definitional problems for borderline cases, these problems are always situated, precisely for this reason, at the margins; they do not touch on the core.

Writers who situate themselves vis-à-vis feminist questions are part of the feminist debate—including those who *oppose* feminism; but even though the latter are discussed, they are not treated in the same category as writers who define themselves as feminist. Feminists have always discussed antifeminists: one could even say that this constitutes a major part of feminist writing. Exposing and analyzing patriarchal ideology has been on the feminist agenda from the very beginnings of feminism. But antifeminists and feminists have distinct places in feminist analysis. Patriarchy and its intellectual productions

35. Judith Stacey, "Are Feminists Afraid to Leave Home? The Challenge of Conservative Pro-Family Feminism," in *What is Feminism?*, ed. Juliet Mitchell and Ann Oakley (Oxford: Blackwell, 1986), 219–49.

36. Maryse Guerlais, "Vers une nouvelle idéologie du droit statuaire: *Le temps de la différence* de Luce Irigaray," *Nouvelles Questions Féministes* 16–18 (1991): 63–93; and Varikas 1993.

are an *object* of study, they are not and cannot be a *means* or a *tool* of feminist analysis.

The case is quite different with writers who are not necessarily hostile to feminism but who *do not* address feminist issues. The question is not: "Friend or foe?" It is: "What do they bring to the discussion?" This is the case in France for Kristeva, who does not address the questions raised by feminism because she does not know what they are. Her only information about feminism is the kind of caricatures circulated by the media. This is the case also for women like Montrelay or Lemoine-Luccioni, who are traditional psychoanalysts and cannot even be described as "antifeminist," since that implies engaging with feminist ideas, which they do not. Their position is best described as a traditional "male-supremacist" or "prefeminist" view; and it is so widely held in France by psychoanalysts that feminists have never felt the need to discuss those three in particular.[37] So here the point is rather: could Jardine, or any other supposedly feminist writer, decide that an English or American author, whose work is not considered relevant and is not discussed by English and American feminists because *she or he does not discuss feminist questions*, represent what is most interesting in the feminist scene of those countries?

This is, in fact, exactly what Jardine, and with her, most other French Feminists are saying: that there is no difference between feminist thinking and patriarchal thinking from the point of view of their use for feminist analysis. Further, they imply that addressing questions which are relevant for feminism is irrelevant for participating in the feminist debate. That makes feminism itself an irrelevant position.

This could not be argued from a domestic position, using domestic examples: straw women had to be invented who, supposedly from *within* feminism, were questioning and invalidating a feminist approach; but it had to be a feminism so strange, so foreign, that this would be as credible as it was improbable. It had to be "French Feminism." The second part of the message is: if the "French" can do it, why can't we? And they did.

---

37. This is why Cixous and Irigaray, who know what feminism is, must be distinguished one from the other, the first being antifeminist, and the second being feminist by her own definition. Furthermore, both must be sharply distinguished from the second group—Kristeva, Montrelay, and Lemoine-Luccioni—who do not know what feminism is and who are neither feminist nor antifeminist, but *pre*-feminist.

Feminism could not be invalidated from within the French Feminists' own culture, i.e. Anglo-American culture; men could not be reinstated as the main interlocutors, as the arbiters of all knowledge, including feminist knowledge, from a domestic position. Introducing "French women" was the way to introduce the idea that to be antifeminist and to be part of the feminist debate was acceptable; the next step was to do away with the women and to reveal the men behind them, according to the purported native women's wishes, so that men could be, once more, center stage, in feminism as well as everywhere else.

Promoting essentialism was the main motive behind the creation of French Feminism; but there was a further, and when one thinks about it, not vastly different, reason for that invention; and that was putting Women's Studies scholars "in dialogue" again with male authors.

EPILOGUE *IN THE FORM OF AN (IMAGINARY) TRANSATLANTIC DIALOGUE*

My undergraduate students assure me that feminism is no longer necessary because we've solved all that, and various female colleagues and graduate students derive it from two white gentlemen, ignoring twenty years of extra-academic feminist work and writing. I would say that we've been betrayed, were not such a remark one of the banalities of history. And so heartbreaking. [Russ, 4]

I want to add: and academic.

The price paid by resistant women is literally incalculable (that is, I know of no currency in which its cost can be counted). It is thus not at all surprising that the temptation to "dilute" the challenge is not always resistible, or resisted.[38]

---

38. Ailbhe Smyth, "Haystacks in My Mind or How to Stay SAFE (Sane, Angry and Feminist) in the 1990s," a paper presented at the WISE Conference, October 1993, Paris.

LAURENT JENNY

Genetic Criticism and its Myths*

Is it possible to conceive of a "science of origins" in literature—not at all in the Darwinian sense of a genealogy of literary "species" but, rather, in the sense intended by Valéry of a study of literary creation rendered scientific by new methods? That is the question that genetic criticism has posed over the past few years. For my part, it is from the outside—from the perspective, let us say, of a hermeneuticist or even a phenomenologist of literature—that I would like to consider how genetic criticism has established itself as a discipline, institutionally as well as theoretically.

It would undoubtedly be easiest to situate genetic criticism in relation to the status of "science" to which it aspires.[1] Genetic criticism has had an undeniable success in research institutions, which do not ordinarily welcome literary scholars and the type of work they do (for research is defined, organized, and encouraged according to criteria specific to the model sciences, the "hard" sciences). Finally, there is a literary discipline that satisfies the requirements pertaining to the methods of research demanded by these model sciences. Genetic criticism has at its disposal palpable materials to work on: the pre-textual documents of the great literary works (drafts, sketches, notes, etc.). It requires research teams to be assembled to conduct the vast deciphering and archival work necessary to its goal. And, in order to work upon the material it studies, genetic criticism can claim to need a sophisticated technological apparatus (scanners, data banks, computer-assisted reading stations, etc.). In these diverse fashions, it establishes its

*From *Yale French Studies* 89 (1996): *Drafts.*
1. Pierre-Marc de Biasi gives the subheading "Vers une science de la littérature" to his presentation of genetic criticism in the *Encyclopedia Universalis* (1991).

YFS 97, *50 Years of Yale French Studies, Part 2,* ed. Porter and Waters, © 2000 by Yale University.

status as a science with the research methods it adopts, whereas solitary, artisanal, and unverifiable critical work cannot be situated according to scientific criteria, rendering the latter form of criticism "invisible" in the former's institutional field. Inasmuch as it has accomplished this, has genetic criticism attained the status of "science"? One can remark that the palpability of the material under study does not necessarily imply the scientific status of that object, nor does the technological refinement of the research instruments guarantee in any evident way the rigor of the inquiry. Genetic criticism's institutional and technical arsenal does not in any way allow one to forget that its object of study escapes almost by definition the category of "science." Genetic criticism is searching for a phenomenon that is in effect unobservable, unobjectifiable: the origin of a literary work. Its object of inquiry is essentially unstable, or rather its object of study is the very instability of the "pre-text" (*l'avant-texte*), where explicit projects, unconscious choices, and the play between what is possible and what is dangerous are intertwined to the point of nonsense. Genetic criticism is admittedly contemporaneous with an age in which the study of opaque phenomena takes precedence over the study of those that are clear, in which the genesis of order is searched for in chaos theory, but only its imagination links it up with these complex disciplines. It is far from sharing their techniques and models.

The ultimate goal of genetic criticism evokes, rather, the concern of a branch of psychology from the late nineteenth century—literary creation—in such a way that it is sometimes difficult to situate it temporally. Sometimes we see in genetic criticism either the resurgence of a literary positivism of the last century or the proclaiming of a discipline "for the twenty-first century," whose activity will lead to a radical redefinition of the notion of the text and of creation, but there is probably some truth to both. If ambiguity is possible, however, it is because genetic criticism was created in a certain conceptual vagueness and imposed as a practice more quickly than it thought out its functions in the field of literary studies. In this respect, it relied perhaps hastily on false evidence. Therefore, it seemed obvious to genetic criticism from the start that it was destined to prepare, enrich, and complexify the interpretation of texts. In supplying the diachronic states of the manuscript, it would allow the confirmation or invalidation of the finished text's meaning and would thus function as an additional hermeneutic guarantee. In addition, genetic criticism envisioned itself as the foundation of a "three-dimensional" poetics, attentive to describing no longer only the immanent structures of the text, but the movements of variance and transformation that rule the different states of the text. However, it is not certain that the logic of its development led it to fulfill such promises. It seems to me, rather, that its premises led it elsewhere entirely. To believe the contrary is to suppose, moreover, that with new practices one renews old conclusions, those precisely of criticism and poetics. Thus, far from preparing the new age of criticism (to remedy what can legitimately be seen as a "breakdown" in critical thought), genetic criticism exacerbates the problem. It does not have the effect of shoring up new interpretations, but of inventing a link with the text that suspends the hermeneutic relationship. It does not have as its primary objective the reading of texts but rather the discovery of their origin. A look at its genealogy may allow us better to establish why.

THE GENEALOGY OF GENETIC CRITICISM

In historical terms, genetic criticism was probably born out of a desire to supersede the structuralist poetics of the 1970s. At the end of that decade, textual theory suddenly found itself constrained by the analysis of the immanent structures of the text, caught in the trap of the dogma of closure, and imprisoned by its games of reflexivity. Critics then questioned if it would not be possible for the "real" to be reinserted into a literary analysis that seemed to be distancing itself from just such a move. How was the text to be reopened to the Other (Life, History, Culture) without a return to biography, historicism, or "source studies"? In fact, some ideas already offered poststructuralist perspectives that distanced themselves from the model of immanence: for example, "writing" (Barthes), the "opening" of a work (Eco), and Julia Kristeva's "intertextuality" and "semiotics." But these notions seemed more like escape routes away from poetics than the foundations of a new poetics. The future practitioners of genetic criticism, concerned with returning in a more concrete fashion to the stuff of literature, began by offering the creation of a more broadly defined poetics.

In this respect, Raymonde Debray-Genette's article "Génétique et poétique. Le cas Flaubert"[2] seems to me a foundational moment.

2. Raymonde Debray-Genette, "Génétique et poétique. Le cas Flaubert," in *Essais de critique génétique*, Louis Aragon et al. (Paris: Flammarion, 1979), 21–68.

Barthes's notion of writing (for Barthes, a dialectical space where "language," which is to say memory, and the detour of this language rise to the surface during the event that is the work) is the object of a reappropriation by a nascent genetic criticism that hoped to create a "poetics of writing." In truth, this cannot occur without bending the notion of "writing" that finds itself henceforth identified with the pre-textual process of the work. Certain of Barthes's formulas can suggest a proximity between "writing" and the genesis of the text, as in the following definition of literature, given on the occasion of his inaugural lecture at the Collège de France, as the "complex graphic symbol of the traces of a practice: the practice of writing." But the context of this passage, which is in fact quoted by Raymonde Debray-Genette, eliminates the possibility of such a relationship: there is no reference to the preparatory work on a text, only to the "fabric of signifiers." Barthes notes as well that the words "literature, writing, or text" can be used interchangeably. The site of "writing" for Barthes is clearly the "text," conceived, it is true, as a site where the play of signifiers is given over to reading its own *poiesis*, which is entirely different from its real genesis. In the same way, Umberto Eco, in *The Open Work*, defines poetics as the study of "the manner in which the work *is made* allowing one to determine the way in which the author *wanted it to be made*."[3] From this perspective, the question of the positive genesis of a work is subverted from the start. It is impossible to measure the distance between a genesis and a finished text. Perhaps, though, it is possible to measure the distance between a *poiesis* and the work in which it appears, since Eco foresees the possibility of a distortion between the implicit poetics and the work: this distortion is then discovered at the heart of the work itself, functioning as a structural imbalance, and not as a confrontation of different projects and rough outlines with the finished text. It is therefore necessary to recognize a fundamental displacement in the redefinition of "writing" by genetic criticism. "Writing" is no longer understood as a dynamic process that is immanent to the text, but as a pre-textual process. Henceforth, "writing" and "text" find themselves separated by a logical and chronological relation of succession. There is no longer a "writing" *of* the text but only of its genesis.

In the transition to genetic criticism, the notion of "writing,"

3. Umberto Eco, *L'oeuvre ouverte* (Paris: Seuil, 1965), 11. [The passage cited here is from the introduction to the French edition. This introduction appears neither in the original nor in the English translation—Translator's note.]

strongly metaphorical for Barthes, becomes literalized. It serves to designate the material generation of the work over the source of a specific period of time. And in the same manner, one can observe in the foundations of genetic criticism a rereading that literalizes the theme of the "open work." In his book by the same name, Eco calls for a poetics that is less strictly structuralist and turned more in the direction of the "consumption" of the work. The "opening" in question thus follows from an acknowledgment of the programs of reception that are inscribed in all texts. However, this "opening" is more readily apparent in certain texts where a strong will to maintain the mobility of structures is evident, texts that have "the project of a message endowed with multiple interpretative possibilities." Nevertheless, this opening has its limits, a fact to which Eco draws our attention:

> Thus, even an art that upholds the values of vitality, action, movement, brute matter, and chance rests on the dialectics between the work itself and the "openness" of the "readings" it invites. A work of art can be open only insofar as it remains a work; beyond a certain boundary, it becomes mere noise.[4]

The relative closure of the work is therefore, according to Eco, the necessary condition for its opening. Here, once again, when genetic criticism appropriates the idea of the "opening" of the work, its meaning is completely different from the one Eco proposed. One can no longer consider the modes of destination inscribed in the structure of the work; one must rather proceed to a *literal* opening of the text onto the textual nebula that is its genesis. It would be this structural indeterminacy that would characterize open "writing" in opposition to the text. Debray-Genette writes, for example:

> If text is defined as anything that shows a certain aptitude to an internal structuring strong enough to resist the forms of preexisting structures (linguistic, social, psychological . . .), writing, on the other hand, is defined as open, fluid, permeable to all outside interventions, both outgrowths and degenerations. ["Génétique et poétique," 48]

Thus one can see genetic criticism putting forth a translation of poststructuralist themes in a material and positive way, "writing" ultimately referring to the handwritten form of the text, and "openness" referring to the expansion of the text to include its pre-textual documents.

---

4. Eco, *The Open Work*, trans. Anna Cancogni (Cambridge, Mass: Harvard University Press, 1989), 100.

This operation of opening brings with it, moreover, a choice of options that are not always clearly distinguished by practitioners of genetic criticism. In effect, genetic criticism can keep as its privileged object either an open form that is witness to a process of genesis ("writing" or, better yet, the "pre-text"), or the articulation of the relations between this open form and the closed form that is the text. In thé first case, genetic criticism is not interested in the text but in "writing," which can be considered on its own, without any teleological relation to the final text (unless the final text is itself considered to be homogeneous to the pre-text, the final creative trace).[5] Genetic criticism therefore seeks in the first instance the very process of creative thought, using the traces of its wanderings, its deletions, its resumptions. In this sense, it is fairly close to a Valérian poetics that is as interested in the expressions of the productive "mind" of literature as it is in literature itself. But we are dealing with a poetics renewed by semiotics and that describes precisely the process of textual production: "the combination of transfers, substitutions, expansions and refractions that the manuscript puts forth in order to locate and systematize the collection of genetic operations: programming, textualization, transformation" (Hay, 152). In the second case, genetic criticism confronts a process and a product, and sets its sights on an interpretation. This is clearly the route Debray-Genette intends to use in "Génétique et poétique" ("Genetic Criticism and Poetics"), where, after a methodological exposé, she attempts an application on a description culled from Flaubert's "Hérodias":

> In more general terms, genetic criticism, inasmuch as it studies the production of the text and the "signifying process," is forced to take into account the double presence of the "genotext" and the "phenotext," the one an "unobstructed route," the other a structure that obeys the rules of communication, stopping at some point the signifying process. ["Génétique et poétique," 42]

It is evident that it will therefore be possible to divide the practitioners of genetic criticism, depending on their sensibilities, into two groups: "geneticists of writing" and "geneticists of the text."

Regardless of which option is chosen, however, the pre-text presents serious methodological problems. For if the production of the text truly constitutes an "unobstructed route," an open form, how

---

5. This seems to be Louis Hay's inclination in his article "Le texte n'existe pas," *Poétique* 62 (1985).

then to transform it into a corpus without distorting it? The formation of the "pre-text" amounts to textualizing that which rightfully should survive as an eternal pre-textuality, fundamentally heterogeneous to the fixed nature of the text. To present a pre-text for reading is obviously to inaugurate it as a text, as Francis Ponge demonstrates in a practical fashion in *La fabrique du pré*. In this sense, a pre-text cannot be read and still remain a pre-text. It is not only materially difficult to assemble an exhaustive pre-text,[6] it is also logically impossible to close it without betraying its essence. It must be added as well that, besides this problem of logic, an exhaustive pre-text is hardly conceivable for reasons that are linked in this case to its "originary" character. It is not only that we are kept from the discovery of another condition of the text that would undermine all known data, it is rather that the traces of "writing" are necessarily incomplete in relation to the process of mental creation (a neuronal writing?) to which they refer and of which they are the irregular evidence.[7]

This essentially indefinite character of the pre-text hardly predisposes it to serving as the foundation of an interpretation of the text. Supposing nevertheless that we provisionally ignore the problem that its material formation constitutes, there remains, for the "geneticists of the text," to construct the relations between an open pre-text and a closed text, between a form that exists only in the dynamic of its transformations and a finished form. Faced with this irreducible heterogeneity, the construction of a poetics of genetic criticism, or a "three-dimensional" poetics, seems problematic. In any case, the problem would not be resolved by the descriptive tools of an intertextual poetics, for it does not deal with a relationship from text to text, except to select one stratum of the pre-text (such as, for example, the *Carnets de Flaubert*), which in effect reduces its dynamism and its openness. In truth, it is difficult to see how it would be possible to establish a relation with an identifiable meaning between a determinate and an indeterminate form. If genetic criticism, then, can hardly hope to prop up interpretation, it certainly has the power to suspend interpretation or render it indeterminate for reasons of a quasi-technical nature.

6. De Biasi, "La critique génétique", in *Introduction aux méthodes critiques pour l'analyse littéraire* (Paris: Bordas, 1990), 21. He sees here a task that in and of itself "could take several years of research and negotiation."

7. There is agreement on this point between Hay ("Le texte n'existe pas," 151,) and Michel Contat, "La question de l'auteur au regard des manuscripts," in Contat, ed., *L'auteur et le manuscrit* (Paris: Presses Universitaires de France, 1991), 24.

THE SUSPENSION OF INTERPRETATION

One could claim, however, that it would be easy to show that genetic criticism has performed critical readings of important texts, and far from precluding interpretation, it has assumed all the risks involved. There is no doubt that, at the very least, it has attempted as much. But the authors genetic criticism favors and the types of readings it offers allow us perhaps to interpret genetic criticism more than to renew our understanding of these works. Let us begin by stating that genetic criticism is limited in theory to a specific literary period: the period during which manuscripts lose their communicating and distributing functions to become "the personal trace of an individual creation,"[8] that is from the end of the eighteenth century to the present, or, rather, a bit before "our time" when the widespread use of word processors relegated the draft to oblivion. This relatively brief period is also probably the richest in the history of literature, but, strictly speaking, most of the studies undertaken by genetic criticism are concerned with a restricted number of works composed between 1850 and 1920, primarily by Hugo and Flaubert (and secondarily Zola, Valéry, Proust, and others). But, in fact, this prioritization is no coincidence. It is a response to the structural or thematic characteristics of these works, either because they manifest in and of themselves a consciousness of formal indeterminacy (Hugo), or because they promote an aesthetic of semantic indeterminacy (Flaubert).

There is no doubt that Hugo waited for, hoped for, and even created genetic criticism. We are familiar with the codicil of his testament of 31 August 1881 in which he bequeathed "all [his] manuscripts and anything else found to have been written or drawn by [him]" to the Bibliothèque Nationale. This broad definition includes anything from ledgers to notes on erotic exploits. With this gesture, the first of its kind, Hugo transformed his pre-textual documents into something of value, into a precious deposit of the traces of genius at work. But Hugo was not aiming solely for the preservation of this inheritance. He fully intended to make it the force behind the deployment of his work above and beyond itself and from beyond the grave. Besides, in so doing he was simply setting in motion the editorial program handed down to him, during a seance held on 29 September 1854, by "Death," who advised him on how to tactfully create regular resurrections of his work through the expedient of posthumous publications. From this perspec-

8. De Biasi, "La critique génétique," 7.

tive, the legacy of the pre-textual documents would challenge the "grave" of the "Complete Works." It would serve interpretation less than it would the infinite vitality of a corpus without closure whose limits can always be redrawn through the integration of new pre-textual documents. In this, the great writer's desire to survive resembles the vitalist conception of writing promoted by genetic criticism. But, in addition to this posthumous narcissism, there exists in certain of Hugo's works (such as *Dieu*) the consciousness of an impossible completion.[9] Nevertheless, in bequeathing the manuscript of these incompletable works, Hugo delegates to posterity the task of ordering this textual infiniteness. It is the responsibility of the "Science of Manuscripts" to present this infiniteness while dispelling the notion of the closure of "Complete Works" championed by some hastily compiled editions, even though this implies proposing other ones, more complete and more coherent, although no less provisional. Genetic criticism has then as its paradoxical task, at the very suggestion of the author, to prevent the closure of the work, and to ensure that it has infinite possibilities for renewal, not in an interpretative sense, but in a material one. The work here truly exists in the future and is always unattainable.

Flaubert offers an even more spectacular case of reflexivity between a critical approach and its object of study. One must first notice the exceptional consistency with which Flaubert's corpus, and certain texts within this corpus, have held the attention of the practitioners of genetic criticism. One of the *Trois contes*, "Hérodias," serves as a primary example, beginning in 1979 with Debray-Genette's analysis in the programmatic *Essais de critique génétique*, which was followed by Philippe Willemart's reexamination—still from the genetic perspective—in 1983,[10] which in turn was given a postscript in the same vein by Pierre-Marc de Biasi in 1993.[11] The story thus constitutes a sort of connecting thread across fifteen years of genetic criticism. Without a doubt, Flaubert involuntarily, but in proportion to his cult of literary labor, supplies the practitioners of genetic criticism with a

9. Jacques Neefs and Claude Mouchard effectively analyze this characteristic in "*Dieu*, manuscrit," in Béatrice Didier and Jacques Neefs, eds., *Hugo. De l'écrit au livre* (St. Denis: Presses Universitaires de Vincennes, 1987).

10. "Le désir du narrateur et l'apparition de Jean-Baptiste dans le manuscrit d'"Hérodias,'" *Littérature* 52 (December 1983).

11. Gustave Flaubert, *Trois contes* (Paris: Editions du Seuil, 1993).

particularly abundant volume of pre-textual documents that de Biasi scrutinizes at ten times the magnitude of the finished text. The monumental edition of Flaubert's *Carnets de travail*[12] is proof positive of this pre-textual richness. But this material predisposition of the works to genetic criticism does not explain everything. There is in Flaubert a strategy of meaning that resembles that of genetic criticism. Debray-Genette already remarked in 1979 that in "Hérodias" the deletions "almost always go in the direction of obscurity and uncertainty." De Biasi echoes this remark in an article entitled "Flaubert et la poétique du non-finito" where he demonstrates, with supporting documents, how Flaubert devotes himself to the work of incompletion at the very heart of the most completed form that exists:

> The Flaubertian manuscript works to define, at each strategic point in the narrative, the zones of incompletion programmed to become the partial space where the reader takes charge of signification.[13]

Hence the obsession with the finished form combines in Flaubert's case with the "demand of the nonconclusive." This result is both indisputable from the perspective of the Flaubertian aesthetic, as well as deceptive from the point of view of genetic criticism's contribution. In the case of Flaubert, the study of the text and the study of the pre-text effectively converge at an identical statement of the indeterminacy of meaning. In truth, a simple stylistic reading would be just as capable of establishing this in the immanent text, where the strategies of incompletion can be formally located. Certainly, genetic criticism is able to do a precise genealogy of the deletions and demonstrate precisely which semantic formations (myths, symbols, rare terms) had been erased or rendered ambiguous by Flaubert. Nonetheless, the study of the pre-textual documents does not provide a fundamental corrective measure to the study of the text; both, in the end, reject totalizing conclusions and, in truth, any conclusion.[14] Given that the text had not guided us toward any certitude, the pre-text does not upset any interpretations, nor does it establish an incompletion since one was already manifest in the final form. One can ask at this point why genetic criti-

12. Flaubert, *Carnets de travail. Edition critique et génétique*, ed. de Biasi (Paris: Balland, 1988).

13. De Biasi, "Flaubert et la poétique du non-finito," in Hay et al., *Le manuscrit in-achevé. Écriture, création, communication* (Paris: Éditions du CNRS, 1986).

14. Note also that the "refusal to conclude"—as formally marked as it is—does not necessarily escape from totalizing interpretations: it also has its historical interpretability that cannot be forgotten.

cism is so fascinated with the case of Flaubert since it is with this kind of aesthetic that it has the smallest chance of presenting original results.

To find the reasons for this attachment, one must examine the specular relationship between the work of genetic criticism and Flaubert's work. When de Biasi evokes, in relation to the second volume of *Bouvard et Pécuchet,* Flaubert's project of "a totally original textual mechanism: an open system fully integrating the means of incompletion in the internal economy of a new type of textualization" ('Flaubert et la poétique du non-finito,' 47), it is impossible not to think of the very principle of the important genetic editions that open the text to its own "archives," or that even, as in the case of Flaubert's *Carnets de travail,* textualize these archives, not without providing them with their own documentary and explicative apparatus. Obviously, a complete genetic edition (which is materially impossible in the medium of paper) should be both "horizontal" (taking into account a complete stratum of the elaboration of the text, such as we find in Zola's *Carnets d'enquête*) and "vertical" (at every moment in the text, producing all the pre-textual strata from the most embryonic to the most complete, such as the "sketches" in the Pléiade edition of *A la Recherche*), thereby constituting an "open book" in which the very process of its genesis emerges at the same time that the form becomes fixed. Hence the aesthetic that the writer was putting forth in the second volume of *Bouvard et Pécuchet* finds itself shouldered and taken over by the critic who becomes in his turn the producer of the open book. The work of genetic criticism, then, is not to establish the interpretations of finished texts through the expedient of an overload of documentary information. It seeks, rather, to undo these same texts and to suspend their interpretations. This can be verified by looking at any number of works of genetic criticism.[15] This is retroactive work that speaks of a new consciousness of the book (since Flaubert and Mallarmé) and propagates its representation over the entire literary field in one great critical movement. In the age of the "virtual" text, one by one all finished texts find themselves rendered potential by the gaze of genetic criticism. This opening of texts responds to a new

15. Debray-Genette already had a strong foreboding that this was the case when she wrote: "That which allows a genetic study to happen, as opposed to a study of the final text, is the fact that it brings to light a greater diversity of tendencies, possibilities, a greater structural opening, which can reach the point of indecision, uncertainty, undecidability" ("Génétique et poétique," 37).

awareness of the contingent nature of the text as object ("The text does not exist"),[16] which has its own historical determination. Effectively, at the precise moment when the book in a paper medium sees its own materiality being contested by immaterial media, Flaubert's and Mallarmé's age-old utopia of the Open Book regains critical topicality.

From this point forward one must consider what the effects of such a metamorphosis on the practice of the Book are. Flaubert's and Mallarmé's open books announced a metamorphosis of reading itself (in rewrites with Flaubert, in ritual with Mallarmé). The "technical" opening of the Book that genetic criticism performs does not leave reading untouched either. In theory, genetic criticism is opposed to reading since reading is performed through the closure of signifying sequences. Reading only exists through partial syntheses and provisional punctuation. On the other hand, the ideal genetic edition defies the linearity of reading, and constrains it to paradigmatic markers (to which hypertextual software seems predisposed). It defers the material closure of the work indefinitely since it does not offer a text to be read, it seeks rather to offer the "real."

THE DREAM OF THE REAL

To identify this "real," we must return to genetic criticism's valorization of the pre-text. From the start, genetic criticism proposed the dethroning of the text in the name of its Other, a pre-textual, eternally anterior, minor, primitive, raw, illogical, but also polysemic, free, and fecund Other. And each critic then gave a different name to this origin, which is irreducible to the text. In 1979, Debray-Genette evoked the "unobstructed route" of pre-textual signification, as opposed to the fixed and inert nature of the text, just as the genotext is opposed to the phenotext in Julia Kristeva's literary semiotics. For Jean Bellemin-Noël or Yves Gohin,[17] the pre-text is the privileged place where the "work of desire" can appear. The indecision of the pre-text preserves the mobility of the fantasy that necessarily reduces the final text.

16. It would work just as well if one were to reverse the formula so that it read "The pre-text does not exist," since the pre-text only takes form during the gesture of textualization.

17. See Jean Bellemin-Noël, "Lecture psychoanalytique d'un brouillon de poème: 'Eté' de Valéry," in *Essais de critique génétique* (103–150), and "En guise de post-face. L'essayage infini," *Littérature* 52 (December 1983), and Yves Gohin, "La plume de l'ange. Analyse du manuscrit d'un poème des *Contemplations*," ibid.

Hence the pre-text is a repository of precious documents on the unconscious. Michel Contat, to take another example, is aware of the progressive temporal dimension of the pre-text (as opposed to the fallacious atemporality of the text): "That which has been traced has been traced *through time,* and it is time that allows us to see, or to reconstitute the manuscript."[18] The pre-text, then, would also be the repository for a duration that reading would have the power to revive by following the meanderings of creative thought. "Time recaptured" is here no longer in the text (produced by narrative figuration) but in the pre-text and as a result of a critical operation. For his part, de Biasi[19] proposes that the pre-text be recognized as "thought in the nascent state." This formula evokes a Bergsonian vitalism[20] and presupposes that a "genetic" continuity exists between the first stages of thought and literary drafts. Thus, all the critics above designate the pre-text as a site of semantic savagery and richness eventually reduced by textual structuring. The pre-text is not the figure but the *very trace* of the genesis of meaning—a positive and identifiable genesis. I would remark, to conclude on this point, that the diverse forms of alterity that are designated in the pre-text by the practitioners of genetic criticism are strangely close to those the critics from the 1970s sought to drive out of the very heart of the text: Kristeva's "signification," Bellemin-Noël's "unconscious of the text," or even Meschonnic's "the writing of lived experience." Nevertheless, in the transfer from the text to the pre-text, there was not just a simple moving of the "real" from one textual site to another. In the move toward drafts, the "real" deserted the text, cut it out of its semantic escape routes to harden it into a fixed and inert structure. The architecture of tensions and gaps that constitute all texts is no longer recognized as such, since the alterity of meaning is localized in a specific site, anterior to the work. As a result, this "real" is identified as positive material (Hugo's trunks full of manuscripts, Flaubert's sealed boxes containing his notebooks, etc.), as a "reality." From this point forth, genetic criticism owns this "reality" and must then transmute it into its editorial

---

18. Contat, "La question de l'auteur," in *L'auteur et le manuscrit,* 23.

19. De Biasi, "Avant-propos," in *Carnets de travail,* 23.

20. The same one that Julien Benda recognized (and denounced in the name of a rigid rationalism) in the taste his contemporaries had for incompleteness: "Let us note that our contemporaries have a proclivity for exhuming drafts and unfinished works, where the author has not yet invoked reason 'to alter his outpouring of emotion.'" Benda, *Belphégor* (Paris: Emile-Paul frères, 1918), 88.

equivalent and give it exposure in the voluminous and indisputable form of monumental editions.

New ways of presenting texts should imply new practices. Faced with this "proof" of creation, we are invited less to decipher documents than to participate in the experience of a genesis. Through reading, we must recreate in ourselves "a state of mind, a way of seeing, feeling, and thinking that entails bringing back all experience to that which is going to be written."[21] The genetic edition of Flaubert's *Carnets de travail* should therefore force us to recognize the profile of "the one through whom literature thinks itself and looks for itself prior to creating itself: a sort of mediation between the possible and the determined, between the always already written and the future of the work" (*Carnets de travail*, 13). De Biasi therefore allows us to witness in the pre-text the emergence, not of the man nor the author, but of an inextricably vital and mental instance, "the man-as-pen" ("*l'homme-plume*").[22] This recognition of the "man-as-pen" implies "a new form of reading." What is it? At the very least it displays a displacement of thematic interest: one considers with new curiosity "the secret of creation; what happens behind the scenes of the artistic enterprise." But this new form of reading goes far beyond that. It incites us less to construct meaning (an enterprise hindered by the complexity of the profuse, contradictory, and nonhierarchizable pre-textual documents) than to envision the real of a creation starting with the written traces. Hence, in relation to the material writing of a certain notebook of Flaubert's, de Biasi, the editor of the *Carnets*, writes:

> The handwriting, jerky, often difficult to decipher, sometimes "seismographic" is clearly characteristic of the uncomfortable positions in which the author took his notes, naturally with a pencil. In certain places one can unmistakably recognize the shaking of the carriage going over cobblestones. [*Carnets de travail*, 49]

By following this seismographic trace, wouldn't readers also be able to return to that very shaking such as it was lived in the moment of a thought? Wouldn't they be able to redynamize the trace so as to relive the event? This is perhaps an allegory of the new pact of reading that genetic criticism proposes to us.

21. De Biasi, "Avant-propos," 12.
22. One might ask if the notion of "man-as-pen" in Alain Borer's edition of Rimbaud did not engender the no less composite notion of "work-as-life." What brings them together is the conjunction of the lived and the written in a single entity where the limits of the work are undone.

Criticism, previously sworn to abstract work on signs and imaginary configurations, has finally touched an archival "reality" through the expedient of genetic criticism: it handles the boxes where the documents are kept, dusts off the manuscripts, scrutinizes ink blotches, compares the texture of different types of paper or the bindings of notebooks, classifies scattered pages left in inextricable disorder by negligent heirs. This archival "reality" that they have finally reached is also, as we have seen, the site of that which would be most "real" in literature: the very origin of meaning, pure creation materialized into concrete evidence. But this apprehension of the "real" is played out against an unsettling background of derealization. Derealization, as we have seen, is primarily concerned with the logic of the symbolic relations between the text and the pre-text. A pre-text derives its value from the consecration of the text that it precedes. But paradoxically, the establishment of the pre-text tends to dissolve the textual entity that was precisely the one that gave it this value. The pre-text is therefore constantly threatened with becoming the antecedent of something nonexistent (which could be formulated, for example, in the following manner: "Proust's *A la recherche du temps perdu* does not exist"). More concretely, at the moment when the "real" of literature is recognized in the pre-textual "reality," the latter appears in all its perishable fragility. In accordance with a structure that, in contemporary culture, characterizes all aspects of origins (virgin lands, preserved Nature, primitive peoples), their recognition as Treasures also signals their virtual destruction. Is it a historical accident that the great age of "drafts" that so interests genetic criticism is the same age in which the most mediocre and destructible paper was used, dooming the inheritance of modern manuscripts to imminent destruction? Faced with this eventuality, a genetic critic such as de Biasi reacts by advocating the transference of the archives onto numerical or optical media.[23] The remedy for the destruction of the materiality of the pre-text would therefore be its computerized dematerialization. Reality and unreality never stop fighting over the originary archive which, first conceived of as the true site of the "real," should soon metamorphose into its own hyperreal simulacrum, endowed with ubiquity and infinite reproducibility. The technique would effectively allow the subversion of the opposition between the original and the copy, be-

23. "Pour une politique d'enrichissement du patrimoine écrit," in *Trésors de l'écrit* (Paris: Ministère de la Culture, 1991).

tween the materiality and the immateriality of the archive. Immaterially downloaded, the original manuscript could travel along computer networks and allow the production of copies by means of a laser printer. De Biasi comments upon this:

> A book or a manuscript is not necessarily an inert object that one must consult in the place where it is kept: it is also a series of images that can circulate at the speed of light, appear at the same moment in a hundred different places, and rematerialize there quite easily by means of a printed copy. ["Pour une politique," 30]

Technology appears here as the instrument of an archival Pentecost that manifests its luminous presence everywhere at the same time and offers the always renewed miracle of its material reincarnation. The binary encoding of the archive would not only make its infinite "transportability" possible, it would also transmute it into hypertextual data (leading not to a syntagmatic reading of signs but to a paradigmatic marking of the different documents that are downloaded). Ultimately, the archive could be seen on a screen (the necessary condition for a contemporary viewing), and would become an "image," an iconic appearance, that is to say an elementary form of cultural communication.

Genetic criticism dreams, then, of "presence" against a background of advanced technology. It emerges in a context that sees not only a contestation of the book by immaterial media, but, in the same movement, the dissolution of the text as a configuration of finished meaning, and the metamorphosis of reading into the processing of information. This entails a serious calling into question of the hermeneutic relationship that literary criticism maintains more or less with literature and that, to my mind, is its only justification. To question the configurations of problematic meanings and to elucidate how one experiences literary forms, to illuminate our own times through our queries, these remain for me the essential tasks of criticism—tasks that cannot be suspended while waiting indefinitely for the *absolute* establishment of the text and its beginnings. We must resolve to admit that each period invents its imaginary and always provisional library, because of the urgency of the questions it seeks to ask of it. It is obvious that genetic criticism, *in practice*, is not necessarily contrary to the work of interpretation. New editions inspired by its methods, and which we all use, bear witness to this fact every day. (It is nevertheless necessary to point out that these editions are only really readable to the extent that they renounce the total accomplishment of the genetic project.) Nonetheless, in *theory* and in the logic of its emergence, genetic criticism renders the critical relationship null and void. For more than fifteen years now, genetic criticism has engaged in enormous archival and methodological work and yet has remained astonishingly uninterested in the meaning of its own practice. We seek here only to break the silence.

—Translated by Richard Watts

III. Indexes to Numbers 1–95

**JAMES AUSTIN, DARYL LEE,
ALYSON WATERS**

Yale French Studies
Volume Index, 1–95

1.1 (Spring–Summer 1948) *Existentialism*

Sartre, Jean-Paul. "Scenes from *Les mains sales*." 3–20.

Peyre, Henri. "Existentialism—A Literature of Despair?" 21–32.

Dieckmann, Herbert. "French Existentialism before Sartre." 33–41.

Slochower, Harry. "The Function of Myth in Existentialism." 42–52.

Fowlie, Wallace. "Existentialist Hero: A Study of *L'âge de raison*." 53–61.

Cohn, Robert G. "Sartre's First Novel: *La nausée*." 62–65.

Bruneau, Jean. "Existentialism and the American Novel." 66–72.

Morris, Edward. "Intimacy." 73–79.

Smith, Madeleine. "The Making of a Leader." 80–83.

Whiting, Charles G. "The Case for 'Engaged' Literature." 84–89.

Boorsch, Jean. "Sartre's View of Cartesian Liberty." 90–96.

Grene, Marjorie. "Sartre's Theory of Emotions." 97–101.

Leavitt, Walter. "Sartre's Theatre." 102–5.

Bays, Gwendolyn. "Simone de Beauvoir: Ethics and Art." 106–12.

Mohrt, Michel. "Ethic and Poetry in the work of Camus." 113–18.

Brombert, Victor. "Camus and the Novel of the 'Absurd.'" 119–23.

Jagger, George. "Camus's *La peste*." 124–27.

1.2 (Fall–Winter 1948) *Modern Poets: Surrealists, Baudelaire, Perse, Laforgue, and Others*

Supervielle, Jules. "'L'escalier.'" 3–4.

Poggioli, Renato. "The Poetry of St.-J. Perse." 5–33.

Peyre, Henri. "The Significance of Surrealism." 34–49.

Apollinaire, Guillaume. "'Phantom of the Clouds' and 'The Gypsy.'" Trans. Roger Shattuck. 50–52.

Michaux, Henri. "Selections ["Projection," "Nausea or Is It Death Coming,"

YFS 97, *50 Years of Yale French Studies, Part 2*, ed. Porter and Waters, © 2000 by Yale University.

2.1 (Spring–Summer 1949) *Criticism and Creation*

2.2 or 4 (1949) *Literature and Ideas*

Spoerri, Theophil. "Mérimée and the Short Story." Trans. Trude Douglas. 3–11.

Béguin, Albert. "Poetry and Occultism." Trans. Robert G. Cohn. 12–25.

St. Aubyn, Frédéric. "The Social Consciousness of Rimbaud." 26–33.

Slochower, Harry. "André Gide's *Theseus* and the French Myth." 34–43.

March, Harold. "The Artist as Seer: Notes on the Esthetic Vision." 44–54.

Kneller, John W. "The Musical Structure of Proust's *Un amour de Swann*." 55–62.

Blanchot, Maurice. "Symbolism and Bergson." Trans. Joel A. Hunt. 63–66.

Niess, Robert L. "Julien Benda: The Poet's Function." 67–78.

Balakian, Anna. "Apollinaire and the Modern Mind." 79–90.

Frohock, W. M. "Camus: Image, Influence and Sensibility." 91–99.

Cornell, Kenneth. "Audiberti and Obscurity." 100–104.

Noth, Ernst Erich. "The Prophetism of Georges Bernanos." 105–19.

Special Monograph no. 1. (1950)

Douglas, Kenneth. *A Critical Bibliography of Existentialism (The Paris School)*.

3.1 or 5 (1950) *The Modern Theatre and Its Background*

Barrault, Jean-Louis. "The Rehearsal, The Performance." 3–4.

Fowlie, Wallace. "Mystery of the Actor." 5–11.

Vilar, Jean. "The Director and the Play." Trans. Richard R. Strawn. 12–26.

Coindreau, Maurice. "The Evolution of the Contemporary French Theatre." Trans. Joel A. Hunt. 27–33.

Collignon, Jean. "Theatre and Talking Pictures in France." Trans. Philip Wadsworth and Charlotte Wadsworth. 34–40.

Picard, Raymond. "Racine Among Us." Trans. John M. Guret. 41–50.

Spoerri, Theophil. "The Smile of Molière." Trans. Kenneth Douglas. 51–65.

Mauriac, François. "A Communication." 66–67.

Vial, Fernand. "François Mauriac as Dramatic Author." 68–74.

Boorsch, Jean. "The Use of Myths in Cocteau's Theatre." 75–81.

Cornell, Kenneth. "Claudel's Plays on the Stage." 82–87.

May, Georges. "Jean Giraudoux: Diplomacy and Dramaturgy." 88–99.

Mohrt, Michel. "Three Plays of the Current Paris Season." 100–104.

Mohrt, Michel. "Jacques Copeau, Charles Dullin." 105–7.

Douglas, Kenneth. "A Note on Mallarmé and the Theatre." 108–12.

Messner, Charles. "The French Theatre: A Bibliography." 113–17.

6 (1950) *France and World Literature*

Quinn, Patrick F. "The Profundities of Edgar Poe." 3–13.

Gilman, Margaret. "Revival and Revolution in English and French Romantic Poetry." 14–26.

Galand, R. "T. S. Eliot and the Impact of Baudelaire." 27–34.

Atkins, Stuart. "Mirages Français—French Literature in German Eyes." 35–44.

Weinberg, Kurt. "Heine and French Poetry." 45–52.

Peyre, Henri. "What Greece Means to Modern France." 53–62.

López-Morillas, Juan. "Ortega y Gasset: Historicism vs. Classicism." 63–74.

Levin, Harry. "From Priam to Birotteau." 75–82.

May, Georges. "Valery Larbaud: Translator and Scholar." 83–90.

Jones, Frank. "Scenes from the Life of Antigone." 91–100.

Shattuck, Roger. "The Doubting of Fiction." 101–8.

H. M. P[eyre]. "English Literature Seen through French Eyes." 109–19.

7 (1951) *André Gide 1869–1951*

Picon, Gaëtan. "Remarks on Gide's Ethics." 3–11.

Noth, Ernst Erich. "The Struggle for Gide's Soul." 12–20.

Turnell, Martin. "André Gide and the Disintegration of the Protestant Cell." 21–31.

Loy, Robert J. "Prometheus, Theseus, The Uncommon Man and an Eagle." 32–43.

Collignon, Jean. "Gide's Sincerity." 44–50.

Brée, Germaine. "Time Sequences and Consequences in the Gidian World." 51–59.

Parnell, Charles. "André Gide and his *Symphonie pastorale*." 60–71.

Stock, Irvin. "A View of *Les faux monnayeurs*." 72–80.

O'Brien, Justin. "Gide's Fictional Technique." 81–90.

Cordle, Thomas. "Gide and the Novel of the Egoist." 91–97.

Lang, René. "Rilke and Gide: Their Reciprocal Translations." 98–106.

Guggenheim, Michel. "Gide and Montaigne." Trans. Richard Strawn. 107–14.

Maurin, Mario. "A Few Notes on the Gide-Suarès Relations." 115–24.

8 (1951) *What's Novel in the Novel*

Zéraffa, Michel. "The Young Novelists: Problems of Style and Technique." 3–8.

Albérès, R. M. "Is There a New Ethic in Fiction?" 9–16.

Hoog, Armand. "The Surrealist Novel." 17–25.

Frohock, W. M. "André Malraux: The Intellectual as Novelist." 26–37.

Guicharnaud, Jacques. "Raymond Queneau's Universe." 38–47.

Picon, Gaëtan. "Concerning Noël Devaulx." 48–50.

Boorsch, Jean. "Romain Gary." 51–55.

Magny, Claude-Edmonde. "Roger Nimier." 56–76.

Poulet, Georges. "Maurice Blanchot as Novelist."77–81.

Botsford, Keith. "Jean Genet." 82–92.

Brée, Germaine. "Albert Camus and *The Plague*." 93–100.

Didier, Pierre. "Bernanos' World." 101–7.

Lynes, Carlos, Jr. "Jean Cayrol and 'Le Romanesque Lazaréen.'" 108–17.

9 (1952) *Symbol and Symbolism*

Auerbach, Erich. "Typological Symbolism in Medieval Literature." 3–10.

Frye, Northrop. "Three Meanings of Symbolism." 11–19.

Fowlie, Wallace. "Legacy of Symbolism." 20–26.

Pucciani, Oreste. "The Universal Language of Symbolism." 27–35.

Steiner, Herbert. "A Note on 'Symbolism.'" 36–39.

Lapp, John C. "Racine's Symbolism." 40–45.

Hubert, Judd D. "Symbolism, Correspondence, and Memory." 46–55.

Oxenhandler, Neal. "'The Balcony' of Charles Baudelaire." 56–62.

Champigny, Robert. "Situation of Jules Laforgue." 63–73.

Whiting, Charles. "Femininity in Valéry's Early Poetry." 74–83.

Wimsatt, W. K. "Prufrock and Maud: From Plot to Symbol." 84- 92.

Vial, Fernand. "Symbols and Symbolism in Paul Claudel." 93–102.

Cook, Bradford. "Jacques Rivière and Symbolism." 103–11.

Ramsey, Warren. "'Words of Light' and 'Somber Leaves': The Poetry of Léon-Paul Fargue." 112–22.

Douglas, Kenneth. "Sartre and the Self-Inflicted Wound." 123–31.

Thorlby, Anthony. "Rilke and the Ideal World of Poetry." 132–42.

Hoog, Armand. "Henri Michaux, or Mythic Symbolism." 143–54.

Ilsley, Marjorie H. "Four Unpublished Letters of Stéphane Mallarmé to Stuart Merrill." 155–61.

Hofmannsthal, Hugo von. "Encounters." Trans. Tanya Stern and James Stern. 162–65.

10 (1952) *French-American Literary Relationships*

La Fontaine, Jean de. "Three Fables from La Fontaine. ["The Fox and the Grapes" III: xi, "Epilogue" VI, "The Head and Tail of the Serpent" VII: xvii]." Trans. Marianne Moore. 3–4.

Sutherland, Donald. "Time on our Hands." 5–13.

11 (1953?) *Eros, Variations on an Old Theme*

12 (Fall–Winter 1953) *God and the Writer*

Maurin, Mario. "Suarès and the Third Kingdom." 34–40.

Oxenhandler, Neal. "Jacob's Struggle with the Angel." 41–46.

Pitou, Spire. "Evil, Grace, and Luc Estang." 47–53.

Frohock, W. M. "Georges Bernanos and his Priest-Hero." 54–61.

Dieckmann, Herbert. "André Gide and the Conversion of Charles Du Bos."
62–72.

Cook, Bradford. "Simone Weil: Art and the Artist under God." 73–80.

Champigny, Robert. "God in Sartrean Light." 81–87.

Pamplume, Louis. "Gabriel Marcel: Existence, Being, and Faith." Trans. Beth
Brombert. 88–100.

13 (Spring–Summer 1954) *Romanticism Revisited*

Brombert, Victor. "T. S. Eliot and the Romantic Heresy." 3–16.

Levin, Harry. "The Ivory Gate." 17–29.

Peyre, Henri. "Romantic Poetry and Rhetoric." 30–41.

Hoog, Armand. "Who Invented the 'Mal du Siècle'?" Trans. Beth Brombert.
42–51.

Smith, John E. "Rousseau, Romanticism, and the Philosophy of Existence."
52–61.

Blanchot, Maurice. "*Adolphe*, or, The Curse of Real Feelings." Trans. Edith
Kern. 62–75.

Boorsch, Jean. "Motion and Rest in *René*." 76–81.

Maritain, Raïssa. "Comme on meurt." 82.

Bays, Gwendolyn. "Balzac as Seer." 83–92.

Cornell, Kenneth. "George Sand: Emotion and Idea." 93–97.

Barrère, Jean-Bertrand. "Character and Fancy in Victor Hugo." Trans. Beth
Brombert. 98–113.

Kneller, John W. "Jean-Jacques the Dynamist." 114–18.

V.H. B[rombert]. "Leopardi versus the Romantic." 119–20.

14 (Winter 1954–55) *Motley: Today's French Theatre*

Kierkegaard, Søren. "Farce is Far More Serious." Trans. Louis Mackey 3–9.

Guicharnaud, Jacques. "Jean Vilar and the TNP." 10–18.

Collignon, Jean. "Paris Audiences, Paris Theatres." 19–22.

Fowlie, Wallace. "The French Theatre and the Concept of Communion." 23–
29.

Fauve, Jacques. "A Drama of Essence: Salacrou and Others." 30–40.

Kern, Edith. "Drama Stripped for Inaction: Beckett's Godot." 41–47.

Lynes, Carlos, Jr. "Adamov and 'le sens littéral' in the Theatre." 48–56.

Champigny, Robert. "Theatre in a Mirror: Anouilh." 57–64.

Brée, Germaine. "Georges Neveux: A Theatre of Adventure." 65–70.

Oxenhandler, Neal. "Jean Cocteau: Theatre as Parade." 71–75.

Jigé [Jacques Guicharnaud]. "Songs of a Season." 76–78.

Giraud, Raymond. "Maulnier: In and above the Conflict." 79–84.

Ricoeur, Paul. "Sartre's *Lucifer and the Lord.*" 85–93.

Peyre, Henri. "Paul Claudel (1868–1955)." 94–97.

Kendo [Kenneth Douglas]. "French-English Theatre Vocabulary." 98–101.

Barrault, Jean-Louis. "A Barrault Breviary [excerpts from *Cahiers de la Compagnie Madelaine Renaud Jean-Louis Barrault*]." 104.

15 (Winter 1954–55) *Social and Political France*

Wright, Gordon. "The Resurgence of the Right in France." 3–11.

Duverger, Maurice. "Generations in Conflict." Trans. Alvis Tinnin. 12–16.

Aron, Raymond. "France: Stability and Instability." Trans. Raymond Giraud. 17–23.

Weil, Eric. "French Complexes." Trans. Josephine Ott. 24–29.

Goguel, François. "The Historical Background of Contemporary French Politics." Trans. Marianna Carlson. 30–37.

Daladier, Edouard. "Europe after the Ratification of the London and Paris Agreements." Trans. Kenneth Cornell. 38–41.

Cogniot, Georges. "France Has Faith in Its Future." Trans. Pierre Barthelémy. 42–48.

Malraux, André. "The 'New Left' Can Succeed!" Trans. Neal Oxenhandler. 49–60.

Siegfried, André. "History of the Mendès-France Government." Trans. Bryant C. Freeman. 61–67.

Mendès-France, Pierre. "Economic Equilibrium and Social Progress." Trans. Imbrie Buffum and Pierre Barthelémy. 68–88.

Philip, André. "France's Economic Situation." Trans. Raymond Giraud. 89–98.

Sauvy, Alfred. "Estimates and Life." Trans. Kenneth Douglas. 99–114.

Williams, L. Pearce. "Robert Aron's History of Vichy." 115–19.

Herr, Richard. "The Memoirs of General de Gaulle." 120–28.

Douglas, Kenneth. "As Others See U.S." 129–36.

Avryl [Georges May]. "Words, Initials, Facts and Figures." 137–43.

16 (Winter 1955–56) *Foray Through Existentialism*

Magnan, Henri. " . . . Said Jean-Paul Sartre." Trans. Rima Drell. 3–7.

Oxenhandler, Neal. "*Nekrassov* and the Critics." 8–12.

Brombert, Victor. "Raymond Aron and the French Intellectuals." 13–23.

17 (Summer 1956) *The Art of Cinema*

18 (Winter 1957) *Passion and the Intellect, or: André Malraux*

Picon, Gaëtan. "Man's Hope." Trans. Rima Drell Reck. 3–6.

Herz, Micheline. "Woman's Fate." 7–19.

Cordle, Thomas. "The Royal Way." 20–26.

Malraux, André. "Three Speeches ["Every Man Endeavors to Think His Life," "Rejoinder to Sixty-Four," "Our Cultural Heritage"]." Trans. Kenneth Douglas. 27–38.

Roedig, Charles F. "Malraux on the Novel (1930–1945)." 39–44.

Albérès, R. M. "André Malraux and the 'Abridged Abyss.'" Trans. Kevin Neilson. 45–54.

Girard, René. "Man, Myth and Malraux." 55–62.

Brombert, Victor. "Malraux: Passion and Intellect." 63–76.

Douthat, Blossom. "Nietzschean Motifs in *Temptation of the Occident*." 77–86.

Hoog, Armand. "Malraux, Möllberg and Frobenius." Trans. Beth Brombert. 87–96.

Blend, Charles D. "The Rewards of Tragedy." 97–106.

Darzins, John. "Malraux and the Destruction of Aesthetics." 107–13.

Hartman, Geoffrey H. "The Taming of History." 114–28.

Roedig, C. F. "A Bibliographic Note on Malraux's Art Criticism." 129–30.

19 & 20 (Spring 1957–Winter 1958) *Contemporary Art*

Dorival, Bernard. "Painting Today: Principles and Practitioners." Trans. Kenneth Douglas. 7–14.

Ragon, Michel. "In Praise of Sculpture." Trans. Howard B. Garey. 15–26.

Herbert, Robert. "A Paris Commentary: The Tough Trend." 27–34.

Habasque, Guy. "Notes on a New Trend: Multidimensional Animated Works." Trans. Mona Tobin. 35–44.

Hess, Thomas B. "The Cigarbox of Napoleon III." 45–49.

Peyre, Henri. "Painters and Sculptors of France Today." 50–74.

Etiemble. "Constant Rey-Millet." Trans. Phyllis Berla. 75–77.

Guth, Paul. "Encounter with Germaine Richier." Trans. Neil Chapman. 78–84.

Schneider, Pierre. "Jean-Paul Riopelle." Trans. Paul Mankin. 85–93.

Cornell, Kenneth. "The Buffet Enigma." 94–7.

Francastel, Pierre. "Criticism and the History of Painting in the Twentieth Century." Trans. Derek Aiken. 98–106.

Scully, Vincent J., Jr. "The Nature of the Classical in Art." 107–24.

21 (Spring–Summer 1958) *Poetry Since the Liberation*

Breunig, L. C. "Picasso's Poets." 3–9.

Apollinaire, Guillaume. "Pablo Picasso." Trans. Noelle Gillmor. 10.

22 (Winter–Spring 1958–59) French Education: Why Jeannot Can Read

23 (Summer 1959) *Humor*

Doubrovsky, J. S. "Ionesco and the Comedy of Absurdity." 3–10.

Cohn, Ruby. "The Comedy of Samuel Beckett: 'Something old, something new. . . .'" 11–17.

Simon, John F. "Hulot, or, The Common Man as Observer and Critic." 18–25.

Jameson, Fredric. "The Laughter of Nausea." 26–32.

Mankin, Paul. "The Humor of Marcel Achard." 33–38.

Sonnenfeld, Albert. "The Yellow Laugh of Tristan Corbière." 39–46.

Moore, Will G. "The French Notion of the Comic." 47–53.

Herz, Micheline. "Gallic Wit in Triumph and Decline." 54–62.

Grossvogel, David I. "The Depths of Laughter: The Subsoil of a Culture." 63–70.

Frohock, W. M. "Panurge as Comic Character." 71–76.

Hall, H. Gaston. "A Comic *Dom Juan*." 77–84.

Hubert, Renée Riese. "The Fleeting World of Humor from Watteau to Fragonard." 85–91.

Temmer, Mark. "Comedy in *The Charterhouse of Parma*." 92–99.

Bowman, Frank. "Benjamin Constant: Humor and Self-Awareness." 100–104.

24 (Summer 1959) *Midnight Novelists and Others*

Girard, René. "Pride and Passion in the Contemporary Novel." 3–10.

Giraud, Raymond. "Unrevolt Among the Unwriters in France Today." 11–17.

Pingaud, Bernard. "The School of Refusal." Trans. Kenneth Douglas. 18–21.

Dort, Bernard. "Are These Novels 'Innocent'?" Trans. Kenneth Douglas. 22–29.

Joyaux, Georges J. "Driss Chraïbi, Mohammed Dib, Kateb Yacine, and Indigenous North African Literature." 30–40.

Bieber, Konrad. "A Do-It-Yourself Novel?" 41–47.

Cohn, Ruby. "Still Novel." 48–53.

Frohock, W. M. "Introduction to Butor." 54–61.

Lynes, Carlos, Jr. "Toward Reconciliation: The World of Jean Cayrol." 62–67.

Hoog, Armand. "The Itinerary of Marguerite Duras: Or, from the Dangers of the American Novel to the Perils of the Abstract Novel, without Mishap." Trans. H. Gaston Hall. 68–73.

Reck, Rima Drell. "Françoise Mallet-Joris and the Anatomy of the Will." 74–79.

May, Georges. "Félicien Marceau: A Modern Romantic Novelist." 80–86.

Brée, Germaine. "*Jalousie*: New Blinds of Old." 87–90.

27 (Spring–Summer 1961) *Women Writers*

Houston, John. "The *Memoirs of Hadrian* by Marguerite Yourcenar." 140–41.

Porter, C[harles] A. "Françoise d'Eaubonne's *Le temps d'apprendre à vivre.*" 142–43.

28 (Fall–Winter 1961–62) *Jean-Jacques Rousseau*

Emery, Léon. "Rousseau and the Foundations of Human Regeneration." 3–12.

Mead, William. "*La nouvelle Héloïse* and the Public of 1761." 13–19.

Hall, H. Gaston. "The Concept of Virtue in *La nouvelle Héloïse.*" 20–33.

Crocker, Lester G. "The Priority of Justice or Law." 34–42.

Osmont, Robert. "J. J. Rousseau and the Idea of Love." Trans. E.R. Porter. 43–47.

Dickstein, Morris. "The Faith of a Vicar: Reason and Morality in Rousseau's Religion." 48–54.

Voisine, Jacques. "Self-Ridicule in *Les confessions.*" 55–63.

Starobinski, Jean. "The Illness of Rousseau." 64–74.

Giraud, Raymond. "Rousseau's Happiness—Triumph or Tragedy?" 75–82.

Jouvenel, Bertrand de. "Rousseau the Pessimistic Evolutionist." 83–96.

McMahon, Joseph H. "Madame de Warens." 97–105.

Burgelin, Pierre. "The Second Education of Emile." 106–11.

Temmer, Mark J. "Rousseau and Thoreau." 112–21.

May, Georges. "Rousseau and France." 122–35.

"Biblio: Recent Publications on Rousseau [Bibliography]." 136–40.

29 (Spring–Summer 1962) *The New Dramatists*

Ionesco, Eugène. "Selections from the Journals ["On Life and Death," "On the Theatre," "On History and Politics," "About Art"]." 3–9.

Hill, Robert E. "Summing Up." 10–15.

Houston, Mona T. "Villiers Vindicated." 16–19.

Reck, Rima Drell. "Appearance and Reality in Genet's *Le balcon.*" 20–25.

McMahon, Joseph H. "Keeping Faith and Holding Firm." 26–32.

Ehrmann, Jacques. "Genet's Dramatic Metamorphosis: From Appearance to Freedom." 33–42.

Cohn, Ruby. "Plays and Players in the Plays of Samuel Beckett." 43–48.

Kern, Edith. "Beckett's Knight of Infinite Resignation." 49–56.

Radke, Judith J. "The Theatre of Samuel Beckett: 'Une durée à animer.'" 57–64.

Schechner, Richard. "The Enactment of the 'Not' in Eugène Ionesco's *Les chaises.*" 65–72.

32 (October 1964) *Paris in Literature*

Cecchi, Annie. "Sartre's Ambiguous Friend." 133–37.

Mahlendorf, Ursula R. "Where the Air Throbs." 138–43.

McMahon, Joseph H. "City for Expatriates." 144–58.

33 (December 1964) *Shakespeare in France*

Voltaire. "A Shakespeare Journal." 5–13.

McMahon, Joseph H. "Ducis: Unkindest Cutter?" 14–25.

Guizot, François. "A Stage for Man Alone." 26–32.

Taine, H. A. "The Brink of an Abyss." 33–36.

Verdier, Philippe. "Delacroix and Shakespeare." 37–45.

Giraud, Raymond. "Stendhal's 'Greatest Bard.'" 46–52.

Haig, Stirling. "Vigny and *Othello*." 53–64.

Boorsch, Jean. "Hugo's Fraternal Genius." 65–71.

Plantinga, Leon B. "Berlioz' Use of Shakespearian Themes." 72–79.

Lamont, Rosette. "The Hamlet Myth." 80–91.

Sonnenfeld, Albert. "Hamlet the German and Jules Laforgue." 92–100.

Price, Jonathan B. "Montherlant's Exemplar." 101–4.

Knapp, Bettina. "A Director's Viewpoint." 105–6.

Peyre, Henri. "Shakespeare's Women: A French View." 107–19.

Bonnefoy, Yves. "Transpose or Translate?" 120–26.

"Shakespeare in France [Annotated Bibliography]." 127–30.

34 (June 1965) *Proust*

McMahon, Joseph H. "From Things to Themes." 5–17.

Pardee, W. Hearne. "The Images of Vision." 19–23.

Lewis, Philip E. "Idealism and Reality." 24–28.

Tolmachev, M. V. "Impressionist-Classicist Tensions." Trans. Harold Beyerly. 29–35.

Philip, Michel. "The Hidden Onlooker." 37–42.

March, Harold. "The Imprisoned." 43–54.

Thibaudeau, Barbara. "Condemned to Lie." 55–63.

Murray, Jack. "The Mystery of Others." 65–72.

Marks, Jonathan E. "The Verdurins and Their Cult." 73–80.

Johnson, J. Theodore, Jr. "From Artistic Celibacy to Artistic Contemplation." 81–90.

Shattuck, Roger. "Proust's Stilts." 91–98.

Jefferson, Louise M. "Proust and Racine." 99–105.

Hicks, Eric C. "Swann's Dream and the World of Sleep." 106–16.

Languth, William. "The World and Life of the Dream." 117–30.

35 (December 1965) *Sade*

May, Georges. "Fiction Reader, Novel Writer." 5–11.

Sade, D. A. F. de. "Notes on the Novel." 12–19.

Temmer, Mark J. "Style and Rhetoric." 20–28.

Guicharnaud, Jacques. "The Wreathed Columns of St. Peter's." 29–38.

Giraud, Raymond. "The First *Justine*." 39–47.

Pastoureau, Henri. "Sado-Masochism and the Philosophies of Ambivalence." 48–60.

Klossowski, Pierre. "A Destructive Philosophy." 61–80.

Mitchell, Jeremy. "Swinburne—The Disappointed Protagonist." 81–88.

Matthews, J. H. "The Right Person for Surrealism." 89–95.

McMahon, Joseph H. "Where Does Real Life Begin?" 96–113.

Beaujour, Michel. "Peter Weiss and the Futility of Sadism." 114–19.

36 & 37 (October 1966) *Structuralism*

Ehrmann, Jacques. "Introduction." 5–9.

Martinet, André. "Structure and Language." Trans. Thomas G. Penchoen. 10–18.

Lewis, Philip E. "Merleau-Ponty and the Phenomenology of Language." 19–40.

Lévi-Strauss, Claude. "Overture to *Le cru et le cuit*." Trans. Joseph H. McMahon. 41–65.

Scheffler, Harold W. "Structuralism in Anthropology." 66–88.

Nodelman, Sheldon. "Structural Analysis in Art and Anthropology." 89–103.

Miel, Jan. "Jacques Lacan and the Structure of the Unconscious." 104–11.

Lacan, Jacques. "The Insistence of the Letter in the Unconscious." 112–47.

Hartmann, Geoffrey. "Structuralism: The Anglo-American Adventure." 148–68.

Ehrmann, Jacques. "Structures of Exchange in *Cinna*." Trans. Joseph H. McMahon. 169–99.

Riffaterre, Michael. "Describing Poetic Structures: Two Approaches to Baudelaire's *Les chats*." 200–42.

Rippere, Victoria L. "Towards an Anthropology of Literature." 243–51.

Barber, Elizabeth. "Linguistics [Annotated Bibliography]." 252–55.

Maxwell, Allen R. "Anthropology [Annotated Bibliography]." 256–62.

Wilden, Anthony G. "Jacques Lacan: A Partial Bibliography [Annotated Bibliography]." 263–68.

Todorov, Tzvetan. "Structuralism and Literary Criticism [Annotated Bibliography]." 269–70.

Ehrmann, Jacques. "Selected General Bibliography." 270.

38 (May 1967) *The Classical Line: Essays in Honor of Henri Peyre*

Hytier, Jean. "The Classicism of the Classics." Trans. June Guicharnaud. 5–17.

Doubrovsky, Serge. "New Critics and Old Myths." 18–26.

McMahon, Joseph H. "More Perfect Souls." 27–46.

Wellek, René. "French 'Classical' Criticism in the Twentieth Century." 47–71.

Boorsch, Jean. "About Some Greek Romances." 72–88.

Lapp, John C. "The Potter and His Clay: Mythological Imagery in Ronsard." 89–108.

Moore, W. G. "Lucretius and Montaigne." 109–14.

Hall, H. Gaston. "Scarron and the Travesty of Virgil." 115–27.

Levin, Harry. "From Terence to Tabarin: A Note on *Les fourberies de Scapin.*" 128–37.

May, Georges. "Corneille and the Classics." 138–50.

Wadsworth, Philip A. "Ovid and La Fontaine." 151–55.

Porter, Charles A. "Chateaubriand's Classicism." 156–71.

Giraud, Raymond. "Winckelmann's Part in Gautier's Perception of Classical Beauty." 172–82.

Brée, Germaine. "Proust's Dormant Gods." 183–94.

Cornell, Kenneth. "Claudel and the Greek Classics." 195–204.

Guicharnaud, Jacques. "Beware of Happiness: Mairet's *Sophonisbe.*" 205–21.

Frohock, W. M. "The 'Picaresque' in France before *Gil Blas.*" 222–29.

Brombert, Victor. "Pascal's Happy Dungeon." 230–42.

Demorest, Jean-Jacques. "Pascal and the Querelle." 243–50.

Weinberg, Kurt. "Nietzsche's Paradox of Tragedy." 251–66.

39 (1967) *Literature and Revolution*

Ehrmann, Jacques. "Foreword." 5–8.

———. "On Articulation: The Language of History and the Terror of Language." Trans. Barry Lydgate. 9–28.

Beaujour, Michel. "Flight out of Time: Poetic Language and the Revolution." Trans. Richard Klein. 29–49.

Blanchot, Maurice. "The Main Impropriety (Excerpts)." Trans. June Guicharnaud. 50–63.

Blanchard, J. M. E. "The French Revolution: A Political Line or a Language Circle?" 64–76.

Barthes, Roland. "Writing and Revolution." Trans. June Guicharnaud. 77–84.

Klein, Richard. "Baudelaire and Revolution: Some Notes." 85–97.

Regalado, Antonio. "The Counterrevolutionary Image of the World." 98–118.

Jakobson, Roman. "The Generation That Squandered Its Poets (Excerpts)." Trans. Dale E. Peterson. 119–25.

Holquist, Michael. "The Mayakovsky Problem." 126–36.

Serge, Victor. "Is a Proletarian Literature Possible?" Trans. Anna Aschenbach. 137–45.

Greeman, Richard. "'The Laws Are Burning': Literary and Revolutionary Realism in Victor Serge." 146–59.

Morel, Jean-Pierre. "A 'Revolutionary' Poetics?" 160–79.

Poggioli, Renato. "The Avant-Garde and Politics." 180–87.

Greene, Naomi. "Antonin Artaud: Metaphysical Revolutionary." 188–97.

Janvier, Ludovic. "Literature and the Rest of the World." 198–99.

Gombrowicz, Witold. "Journal Excerpts." Trans. June Guicharnaud. 200–209.

———. "Operetta." Trans. June Guicharnaud. 210–14.

Spence, Jonathan. "On Chinese Revolutionary Literature." 215–25.

Chisolm, Lawrence W. "Lu Hsun and Revolution In Modern China." 226–41.

40 (1968) *Literature and Society: Eighteenth Century*

Grimsley, Ronald. "Rousseau as a Critic of Society." 5–17.

Havens, George R. "The Road to Rousseau's *Discours sur l'inégalité*." 18–31.

Katz, Eve. "Chamfort." 32–46.

Starobinski, Jean. "Reflections on Some Symbols of the Revolution." Trans. John D. Lyons. 47–61.

Mortier, Roland. "The 'Philosophes' and Public Education." 62–76.

Guy, Basil. "Toward an Appreciation of the *abbé de cour*." 77–90.

Gossman, Lionel. "Prévost's *Manon*: Love in the New World." 91–102.

Porter, Charles A. "Life in Restif Country." 103–17.

Showalter, English, Jr. "Money Matters and Early Novels." 118–33.

Stewart, Philip. "The Child Comes of Age." 134–41.

Pizzorusso, Arnaldo. "Situations and Environment in *Margot la ravaudeuse*." 142–55.

Alstad, Dianne. "*Les liaisons dangereuses*: Hustlers and Hypocrites." 156–67.

41 (1968) *Game, Play, Literature*

Ehrmann, Jacques. "Introduction." 5.

Axelos, Kostas. "Planetary Interlude." Trans. Sally Hess. 6–18.

Fink, Eugen. "The Oasis of Happiness: Toward an Ontology of Play." Trans. Ute Saine and Thomas Saine. 19–30.

Ehrmann, Jacques. "Homo Ludens Revisited." Trans. Cathy Lewis and Phil Lewis. 31–57.

42 (1969) *Zola*

43 (1969) *The Child's Part*

Durand, Marion. "One Hundred Years of Illustrations in French Children's Books." Trans. Diana Wormuth. 85–96.

Winandy, André. "The Twilight Zone: Imagination and Reality in Jules Verne's *Strange Journeys.*" Trans. Rita Winandy. 97–110.

Chesneaux, Jean. "Jules Verne's Image of the United States." Trans. Frances Chew. 111–27.

Flescher, Jacqueline. "The Language of Nonsense in *Alice.*" 128–44.

Holquist, Michael. "What is a Boojum? Nonsense and Modernism." 145–64.

Howard, Richard. "Childhood Amnesia." 165–69.

44 (1970) *Paul Valéry*

Robinson, Judith. "Valéry's View of Mental Creativity." 3–18.

Austin, Lloyd James. "Modulation and Movement in Valéry's Verse." 19–38.

Noulet, E. "Tone in the Poems of Paul Valéry." Trans. Georges Bernauer. 39–50.

Jallat, Jeannine. "Valéry and the Mathematical Language of Identity and Difference." Trans. Ann Smock. 51–64.

Todorov, Tzvetan. "Valéry's Poetics." Trans. Elizabeth Willis. 65–71.

Chisholm, A. R. "Moods of the Intellect in *Le cimetière marin.*" 72–86.

Duchesne-Guillemin, Jacques. "Introduction to 'La jeune Parque.'" Trans. Emmett Gossen. 87–105.

Sabbagh, Céline. "Calypso: A Theme of Ambiguity, a Theme of Fascination." 106–18.

Whiting, Charles G. "Préciosité in 'La jeune Parque' and *Charmes.*" 119–27.

Bastet, N. "*Stratonice* and the Rejection of Tragedy." Trans. Julia Bloch Frey and Rita Winandy. 128–47.

Hackett, C. A. "Valéry and the Swans." 148–56.

Crow, Christine M. "'Teste parle': The question of a potential artist in Valéry's *M. Teste.*" 157–68.

Ince, W. N. "*La promenade avec Monsieur Teste.*" 169–84.

Lawler, James R. "Saint Mallarmé." 185–98.

Gershman, Herbert S. "Valéry and Breton." 199–206.

Champigny, Robert. "Valéry on History and the Novel." 207–14.

Walzer, P. O. "The Physiology of Sex." Trans. A.A. Littauer and J.L. Logan. 215–30.

45 (1970) *Language as Action*

Parry, Adam. "Thucydides' Use of Abstract Language." 3–20.

Putnam, Michael. "Simple Tibullus and the Ruse of Style." 21–32.

Vance, Eugene. "The Word at Heart: *Aucassin et Nicolette* as a Medieval Comedy of Language." 33–51.

Beaujour, Michel. "The Unicorn in the Carpet." 52–63.

Klein, Richard. "Straight Lines and Arabesques: Metaphors of Metaphor." 64–86.

Reiss, T. J. "The Dialectic of Language in the Theater: Corneille from *Mélite* to *Le Cid*." 87–101.

Delft, Louis van. "Language and Power: Eyes and Words in *Britannicus*." Trans. Paul Schwartz. 102–12.

Todorov, Tzvetan. "The Discovery of Language: *Les liaisons dangereuses* and *Adolphe*." Trans. Frances Chew. 113–26.

Vance, Christie. "*La nouvelle Héloïse*: The Language of Paris." 127–36.

Godin, Jean-Cléo. "Anne Hébert: Rebirth in the Word." Trans. Rosemary Brown. 137–53.

Lewis, Philip. "Language and French Critical Debate." 154–65.

46 (1971) *From Stage to Street*

Guicharnaud, Jacques. "Foreword." 3–4.

Reiss, Timothy J. "Psychical Distance and Theatrical Distancing in Sartre's Drama." 5–16.

Kern, Edith. "Structure in Beckett's Theatre." 17–27.

Israel, Abigail. "The Aesthetic of Violence: Rimbaud and Genet." 28–40.

Cohn, Ruby. "Black Power on Stage: *Emperor Jones* and *King Christophe*." 41–47.

Dietemann, Margaret. "Departure from the Absurd: Adamov's Last Plays." 48–59.

Coe, Richard N. "Armand Gatti's Carnival of Compassion: *La deuxième existence du camp de Tatenberg*." 60–74.

Knapp, Bettina L. "Witold Gombrowicz: A Faceless Theatre." 75–87.

Lemarchand, Jacques. "The Dramatic Career of Jean Vauthier." Trans. Ralph Albanese, Jr. 88–101.

Goitein, Denise. "Nathalie Sarraute as Dramatist." 102–12.

Guicharnaud, Jacques. "The Terrorist Marivaudage of Marguerite Duras." 113–24.

Lamont, Rosette C. "Jean-Louis Barrault's *Rabelais*." 125–38.

Simon, Alfred. "The Theatre in May." 139–48.

Denis, Romain et al. "Offstage." Trans. Wyley L. Powell. 149–53.

Farmer, R. L. [Rosette C. Lamont]. "Fernando Arrabal's Guerrilla Theatre." 154–66.

Shank, Theodore. "The Theatre of the Cultural Revolution." Trans. Wyley L. Powell. 167–85.

47 (1972) *Image and Symbol in the Renaissance*

Winandy, André. "Foreword." 3.

Stegmann, André. "Richness and Ambivalence of the Symbol in the Renaissance." Trans. Jean-Pierre Coursodon and Edward Miller. 5–18.

Sharrat, Peter. "Peter Ramus and Imitation: Image, Sign, and Sacrament." 19–32.

Margolin, Jean-Claude. "Mathias Ringmann's *Grammatica figurata*, or, Grammar as a Card Game." Trans. Diana Wormuth. 33–46.

Radcliff-Umstead, Douglas. "Giulio Camillo's Emblems of Memory." 47–56.

Greene, Thomas M. "Styles of Experience in Scève's *Délie*." 57–75.

Cave, Terence C. "Ronsard as Apollo: Myth, Poetry, and Experience in a Renaissance Sonnet-Cycle." 76–89.

Ortali, Ray. "Ronsard: From *Chevelure* to *Rond Parfait*." Trans. Buford Norman. 90–97.

Russell, Daniel. "Du Bellay's Emblematic Vision of Rome." 98–109.

Castan, Félix. "The Realm of the Imaginary in Du Bellay/Ronsard and Du Bartas/La Ceppède." Trans. William Franklin Panici. 110–23.

Kushner, Eva. "The Role of Platonic Symbols in the Poetry of Pontus de Tyard." 124–44.

Winandy, André. "Piety and Humanistic Symbolism in the Works of Marguerite d'Angoulême, Queen of Navarre." 145–69.

Martz, Louis L. "Who is Lycidas?" 170–88.

Wardropper, Bruce W. "The Dramatization of Figurative Language in the Spanish Theater." 189–98.

Reiss, Timothy J. "Jodelle's *Cléopâtre* and the Enchanted Circle." 199–210.

Sobel, Eli. "The Earliest Allegories and Imagery of Hans Sachs: An Introductory Essay." 211–17.

Vaccaro, Jean-Michel. "Metrical Symbolism in Schütz' *Historia der Geburt Jesu Christi*." Trans. Charles S. Fineman. 218–31.

Schwartz, Jerome. "Gargantua's Device and the Abbey of Theleme: A Study in Rabelais' Iconography." 232–42.

Berger, Harry, Jr. "Conspicuous Exclusion in Vermeer: An Essay in Renaissance Pastoral." 243–65.

Bensimon, Marc. "The Significance of Eye Imagery in the Renaissance from Bosch to Montaigne." 266–90.

48 (1972) *French Freud: Structural Studies in Psychoanalysis*

Mehlman, Jeffrey. "French Freud." 5–9.

———. "The 'Floating Signifier': From Lévi-Strauss to Lacan." 10–37.

———. "Jacques Lacan: Introductory Note." 38.

49 (1974) *Science, Language, and the Perspective Mind: Studies in Literature and Thought from Campanella to Bayle*

50 (1974) *Intoxication and Literature*

Peschel, Enid Rhodes. "Foreword." 5–7.

Winandy, André. "Rabelais' Barrel." 8–25.

Cooke, Michael G. "De Quincey, Coleridge, and the Formal Uses of Intoxication." 26–40.

Cockerham, Harry. "Gautier: From Hallucination to Supernatural Vision." 42–53.

Brombert, Victor. "The Will to Ecstasy: The Example of Baudelaire's 'La chevelure.'" 55–63.

Peschel, Enid Rhodes. "Arthur Rimbaud: The Aesthetics of Intoxication." 65–80.

Logan, John Frederick. "The Age of Intoxication." 81–94.

Balakian, Anna. "Breton and Drugs." 96–107.

Caws, Mary Ann. "Robert Desnos and the Flasks of Night." 108–19.

Lyons, John D. "Artaud: Intoxication and its Double." 120–29.

Kuhn, Reinhard. "The Hermeneutics of Silence: Michaux and Mescaline." 130–41.

Grecco, Stephen R. "High Hopes: Eugene O'Neill and Alcohol." 142–49.

Brooks, Peter. "Virtue-Tripping: Notes on *Le lys dans la vallée*." 150–62.

Bloom, Harold. "Walter Pater: The Intoxication of Belatedness." 163–89.

Solomon, Philip H. "Céline's *Death on the Installment Plan*: The Intoxications of Delirium." 191–203.

51 (1974) *Approaches to Medieval Romance*

Haidu, Peter. "Introduction." 3–11.

Jackson, W. T. H. "The Nature of Romance." 12–25.

Ollier, Marie-Louise. "The Author in the Text: The Prologues of Chrétien de Troyes." Trans. David Baker. 26–41.

Batany, Jean. "Home and Rome, A Device in Epic and Romance: *Le Couronnement de Louis* and *Ille et Galeron*." Trans. Joel H. Reader. 42–60.

Bloch, R. Howard. "Tristan, the Myth of the State and the Language of the Self." 61–81.

Hanning, Robert W. "*Engin* in Twelfth-Century Romance: An Examination of the *Roman d'Enéas* and Hue de Rotelande's *Ipomedon*." 82–101.

Dembowski, Peter F. "Monologue, Author's Monologue and Related Problems in the Romances of Chrétien de Troyes." 102–14.

Gallais, Pierre. "Hexagonal and Spiral Structure in Medieval Narrative." Trans. Vincent Pollina. 115–32.

Haidu, Peter. "Narrativity and Language in Some Twelfth-Century Romances." 133–46.

52 (1975) *Graphesis: Perspectives in Literature and Philosophy*

53 (1976) *Traditional and Contemporary African Literature*

Okam, Hilary H. "Introduction." 3–4.

Adedeji, Joel A. "The Genesis of African Folkloric Literature." 5–18.

Lee, Sonia. "The Image of the Woman in the African Folktale From the Sub-Saharan Francophone Area." 19–28.

Michelman, Fredric. "The West African Novel Since 1911." 29–44.

Moore, Gerald. "Colonial Portraits in a Changing Frame." 45–63.

Linnemann, Russell. "The Anticolonialism of Ferdinand Oyono." 64–77.

Lambert, Fernando. "Narrative Perspectives in Mongo Beti's *Le pauvre Christ de Bomba*." Trans. Daniel R. Cianfarini. 78–91.

Erickson, John D. "Cheikh Hamidou Kane's *L'aventure ambiguë*." 92–101.

Priebe, Richard. "Demonic Imagery and the Apocalyptic Vision in the Novels of Ayi Kwei Armah." 102–36.

Sellin, Eric. "The Unknown Voice of Yambo Ouologuem." 137–62.

Hale, Thomas A. "Structural Dynamics in a Third World Classic: Aimé Césaire's *Cahier d'un retour au pays natal*." 163–74.

Okam, Hilary. "Aspects of Imagery and Symbolism in the Poetry of Aimé Césaire." 175–96.

Lindfors, Bernth. "Wole Soyinka, When Are You Coming Home?" 197–210.

54 (1977) *Mallarmé*

Halpern, Joseph. "Foreword." 5–8.

Bonnefoy, Yves. "The Poetics of Mallarmé." Trans. Elaine Ancekewicz. 9–21.

Cohn, Robert Greer. "Mallarmé's Windows." 23–31.

Crowley, Roseline. "Toward the Poetics of Juxtaposition: 'L'après-midi d'un faune.'" 32–44.

Frey, Hans-Jost. "The Tree of Doubt." 45–54.

Burt, Ellen. "Mallarmé's 'Sonnet en yx': The Ambiguities of Speculation." 55–82.

Lawler, James. "Three Sonnets." 83–95.

Stierle, Karlheinz. "Position and Negation in Mallarmé's 'Prose pour des Esseintes.'" Trans. Sibylle Kisro. 96–117.

Dragonetti, Roger. "'Le Nénuphar blanc': A Poetic Dream with Two Unknowns." Trans. Kathryn Crecelius. 118–39.

Johnson, Barbara. "Poetry and Performative Language." 140–58.

Sonnenfeld, Albert. "Mallarmé: The Poet as Actor as Reader." 159–72.

Barko, Carol. "The Dancer and the Becoming of Language." 173–87.

Knapp, Bettina. "'Igitur or Elbehnon's Folly': The Depersonalization Process and the Creative Encounter." 188–214.

Hanson, Thomas. "Mallarmé's Hat." 215–27.

55 & 56 (1977) *Literature and Psychoanalysis: The Question of Reading: Otherwise*

Felman, Shoshana. "Foreword." 2.

———. "To Open the Question." 5–10.

Lacan, Jacques. "Desire and the Interpretation of Desire in *Hamlet*." Ed. Jacques-Alain Miller. Trans. James Hulbert. 11–52.

Sibony, Daniel. "*Hamlet*: A Writing-Effect." Trans. James Hulbert with the assistance of Joshua Wilner. 53–93.

Felman, Shoshana. "Turning the Screw of Interpretation." 94–207.

Spivak, Gayatri Chakravorty. "The Letter as Cutting Edge." 208–26.

Dragonetti, Roger. "The Double Play of Arnaut Daniel's *Sestina* and Dante's *Divina Commedia*." Trans. Timothy Bahti. 227–52.

Méla, Charles. "Perceval." 253–79.

Brooks, Peter. "Freud's Masterplot: Questions of Narrative." 280–300.

Rey, Jean-Michel. "Freud's Writing on Writing." Trans. G.W. Most and James Hulbert. 301–28.

Sollers, Philippe. "Freud's Hand." Trans. Barbara Johnson. 329–37.

Jameson, Fredric. "Imaginary and Symbolic in Lacan: Marxism, Psychoanalytic Criticism, and the Problem of the Subject." 338–95.

Brenkman, John. "The Other and the One: Psychoanalysis, Reading, the *Symposium*." 396–456.

Johnson, Barbara. "The Frame of Reference: Poe, Lacan, Derrida." 457–505.

57 (1979) *Locus: Space, Landscape, Decor in Modern French Fiction*

Solomon, Philip H. "Foreword." 3–4.

———. "The View from a Rump: America as Journey and Landscape of Desire in Céline's *Voyage au bout de la nuit*." 5–22.

Andermatt, Verena. "Rodomontages of *Le ravissement de Lol V. Stein*." 23–35.

Loubère, J. A. E. "Views Through the Screen: In-Site in Claude Simon." 36–47.

Smith, Stephen. "Fragments of Landscape, Scraps of Décor: Maurice Roche's *Compact*." 48–57.

Halpern, Joseph. "Sartre's Enclosed Space." 58–71.

Livingston, Beverly. "From A to F and Back: Pinget's Fictive Arena." 72–85.

Dobbs, Annie-Claude. "The Problematics of Space in Julien Gracq: Fiction and Narration in a Chapter of *Au château d'Argol*." Trans. Kathleen Flosi Good. 86–108.

Ladimer, Bethany. "Camus' Chenoua Landscape." 109–23.

Ungar, Steven. "Night Moves: Spatial Perception and the Place of Blanchot's Early Fiction." 124–35.

Paganini, Maria. "Intertextuality and the Strategy of Desire: Proust's 'Mélancolique Villégiature de Mme de Breyves.'" Trans. Janet Beizer. 136–63.

60 (1980) *Cinema/Sound*

Insdorf, Annette. "Maurice Jaubert and François Truffaut: Musical Continuities from *L'Atalante* to *L'histoire d'Adèle H.*" 204–18.

Marie, Michel. "The Poacher's Aged Mother: On Speech in *La chienne* by Jean Renoir." Trans. Marguerite Morley. 219–32.

Browne, Nick. "Film Form/Voice-Over: Bresson's *The Diary of a Country Priest.*" 233–40.

Ropars-Wuilleumier, Marie-Claire. "The Disembodied Voice: *India Song.*" Trans. Kimberly Smith. 241–68.

Gorbman, Claudia. "Bibliography on Sound in Film." 269–86.

61 (1981) *Towards a Theory of Description*

Kittay, Jeffrey. "Introduction." i–v.

Hamon, Philippe. "Rhetorical Status of the Descriptive." Trans. Patricia Baudoin. 1–26.

Beaujour, Michel. "Some Paradoxes of Description." 27–59.

Sternberg, Meir. "Ordering the Unordered: Time, Space, and Descriptive Coherence." 60–88.

Halpern, Joseph. "Describing the Surreal." 89–106.

Riffaterre, Michael. "Descriptive Imagery." 107–25.

Conley, Tom. "Retz of Love." 126–44.

Bonnefis, Philippe. "The Melancholic Describer." Trans. Jeremy Raw. 145–75.

Casey, Edward S. "Literary Description and Phenomenological Method." 176–201.

Talarico, Kathryn Marie. "Fundare domum: Medieval Modes and the *Roman d'Eneas.*" 202–24.

Kittay, Jeffrey. "Descriptive Limits." 225–43.

Owen, Stephen. "A Monologue of the Senses." 244–60.

Buisine, Alain. "The First Eye." Trans. Carla Freccero. 261–75.

Blanchard, Marc Eli. "On Still Life." 276–98.

Perec, Georges. "Still Life/Style Leaf." Trans. Harry Mathews. 299–305.

62 (1981) *Feminist Readings: French Texts/American Contexts*

Gaudin, Colette, Mary Jean Green, Lynn Anthony Higgins, Marianne Hirsch, Vivian Kogan, Claudia Reeder, and Nancy Vickers. "Introduction." 2–18.

Felman, Shoshana. "Rereading Femininity." 19–44.

Sivert, Eileen Boyd. "*Lélia* and Feminism." 45–66.

Hirsch, Marianne. "A Mother's Discourse: Incorporation and Repetition in *La Princesse de Clèves.*" 67–87.

Scharfman, Ronnie. "Mirroring and Mothering in Simone Schwartz-Bart's

Compagnon, Antoine. "A Long Short Story: Montaigne's Brevity." Trans. Carla Freccero. 24–50.

Tournon, André. "Self-Interpretation in Montaigne's *Essais*." Trans. Matthew Senior. 51–72.

Defaux, Gérard. "Readings of Montaigne." Trans. John A. Gallucci. 73–92.

Duval, Edwin M. "Lessons of the New World: Design and Meaning in Montaigne's 'Des cannibales' (I:31) and 'Des coches' (III:6)." 95–112.

Todorov, Tzvetan. "L'être et l'autre: Montaigne." Trans. Pierre Saint-Amand. 113–44.

Rigolot, François. "Montaigne's Purloined Letters." 145–66.

Meijer, Marianne S. "Guesswork or Facts: Connections between Montaigne's Last Three Chapters (III:11, 12 and 13)." 167–79.

Gutwirth, Marcel. "'By Diverse Means . . . ' (I:1)." 180–87.

Demure, Catherine. "Montaigne: The Paradox and the Miracle—Structure and Meaning in 'The Apology for Raymond Sebond' (*Essais* II:12)." Trans. Dianne Sears. 188–208.

Scodel, Joshua. "The Affirmation of Paradox: A Reading of Montaigne's 'De la Phisionomie' (III:12)." 209–37.

Brody, Jules. "'Du repentir' (III:2): A Philological Reading." 238–72.

Starobinski, Jean. "The Body's Moment." Trans. John A. Gallucci. 273–305.

65 (1983) *The Language of Difference: Writing in QUEBEC(ois)*

Sarkonak, Ralph. "Editor's Preface." iii–vi.

———. "Accentuating the Differences." 3–20.

Melançon, Joseph. "The Writing of Difference in Québec." Trans. Lisa Gosselin. 21–29.

Gauvin, Lise. "From Octave Crémazie to Victor-Lévy Beaulieu: Language, Literature, and Ideology." Trans. Emma Henderson. 30–49.

Schendel, Michel van. "*Refus global*, or the Formula and History." Trans. Ruth G. Koizim. 53–73.

Mailhot, Laurent. "The Writing of the Essay." Trans. Jay Lutz. 74–89.

Nepveu, Pierre. "A (Hi)story that Refuses the Telling: Poetry and the Novel in Contemporary Québécois Literature." Trans. Karen McPherson. 90–105.

Gobin, Pierre. "Michel Tremblay: An Interweave of Prose and Drama." Trans. Richard Deshaies. 106–23.

Green, Mary Jean. "Structures of Liberation: Female Experience and Autobiographical Form in Québec." 124–36.

Hajdukowski-Ahmed, Maroussia. "The Unique, Its Double, and the Multiple: The Carnivalesque Hero in the Québécois Novel." Trans. Jan Marta. 139–53.

Laflèche, Guy. "Ringuet's *Trente arpents*: For Different Men But Always the Same Literature." Trans. Erec Koch. 155–71.

66 (1984) *The Anxiety of Anticipation*

67 (1984) *Concepts of Closure*

68 (1985) *Sartre after Sartre*

Felperin, Howard. "The Anxiety of Deconstruction." 254–66.

Warminski, Andrzej. "Dreadful Reading: Blanchot on Hegel." 267–75.

Hamacher, Werner. "The Second of Inversion: Movements of a Figure through Celan's Poetry." Trans. William D. Jewett. 276–311.

Keenan, Tom. "Bibliography of Texts by Paul de Man." 315–22.

70 (1986) *Images of Power: Medieval History/Discourse/Literature*

Brownlee, Kevin, and Stephen G. Nichols. "Editor's Preface." 1–4.

Stock, Brian. "History, Literature, and Medieval Textuality." 7–17.

Nichols, Stephen G. "Fission and Fusion: Mediations of Power in Medieval History and Literature." 21–41.

Vance, Eugene. "Chrétien's *Yvain* and the Ideologies of Change and Exchange." 42–62.

Regalado, Nancy Freeman. "Effet de réel, Effet du réel: Representation and Reference in Villon's *Testament*." 63–77.

Bloch, R. Howard. "Silence and Holes: The *Roman de silence* and the Art of the Trouvère." 81–99.

Zink, Michel. "The Allegorical Poem as Interior Memoir." Trans. Margaret Miner and Kevin Brownlee. 100–26.

Leupin, Alexandre. "The Powerlessness of Writing: Guillaume de Machaut, the Gorgon, and Ordenance." Trans. Peggy McCracken. 127–49.

Lyons, John D. "The *Heptaméron* and the Foundation of Critical Narrative." 150–63.

Brownlee, Kevin. "Discourse as *Proueces* in *Aucassin et Nicolette*." 167–82.

Cerquiglini, Bernard. "The Syntax of Discursive Authority: The Example of Feminine Discourse." Trans. Cynthia Hoffman, David Pelizzari, and Stephen G. Nichols. 183–98.

Fleischman, Suzanne. "Evaluation in Narrative: The Present Tense in Medieval 'Performed Stories.'" 199–251.

71 (1986) *Men/Women of Letters*

Porter, Charles A. "Foreword." 1–14.

Altman, Janet Gurkin. "The Letter Book as a Literary Institution 1539–1789: Toward a Cultural History of Published Correspondences in France." 17–62.

Bossis, Mireille. "Methodological Journeys through Correspondences." Trans. Karen McPherson. 63–75.

Grassi, Marie-Claire. "Friends and Lovers (or The Codification of Intimacy)." Trans. Neil Gordon. 77–92.

Dawson, Deidre. "In Search of the Real Pangloss: The Correspondence of Voltaire with the Duchess of Saxe-Gotha." 93–112.

Showalter, English, Jr. "Authorial Self-Consciousness in the Familiar Letter: The Case of Madame de Graffigny." 113–30.

Riberette, Pierre. "On Editing Chateaubriand's Correspondence." Trans. Charles A. Porter. 131–47.

Reid, Martine. "Correspondences: *Stendhal en toutes lettres.*" Trans. Mark Gross with Alan Stoekl. 149–68.

Le Guillou, Louis. "Lamennais: A Happy Ending." Trans. Erec Koch. 169–76.

Gaudon, Sheila. "On Editing Victor Hugo's Correspondence." 177–98.

Kolb, Philip. "Proust's Letters." 199–210.

72 (1986) *Simone de Beauvoir: Witness to a Century*

Wenzel, Hélène V. "Introduction." v–xiv.

———. "Interview with Simone de Beauvoir." Trans. Hélène V. Wenzel. 5–32.

Butler, Judith. "Sex and Gender in Simone de Beauvoir's *Second Sex.*" 35–49.

Fichera, Virginia M. "Simone de Beauvoir and 'The Woman Question': *Les bouches inutiles.*" 51–64.

Evans, Martha Noel. "Murdering *L'invitée*: Gender and Fictional Narrative." 67–86.

Patterson, Yolanda Astarita. "Simone de Beauvoir and the Demystification of Motherhood." 87–105.

Portuges, Catherine. "Attachment and Separation in *The Memoirs of a Dutiful Daughter.*" 107–18.

Kaufmann, Dorothy. "Simone de Beauvoir: Questions of Difference and Generation." 121–31.

Courtivron, Isabelle de. "From Bastard to Pilgrim: Rites and Writing for Madame." 133–48.

Bair, Deirdre. "Simone de Beauvoir: Politics, Language, and Feminist Identity." 149–62.

Simons, Margaret A. "Beauvoir and Sartre: The Philosophical Relationship." 165–79.

Marks, Elaine. "Transgressing the (In)cont(in)ent Boundaries: The Body in Decline." 181–200.

Simons, Margaret A. ["In Memoriam"]. 203–5.

Patterson, Yolanda Astarita. "Some Personal Reflections [In Memoriam"]. 207–9.

Bair, Deirdre. ["In Memoriam"]. 211–15.

73 (1987) *Everyday Life*

Kaplan, Alice, and Kristin Ross. "Introduction." 1–4.

Lefebvre, Henri. "The Everyday and Everydayness." Trans. Christine Levich, with Alice Kaplan and Kristin Ross. 7–11.

74 (1988) *Phantom Proxies: Symbolism and the Rhetoric of History*

75 (1988) *The Politics of Tradition: Placing Women in French Literature*

DeJean, Joan, and Nancy K. Miller. "Editors' Preface." 1–6.

Jones, Ann R., and Nancy J. Vickers. "Canon, Rule and the Restoration Renaissance." 9–25.

DeJean, Joan. "Classical Reeducation: Decanonizing the Feminine." 26–39.

Miller, Nancy K. "Men's Reading, Women's Writing: Gender and the Rise of the Novel." 40–55.

Schor, Naomi. "Idealism in the Novel: Recanonizing Sand." 56–73.

Nichols, Stephen G. "Medieval Women Writers: *Aisthesis* and the Powers of Marginality." 77–94.

Showalter, English, Jr. "Writing off the Stage: Women Authors and Eighteenth-Century Theater." 95–111.

Frappier-Mazur, Lucienne. "Marginal Canons: Rewriting the Erotic." 112–28.

Danahy, Michael. "Marceline Desbordes-Valmore and the Engendered Canon." 129–47.

Suleiman, Susan Rubin. "A Double Margin: Reflections on Women Writers and the Avant-garde in France." 148–72.

Marks, Elaine. "'Sapho 1900': Imaginary Renée Viviens and the Rear of the Belle Epoque." 175–89.

Makward, Christiane, with Odile Cazenave. "The Others' Others: 'Francophone' Women and Writing." 190–207.

Thiesse, Anne-Marie, and Hélène Mathieu. "The Decline of the Classical Age and the Birth of the Classics." Trans. Lauren Doyle-McCombs. 208–28.

Jardine, Alice A., and Anne M. Menke. "Exploding the Issue: 'French' 'Women' 'Writers' and 'the Canon'? Fourteen Interviews." 229–58.

Special Issue (1988): *After the Age of Suspicion: The French Novel Today*

Porter, Charles A. "Foreword." 1–4.

Sarraute, Nathalie. *Disent les imbéciles* [excerpt]. Trans. Maria Jolas. *L'usage de la parole* [excerpt]. Trans. Barbara Wright in consultation with the author. *Elle est là* [excerpt]. Trans. Marie-Anne Fleming. *Enfance* [excerpt]. Trans. Barbara Wright in consultation with the author. Intro. Eric Eigenmann. 7–24.

Thomas, Henri. *Le croc des chiffoniers* [excerpts]. Trans. and intro. Michael Syrotinski. 25–44.

Simon, Claude. *Leçon de choses*. Trans. Daniel Weissbort. Intro. Barbara Vinken. 45–60.

Duras, Marguerite. *Un barrage contre le Pacifique* [excerpt]. Trans. Herma

76 (1989) *Autour de Racine: Studies in Intertextuality*

3261

———. "Letter to René Char on the Incompatabilities of the Writer." Trans. Christopher Carsten. 29–43.

Nancy, Jean-Luc. "Exscription." Trans. Katherine Lydon. 47–65.

Comay, Rebecca. "Gifts without Presents: Economies of 'Experience' in Bataille and Heidegger." 66–89.

Guerlac, Suzanne. "'Recognition' by a Woman!: A Reading of Bataille's *L'érotisme*." 90–105.

Strauss, Jonathan. "The Inverted Icarus." 106–23.

Hollier, Denis. "The Dualist Materialism of Georges Bataille." Trans. Hilari Allred. 124–39.

Richman, Michèle. "Bataille Moralist?: *Critique* and the Postwar Writings." 143–68.

Besnier, Jean-Michel. "Georges Bataille in the 1930s: A Politics of the Impossible." Trans. Amy Reid. 169–80.

Stoekl, Allan. "Truman's Apotheosis: Bataille, 'Planisme,' and Headlessness." 181–205.

Goux, Jean-Joseph. "General Economics and Postmodern Capitalism." Trans. Kathryn Aschheim and Rhonda Garelick. 206–24.

Heimonet, Jean-Michel. "Recoil in Order to Leap Forward: Two Values of Sade in Bataille's Text." Trans. Joaniko Kohchi. 227–36.

Lala, Marie-Christine. "The Conversations of Writing in Georges Bataille's *L'impossible*." Trans. Robert Livingston. 237–45.

Ungar, Steven. "Phantom Lascaux: Origin of the Work of Art." 246–62.

79 (1991) *Literature and the Ethical Question*

Nouvet, Claire. "Foreword." 1–2.

Blanchot, Maurice. "Enigme." 5–7.

———. "Enigma." Trans. Paul Weidmann. 8–10.

Bataille, Georges. "The Reasons for Writing a Book . . . " Trans. Elizabeth Rottenberg. 11.

———. "Reflections on the Executioner and the Victim." Trans. Elizabeth Rottenberg. 15–19.

Nancy, Jean-Luc. "The Unsacrificeable." Trans. Richard Livingston. 20–38.

Felman, Shoshana. "In an Era of Testimony: Claude Lanzmann's *Shoah*." 39–81.

Lanzmann, Claude. "Seminar on *Shoah*." Ed. David Rodowick. 82–99.

Nouvet, Claire. "An Impossible Response: The Disaster of Narcissus." 103–34.

Robbins, Jill. "*Visage, Figure*: Reading Levinas's *Totality and Infinity*." 135–49.

Newmark, Kevin. "Ingesting the Mummy: Proust's Allegory of Memory." 150–77.

Fassler, Margot. "Representations of Time in *Ordo representacionis Ade.*" 97–113.

Hindman, Sandra. "King Arthur, His Knights, and the French Aristocracy in Picardy." 114–33.

Nichols, Stephen G. "Marie de France's Commonplaces." 134–48.

Camille, Michael. "Gothic Signs and the Surplus: The Kiss on the Cathedral." 151–70.

Thomasset, Claude. "Toward an Understanding of 'Truthfulness' in the French Version of the *Pratique* by Maître Bernard de Gordon." Trans. Sahar Amer. 171–81.

Evans, Beverly J. "Music, Text, and Social Context: Reexamining Thirteenth-Century Styles." 183–95.

Nouvet, Claire. "Dangerous Resemblances: The *Romance of the Rose.*" 196–209.

Berthelot, Anne. "The Other-World Incarnate: 'Chastel Mortel' and 'Chastel des Armes' in the *Perlesvaus.*" Trans. Amy Reed. Translations from the Old French by John Jay Thompson. 210–22.

Cerquiglini-Toulet, Jacqueline. "Fullness and Emptiness: Shortages and Storehouses of Lyric Treasure in the Fourteenth and Fifteenth Centuries." Trans. Christine Cano. Translations from the Middle French by John Jay Thompson. 224–39.

Huot, Sylvia. "The Daisy and the Laurel: Myths of Desire and Creativity in the Poetry of Jean Froissart." 240–51.

Newels, Margarete. "From Narrative Style to Dramatic Style in *Les moralités.*" Trans. Joe Breines. 252–68.

Zink, Michel. "The Time of the Plague and the Order of Writing: Jean le Bel, Froissart, Machaut." Trans. Katherine Lydon. 269–80.

Poirion, Daniel. "Afterword." Trans. Sahar Amer. 281–86.

81 (1992) *On Leiris*

Blanchard, Marc. "Editor's Preface: Michel Leiris (1901–1990) in Perspective." 1–2.

Leiris, Michel. "An Excerpt from *Fourbis.*" Trans. Lydia Davis. 3–20.

Glissant, Edouard. "Michel Leiris: The *Repli* and the *Dépli.*" Trans. Cynthia Mesh. 21–27.

Marmande, Francis. "Michel Leiris: The Letter to Louise." Trans. Abigail S. Rischin. 28–34.

Bailly, Jean-Christophe. "A River with No Novel." Trans. Benjamin Elwood. 35–45.

Nancy, Jean-Luc. "Les iris." Trans. Michael Syrotinski. 46–63.

Hollier, Denis. "Poetry . . . up to Z." Trans. Betsy Wing. 64–76.

Hewitt, Leah D. "Between Movements: Leiris in Literary History." 77–90.

Richman, Michèle. "Leiris's *L'âge d'homme:* Politics and the Sacred in Everyday Ethnography." 91–110.

82 (1993) *Post/Colonial Conditions: Exiles, Migrations, and Nomadisms.* Vol. 1

83 (1993) *Post/Colonial Conditions: Exiles, Migrations, and Nomadisms.* Vol. 2

84 (1994) Boundaries: Writing and Drawing

85 (1994) *Discourses of Jewish Identity in Twentieth-Century France*

Jacobson, David J. "Jews for Genius: The Unholy Disorders of Maurice Sachs." 181–200.

Haddad, Gérard. "Judaism in the Life and Work of Jacques Lacan: A Preliminary Study." Trans. Noah Guynn. 201–16.

Fontenay, Élisabeth de. "On the quant-à-soi." Trans. Françoise Rosset. 217–23.

Ertel, Rachel. "A Minority Literature." Trans. Alan Astro. 224–26.

Avni, Ora. "Patrick Modiano: A French Jew?" 227–47.

Abitbol, Michel. "The Integration of North African Jews in France." Trans. Alan Astro. 248–61.

86 (1994) Corps Mystique, Corps Sacré: Textual Transfigurations of the Body from the Middle Ages to the Seventeenth Century

Jaouën, Françoise, and Benjamin Semple. "Editors' Preface: The Body into Text." 1–4.

Boureau, Alain. "The Sacrality of One's Own Body in the Middle Ages." Trans. Benjamin Semple. 5–17.

Brownlee, Kevin. "Mélusine's Hybrid Body and the Poetics of Metamorphosis." 18–38.

Cantillon, Alain. "Corpus Pascalis." Trans. Françoise Jaouën. 39–55.

Cazelles, Brigitte. "Bodies on Stage and the Production of Meaning." 56–74.

Greene, Thomas M. "The King's One Body in the Balet comique de la royne." 94–108.

Lestringant, Frank. "Travels in Eucharistia: Formosa and Ireland from George Psalmanaazaar to Jonathan Swift." Trans. Noah Guynn. 109–25.

Merlin, Hélène. "Fables of the 'Mystical Body' in Seventeenth-Century France." Trans. Allison Tait. 126–42.

Murray, Timothy. "Philosophical Antibodies: Grotesque Fantasy in a French Stoic Fiction." 143–63.

Semple, Benjamin. "The Male Psyche and the Female Sacred Body in Marie de France and Christine de Pizan." 164–86.

Zanger, Abby. "Making Sweat: Sex and the Gender of National Reproduction in the Marriage of Louis XIII." 187–205.

87 (1995) Another Look, Another Woman: Retranslations of French Feminism

Huffer, Lynne. "Editor's Preface." 1–3.

Irigaray, Luce. "The Question of the Other." Trans. Noah Guynn. 7–19.

Huffer, Lynne. "Luce et veritas: Toward an Ethics of Performance." 20–41.

Jones, Serene. "Divining Women: Irigaray and Feminist Theologies." 42–67.

Kamuf, Peggy. "To Give Place: Semi-Approaches to Hélène Cixous." 68–89.

88 (1995) *Depositions: Althusser, Balibar, Macherey, and the Labor of Reading*

89 (1996) *Drafts*

90 (1996) *Same Sex / Different Text? Gay and Lesbian Writing in French*

Garréta, Anne F. "In Light of Invisibility." 205–13.

Garréta, Anne F., and Josyane Savigneau. "A Conversation." 214–34.

Garréta, Anne F. "A Questionnaire: French Lesbian Writers? [Answers from Monique Wittig, Jocelyne François, and Mireille Best]." 235–41.

Robichon, Suzanne, and Anne F. Garréta. "Select Bibliography of Works in French Related to Lesbian Issues and Problematics." 242–52.

91 (1997) *Genet: In the Language of the Enemy*

Durham, Scott. "Editor's Preface: In the Language of the Enemy." 1–6.

Ross, Kristin. "Schoolteachers, Maids, and Other Paranoid Histories." 7–27.

Weber, Samuel. "Double Take: Acting and Writing in Genet's 'L'étrange mot de . . .'" 28–48.

Conley, Tom. "From Image to Event: Reading Genet through Deleuze." 49–63.

Hardt, Michael. "Prison Time." 64–79.

Lucey, Michael. "Genet's *Notre-Dame-des-Fleurs*: Fantasy and Sexual Identity." 80–102.

Harvey, Robert. "Genet's Open Enemies: Sartre and Derrida." 103–16.

Creech, James. "Outing Jean Genet." 117–140.

Bougon, Patrice. "The Politics of Enmity." Trans. Susan Marson. 141–58.

Durham, Scott. "The Deaths of Jean Genet." 159–184.

92 (1997) *Exploring the Conversible World: Text and Sociability from the Classical Age to the Enlightenment*

Russo, Elena. "Editor's Preface." 1–7.

Viala, Alain. "*Les Signes Galants:* A Historical Reevaluation of *Galanterie.*" Trans. Daryl Lee. 11–29.

Klein, Lawrence E. "The Figure of France: The Politics of Sociability in England, 1660–1715." 30–45.

Force, Pierre. "Self-Love, Identification, and the Origin of Political Economy." 46–64.

Gordon, Daniel. "The City and the Plague in the Age of Enlightenment." 67–87.

Vila, Anne C. "Beyond Sympathy: Vapors, Melancholia, and the Pathologies of Sensibility in Tissot and Rousseau." 88–101.

Jaouën, Françoise. "Civility and the Novel: De Pure's *La prétieuse ou le mystère des ruelles.*" 105–25.

Russo, Elena. "The Self, Real and Imaginary: Social Sentiment in Marivaux and Hume." 126–48.

Pucci, Suzanne Rodin. "The Spectator Surfaces: Tableau and Tabloid in Marivaux's *Spectateur français.*" 149–70.

95 (1999) *Rereading Allegory: Essays in Memory of Daniel Poirion*

JAMES AUSTIN, DARYL LEE, ALYSON WATERS

Yale French Studies
Author Index, 1–95

YFS 97, *50 Years of Yale French Studies, Part 2*, ed. Porter and Waters, © 2000 by Yale University.

Andrew, Dudley. "Sound in France: The Origins of a Native School." 60 (1980): 94–114.

Anglès, Auguste. "Sartre versus Baudelaire." Trans. Charles Messner. 1.2 (Fall–Winter 1948): 119–124.

———. "The Critic: Trends and Temptations." Trans. Charles Messner. 2.1 (Spring–Summer 1949): 3–13.

———. "Aragon the Inopportune." Trans. Henry B. Richardson. 21 (Spring–Summer 1958): 90–94.

Apollinaire, Guillaume. "'Phantom of the Clouds' and 'The Gypsy.'" Trans. Roger Shattuck. 1.2 (Fall–Winter 1948): 50–52.

———. "Pablo Picasso." Trans. Noelle Gillmor. 21 (Spring–Summer 1958): 10.

Archer, Eugene. "Ophuls and the Romantic Tradition." 17 (Summer 1956): 3–5.

Ariès, Philippe. "At the Point of Origin." Trans. Margaret Brooks. 43 (1969): 15–23.

Armstrong, Grace M. "Questions of Inheritance: *Le Chevalier au lion* and *La Queste del Saint Graal.*" 95 (1999): 171–92.

Arnaud, Pierre. "Aftermath—A Young Philosopher's View." Trans. Derek Aiken. 16 (Winter 1955–56): 106–10.

Aron, Raymond. "France: Stability and Instability." Trans. Raymond Giraud. 15 (Winter 1954–55): 17–23.

Aronson, Ronald. "Sartre and the Dialectic: The Purposes of *Critique, II.*" 68 (1985): 85–107.

Aschheim, Kathryn. "Belles-lettres and the University: Diderot's *Plan d'une université ou d'une éducation publique dans toutes les sciences.*" 77 (1990): 61–75.

Ashbery, John. "Drame bourgeois (Poem)." 52 (1975): 3.

Astro, Alan. "Editor's Preface: Jewish Discretion in French Literature [*Discourses of Jewish Identity in Twentieth-Century France*]." 85 (1994): 1–14.

Atkins, Stuart. "Mirages Français—French Literature in German Eyes." 6 (1950): 35–44.

Auerbach, Erich. "Typological Symbolism in Medieval Literature." 9 (1952): 3–10.

Auster, Paul, and Michel Contat. "The Manuscript in the Book: A Conversation." Trans. Alyson Waters. 89 (1996): 160–87.

Austin, Lloyd James. "Modulation and Movement in Valéry's Verse." 44 (1970): 19–38.

Avni, Ora. "Patrick Modiano:A French Jew?" 85 (1994): 227–47.

Avryl [Georges May]. "Words, Initials, Facts and Figures." 15 (Winter 1954–55): 137–43.

———. "'A Great Critic in His Leisure Moments.'" 26 (Fall–Winter 1960–1961): 119–27.

Axelos, Kostas. "Planetary Interlude." Trans. Sally Hess. 41 (1968): 6–18.

———. "The Set's Game-Play of Sets." Trans. Beverly Livingston. 58 (1979): 95–101.

Baelen, Jacqueline van. "Reality and Illusion in *L'autre monde*: The Narrative Voyage." 49 (1974): 178–84.

Baetens, Jan. "Latent Violence (Escher, Franc, Vaughn-James)." Trans. Caren Litherland. 84 (1994): 222–41.

Bailly, Jean-Christophe. "A River with No Novel." Trans. Benjamin Elwood. 81 (1992): 35–45.

Bair, Deirdre. "Simone de Beauvoir: Politics, Language, and Feminist Identity." 72 (1986): 149–62.

———. ["In Memoriam: Simone de Beauvoir."] 72 (1986): 211–15.

Bakhtin, Mikhail. "The Role of Games in Rabelais." Trans. Helene Iswolsky. 41 (1968): 124–32.

Balakian, Anna. "The Post-Surrealism of Aragon and Eluard." 1.2 (Fall–Winter 1948): 93–102.

———. "Apollinaire and the Modern Mind." 2.2 or 4 (1949): 79–90.

———. "André Breton as Philosopher." 31 (May 1964): 37–44.

———. "Breton and Drugs." 50 (1974): 96–107.

Balibar, Etienne. "The Infinite Contradiction." Trans. Jean-Marc Poisson with Jacques Lezra. 88 (1995): 142–64.

Ball, Edward. "The Great Sideshow of the Situationist International." 73 (1987): 21–37.

Bandy, W. T. "New Light on Baudelaire and Poe." 10 (1952): 65–69.

Banfield, Ann. "The Name of the Subject: The 'il'?" 93 (1998): 133–74.

Barber, Elizabeth. "Linguistics [Annotated Bibliography]." 36 & 37 (October 1966): 252–55.

Barko, Carol. "The Dancer and the Becoming of Language." 54 (1977): 173–87.

Barrault, Jean-Louis. "A Barrault Breviary [excerpts from *Cahiers de la Compagnie Madelaine Renaud Jean-Louis Barrault*]." 14 (Winter 1954–55): 104.

———. "The Rehearsal, The Performance." 3.1 or 5 (1950): 3–4.

Barrère, Jean-Bertrand. "Character and Fancy in Victor Hugo." Trans. Beth Brombert. 13 (Spring–Summer 1954): 98–113.

Barthes, Roland. "Writing and Revolution." Trans. June Guicharnaud. 39 (1967): 77–84.

Barzilai, Shuli. "A Review of Paul de Man's 'Review of Harold Bloom's *Anxiety of Influence*.'" 69 (1985): 134–41.

Bastet, N. "*Stratonice* and the Rejection of Tragedy." Trans. Julia Bloch Frey and Rita Winandy. 44 (1970): 128–47.

Bataille, Georges. "Hegel, Death, and Sacrifice." Trans. Jonathan Strauss. 78 (1990): 9–28.

———. "Letter to René Char on the Incompatabilities of the Writer." Trans. Christopher Carsten. 78 (1990): 29–43.

———. "The Reasons for Writing a Book . . . " Trans. Elizabeth Rottenberg. 79 (1991): 11.

———. "Home and Rome, A Device in Epic and Romance: *Le Couronnement de Louis* and *Ille et Galeron*." Trans. Joel H. Reader. 51 (1974): 42–60.

Batany, Jean. "Reflections on the Executioner and the Victim." Trans. Elizabeth Rottenberg. 79 (1991): 15–19.

Bauer, George H. "Just Desserts." 68 (1985): 3–14.

Baym, Max I. "The Garret on the Avenue du Bois: An Essay on Henry Adams and France." 10 (1952): 43–53.

Bays, Gwendolyn M. "Simone de Beauvoir: Ethics and Art." 1.1 (Spring–Summer 1948): 106–112.

———. "Balzac as Seer." 13 (Spring–Summer 1954): 83–92.

———. "Rimbaud—Father of Surrealism?" 31 (May 1964): 45–51.

Beaujour, Michel. "An Introduction to the Theatre of Jean Vauthier." 29 (Spring–Summer 1962): 125–31.

———. "Sartre and Surrealism." 30 (1963): 86–95.

———. "The Stone Age." 31 (May 1964): 61–65.

———. "The Surrealist Map of Love." 32 (October 1964): 124–32.

———. "Peter Weiss and the Futility of Sadism." 35 (December 1965): 114–19.

———. "Flight out of Time: Poetic Language and the Revolution." Trans. Richard Klein. 39 (1967): 29–49.

———. "The Game of Poetics." 41 (1968): 58–67.

———. "The Unicorn in the Carpet." 45 (1970): 52–63.

———. "Introduction [*In Memory of Jacques Ehrmann: Inside Play Outside Game*]." 58 (1979): 6–14.

———. "Some Paradoxes of Description." 61 (1981): 27–59.

Becker, Lucille. "Pessimism and Nihilism in the Plays of Henri de Montherlant." 29 (Spring–Summer 1962): 88–91.

Béguin, Albert. "Poetry and Occultism." Trans. Robert G. Cohn. 2.2 or 4 (1949): 12–25.

Belaval, Yvon. "The Author and Love." 11 (1953?): 5–11.

Ben Aych, Gil. "*The Chant of Being* (Excerpts)." Trans. Alan Astro. 85 (1994): 17–24.

Benamou, Michel. "Romantic Counterpoint: Nature and Style." 25 (Spring 1960): 44–51.

Benrekassa, Georges. "Libertinage and Figurations of Desire: The Legend of a Century." Trans. Sophie Aslanides. 94 (1998): 29–51.

Bensimon, Marc. "The Significance of Eye Imagery in the Renaissance from Bosch to Montaigne." 47 (1972): 266–90.

Bensmaïa, Réda. "The Exiles of Nabile Farès: Or, How to Become a Minority." Trans. Jennifer Curtiss Gage. 83 (1993): 44–70.

Béranger, Jean. "The Illustrious Career of Jean Renoir." Trans. Howard B. Garey. 17 (Summer 1956): 27–37.

———. "Books in French on the Cinema." 17 (Summer 1956): 109–10.

Berger, Harry, Jr. "Conspicuous Exclusion in Vermeer: An Essay in Renaissance Pastoral." 47 (1972): 243–65.

Berthelot, Anne. "The Other-World Incarnate: 'Chastel Mortel' and 'Chastel des Armes' in the *Perlesvaus*." Trans. Amy Reed. Translations from the Old French by John Jay Thompson. Special Issue (1991): 210–22.

Bertocci, Angelo P. "Tensions in the Criticism of Charles Du Bos." 2.1 (Spring–Summer 1949): 79–84.

Besnier, Jean-Michel. "Georges Bataille in the 1930s: A Politics of the Impossible." Trans. Amy Reid. 78 (1990): 169–80.

Bessette, Gérard. "Rêveries Narcotowniennes." Trans. Fredric Jameson. 65 (1983): 256–71.

Bianchi, Pietro. "Henri-Georges Clouzot." Trans. Rigo Mignani. 17 (Summer 1956): 21–26.

Biasi, Pierre-Marc de. "What Is a Literary Draft? Toward a Functional Typology of Genetic Documentation." Trans. Ingrid Wassenaar. 89 (1996): 26–58.

Bieber, Konrad. "*Engagement* as a Professional Risk." 16 (Winter 1955–56): 29–39.

———. "A Do-It-Yourself Novel?" 24 (Summer 1959): 41–47.

———. "Ups and Downs in Elsa Triolet's Prose." 27 (Spring–Summer 1961): 81–85.

Blanchard, Marc "The French Revolution: A Political Line or a Language Circle?" 39 (1967): 64–76.

———. "On Still Life." 61 (1981): 276–98.

———. "Editor's Preface: Michel Leiris (1901–1990) in Perspective [*On Leiris*]." 81 (1992): 1–2.

———. "'N stuff . . . ': Practices, Equipment, Protocols in Twentieth-Century Ethnography." 81 (1992): 111–27.

Blanchot, Maurice. "Symbolism and Bergson." Trans. Joel A. Hunt. 2.2 or 4 (1949): 63–66.

———. "*Adolphe*, or, The Curse of Real Feelings." Trans. Edith Kern. 13 (Spring–Summer 1954): 62–75.

———. "The Main Impropriety (Excerpts)." Trans. June Guicharnaud. 39 (1967): 50–63.

———. "Everyday Speech." Trans. Susan Hanson. 73 (1987): 12–20.

———. "Enigme." 79 (1991): 5–7.

———. "Enigma." Trans. Paul Weidmann. 79 (1991): 8–10.

———. "Glances from Beyond the Grave." Trans. Hilari Allred. 81 (1992): 151–61.

Blend, Charles D. "The Rewards of Tragedy." 18 (Winter 1957): 97–106.

Bloch, Olivier René. "Gassendi and the Transition from the Middle Ages to the Classical Era." Trans. Timothy J. Reiss. 49 (1974): 43–55.

Bloch, R. Howard. "Tristan, the Myth of the State and the Language of the Self." 51 (1974): 61–81.

———. "Silence and Holes: The *Roman de silence* and the Art of the Trouvère." 70 (1986): 81–99.

———. "Medieval French Literature and its Devices." 95 (1999): 237–59

Bloom, Harold. "Napoleon and Prometheus: The Romantic Myth of Organic Energy." 26 (Fall–Winter 1960–1961): 79–82.

———. "Walter Pater: The Intoxication of Belatedness." 50 (1974): 163–89.

Bonnefis, Philippe. "The Melancholic Describer." Trans. Jeremy Raw. 61 (1981): 145–75.

Bonnefoy, Yves. "The Feeling of Transcendency." 31 (May 1964): 135–37.

———. "Transpose or Translate?" 33 (December 1964): 120–26.

———. "The Poetics of Mallarmé." Trans. Elaine Ancekewicz. 54 (1977): 9–21.

———. "Paul de Man." 69 (1985): 17–21. [English translation: 327–30. Trans. Peggy McCracken.]

———. "Poetry and Liberty." Trans. Alfredo Monferré with the collaboration of Yves Bonnefoy. 79 (1991): 255–69.

———. "Overture: The Narrow Path toward the Whole." Trans. John T. Naughton. 84 (1994): 13–16.

Boorsch, Jean. "Sartre's View of Cartesian Liberty." 1.1 (Spring–Summer 1948): 90–96.

———. "The Use of Myths in Cocteau's Theatre." 3.1 or 5 (1950): 75–81.

———. "Romain Gary." 8 (1951): 51–55.

———. "Motion and Rest in *René*." 13 (Spring–Summer 1954): 76–81.

———. "Primary Education." 22 (Winter-Spring 1958–59): 17–46.

———. "Chateaubriand and Napoleon." 26 (Fall–Winter 1960–1961): 55–62.

———. "Hugo's Fraternal Genius." 33 (December 1964): 65–71.

———. "About Some Greek Romances." 38 (May 1967): 72–88.

Bordwell, David. "The Musical Analogy." 60 (1980): 141–56.

Bossis, Mireille. "Methodological Journeys through Correspondences." Trans. Karen McPherson. 71 (1986): 63–75.

Botsford, Keith. "Jean Genet." 8 (1951): 82–92.

Bougon, Patrice. "The Politics of Enmity." Trans. Susan Marson. 91 (1997): 141–58.

Bourdieu, Pierre. "The Invention of the Artist's Life." Trans. Erec R. Koch. 73 (1987): 75–103.

Boureau, Alain. "The Sacrality of One's Own Body in the Middle Ages." Trans. Benjamin Semple. 86 (1994): 5–17.

Bourjea, Serge. "Rhombos. Eye, Dance, Trace: The Writing Process in Valéry's Rough Drafts." Trans. Liliane Greene and Serge Bourjea. 84 (1994): 136–53.

Bowman, Frank. "Irredentist Existentialism: Fondane and Shestov." 16 (Winter 1955–56): 111–17.

———. "Benjamin Constant: Humor and Self-Awareness." 23 (Summer 1959): 100–104.

Brandt, Joan. "The Theory and Practice of a 'Revolutionary' Text: Denis Roche's 'Le mécrit.'" 67 (1984): 203–21.

Braudy, Leo. "Zola on Film: The Ambiguities of Naturalism." 42 (1969): 68–88.

Brée, Germaine. "Time Sequences and Consequences in the Gidian World." 7 (1951): 51–59.

———. "Albert Camus and The Plague." 8 (1951): 93–100.

———. "Georges Neveux: A Theatre of Adventure." 14 (Winter 1954–55): 65–70.

———. "Jalousie: New Blinds of Old." 24 (Summer 1959): 87–90.

———. "A Grain of Salt." 25 (Spring 1960): 41–43.

———. "Proust's Dormant Gods." 38 (May 1967): 183–94.

Brenkman, John. "The Other and the One: Psychoanalysis, Reading, the Symposium." 55 & 56 (1977): 396–456.

Breton, André. "The Situation of Surrealism Between the Two Wars." Trans. Robert Greer Cohn. 1.2 (Fall–Winter 1948): 67–78.

———. "The Situation of Surrealism Between the Two Wars." [excerpt] Trans. Robert Greer Cohn. Reprint from Yale French Studies 1.2 (Fall–Winter 1948). 31 (May 1964): 3–4.

Breunig, L. C. "Picasso's Poets." 21 (Spring–Summer 1958): 3–9.

———. "The Laughter of Apollinaire." 31 (May 1964): 66–73.

Brodsky, Claudia. "'The Impression of Movement': Jean Racine, Architecte." 76 (1989): 162–81.

Brody, Jules. "'Du repentir' (III:2): A Philological Reading." 64 (1983): 238–72.

Brodzki, Bella. "Nomadism and the Textualization of Memory in André Schwarz-Bart's La mulâtresse solitude." 83 (1993): 213–30.

Brombert, Victor. "Camus and the Novel of the 'Absurd.'" 1.1 (Spring–Summer 1948): 119–23.

———. "Stendhal, Analyst or Amorist?" 11 (1953?): 39–48.

———. "T. S. Eliot and the Romantic Heresy." 13 (Spring–Summer 1954): 3–16.

———. "Leopardi versus the Romantic." 13 (Spring–Summer 1954): 119–20.

———. "Raymond Aron and the French Intellectuals." 16 (Winter 1955–56): 13–23.

———. "Malraux: Passion and Intellect." 18 (Winter 1957): 63–76.

————. "Secondary Education." 22 (Winter–Spring 1958–59): 47–78.

————. "'The Renegade' or the Terror of the Absolute." 25 (Spring 1960): 81–84.

————. "Baudelaire: City Images and the 'Dream of Stone.'" 32 (October 1964): 99–105.

————. "Pascal's Happy Dungeon." 38 (May 1967): 230–42.

————. "The Will to Ecstasy: The Example of Baudelaire's 'La chevelure.'" 50 (1974): 55–63.

————. "Sartre, Hugo, a Grandfather." 68 (1985): 73–81.

Brooks, Peter. "Foreword [*The Child's Part*]." 43 (1969): 3.

————. "Toward Supreme Fictions." 43 (1969): 5–14.

————. "Virtue-Tripping: Notes on *Le lys dans la vallée*." 50 (1974): 150–62.

————. "Freud's Masterplot: Questions of Narrative." 55 & 56 (1977): 280–300.

Brooks, Peter, Shoshana Felman, and J. Hillis Miller. "Foreword [*The Lesson of Paul de Man*]." 69 (1985): iii.

Brooks, Peter. "In Memoriam [Paul de Man]." 69 (1985): 4–6.

Brossard, Nicole. "The Textured Angle of Desire." Trans. Barbara Godard. 87 (1995): 105–14.

Browne, Nick. "Film Form/Voice-Over: Bresson's *The Diary of a Country Priest*." 60 (1980): 233–40.

Brownlee, Kevin, and Stephen G. Nichols. "Editor's Preface [*Images of Power: Medieval History/Discourse/Literature*]." 70 (1986): 1–4.

Brownlee, Kevin. "Discourse as *Proueces* in *Aucassin et Nicolette*." 70 (1986): 167–82.

————. "The Image of History in Christine de Pizan's *Livre de la mutacion de Fortune*." Special Issue (1991): 44–56.

————. "Mélusine's Hybrid Body and the Poetics of Metamorphosis." 86 (1994): 18–38.

————. "Pygmalion, Mimesis, and the Multiple Endings of the *Roman de la Rose*." 95 (1999): 193–211.

Bruneau, Jean. "Existentialism and the American Novel." 1.1 (Spring–Summer 1948): 66–72.

Buffum, Imbrie. "The Critical Principles of Paul Claudel." 2.1 (Spring–Summer 1949): 34–42.

Bugbee, Henry G., Jr. "From an American Philosophical Journal." 16 (Winter 1955–56): 89–95.

Buisine, Alain. "The First Eye." Trans. Carla Frecerro. 61 (1981): 261–75.

————. "Crossed Drawings (Rimbaud, Verlaine, and Some Others)." Trans. Madeleine Dobie. 84 (1994): 95–117.

Burgelin, Pierre. "Existentialism and the Tradition of French Thought." 16 (Winter 1955–56): 103–5.

————. "The Second Education of Emile." 28 (Fall–Winter 1961–62): 106–11.

Burt, E. S. "In Memoriam [Paul de Man]." 69 (1985): 10–12.

———. "Developments in Character: Reading and Interpretation in 'The Children's Punishment' and 'The Broken Comb.'" 69 (1985): 192–210.

———. "Mapping City Walks: The Topography of Memory in Rousseau's Second and Seventh *Promenades*." 74 (1988): 231–47.

Burt, E. S., and Janie Vanpée. "Editors' Preface [*Reading the Archive: On Texts and Institutions*]." 77 (1990): 1–4.

Burt, E. S. "Cracking the Code: The Poetical and Political Legacy of Chénier's 'Antique Verse.'" 77 (1990): 210–42.

Burt, Ellen. "Mallarmé's 'Sonnet en yx': The Ambiguities of Speculation." 54 (1977): 55–82.

Butler, Judith. "Sex and Gender in Simone de Beauvoir's *Second Sex*." 72 (1986): 35–49.

———. "'Conscience Doth Make Subjects of Us All.'" 88 (1995): 6–26.

Butor, Michel. "Zola's Blue Flame." Trans. Michael Saklad. 42 (1969): 9–25.

Cahn, Walter. "Medieval Landscape and the Encyclopedic Tradition." Special Issue (1991): 11–24.

Caillois, Roger. "Riddles and Images." Trans. Jeffrey Mehlman. 41 (1968): 148–58.

Calas, Nicolas. "The Rose and the Revolver." 1.2 (Fall–Winter 1948): 106–111.

Calin, Françoise, and William Calin. "Medieval Fiction and New Novel: Some Polemical Remarks on the Subject of Narrative." 51 (1974): 235–50.

Calin, William, and Françoise Calin. "Medieval Fiction and New Novel: Some Polemical Remarks on the Subject of Narrative." 51 (1974): 235–50.

Calleo, David. "Coleridge on Napoleon." 26 (Fall–Winter 1960–1961): 83–93.

Camille, Michael. "Gothic Signs and the Surplus: The Kiss on the Cathedral." Special Issue (1991): 151–70.

Camus, Renaud. *Buena Vista Park, Journal d'un voyage en France, Été, Roman roi, Notes sur les manières du temps* [excerpts]. Trans. Christopher Rivers. Intro. Pierre Force and Dominique Jullien. Special Issue (1988): 285–315.

Cantillon, Alain. "Corpus Pascalis." Trans. Françoise Jaouën. 86 (1994): 39–55.

Carré, Marie-Rose. "René Crevel: Surrealism and the Individual." 31 (May 1964): 74–86.

Carroll, David. "Representation of the End(s) of History: Dialectics and Fiction." 59 (1980): 201–29.

Caruth, Cathy. "The Force of Example: Kant's Symbols." 74 (1988): 17–37.

———. "Unclaimed Experience: Trauma and the Possibility of History." 79 (1991): 181–92.

Casey, Edward S. "Imagination and Repetition in Literature: A Reassessment." 52 (1975): 249–67.

———. "Literary Description and Phenomenological Method." 61 (1981): 176–201.

Cassou, Jean. "Prison Sonnets: XIII." Trans. Kenneth Cornell. 1.2 (Fall–Winter 1948): 92.

Castan, Félix. "The Realm of the Imaginary in Du Bellay/Ronsard and Du Bartas/La Ceppède." Trans. William Franklin Panici. 47 (1972): 110–23.

Cave, Terence C. "Ronsard as Apollo: Myth, Poetry, and Experience in a Renaissance Sonnet-Cycle." 47 (1972): 76–89.

Caws, Mary Ann. "Péret: Plausible Surrealist." 31 (May 1964): 105–11.

———. "Robert Desnos and the Flasks of Night." 50 (1974): 108–19.

———. "Winging It, or Catching Up with Kierkegaard and Some Swans." 66 (1984): 83–90.

Cazelles, Brigitte. "Bodies on Stage and the Production of Meaning." 86 (1994): 56–74.

———. "Arthur as Barbe-Bleue: The Martyrdom of Saint Tryphine (Breton Mystery)." 95 (1999): 134–51.

Cecchi, Annie. "Sartre's Ambiguous Friend." 32 (October 1964): 133–37.

Cerquiglini, Bernard. "The Syntax of Discursive Authority: The Example of Feminine Discourse." Trans. Cynthia Hoffman, David Pelizzari, and Stephen G. Nichols. 70 (1986): 183–98.

Cerquiglini-Toulet, Jacqueline. "Fullness and Emptiness: Shortages and Storehouses of Lyric Treasure in the Fourteenth and Fifteenth Centuries." Trans. Christine Cano. Translations from the Middle French by John Jay Thompson. Special Issue (1991): 224–39.

Certeau, Michel de. "Writing vs. Time: History and Anthropology in the Works of Lafitau." Trans. James Hovde. 59 (1980): 37–64.

Chadbourne, Richard M. "Renan or the Contemptuous Approach to Literature." 2.1 (Spring–Summer 1949): 96–104.

Chadourne, Marc. "Eros and Restif." 11 (1953?): 12–17.

Chambers, Ross. "Poetry in the Asiatic Mode: Baudelaire's 'Au lecteur.'" 74 (1988): 97–116.

Champigny, Robert. "Situation of Jules Laforgue." 9 (1952): 63–73.

———. "Way of Flesh." 11 (1953?): 73–79.

———. "God in Sartrean Light." 12 (Fall–Winter 1953): 81–87.

———. "Theatre in a Mirror: Anouilh." 14 (Winter 1954–55): 57–64.

———. "The Comedy of Ethics." 25 (Spring 1960): 72–74.

———. "Valéry on History and the Novel." 44 (1970): 207–14.

Chapsal, Madeleine. "'To Show, to Demonstrate . . .'" 30 (1963): 30–44.

Char, René. "The Journey is Done." 31 (May 1964): 126.

Charpier, Jacques. "Saint-John Perse and the Fertile Woman." Trans. Neal Oxenhandler. 11 (1953?): 101–5.

Chesneaux, Jean. "Jules Verne's Image of the United States." Trans. Frances Chew. 43 (1969): 111–27.

Chisholm, A. R. "Moods of the Intellect in *Le cimetière marin*." 44 (1970): 72–86.

Chisolm, Lawrence W. "Lu Hsun and Revolution In Modern China." 39 (1967): 226–41.

Cixous, Hélène. "'An Error of Calculation.'" Trans. Eric Prenowitz. 89 (1996): 151–54.

Clark, Charles N. "Love and Time: The Erotic Imagery of Marcel Proust." 11 (1953?): 80–90.

Cockerham, Harry. "Gautier: From Hallucination to Supernatural Vision." 50 (1974): 42–53.

Cocteau, Jean. "Broken Poem for Picasso." Trans. Noelle Gillmor. 21 (Spring–Summer 1958): 14.

Coe, Richard N. "Armand Gatti's Carnival of Compassion: *La deuxième existence du camp de Tatenberg*." 46 (1971): 60–74.

Cogniot, Georges. "France Has Faith in Its Future." Trans. Pierre Barthelémy. 15 (Winter 1954–55): 42–48.

Cohen, Alain. "Proust and the President Schreber: A Theory of Primal Quotation or *For a Psychoanalytics of (-desire-in) Philosophy*." Trans. Catherine Lowe. 52 (1975): 189–205.

Cohn, Robert Greer. "Sartre's First Novel: *La nausée*." 1.1 (Spring–Summer 1948): 62–65.

———. "Sartre-Camus Resartus." 30 (1963): 73–77.

———. "Mallarmé's Windows." 54 (1977): 23–31.

Cohn, Ruby. "The Comedy of Samuel Beckett: 'Something old, something new . . .'" 23 (Summer 1959): 11–17.

———. "Still Novel." 24 (Summer 1959): 48–53.

———. "A Diminishing Difference." 27 (Spring–Summer 1961): 99–105.

———. "Plays and Players in the Plays of Samuel Beckett." 29 (Spring–Summer 1962):43–48.

———. "Surrealism and Today's French Theatre." 31 (May 1964): 159–65.

———. "Black Power on Stage: *Emperor Jones* and *King Christophe*." 46 (1971): 41–47.

Coindreau, Maurice Edgar. "The Evolution of the Contemporary French Theatre." Trans. Joel A. Hunt. 3.1 or 5 (1950): 27–33.

———. "William Faulkner in France." 10 (1952): 85–91.

Colby-Hall, Alice M. "Frustration and Fulfillment: The Double Ending of the *Bel inconnu*." 67 (1984): 120–34.

Coleman, Patrick. "Rousseau and Preromanticism: Anticipation and Oeuvre." 66 (1984): 67–82.

Collignon, Jean. "Theatre and Talking Pictures in France." Trans. Philip Wadsworth and Charlotte Wadsworth. 3.1 or 5 (1950): 34–40.

———. "Gide's Sincerity." 7 (1951): 44–50.

———. "Paris Audiences, Paris Theatres." 14 (Winter 1954–55): 19–22.

———. "Kafka's Humor." 16 (Winter 1955–56): 53–62.

Comay, Rebecca. "Gifts without Presents: Economies of 'Experience' in Bataille and Heidegger." 78 (1990): 66–89.

Compagnon, Antoine. "A Long Short Story: Montaigne's Brevity." Trans. Carla Freccero. 64 (1983): 24–50.

———. "Proust on Racine." Trans. Richard E. Goodkin and Charles G. Gillespie. 76 (1989): 21–58.

Condé, Maryse. "Order, Disorder, Freedom, and the West Indian Writer." 83 (1993): 121–35.

———. "No Woman No Cry." Trans. Karl Britto. 87 (1995): 122–37.

Conley, Tom. "Retz of Love." 61 (1981): 126–44.

———. "Le quotidien météorologique." 73 (1987): 215–28.

———. "From Image to Event: Reading Genet through Deleuze." 91 (1997): 49–63.

Contat, Michel, Denis Hollier, and Jacques Neefs. "Editors' Preface [*Drafts*]." Trans. Alyson Waters. 89 (1996): 1–5.

Contat, Michel, and Paul Auster. "The Manuscript in the Book: A Conversation." Trans. Alyson Waters. 89 (1996): 160–87.

Cook, Bradford. "Jacques Rivière and Symbolism." 9 (1952): 103–11.

———. "Simone Weil: Art and the Artist under God." 12 (Fall–Winter 1953): 73–80.

Cooke, Michael G. "De Quincey, Coleridge, and the Formal Uses of Intoxication." 50 (1974): 26–40.

Cordle, Thomas. "Gide and the Novel of the Egoist." 7 (1951): 91–97.

———. "The Royal Way." 18 (Winter 1957): 20–26.

Cornell, Kenneth. "Audiberti and Obscurity." 2.2 or 4 (1949): 100–104.

———. "Claudel's Plays on the Stage." 3.1 or 5 (1950): 82–87.

———. "George Sand: Emotion and Idea." 13 (Spring–Summer 1954): 93–97.

———. "*Les temps modernes*: Peep Sights across the Atlantic." 16 (Winter 1955–56): 24–28.

———. "The Buffet Enigma." 19 & 20 (Spring 1957–Winter 1958): 94–97.

———. "May 5, 1821 and the Poets." 26 (Fall–Winter 1960–1961): 50–54.

———. "On the Difficulty of a Label." 31 (May 1964): 138–44.

———. "Zola's City." 32 (October 1964): 106–11.

———. "Claudel and the Greek Classics." 38 (May 1967): 195–204.

Couch, John Philip. "Camus and Faulkner: The Search for the Language of Modern Tragedy." 25 (Spring 1960): 120–25.

Courtivron, Isabelle de. "From Bastard to Pilgrim: Rites and Writing for Madame." 72 (1986): 133–48.

Creech, James. "'Chasing after Advances': Diderot's Article 'Encyclopedia.'" 63 (1982): 183–97.

———. "Outing Jean Genet." 91 (1997): 117–140.

Critchley, Simon. "Who Speaks in the Work of Samuel Beckett?" 93 (1998): 114–30.

Crocker, Lester G. "The Priority of Justice or Law." 28 (Fall–Winter 1961–62): 34–42.

Crow, Christine M. "'Teste parle': The question of a potential artist in Valéry's *M. Teste*." 44 (1970): 157–68.

Crowley, Roseline. "Toward the Poetics of Juxtaposition: 'L'après-midi d'un faune.'" 54 (1977): 32–44.

Culler, Jonathan. "Reading Lyric." 69 (1985): 98–106.

Curtis, D. E. "Pierre Bayle and the Range of Cartesian Reason." 49 (1974): 71–81.

Cusset, Catherine. "A Different Measure of Time: Writing or the Consciousness of Pleasure: Interview with Philippe Sollers." Trans. Marie-Anne Fleming. Special Issue (1988): 155–62.

———. "Editor's Preface: The Lesson of Libertinage [*Libertinage and Modernity*]." 94 (1998): 1–14.

D. Z. H. "Thibaudet, or the Critic as Mediator." 2.1 (Spring–Summer 1949): 74–78.

Daladier, Edouard. "Europe after the Ratification of the London and Paris Agreements." Trans. Kenneth Cornell. 15 (Winter 1954–55): 38–41.

Danahy, Michael. "Marceline Desbordes-Valmore and the Engendered Canon." 75 (1988): 129–47.

Darzins, John. "Malraux and the Destruction of Aesthetics." 18 (Winter 1957): 107–13.

———. "Transparence in Camus and Kafka." 25 (Spring 1960): 98–103.

Davies, Howard. "*Les mots* as *Essai sur le don*: Contribution to an Origin Myth." 68 (1985): 57–72.

Davis, Lennard J. "Wicked Actions and Feigned Words: Criminals, Criminality, and the Early English Novel." 59 (1980): 106–18.

Dawson, Deidre. "In Search of the Real Pangloss: The Correspondence of Voltaire with the Duchess of Saxe-Gotha." 71 (1986): 93–112.

Dayan, Joan. "France Reads Haiti: An Interview with René Depestre." 83 (1993): 136–53.

———. "France Reads Haiti: René Depestre's *Hadriana dans tous mes rêves*." 83 (1993): 154–75.

De Ley, Herbert. "Two Modes of Thought in *L'astrée*." 49 (1974): 143–53.

de Man, Paul. "Action and Identity in Nietzsche." 52 (1975): 16–30.

———. "The Resistance to Theory." 63 (1982): 3–20.

———. "'Conclusions' on Walter Benjamin's 'The Task of the Translator.'" Ed. William D. Jewett. 69 (1985): 25–46.

———. "The Double Aspect of Symbolism." 74 (1988): 3–16.

———. "Roland Barthes and the Limits of Structuralism." 77 (1990): 177–90.

Dean, Carolyn J. "Claude Cahun's Double." 90 (1996): 71–92.

Debrix, Jean. "Cinema and Poetry." 17 (Summer 1956): 86–104.

Defaux, Gérard. "Editor's Preface [*Montaigne: Essays in Reading*]." Trans. John Gallucci. 64 (1983): iii–viii.

———. "Readings of Montaigne." Trans. John A. Gallucci. 64 (1983): 73–92.

———. "The Case of *Bérénice*: Racine, Corneille and Mimetic Desire." Trans. Michael Metteer. 76 (1989): 211–39.

Deguy, Michel. "Complications, Intricacies." Trans. Janie Vanpee and Marie-Rose Logan. 52 (1975): 303–10.

DeJean, Joan. "*La nouvelle Héloïse*, or the Case for Pedagogical Deviation." 63 (1982): 98–116.

———. "No Man's Land: The Novel's First Geography." 73 (1987): 175–89.

DeJean, Joan, and Nancy K. Miller. "Editors' Preface [*The Politics of Tradition: Placing Women in French Literature*]." 75 (1988): 1–6.

DeJean, Joan. "Classical Reeducation: Decanonizing the Feminine." 75 (1988): 26–39.

———. "Sappho, c'est moi, selon Racine: Coming of Age in Neo-Classical Theater." 76 (1989): 3–20.

Delattre, André. "Personal Notes on Paul Eluard." 1.2 (Fall–Winter 1948): 103–5.

Delattre, Geneviève. "Mirrors and Masks in the World of Françoise Mallet-Joris." 27 (Spring–Summer 1961): 121–26.

Deleuze, Gilles. "The Fold." Trans. Jonathan Strauss. 80 (1991): 227–47.

Delft, Louis van. "Language and Power: Eyes and Words in *Brittanicus*." Trans. Paul Schwartz. 45 (1970): 102–12.

Delphy, Christine. "The Invention of French Feminism: An Essential Move." 87 (1995): 190–221.

Dembowski, Peter F. "Monologue, Author's Monologue and Related Problems in the Romances of Chrétien de Troyes." 51 (1974): 102–14.

Demorest, Jean-Jacques. "Pascal and the Querelle." 38 (May 1967): 243–50.

Demure, Catherine. "Montaigne: The Paradox and the Miracle—Structure and Meaning in 'The Apology for Raymond Sebond' (*Essais* II:12)." Trans. Dianne Sears. 64 (1983): 188–208.

Denis, Romain et al. "Offstage." Trans. Wyley L. Powell. 46 (1971): 149–53.

Derrida, Jacques. "Freud and the Scene of Writing." Trans. Jeffrey Mehlman. 48 (1972): 74–117.

———. "The Purveyor of Truth." Trans. Willis Domingo, James Hulbert, Moshe Ron, and Marie-Rose Logan. 52 (1975): 31–113.

———. "Scribble (Writing-Power)." Trans. Cary Plotkin. 58 (1979): 116–47.

———. "All Ears: Nietzsche's Otobiography." Trans. Avital Ronell. 63 (1982): 245–50.

———. "In Memoriam [Paul de Man]." 69 (1985): 13–16. [English translation: 323–26. Trans. Kevin Newmark with the approval of the author.]

———. "Sendoffs." Ed. Deborah Esch and Thomas Keenan. Trans. Thomas Pepper. 77 (1990): 7–43.

———. "Maddening the Subjectile." Trans. Mary Ann Caws. 84 (1994): 154–71.

des Forêts, Louis-René. *Ostinato* [excerpt]. Trans. Joaniko Kohchi. Intro. Rindala El-Khoury. Special Issue (1988): 77–95.

Dickstein, Morris. "The Faith of a Vicar: Reason and Morality in Rousseau's Religion." 28 (Fall–Winter 1961–62): 48–54.

Didier, Pierre. "Bernanos' World." 8 (1951): 101–7.

Dieckmann, Herbert. "French Existentialism before Sartre." 1.1 (Spring–Summer 1948): 33–41.

———. "André Gide and the Conversion of Charles Du Bos." 12 (Fall–Winter 1953): 62–72.

Dietemann, Margaret. "Departure from the Absurd: Adamov's Last Plays." 46 (1971): 48–59.

Djebar, Assia. "The White of Algeria." With an introduction by Clarisse Zimra. Trans. Andrew Benson. 87 (1995): 138–48.

Doane, Mary Ann. "The Voice in the Cinema: The Articulation of Body and Space." 60 (1980): 33–50.

Dobbs, Annie-Claude. "The Problematics of Space in Julien Gracq: Fiction and Narration in a Chapter of *Au château d'Argol*." Trans. Kathleen Flosi Good. 57 (1979): 86–108.

Donato, Eugenio. "Ending/Closure: On Derrida's Edging of Heidegger." 67 (1984): 3–22.

Doolittle, James. "Criticism as Creation in the Work of Diderot." 2.1 (Spring–Summer 1949): 14–23.

Dorival, Bernard. "Painting Today: Principles and Practitioners." Trans. Kenneth Douglas. 19 & 20 (Spring 1957-Winter 1958): 7–14.

Dort, Bernard. "Are These Novels 'Innocent'?" Trans. Kenneth Douglas. 24 (Summer 1959): 22–29.

Doubrovsky, Serge. "Ionesco and the Comedy of Absurdity." 23 (Summer 1959): 3–10.

———. "Sartre and Camus: A Study in Incarceration." 25 (Spring 1960): 85–92.

———. "New Critics and Old Myths." 38 (May 1967): 18–26.

Douglas, Kenneth. "René Char." 1.2 (Fall–Winter 1948): 79–84.

———. "Blanchot and Sartre." 2.1 (Spring–Summer 1949): 85–95.

———. "A Note on Mallarmé and the Theatre." 3.1 or 5 (1950): 108–112.

———. *A Critical Bibliography of Existentialism (The Paris School)*. Special Monograph no. 1. (1950).

———. "Sartre and the Self-Inflicted Wound." 9 (1952): 123–31.

———. "French-English Theatre Vocabulary." 14 (Winter 1954–55): 98–101.

———. "As Others See U.S." 15 (Winter 1954–55): 129–36.

———. "Film Facts and Figures." 17 (Summer 1956): 107–8.

Douthat, Blossom Margaret. "Nietzschean Motifs in *Temptation of the Occident*." 18 (Winter 1957): 77–86.

———. "Francis Ponge's Untenable Goat." 21 (Spring–Summer 1958): 172–81.

Dragonetti, Roger. "'Le Nénuphar blanc': A Poetic Dream with Two Unknowns." Trans. Kathryn Crecelius. 54 (1977): 118–39.

———. "The Double Play of Arnaut Daniel's *Sestina* and Dante's *Divina Commedia*." Trans. Timothy Bahti. 55 & 56 (1977): 227–52.

———. "Joufroi, Count of Poitiers and Lord of Cocaigne." Trans. Karen McPherson. 67 (1984): 95–119.

Drake, Stillman. "Galileo's Language: Mathematics and Poetry in a New Science." 49 (1974): 13–27.

Dubost, Jean-Pierre. "Libertinage and Rationality: From the 'Will to Knowledge' to Libertine Textuality." 94 (1998): 52–78.

Duby, Georges. "Memories With No Historian." Trans. Jennifer Wicke and Dan Moschenberg. 59 (1980): 7–16.

Duchesne-Guillemin, Jacques. "'Introduction to 'La jeune Parque.''" Trans. Emmett Gossen. 44 (1970): 87–105.

Duchet, Claude. "The Object-Event of the Ram's Charge: An Ideological Reading of an Image." Trans. J. Ellen Evans and Wendy Greenberg. 59 (1980): 155–74.

Dunn, Kevin. "'A Great City is a Great Solitude': Descartes's Urban Pastoral." 80 (1991): 93–107.

Durán, Manuel. "Camus and the Spanish Theatre." 25 (Spring 1960): 126–31.

Durand, Marion. "One Hundred Years of Illustrations in French Children's Books." Trans. Diana Wormuth. 43 (1969): 85–96.

Duras, Marguerite. *Un barrage contre le Pacifique* [excerpt]. Trans. Herma Briffault. *Le ravissement de Lol V. Stein* [excerpt]. Trans. Richard Seaver. *L'amant* [excerpt]. Trans. Barbara Bray. *La vie matérielle* [excerpt]. Trans. Lauren Doyle-McCombs. Intro. Catherine Cusset. Trans. Deidre Dawson. Special Issue (1988): 61–76.

Durham, Scott. "Editor's Preface: In the Language of the Enemy [*Genet: In the Language of the Enemy*]." 91 (1997): 1–6.

———. "The Deaths of Jean Genet." 91 (1997): 159–184.

Duval, Edwin M. "Lessons of the New World: Design and Meaning in Montaigne's 'Des cannibales' (I:31) and 'Des coches' (III:6)." 64 (1983): 95–112.

———. "The Place of the Present: Ronsard, Aubigné, and the 'Misères de ce temps.'" 80 (1991): 13–29.

Duverger, Maurice. "Generations in Conflict." Trans. Alvis Tinnin. 15 (Winter 1954–55): 12–16.

Echenoz, Jean. *L'équipée malaise* [excerpt]. Trans. Mark Polizzotti. Intro. Dominique Jullien. Special Issue (1988): 337–51.

Echevarría, Roberto González. "Threats in Calderón: *Life Is a Dream* 1, 303–8." 69 (1985): 180–91.

Ehrmann, Jacques. "Camus and the Existentialist Venture." 25 (Spring 1960): 93–97.

———. "Simone de Beauvoir and the Related Destinies of Woman and Intellectual." 27 (Spring–Summer 1961): 26–32.

———. "Genet's Dramatic Metamorphosis: From Appearance to Freedom." 29 (Spring–Summer 1962): 33–42.

———. "Of Rats and Men: Notes on the Prefaces." 30 (1963): 78–85.

———. "Introduction [*Structuralism*]." 36 & 37 (October 1966): 5–9.

———. "Structures of Exchange in *Cinna*." Trans. Joseph H. McMahon. 36 & 37 (October 1966): 169–99.

———. "Selected General Bibliography [*Structuralism*]." 36 & 37 (October 1966): 270.

———. "Foreword [*Literature and Revolution*]." 39 (1967): 5–8.

———. "On Articulation: The Language of History and the Terror of Language." Trans. Barry Lydgate. 39 (1967): 9–28.

———. "Introduction [*Game, Play, Literature*]." 41 (1968): 5.

———. "Homo Ludens Revisited." Trans. Cathy Lewis and Phil Lewis. 41 (1968): 31–57.

———. "The Tragic/Utopian Meaning of History." Trans. Jay Caplan. 58 (1979): 15–30.

———. "Selections from *Texts II*." Trans. M[ichel] B[eaujour]. 58 (1979): 31–43.

———. "About origin . . . " Trans. M[ichel] B[eaujour]. 58 (1979): 44–54.

Ellison, David R. "Narrative and Music in Kafka and Blanchot: The 'Singing' of Josefine." 93 (1990): 196–218.

Éluard, Paul. "To Pablo Picasso." Trans. Noelle Gillmor. 21 (Spring–Summer 1958): 11–12.

———. "Victory at Guernica." Trans. Noelle Gillmor. 21 (Spring–Summer 1958): 12–13.

Emery, Léon. "Rousseau and the Foundations of Human Regeneration." 28 (Fall–Winter 1961–62): 3–12.

Enders, Jody. "Memory, Allegory, and the Romance of Rhetoric." 95 (1999): 49–64.

Erickson, John D. "Cheikh Hamidou Kane's *L'aventure ambiguë*." 53 (1976): 92–101.

Ertel, Rachel. "A Minority Literature." Trans. Alan Astro. 85 (1994): 224–26.

Etiemble. "Constant Rey-Millet." Trans. Phyllis Berla. 19 & 20 (Spring 1957–Winter 1958): 75–77.

———. "The Tibetan Dog." 31 (May 1964): 127–34.

Evans, Beverly J. "Music, Text, and Social Context: Reexamining Thirteenth-Century Styles." Special Issue (1991): 183–95.

Evans, Martha Noel. "Murdering *L'invitée*: Gender and Fictional Narrative." 72 (1986): 67–86.

Exner, Richard. "A Note on Post-War German Poetry." 21 (Spring–Summer 1958): 135–44.

Farmer, R. L. See Lamont, Rosette C.

Fassler, Margot. "Representations of Time in *Ordo representacionis Ade*." Special Issue (1991): 97–113.

Fauve, Jacques. "A Drama of Essence: Salacrou and Others." 14 (Winter 1954–55): 30–40.

Felman, Shoshana. "Madness and Philosophy *or* Literature's Reason." 52 (1975): 206–28.

———. "Foreword [*Literature and Psychoanalysis: The Question of Reading: Otherwise*]." 55 & 56 (1977): 2.

———. "To Open the Question." 55 & 56 (1977): 5–10.

———. "Turning the Screw of Interpretation." 55 & 56 (1977): 94–207.

———. "Rereading Femininity." 62 (1981): 19–44.

———. "Psychoanalysis and Education: Teaching Terminable and Interminable." 63 (1982): 21–44.

Felman, Shoshana, Peter Brooks, and J. Hillis Miller. "Foreword [*The Lesson of Paul de Man*]." 69 (1985): iii.

Felman, Shoshana. "In Memoriam [Paul de Man]." 69 (1985): 8–9.

———. "Postal Survival, or The Question of the Navel." 69 (1985): 49–72.

———. "In an Era of Testimony: Claude Lanzmann's *Shoah*." 79 (1991): 39–81.

Felperin, Howard. "The Anxiety of Deconstruction." 69 (1985): 254–66.

Ferrer, Daniel. "Clementis's Cap: Retroaction and Persistence in the Genetic Process." Trans. Marlena G. Corcoran. 89 (1996): 223–36.

Fichera, Virginia M. "Simone de Beauvoir and 'The Woman Question': *Les bouches inutiles*." 72 (1986): 51–64.

Fink, Eugen. "The Oasis of Happiness: Toward an Ontology of Play." Trans. Ute Saine and Thomas Saine. 41 (1968): 19–30.

Fitz, Brewster E. "Desire and Interpretation: Marie de France's 'Chievrefoil.'" 58 (1979): 182–89.

Fleischman, Cyrille. "Two from *The Main Attraction*." Trans. Alan Astro. 85 (1994): 25–31.

Fleischman, Suzanne. "Evaluation in Narrative: The Present Tense in Medieval 'Performed Stories.'" 70 (1986): 199–251.

Flescher, Jacqueline. "The Language of Nonsense in *Alice*." 43 (1969): 128–44.

Fontenay, Élisabeth de. "On the quant-à-soi." Trans. Françoise Rosset. 85 (1994): 217–23.

Force, Pierre. "Self-Love, Identification, and the Origin of Political Economy." 92 (1997): 46–64.

Fort, Bernadette. "Accessories of Desire: On Indecency in a Few Paintings by Jean-Baptiste Greuze." 94 (1998): 146–62.

Fourny, Jean-François. "Laziness and Technology according to a Storyteller of Cairo." 82 (1993): 158–71.

Fowlie, Wallace. "Existentialist Hero: A Study of L'âge de raison." 1.1 (Spring–Summer 1948): 53–61.

———. "Mystery of the Actor." 3.1 or 5 (1950): 5–11.

———. "Legacy of Symbolism." 9 (1952): 20–26.

———. "The French Theatre and the Concept of Communion." 14 (Winter 1954–55): 23–29.

———. "René Char and the Poet's Vocation." 21 (Spring–Summer 1958): 83–89.

Francastel, Pierre. "Criticism and the History of Painting in the Twentieth Century." Trans. Derek Aiken. 19 & 20 (Spring 1957-Winter 1958): 98–106.

Frank, Bernard. "An Age of Excess (Excerpts)." Trans. Alan Astro. 85 (1994): 32–40.

Frappier-Mazur, Lucienne. "Marginal Canons: Rewriting the Erotic." 75 (1988): 112–28.

———. "Sadean Libertinage and the Esthetics of Violence." 94 (1998): 184–98.

Frey, Hans-Jost. "The Tree of Doubt." 54 (1977): 45–54.

———. "Undecidability." Trans. Robert Livingston. 69 (1985): 124–33.

———. "Spume." Trans. Bruce Lawder. 74 (1988): 249–60.

———. "The Last Man and the Reader." Trans. Georgia Albert. 93 (1998): 252–79.

Friedman, Geraldine. "The Spectral Legacy of Althusser: The Symptom and Its Return." 88 (1995): 165–82.

Friedman, Melvin. "Valery Larbaud: The Two Traditions of Eros." 11 (1953?): 91–100.

Frohock, W. M. "Camus: Image, Influence and Sensibility." 2.2 or 4 (1949): 91–99.

———. "André Malraux: The Intellectual as Novelist." 8 (1951): 26–37.

———. "Georges Bernanos and his Priest-Hero." 12 (Fall–Winter 1953): 54–61.

———. "Panurge as Comic Character." 23 (Summer 1959): 71–76.

———. "Introduction to Butor." 24 (Summer 1959): 54–61.

———. "The 'Picaresque' in France before Gil Blas." 38 (May 1967): 222–29.

Froula, Christine. "Modernity, Drafts, Genetic Criticism: On the Virtual Lives of James Joyce's Villanelle." 89 (1996): 113–29.

Frye, Northrop. "Three Meanings of Symbolism." 9 (1952): 11–19.

Gaillard, Françoise. "An Unspeakable (Hi)story." Trans. Timothy J. Reiss. 59 (1980): 137–54.

Galand, R. "T. S. Eliot and the Impact of Baudelaire." 6 (1950): 27–34.

Gallais, Pierre. "Hexagonal and Spiral Structure in Medieval Narrative." Trans. Vincent Pollina. 51 (1974): 115–32.

Gallop, Jane. "The Immoral Teachers." 63 (1982): 117–28.

Gandelman, Claude. "The Artist as 'Traumarbeiter': On Sketches of Dreams by Marcel Proust." 84 (1994): 118–35.

García-Abrines, Luis. "Rebirth of Buñuel." Trans. Daniel de Guzmán. 17 (Summer 1956): 54–66.

Garréta, Anne F. "In Light of Invisibility." 90 (1996): 205–13.

Garréta, Anne F., and Josyane Savigneau. "A Conversation." 90 (1996): 214–34.

Garréta, Anne F. "A Questionnaire: French Lesbian Writers? [Answers from Monique Wittig, Jocelyne François, and Mireille Best]." 90 (1996): 235–41.

Garréta, Anne F., and Suzanne Robichon. "Select Bibliography of Works in French Related to Lesbian Issues and Problematics." 90 (1996): 242–52.

Gasché, Rodolphe. "The Falls of History: Huysmans's *A rebours*." 74 (1988): 183–204.

Gaudin, Colette, Mary Jean Green, Lynn Anthony Higgins, Marianne Hirsch, Vivian Kogan, Claudia Reeder, and Nancy Vickers. "Introduction [*Feminist Readings: French Texts/American Contexts*]." 62 (1981): 2–18.

Gaudon, Jean. "One of Victor Hugo's Discarded Drafts." 89 (1996): 130–48.

Gaudon, Sheila. "On Editing Victor Hugo's Correspondence." 71 (1986): 177–98.

Gauvin, Lise. "From Octave Crémazie to Victor-Lévy Beaulieu: Language, Literature, and Ideology." Trans. Emma Henderson. 65 (1983): 30–49.

Gearhart, Suzanne. "Reading *De l'esprit des lois*: Montesquieu and the Principles of History." 59 (1980): 175–200.

Gelfand, Elissa. "Imprisoned Women: Toward a Socio-Literary Feminist Analysis." 62 (1981): 185–203.

Genette, Gérard. "'One of My Favourite Writers.'" Trans. Ingrid Wassenaar. 89 (1996): 208–22.

Gershman, Herbert S. "L'Affaire Pastoureau." 31 (May 1964): 154–58.

———. "Valéry and Breton." 44 (1970): 199–206.

Gezari, Janet K., and W. K. Wimsatt. "Vladimir Nabokov: More Chess Problems and the Novel." 58 (1979): 102–15.

Giamatti, A. Bartlett. "In Memoriam [Paul de Man]." 69 (1985): 6.

Gibbon, Edward, et al. "City of Fact, City of Fable: An Early Portrait." 32 (October 1964): 5–11.

Gilman, Margaret. "Revival and Revolution in English and French Romantic Poetry." 6 (1950): 14–26.

Girard, René. "The Role of Eroticism in Malraux's Fiction." 11 (1953?): 49–54.

———. "Existentialism and Literary Criticism." 16 (Winter 1955–56): 45–52.

———. "Man, Myth and Malraux." 18 (Winter 1957): 55–62.

———. "Pride and Passion in the Contemporary Novel." 24 (Summer 1959): 3–10.

———. "Memoirs of a Dutiful Existentialist." 27 (Spring–Summer 1961): 41–46.

Giraud, Raymond. "Maulnier: In and above the Conflict." 14 (Winter 1954–55): 79–84.

———. "Unrevolt Among the Unwriters in France Today." 24 (Summer 1959): 11–17.

———. "Rousseau's Happiness—Triumph or Tragedy?" 28 (Fall–Winter 1961–62): 75–82.

———. "Stendhal's 'Greatest Bard.'" 33 (December 1964): 46–52.

———. "The First *Justine*." 35 (December 1965): 39–47.

———. "Winckelmann's Part in Gautier's Perception of Classical Beauty." 38 (May 1967): 172–82.

Giroud, Françoise. "The Second Sex." 27 (Spring–Summer 1961): 22–25.

Glissant, Edouard. "Michel Leiris: The *Repli* and the *Dépli*." Trans. Cynthia Mesh. 81 (1992): 21–27.

Gobin, Pierre. "Michel Tremblay: An Interweave of Prose and Drama." Trans. Richard Deshaies. 65 (1983): 106–23.

Godfrey, Sima. "Editor's Preface [*The Anxiety of Anticipation*]." 66 (1984): iii–ix.

———. "The Anxiety of Anticipation: Ulterior Motives in French Poetry." 66 (1984): 1–26.

Godin, Jean-Cléo. "Anne Hébert: Rebirth in the Word." Trans. Rosemary Brown. 45 (1970): 137–53.

Goguel, François. "The Historical Background of Contemporary French Politics." Trans. Marianna Carlson. 15 (Winter 1954–55): 30–37.

Goitein, Denise. "Nathalie Sarraute as Dramatist." 46 (1971): 102–12.

Gombrowicz, Witold. "Journal Excerpts." Trans. June Guicharnaud. 39 (1967): 200–209.

———. "Operetta." Trans. June Guicharnaud. 39 (1967): 210–14.

Gomery, Douglas. "Economic Struggle and Hollywood Imperialism: Europe Converts to Sound." 60 (1980): 80–93.

Goodkin, Richard E. "A Choice of Andromache's." 67 (1984): 225–47.

———. "Zeno's Paradox: Mallarmé, Valéry, and the Symbolist 'Movement.'" 74 (1988): 133–56.

———. "Editor's Preface [*Autour de Racine: Studies in Intertextuality*]." 76 (1989): iii–v.

———. "*Killing Order(s)*: Iphigenia and the Direction of Tragic Intertextuality." 76 (1989): 81–107.

———. "T(r)yptext: Proust, Mallarmé, Racine." 76 (1989): 284–314.

Gorbman, Claudia. "Narrative Film Music." 60 (1980): 183–203.

———. "Bibliography on Sound in Film." 60 (1980): 269–86.

Gordon, Daniel. "The City and the Plague in the Age of Enlightenment." 92 (1997): 67–87.

Gossman, Lionel. "Prévost's *Manon*: Love in the New World." 40 (1968): 91–102.

Goulemot, Jean-Marie. "Toward a Definition of Libertine Fiction and Pornographic Novels." Trans. Arthur Greenspan. 94 (1998): 133–45.

Goux, Jean-Joseph. "General Economics and Postmodern Capitalism." Trans. Kathryn Aschheim and Rhonda Garelick. 78 (1990): 206–24.

Graham, Joseph. "Time and Place for Criticism." 58 (1979): 84–94.

Grassi, Marie-Claire. "Friends and Lovers (or The Codification of Intimacy)." Trans. Neil Gordon. 71 (1986): 77–92.

Grecco, Stephen R. "High Hopes: Eugene O'Neill and Alcohol." 50 (1974): 142–49.

Greeman, Richard. "'The Laws Are Burning': Literary and Revolutionary Realism in Victor Serge." 39 (1967): 146–59.

Green, Mary Jean, Colette Gaudin, Lynn Anthony Higgins, Marianne Hirsch, Vivian Kogan, Claudia Reeder, and Nancy Vickers. "Introduction [*Feminist Readings: French Texts/American Contexts*]." 62 (1981): 2–18.

Green, Mary Jean. "Structures of Liberation: Female Experience and Autobiographical Form in Québec." 65 (1983): 124–36.

Greene, Naomi. "Antonin Artaud: Metaphysical Revolutionary." 39 (1967): 188–97.

Greene, Thomas M. "Styles of Experience in Scève's *Delie*." 47 (1972): 57–75.

———. "Dangerous Parleys—*Essais* I:5 and 6." 64 (1983): 3–23.

———. "The End of Discourse in Machiavelli's *Prince*." 67 (1984): 57–71.

———. "The King's One Body in the *Balet comique de la royne*." 86 (1994): 75–93.

Greimas, A. J., and François Rastier. "The Interaction of Semiotic Constraints." 41 (1968): 86–105.

Grene, Marjorie. "Sartre's Theory of Emotions." 1.1 (Spring–Summer 1948): 97–101.

Grimsley, Ronald. "Rousseau as a Critic of Society." 40 (1968): 5–17.

Grosjean, Jean. "Two Poems from *Fils de l'homme* ["Final Instance," "The Counsel of Woman"]." Trans. Blanche Price. 21 (Spring–Summer 1958): 30–31.

Gross, David S. "Sartre's (Mis)Reading of Flaubert's Politics: An Unacknowledged Dialectic of Misanthropy and Utopian Desire." 68 (1985): 127–51.

Gross, Mark. "*Bajazet* and Intertextuality." 76 (1989): 146–61.

Grossvogel, David I. "The Play of Light and Shadow: A Directional Error." 17 (Summer 1956): 75–85.

———. "Pierre Reverdy: The Fabric of Reality." 21 (Spring–Summer 1958): 95–106.

———. "The Depths of Laughter: The Subsoil of a Culture." 23 (Summer 1959): 63–70.

Grubbs, Henry A. "The Essence of Poetry: A Concept and a Dilemma." 2.1 (Spring–Summer 1949): 43–52.

Guerlac, Suzanne. "Lautréamont-Ducasse: At the Edge." 74 (1988): 117–31.

———. "'Recognition' by a Woman!: A Reading of Bataille's *L'érotisme*." 78 (1990): 90–105.

Guetti, Barbara Jones. "The Old Régime and the Feminist Revolution: Laclos' *De l'éducation des femmes*." 63 (1982): 139–62.

———. "'Travesty' and 'Usurpation' in Mme de Lafayette's Historical Fiction." 69 (1985): 211–21.

Guggenheim, Michel. "Gide and Montaigne." Trans. Richard Strawn. 7 (1951): 107–14.

———. "*Aimez-vous Brahms*: Solitude and the Quest for Happiness." 24 (Summer 1959): 91–95.

Guicharnaud, Jacques. "Raymond Queneau's Universe." 8 (1951): 38–47.

———. "Jean Vilar and the TNP." 14 (Winter 1954–55): 10–18.

———. "Songs of a Season." 14 (Winter 1954–55): 76–78.

———. "Those Years: Existentialism 1943–1945." Trans. Kevin Neilson. 16 (Winter 1955–56): 127–45.

———. "Of Grisbi, Chnouf and Rififi." Trans. Cynthia Goldman. 17 (Summer 1956): 6–13.

———. "Renoir's Latest." 17 (Summer 1956): 105–6.

———. "Vowels of the Sea: 'Amers,' by Saint-John Perse." Trans. June Beckelman. 21 (Spring–Summer 1958): 72–82.

———. "Souvenirs of a Greenhorn." 22 (Winter-Spring 1958–59): 83–88.

———. "Higher Education." 22 (Winter-Spring 1958–59): 89–115.

———. "Remembrance of Things Passing: Claude Simon." Trans. June Beckelman. 24 (Summer 1959): 101–8.

———. "Woman's Fate: Marguerite Duras." Trans. June Beckelman. 27 (Spring–Summer 1961): 106–13.

———. "Forbidden Games: Arrabal." 29 (Spring–Summer 1962): 116–20.

———. "The Wreathed Columns of St. Peter's." 35 (December 1965): 29–38.

———. "Beware of Happiness: Mairet's *Sophonisbe*." 38 (May 1967): 205–21.

———. "Foreword [*From Stage to Street*]." 46 (1971): 3–4.

———. "The Terrorist Marivaudage of Marguerite Duras." 46 (1971): 113–24.

Guizot, François. "A Stage for Man Alone." 33 (December 1964): 26–32.

Gumbrecht, Hans Ulrich. "Literary Translation and Its Social Conditioning in the Middle Ages: Four Spanish Romance Texts of the Thirteenth Century." Trans. Helga Bennett. 51 (1974): 205–22.

Guth, Paul. "Encounter with Germaine Richier." Trans. Neil Chapman. 19 & 20 (Spring 1957-Winter 1958): 78–84.

Gutwirth, Marcel. "'By Diverse Means . . . ' (I:1)." 64 (1983): 180–87.

Guy, Basil. "Toward an Appreciation of the *abbé de cour*." 40 (1968): 77–90.

Habasque, Guy. "Notes on a New Trend: Multidimensional Animated Works." Trans. Mona Tobin. 19 & 20 (Spring 1957–Winter 1958): 35–44.

Hackett, C. A. "Valéry and the Swans." 44 (1970): 148–56.

Haddad, Gérard. "Judaism in the Life and Work of Jacques Lacan: A Preliminary Study." Trans. Noah Guynn. 85 (1994): 201–16.

Haidu, Peter. "Introduction [*Approaches to Medieval Romance*]." 51 (1974): 3–11.

———. "Narrativity and Language in Some Twelfth Century Romances." 51 (1974): 133–46.

Haig, Stirling. "Vigny and *Othello*." 33 (December 1964): 53–64.

Hajdukowski-Ahmed, Maroussia. "The Unique, Its Double, and the Multiple: The Carnivalesque Hero in the Québécois Novel." Trans. Jan Marta. 65 (1983): 139–53.

Hale, Thomas A. "Structural Dynamics in a Third World Classic: Aimé Césaire's *Cahier d'un retour au pays natal*." 53 (1976): 163–74.

Hall, H. Gaston. "French in the Oxford Honour School of Modern Languages." 22 (Winter–Spring 1958–59): 116–21.

———. "A Comic *Dom Juan*." 23 (Summer 1959): 77–84.

———. "Aspects of the Absurd." 25 (Spring 1960): 26–32.

———. "The Concept of Virtue in *La nouvelle Héloïse*." 28 (Fall–Winter 1961–62): 20–33.

———. "Scarron and the Travesty of Virgil." 38 (May 1967): 115–27.

Halpern, Joseph. "Foreword [*Mallarmé*]." 54 (1977): 5–8.

———. "Sartre's Enclosed Space." 57 (1979): 58–71.

———. "Describing the Surreal." 61 (1981): 89–106.

Hamacher, Werner. "The Second of Inversion: Movements of a Figure through Celan's Poetry." Trans. William D. Jewett. 69 (1985): 276–311.

———. "History, Teary: Some Remarks on 'La jeune parque.'" Trans. Michael Shae. 74 (1988): 67–94.

Hamon, Philippe. "Rhetorical Status of the Descriptive." Trans. Patricia Baudoin. 61 (1981): 1–26.

Hampton, Timothy. "Introduction: Baroques." 80 (1991): 1–9.

Hanning, Robert W. "*Engin* in Twelfth-Century Romance: An Examination of the *Roman d'Enéas* and Hue de Rotelande's *Ipomedon*." 51 (1974): 82–101.

Hanson, Thomas. "Mallarmé's Hat." 54 (1977): 215–27.

Harari, Josué. "The Pleasures of Science and the Pains of Philosophy: Balzac's *Quest for the Absolute*." 67 (1984): 135–63.

Hardt, Michael. "Prison Time." 91 (1997): 64–79.

Hare, John E. "A Bibigraphical Guide to Québécois Literature and Culture." 65 (1983): 283–95.

Harries, Karsten. "Descartes, Perspective, and the Angelic Eye." 49 (1974): 28–42.

Harth, Erica. "Classical Innateness." 49 (1974): 212–30.

———. "Cartesian Women." 80 (1991): 146–64.

Hartman, Geoffrey H. "The Fullness and Nothingness of Literature." 16 (Winter 1955–56): 63–78.

———. "The Taming of History." 18 (Winter 1957): 114–28.

———. "Camus and Malraux: The Common Ground." 25 (Spring 1960): 104–10.

———. "Structuralism: The Anglo-American Adventure." 36 & 37 (October 1966): 148–68.

———. "In Memoriam [Paul de Man]." 69 (1985): 6–8.

———. "Meaning, Error, Text." 69 (1985): 145–49.

Harvey, Robert. "Genet's Open Enemies: Sartre and Derrida." 91 (1997): 103–16.

Hatzfeld, Helmut. "Stylistic Criticism as Art-Minded Philology." 2.1 (Spring–Summer 1949): 62–70.

Havens, George R. "The Road to Rousseau's *Discours sur l'inégalité*." 40 (1968): 18–31.

Haverkamp, Anselm. "Error in Mourning—A Crux in Hölderlin: 'Dem gleich fehlet die Trauer' ('Mnemosyne')." Trans. Vernon Chadwick in collaboration with Anselm Haverkamp, and Bill Jewett. 69 (1985): 238–53.

Hay, Louis. "History or Genesis." Trans. Ingrid Wassenaar. 89 (1996): 191–207.

Heimonet, Jean-Michel. "Recoil in Order to Leap Forward: Two Values of Sade in Bataille's Text." Trans. Joaniko Kohchi. 78 (1990): 227–36.

Heinrichs, T. A. "Language and Mind in Hobbes." 49 (1974): 56–70.

Hemmings, F. W. J. "Fire in Zola's Fiction: Variations on an Elemental Theme." 42 (1969): 26–37.

Herbert, Robert. "A Paris Commentary: The Tough Trend." 19 & 20 (Spring 1957-Winter 1958): 27–34.

Herr, Richard. "The Memoirs of General de Gaulle." 15 (Winter 1954–55): 120–28.

Hertz, Neil. "Two Extravagant Teachings." 63 (1982): 59–71.

Herz, Micheline. "Woman's Fate." 18 (Winter 1957): 7–19.

———. "A Prophet of Israel: Edmond Fleg." 21 (Spring–Summer 1958): 107–13.

———. "Gallic Wit in Triumph and Decline." 23 (Summer 1959): 54–62.

———. "From 'The Little Corporal' to 'Mongénéral': A Comparison of Two Myths." 26 (Fall–Winter 1960–1961): 37–44.

———. "The Angelism of Madame de Ségur." 27 (Spring–Summer 1961): 12–21.

———. "Tragedy, Poetry and the Burlesque in Ghelderode's Theatre." 29 (Spring–Summer 1962): 92–101.

Hess, Thomas B. "The Cigarbox of Napoleon III." 19 & 20 (Spring 1957–Winter 1958): 45–49.

Hewitt, Leah D. "Between Movements: Leiris in Literary History." 81 (1992): 77–90.

Hicks, Eric. "Swann's Dream and the World of Sleep." 34 (June 1965): 106–16.

———. "*Le livre des trois vertus* of Christine de Pizan: Beinecke MS. 427." Special Issue (1991): 57–71.

———. "*Donner à voir*: Guillaume de Lorris or the Impossible Romance." 95 (1999): 65–80.

Higgins, Lynn Anthony. "Typographical Eros: Reading Ricardou in the Third Dimension." 57 (1979): 180–94.

Higgins, Lynn Anthony, Colette Gaudin, Mary Jean Green, Marianne Hirsch, Vivian Kogan, Claudia Reeder, and Nancy Vickers. "Introduction [*Feminist Readings: French Texts/American Contexts*]." 62 (1981): 2–18.

Hill, Robert E. "Summing Up." 29 (Spring–Summer 1962): 10–15.

Hindman, Sandra. "King Arthur, His Knights, and the French Aristocracy in Picardy." Special Issue (1991): 114–33.

Hirsch, Marianne, Colette Gaudin, Mary Jean Green, Lynn Anthony Higgins, Vivian Kogan, Claudia Reeder, and Nancy Vickers. "Introduction [*Feminist Readings: French Texts/American Contexts*]." 62 (1981): 2–18.

Hirsch, Marianne. "A Mother's Discourse: Incorporation and Repetition in *La Princesse de Clèves*." 62 (1981): 67–87.

Hirschman, Sarah. "Simone de Beauvoir, Lycée Teacher." 22 (Winter–Spring 1958–59): 79–82.

Hoffmann, François. "French Negro Poetry." 21 (Spring–Summer 1958): 60–71.

Hoffmann, Léon-François. "Notes on Zoé Oldenbourg's *Destiny of Fire*." 27 (Spring–Summer 1961): 127–30.

Hofmannsthal, Hugo von. "Encounters." Trans. Tanya Stern and James Stern. 9 (1952): 162–65.

Hollier, Denis. "The Dualist Materialism of Georges Bataille." Trans. Hilari Allred. 78 (1990): 124–39.

———. "Poetry . . . up to Z." Trans. Betsy Wing. 81 (1992): 64–76.

Hollier, Denis, Michel Contat, and Jacques Neefs. "Editors' Preface [*Drafts*]." Trans. Alyson Waters. 89 (1996): 1–5.

Hollier, Denis. "Timeliness and Timelessness." Trans. Deborah Treisman. 93 (1998): 99–113.

Holquist, Michael. "The Mayakovsky Problem." 39 (1967): 126–36.

———. "How to Play Utopia: Some Brief Notes on the Distinctiveness of Utopian Fiction." 41 (1968): 106–23.

———. "What is a Boojum? Nonsense and Modernism." 43 (1969): 145–64.

Hoog, Armand. "The Surrealist Novel." 8 (1951): 17–25.

———. "Henri Michaux, or Mythic Symbolism." 9 (1952): 143–54.

———. "The Romantic Spirit and the American 'Elsewhere.'" 10 (1952): 14–28.

———. "Who Invented the 'Mal du Siècle'?" Trans. Beth Brombert. 13 (Spring–Summer 1954): 42–51.

———. "Malraux, Möllberg and Frobenius." Trans. Beth Brombert. 18 (Winter 1957): 87–96.

———. "The Itinerary of Marguerite Duras: Or, from the Dangers of the American Novel to the Perils of the Abstract Novel, without Mishap." Trans. H. Gaston Hall. 24 (Summer 1959): 68–73.

———. "Today's Woman: Has She a Heart?" 27 (Spring–Summer 1961): 66–73.

Houston, John. "Waterloo: From Fact to Myth." 26 (Fall–Winter 1960–1961): 45–49.

———. "The *Memoirs of Hadrian* by Marguerite Yourcenar." 27 (Spring–Summer 1961): 140–41.

Houston, Mona Tobin. "Villiers Vindicated." 29 (Spring–Summer 1962): 16–19.

———. "The Sartre of Madame de Beauvoir." 30 (1963): 23–29.

Howard, Richard. "Childhood Amnesia." 43 (1969): 165–69.

Howe, Virginia K. "*Les pensées*: Paradox and Signification." 49 (1974): 120–31.

Hoy, David. "Literary History: Paradox or Paradigm." 52 (1975): 268–86.

Hubert, J. D. "Symbolism, Correspondence, and Memory." 9 (1952): 46–55.

———. "Myth and Status: Malherbe's Swan Song." 49 (1974): 132–42.

Hubert, Renée Riese. "Three Women Poets: Renée Rivet, Joyce Mansour, Yvonne Caroutch." 21 (Spring–Summer 1958): 40–48.

———. "The Fleeting World of Humor from Watteau to Fragonard." 23 (Summer 1959): 85–91.

———. "Jules Supervielle in Stageland." 29 (Spring–Summer 1962): 102–27.

———. "Miró and Breton." 31 (May 1964): 52–60.

———. "The Tableau-Poème: Open Work." Trans. Kathryn Aschheim. 67 (1984): 43–56.

———. "Derrida, Dupin, Adami: 'Il faut être plusieurs pour écrire.'" 84 (1994): 242–64.

Hudon, E. Sculley. "Love and Myth in *Les liaisons dangereuses*." 11 (1953?): 25–38.

Hudon, Louis. "*The Stranger* and the Critics." 25 (Spring 1960): 59–64.

Huet, Marie-Hélène. "Social Entropy." 92 (1997): 171–83.

Huffer, Lynne. "Editor's Preface [*Another Look, Another Woman: Retranslations of French Feminism*]." 87 (1995): 1–3.

——. "Luce *et veritas*: Toward an Ethics of Performance." 87 (1995): 20–41.

——. "An Interview with Nicole Brossard. Montreal, October 1993." Trans. David Dean. 87 (1995): 115–21.

——. "From Lesbos to Montreal: Nicole Brossard's Urban Fictions." 90 (1996): 95–114.

——. "Blanchot's Mother." 93 (1998): 175–95.

Hult, David F. "Editor's Preface [*Concepts of Closure*]." 67 (1984): iii–vi.

——. "Closed Quotations: The Speaking Voice in the *Roman de la Rose*." 67 (1984): 248–69.

——. "The Allegoresis of Everyday Life." 95 (1999): 212–33.

Huot, Sylvia. "The Daisy and the Laurel: Myths of Desire and Creativity in the Poetry of Jean Froissart." Special Issue (1991): 240–51.

Hyppolite, Jean. "A Chronology of French Existentialism." 16 (Winter 1955–56): 100–102.

Hytier, Jean. "The Refusals of Valéry." Trans. Reed Law. 2.1 (Spring–Summer 1949): 105–36.

——. "The Classicism of the Classics." Trans. June Guicharnaud. 38 (May 1967): 5–17.

Hyvrard, Jeanne. *Mère la mort, Le corps défunt de la comédie* [excerpts]. Trans. Lauren Doyle-McCombs. Intro. Martine Reid. Special Issue (1988): 317–35.

Ibert, Jean-Claude. "Today's Poetry." Trans. Rima Drell Reck. 21 (Spring–Summer 1958): 114–17.

Ilsley, Marjorie H. "Four Unpublished Letters of Stéphane Mallarmé to Stuart Merrill." 9 (1952): 155–61.

Ince, W. N. "*La promenade avec Monsieur Teste*." 44 (1970): 169–84.

Insdorf, Annette. "Maurice Jaubert and François Truffaut: Musical Continuities from *L'Atalante* to *L'histoire d'Adèle H*." 60 (1980): 204–18.

Ionesco, Eugène. "Selections from the Journals ["On Life and Death," "On the Theatre," "On History and Politics," "About Art"]." 29 (Spring–Summer 1962): 3–9.

Irigaray, Luce. "The Question of the Other." Trans. Noah Guynn. 87 (1995): 7–19.

Israel, Abigail. "The Aesthetic of Violence: Rimbaud and Genet." 46 (1971): 28–40.

Jabès, Edmond. "Rainbow, II (From *Le Livre de l'hospitalité*)." Trans. Rosmarie Waldrop. 82 (1993): 115–17.

Jackson, Robert L. "Napoleon in Russian Literature." 26 (Fall–Winter 1960–1961): 106–18.

Jackson, W. T. H. "The Nature of Romance." 51 (1974): 12–25.

Jacob, Christian. "The Greek Traveler's Areas of Knowledge: Myths and Other Discourses in Pausanias' *Description of Greece.*" Trans. Anne Mullen-Hohl. 59 (1980): 65–85.

Jacobs, Carol. "On Looking at Shelley's Medusa." 69 (1985): 163–79.

Jacobson, David J. "Jews for Genius: The Unholy Disorders of Maurice Sachs." 85 (1994): 181–200.

Jacques, Paula. "*Aunt Carlotta's Legacy* (Excerpt from a Novel)." Trans. Michael T. Ward. 85 (1994): 41–50.

Jagger, George. "Camus's *La peste.*" 1.1 (Spring–Summer 1948): 124–27.

Jaïs, Meyer. "Report on Jewish Culture (Excerpt)." Trans. Madeleine Dobie. 85 (1994): 174–80.

Jakobson, Roman. "The Generation That Squandered Its Poets (Excerpts)." Trans. Dale E. Peterson. 39 (1967): 119–25.

Jallat, Jeannine. "Valéry and the Mathematical Language of Identity and Difference." Trans. Ann Smock. 44 (1970): 51–64.

Jameson, Fredric. "The Laughter of Nausea." 23 (Summer 1959): 26–32.

———. "Imaginary and Symbolic in Lacan: Marxism, Psychoanalytic Criticism, and the Problem of the Subject." 55 & 56 (1977): 338–95.

———. "Euphorias of Substitution: Hubert Aquin and the Political Novel in Québec." 65 (1983): 214–223.

———. "Introduction [*Sartre after Sartre*]." 68 (1985): iii–xi.

Jan, Isabelle. "Children's Literature and Bourgeois Society since 1860." Trans. Wyley L. Powell. 43 (1969): 57–72.

Janvier, Ludovic. "Literature and the Rest of the World." 39 (1967): 198–99.

Jaouën, Françoise, and Benjamin Semple. "Editors' Preface: The Body into Text [*Corps Mystique, Corps Sacré: Textual Transfigurations of the Body from the Middle Ages to the Seventeenth Century*]." 86 (1994): 1–4.

Jaouën, Françoise. "Civility and the Novel: De Pure's *La prétieuse ou le mystère des ruelles.*" 92 (1997): 105–25.

Japrisot, Sébastien. *L'été meurtrier* [excerpts]. Trans. Alan Sheridan. Intro. Marina Kundu. Special Issue (1988): 133–52.

Jardine, Alice A. "Pre-Texts for the Transatlantic Feminist." 62 (1981): 220–36.

Jardine, Alice A., and Anne M. Menke. "Exploding the Issue: 'French' 'Women' 'Writers' and 'the Canon'? Fourteen Interviews." 75 (1988): 229–58.

Jauss, Hans-Robert. "1912: Threshold to an Epoch. Apollinaire's 'Zone' and 'Lundi rue Christine.'" Trans. Roger Blood. 74 (1988): 39–66.

Jay, Salim. "A Star is Worn." Trans. Alan Astro. 85 (1994): 51–61.

Jeanson, Francis. "Hell and Bastardy." 30 (1963): 5–22.

Jefferson, Louise M. "Proust and Racine." 34 (June 1965): 99–105.

Jenny, Laurent. "Genetic Criticism and Its Myths." Trans. Richard Watts. 89 (1996): 9–25.

Jigé. See Guicharnaud, Jacques.

Johnson, Barbara. "Poetry and Performative Language." 54 (1977): 140–58.

———. "The Frame of Reference: Poe, Lacan, Derrida." 55 & 56 (1977): 457–505.

———. "Editor's Preface [*The Pedagogical Imperative: Teaching as a Literary Genre*]." 63 (1982): iii–vii.

———. "Teaching Ignorance: *L'école des femmes*." 63 (1982): 165–82.

———. "In Memoriam [Paul de Man]." 69 (1985): 9–10.

———. "Rigorous Unreliability." 69 (1985): 73–80.

Johnson, J. Theodore, Jr. "From Artistic Celibacy to Artistic Contemplation." 34 (June 1965): 81–90.

Jones, Ann Rosalind, and Nancy J. Vickers. "Canon, Rule and the Restoration Renaissance." 75 (1988): 9–25.

Jones, Ann Rosalind. "Assimilation with a Difference: Renaissance Women Poets and Literary Influence." 62 (1981): 135–53.

Jones, Frank. "Scenes from the Life of Antigone." 6 (1950): 91–100.

Jones, Serene. "Divining Women: Irigaray and Feminist Theologies." 87 (1995): 42–67.

Jordan, Robert M. "Chaucerian Romance?" 51 (1974): 223–34.

Jouhaud, Christian. "Richelieu, or 'Baroque' Power in Action." Trans. Suzanne Toczyski. 80 (1991): 183–201.

Jouvenel, Bertrand de. "Rousseau the Pessimistic Evolutionist." 28 (Fall–Winter 1961–62): 83–96.

Joyaux, Georges J. "Driss Chraïbi, Mohammed Dib, Kateb Yacine, and Indigenous North African Literature." 24 (Summer 1959): 30–40.

———. "Albert Camus and North Africa." 25 (Spring 1960): 10–19.

Jullien, Dominique. "Intertextuality as Labyrinth: The Presence of Racine in Michel Butor's *L'emploi du temps*." 76 (1989): 108–24.

Kahn, Gustave. "One Yom Kippur." Trans. Glenn Swiadon. 85 (1994): 62–66.

Kamuf, Peggy. "To Give Place: Semi-Approaches to Hélène Cixous." 87 (1995): 68–89.

Kanipe, Esther S. "Hetzel and the Bibliothèque d'Éducation et de Récréation." 43 (1969): 73–84.

Kaplan, Alice, and Kristin Ross. "Introduction [*Everyday Life*]." 73 (1987): 1–4.

Kaplan, Alice. "Taste Wars: American Professions of French Culture." 73 (1987): 156–72.

———. "Working in the Archives." 77 (1990): 103–16.

Kaplan, Alice, and Philippe Roussin. "A Changing Idea of Literature: The Bibliothèque de la Pléiade." 89 (1996): 237–62.

Katz, Eve. "Chamfort." 40 (1968): 32–46.

Kaufmann, Dorothy. "Simone de Beauvoir: Questions of Difference and Generation." 72 (1986): 121–31.

Kaufmann, Vincent. "Valéry's Garbage Can." Trans. Deborah Treisman. 89 (1996): 67–81.

Kavanagh, Thomas M. "The Libertine Moment." 94 (1998): 79–100.

Kay, Sarah. "The Life of the Dead Body: Death and the Sacred in the Chansons de Geste." 86 (1994): 94–108.

Keenan, Thomas. "Bibliography of Texts by Paul de Man." 69 (1985): 315–22.

———. "Freedom, the Law of Another Fable." 79 (1991): 231–51.

Kelly, Douglas. "*Matiere* and *Genera Dicendi* in Medieval Romance." 51 (1974): 147–59.

Kendo. See Douglas, Kenneth.

Kenner, Hugh. "Ezra Pound and the Light of France." 10 (1952): 54–64.

Kern, Edith. "Drama Stripped for Inaction: Beckett's Godot." 14 (Winter 1954–55): 41–47.

———. "The Television Teacher—How Near, How Far?" 22 (Winter–Spring 1958–59): 122–27.

———. "Author or Authoress?" 27 (Spring–Summer 1961): 3–11.

———. "Beckett's Knight of Infinite Resignation." 29 (Spring–Summer 1962): 49–56.

———. "Abandon Hope, All Ye . . . " 30 (1963): 56–62.

———. "Structure in Beckett's Theatre." 46 (1971): 17–27.

Khatibi, Abdelkebir. "A Colonial Labyrinth." Trans. Catherine Dana. 83 (1993): 5–11.

Kierkegaard, Søren. "Farce is Far More Serious." Trans. Louis Mackey 14 (Winter 1954–55): 3–9.

Kirsner, Douglas. "Sartre and the Collective Neurosis of Our Time." 68 (1985): 206–25.

Kittay, Jeffrey. "Introduction [*Towards a Theory of Description*]." 61 (1981): i–v.

———. "Descriptive Limits." 61 (1981): 225–43.

Klein, Lawrence E. "The Figure of France: The Politics of Sociability in England, 1660–1715." 92 (1997): 30–45.

Klein, Richard. "Baudelaire and Revolution: Some Notes." 39 (1967): 85–97.

———. "Straight Lines and Arabesques: Metaphors of Metaphor." 45 (1970): 64–86.

———. "Under 'Pragmatic' Paradoxes." 66 (1984): 91–109.

———. "The Future of Nuclear Criticism." 77 (1990): 76–100.

Klossowski, Pierre. "A Destructive Philosophy." 35 (December 1965): 61–80.

Knapp, Bettina. "Georges Schehade: 'He who dreams diffuses into air . . . '" 29 (Spring–Summer 1962): 108–15.

———. "Artaud: A New Type of Magic." 31 (May 1964): 87–98.

———. "The Golden Age of Chanson." 32 (October 1964): 82–98.

———. "A Director's Viewpoint." 33 (December 1964): 105–6.

———. "Witold Gombrowicz: A Faceless Theatre." 46 (1971): 75–87.

———. "'Igitur or Elbehnon's Folly': The Depersonalization Process and the Creative Encounter." 54 (1977): 188–214.

Kneller, John W. "The Musical Structure of Proust's *Un amour de Swann*." 2.2 or 4 (1949): 55–62.

———. "Jean-Jacques the Dynamist." 13 (Spring–Summer 1954): 114–18.

———. "Elective Empathies and Musical Affinities." 27 (Spring–Summer 1961): 114–20.

Kofman, Sarah. "The Psychologist of the Eternal Feminine (Why I Write Such Good Books, 5)." Trans. Madeleine Dobie. 87 (1995): 173–89.

Kogan, Vivian, Colette Gaudin, Mary Jean Green, Lynn Anthony Higgins, Marianne Hirsch, Claudia Reeder, and Nancy Vickers. "Introduction [*Feminist Readings: French Texts/American Contexts*]." 62 (1981): 2–18.

Kolb, Philip. "Proust's Letters." 71 (1986): 199–210.

Kritzman, Lawrence D. "Barthesian Free Play." 66 (1984): 189–210.

Kuhn, Reinhard. "The Hermeneutics of Silence: Michaux and Mescaline." 50 (1974): 130–41.

Kushner, Eva. "The Role of Platonic Symbols in the Poetry of Pontus de Tyard." 47 (1972): 124–44.

La Bruyère, Jean de, et al. "Persons, Places, Peccadilloes: A Seventeenth-Century Portrait." 32 (October 1964): 23–27.

La Fontaine, Jean de. "Three Fables from La Fontaine. ["The Fox and the Grapes" III: xi, "Epilogue" VI, "The Head and Tail of the Serpent" VII: xvii]." Trans. Marianne Moore. 10 (1952): 3–4.

Lacan, Jacques. "The Insistence of the Letter in the Unconscious." 36 & 37 (October 1966): 112–47.

———. "Seminar on 'The Purloined Letter.'" Trans. Jeffrey Mehlman. 48 (1972): 39–72.

———. "Desire and the Interpretation of Desire in *Hamlet*." Ed. Jacques-Alain Miller. Trans. James Hulbert. 55 & 56 (1977): 11–52.

Lacy, Norris J. "Spatial Form in Medieval Romance." 51 (1974): 160–69.

Ladenson, Elisabeth. "Colette for Export Only." 90 (1996): 25–46.

Ladimer, Bethany. "Camus' Chenoua Landscape." 57 (1979): 109–23.

Lafarge, Catherine. "The Emergence of the Bourgeoisie." 32 (October 1964): 40–49.

Laflèche, Guy. "Ringuet's *Trente arpents*: For Different Men But Always the Same Literature." Trans. Erec Koch. 65 (1983): 155–71.

Lala, Marie-Christine. "The Conversations of Writing in Georges Bataille's *L'impossible*." Trans. Robert Livingston. 78 (1990): 237–45.

Lambert, Fernando. "Narrative Perspectives in Mongo Beti's *Le pauvre Christ de Bomba*." Trans. Daniel R. Cianfarini. 53 (1976): 78–91.

Lamont, Rosette C. "The Hero in Spite of Himself." 29 (Spring–Summer 1962): 73–81.

———. "The Hamlet Myth." 33 (December 1964): 80–91.

———. "Jean-Louis Barrault's *Rabelais*." 46 (1971): 125–38.

———. "Fernando Arrabal's Guerrilla Theatre." 46 (1971): 154–66.

Lang, René. "Rilke and Gide: Their Reciprocal Translations." 7 (1951): 98–106.

Languth, William. "The World and Life of the Dream." 34 (June 1965): 117–30.

Lanzmann, Claude. "Seminar on *Shoah*." Ed. David Rodowick. 79 (1991): 82–99.

Laor, Nathaniel. "The Moral Import of Madness to Literature." 79 (1991): 193–202.

Lapacherie, Jean-Gérard. "Typographic Characters: Tension between Text and Drawing." Trans. Anna Lehmann. 84 (1994): 63–77.

Laplanche, Jean, and J.-B. Pontalis. "Appendices ["Anaclisis," "Deferred Action," "Foreclosure," "Imaginary," "Mirror Stage," "Narcissism," "Phallus," "Symbolic"]." Selected articles from *Vocabulaire de la psychanalyse*. Trans. Peter Kussel and Jeffrey Mehlman. 48 (1972): 179–202.

Laplanche, Jean, and Serge Leclaire. "The Unconscious: A Psychoanalytic Study." Trans. Patrick Coleman. 48 (1972): 118–75.

Laplanche, Jean. "Postscript." 48 (1972): 176–78.

Lapp, John C. "Racine's Symbolism." 9 (1952): 40–45.

———. "The Potter and His Clay: Mythological Imagery in Ronsard." 38 (May 1967): 89–108.

Laugaa, Maurice. "The City and Its Poets." 32 (October 1964): 68–75.

———. "Cyrano: Sound and Language." Trans. Marla Kaplan. 49 (1974): 199–211.

Lawler, James R. "Saint Mallarmé." 44 (1970): 185–98.

———. "Three Sonnets." 54 (1977): 83–95.

———. "'An Ever Future Hollow in the Soul.'" 66 (1984): 110–20.

Le Clézio, J. M. G. *Désert* [excerpt]. Trans. Katrine Pflanze. Intro. Françoise Dubor. Trans. Deidre Dawson. Special Issue (1988): 209–36.

Le Guillou, Louis. "Lamennais: A Happy Ending." Trans. Erec Koch. 71 (1986): 169–76.

Leavitt, Walter. "Sartre's Theatre." 1.1 (Spring–Summer 1948): 102–5.

Leclaire, Serge, and Jean Laplanche. "The Unconscious: A Psychoanalytic Study." Trans. Patrick Coleman. 48 (1972): 118–75.

Leduc-Park, Renée. "Repetition with a Difference in Réjean Ducharme." Trans. Margaret Gray McDonald and Renée Leduc-Park. 65 (1983): 201–13.

Lee, Sonia. "The Image of the Woman in the African Folktale From the Sub-Saharan Francophone Area." 53 (1976): 19–28.

Leenhardt, Jacques. "See and Describe: On a Few Drawings by Stendhal." Trans. John Thompson. 84 (1994): 81–94.

Lefebvre, Henri. "The Everyday and Everydayness." Trans. Christine Levich, with Alice Kaplan and Kristin Ross. 73 (1987): 7–11.

Leiris, Michel. "An Excerpt from *Fourbis.*" Trans. Lydia Davis. 81 (1992): 3–20.

Lemarchand, Jacques. "The Dramatic Career of Jean Vauthier." Trans. Ralph Albanese, Jr. 46 (1971): 88–101.

Lestringant, Frank. "Travels in Eucharistia: Formosa and Ireland from George Psalmanaazaar to Jonathan Swift." Trans. Noah Guynn. 86 (1994): 109–25.

Leupin, Alexandre. "A New Sartre." Trans. Peggy McCracken. 68 (1985): 226–38.

———. "The Powerlessness of Writing: Guillaume de Machaut, the Gorgon, and Ordenance." Trans. Peggy McCracken. 70 (1986): 127–49.

Lévi-Strauss, Claude. "Overture to *Le cru et le cuit.*" Trans. Joseph H. McMahon. 36 & 37 (October 1966): 41–65.

Levin, Harry. "From Priam to Birotteau." 6 (1950): 75–82.

———. "The Ivory Gate." 13 (Spring–Summer 1954): 17–29.

———. "From Terence to Tabarin: A Note on *Les fourberies de Scapin.*" 38 (May 1967): 128–37.

Lévinas, Emmanuel. "Transcending Words: Concerning Word-Erasing." Trans. Didier Maleuvre. 81 (1992): 145–50.

Levitan, William. "Seneca in Racine." 76 (1989): 185–210.

Lévy, Sarah. "*My Beloved France* (Excerpt)." Trans. Glenn Swiadon. 85 (1994): 67–72.

Lewis, Philip E. "Idealism and Reality." 34 (June 1965): 24–28.

———. "Merleau-Ponty and the Phenomenology of Language." 36 & 37 (October 1966): 19–40.

———. "La Rochefoucauld: The Rationality of Play." 41 (1968): 133–47.

———. "Language and French Critical Debate." 45 (1970): 154–65.

Lewis, R. W. B. "*Caligula*: or the Realm of the Impossible." 25 (Spring 1960): 52–58.

Lezra, Jacques. "Editor's Preface: Labors of Reading [*Depositions: Althusser, Balibar, Macherey, and the Labor of Reading*]." 88 (1995): 1–5.

———. "Spontaneous Labor." 88 (1995): 78–117.

Lichtenstein, Jacqueline. "What Is the Subject of *La place royale?*" Trans. Madeleine Dobie. 80 (1991): 41–69.

Lindfors, Bernth. "Wole Soyinka, When Are You Coming Home?" 53 (1976): 197–210.

Linnemann, Russell. "The Anticolonialism of Ferdinand Oyono." 53 (1976): 64–77.

Lionnet, Françoise, and Ronnie Scharfman. "Editors' Preface [Post/Colonial Conditions: Exiles, Migrations, and Nomadisms. Vol. 1]." 82 (1993): 1–3.

Lionnet, Françoise. "Créolité in the Indian Ocean: Two Models of Cultural Diversity." 82 (1993): 101–12.

Lionnet, Françoise, and Ronnie Scharfman. "Editors' Preface [Post/Colonial Conditions: Exiles, Migrations, and Nomadisms. Vol. 2]." 83 (1993): 1–2.

Livingston, Beverly. "From A to F and Back: Pinget's Fictive Arena." 57 (1979): 72–85.

———. "An Interview with Alain Robbe-Grillet." Trans. Beverly Livingston. 57 (1979): 228–37.

Logan, John Frederick. "The Age of Intoxication." 50 (1974): 81–94.

Logan, Marie-Rose. "Graphesis . . . " 52 (1975): 4–15.

———. "Rethinking History . . . " 59 (1980): 3–6.

Lombardo, Patrizia. "Hippolyte Taine between Art and Science." 77 (1990): 117–33.

López-Morillas, Juan. "Ortega y Gasset: Historicism vs. Classicism." 6 (1950): 63–74.

Loreau, Max. "Premisses for a Pictorial Logic." Trans. James Hulbert. 52 (1975): 288–302.

Loubère, J. A. E. "Views Through the Screen: In-Site in Claude Simon." 57 (1979): 36–47.

Lowe, Lisa. "Literary Nomadics in Francophone Allegories of Postcolonialism: Pham Van Ky and Tahar Ben Jelloun." 82 (1993): 43–61.

Loy, Robert J. "Prometheus, Theseus, The Uncommon Man and an Eagle." 7 (1951): 32–43.

Lucey, Michael. "Genet's Notre-Dame-des-Fleurs: Fantasy and Sexual Identity." 91 (1997): 80–102.

Lunel, Armand. "Nicolo-Peccavi, or the Dreyfus Affair at Carpentras (Excerpt)." Trans. Michael T. Ward. 85 (1994): 73–80.

Lydon, Mary. "Skirting the Issue: Mallarmé, Proust, and Symbolism." 74 (1988): 157–81.

———. "Re-Translating no Re-Reading no, rather: Rejoycing (with) Hélène Cixous." 87 (1995): 90–102.

Lynes, Carlos, Jr. "Jean Cayrol and 'Le Romanesque Lazaréen.'" 8 (1951): 108–17.

———. "Adamov and 'le sens littéral' in the Theatre." 14 (Winter 1954–55): 48–56.

———. "Toward Reconciliation: The World of Jean Cayrol." 24 (Summer 1959): 62–67.

Lyons, John D. "Artaud: Intoxication and its Double." 50 (1974): 120–29.

———. "The Heptaméron and the Foundation of Critical Narrative." 70 (1986): 150–63.

————. "Unseen Space and Theatrical Narrative: The 'Récit de Cinna.'" 80 (1991): 70–90.

Lyotard, Jean-François. "For a Pseudo-theory." Trans. Moshe Ron. 52 (1975): 115–27.

————. "Endurance and the Profession." Trans. Christophe Gallier, Steven Ungar, and Barbara Johnson. 63 (1982): 72–77.

Macarthur, Elizabeth J. "Trading Genres: Epistolarity and Theatricality in *Britannicus* and *Les liaisons dangereuses*." 76 (1989): 243–64.

————. "Between the Republic of Virtue and the Republic of Letters: Marie-Jeanne Roland Practices Rousseau." 92 (1997): 184–203.

Macherey, Pierre. "A Production of Subjectivity." Trans. Roger Celestin. 88 (1995): 42–52.

Mackenzie, Louis A., Jr. "To the Brink: The Dialectic of Anxiety in the *Pensées*." 66 (1984): 57–66.

Madou, Jean-Pol. "The Law, the Heart: Blanchot and the Question of Community." Trans. Thomas Pepper. 93 (1998): 60–65.

Magnan, Henri. " . . . Said Jean-Paul Sartre." Trans. Rima Drell. 16 (Winter 1955–56): 3–7.

Magny, Claude-Edmonde. "Roger Nimier." 8 (1951): 56–76.

Mahlendorf, Ursula R. "Where the Air Throbs." 32 (October 1964): 138–43.

Mahuzier, Brigitte, Karen McPherson, Charles A. Porter, and Ralph Sarkonak. "Editors' Preface [*Same Sex / Different Text? Gay and Lesbian Writing in French*]." 90 (1996): 1–4.

Mailhot, Laurent. "The Writing of the Essay." Trans. Jay Lutz. 65 (1983): 74–89.

Makward, Christiane, with Odile Cazenave. "The Others' Others: 'Francophone' Women and Writing." 75 (1988): 190–207.

Mallarmé, Stéphane. "Four Unpublished Letters to Stuart Merrill." 9 (1952): 155–61.

Malraux, André. "A Preface for Faulkner's *Sanctuary*." 10 (1952): 92–93.

————. "D. H. Lawrence and Eroticism: Concerning *Lady Chatterley's Lover*." Trans. Melvin Friedman. 11 (1953?): 55–58.

————. "The 'New Left' Can Succeed!" Trans. Neal Oxenhandler. 15 (Winter 1954–55): 49–60.

————. "Three Speeches ["Every Man Endeavors to Think His Life," "Rejoinder to Sixty-Four," "Our Cultural Heritage"]." Trans. Kenneth Douglas. 18 (Winter 1957): 27–38.

Mankin, Paul. "The Humor of Marcel Achard." 23 (Summer 1959): 33–38.

————. "Blue Note from Billetdoux." 29 (Spring–Summer 1962): 121–24.

March, Harold. "The Artist as Seer: Notes on the Esthetic Vision." 2.2 or 4 (1949): 44–54.

————. "The Imprisoned." 34 (June 1965): 43–54.

Marder, Elissa. "The Mother Tongue in *Phèdre* and *Frankenstein*." 76 (1989): 59–77.

Margolin, Jean-Claude. "Mathias Ringmann's *Grammatica figurata*, or, Grammar as a Card Game." Trans. Diana Wormuth. 47 (1972): 33–46.

Marías, Julián. "Metaphysics: Existence and Human Life." 16 (Winter 1955–56): 118–26.

Marie, Michel. "The Poacher's Aged Mother: On Speech in *La chienne* by Jean Renoir." Trans. Marguerite Morley. 60 (1980): 219–32.

Marin, Louis. "'Pascal': Text, Author, Discourse . . . " Trans. María Minich Brewer and Daniel August Brewer. 52 (1975): 129–51.

———. "The Inscription of the King's Memory: On the Metallic History of Louis XIV." Trans. Mark Franko. 59 (1980): 17–36.

———. "Classical, Baroque: Versailles, or the Architecture of the Prince." Trans. Anna Lehman. 80 (1991): 167–82.

Maritain, Raïssa. "Three Poems from *Portes de l'horizon* ["La présence de Dieu," "The Presence of God," "Comme on meurt," "As One Dies," "De Profondis," "De Profondis (English)"]." 12 (Fall–Winter 1953): 4–7.

———. "Comme on meurt." 13 (Spring–Summer 1954): 82.

Marks, Elaine. "Transgressing the (In)cont(in)ent Boundaries: The Body in Decline." 72 (1986): 181–200.

———. "'Sapho 1900': Imaginary Renée Viviens and the Rear of the Belle Epoque." 75 (1988): 175–89.

Marks, Jonathan E. "The Verdurins and Their Cult." 34 (June 1965): 73–80.

Marmande, Francis. "Michel Leiris: The Letter to Louise." Trans. Abigail S. Rischin. 81 (1992): 28–34.

———. "The Laws of Improvisation, or the Nuptial Destruction of Jazz." Trans. Carol Johnson. 89 (1996): 155–59.

Martin, Carole F. "From the Mark to the Mask: Notes on Libertinage and Utopianism." 94 (1998): 101–15.

Martinet, André. "Structure and Language." Trans. Thomas G. Penchoen. 36 & 37 (October 1966): 10–18.

Martz, Louis L. "Who is Lycidas?" 47 (1972): 170–88.

Marx-Scouras, Danielle. "Muffled Scream/Stifled Voices." 82 (1993): 172–82.

Masson, André. "Painting is a Wager." 31 (May 1964): 123–25.

Mathieu, Hélène, and Anne-Marie Thiesse. "The Decline of the Classical Age and the Birth of the Classics." Trans. Lauren Doyle-McCombs. 75 (1988): 208–28.

Mathieu-Castellani, Gisèle. "The Poetics of Place: The Space of the Emblem (Sponde)." Trans. Katherine Lydon. 80 (1991): 30–40.

Matthews, J. H. "Some Post-War Surrealist Poets." 31 (May 1964): 145–53.

———. "The Right Person for Surrealism." 35 (December 1965): 89–95.

Mauriac, François. "A Communication." 3.1 or 5 (1950): 66–67.

Maurin, Mario. "Suarès' Critical Method: The Search." 2.1 (Spring–Summer 1949): 71–73.

———. "A Few Notes on the Gide-Suarès Relations." 7 (1951): 115–24.

———. "Suarès and the Third Kingdom." 12 (Fall–Winter 1953): 34–40.

———. "On Bonnefoy's Poetry." 21 (Spring–Summer 1958): 16–22.

———. "Zola's Labyrinths." 42 (1969): 89–104.

Maxwell, Allen R. "Anthropology [Annotated Bibliography]." 36 & 37 (October 1966): 256–62.

May, Georges [see also under Avryl]. "Jean Giraudoux: Academicism and Idiosyncracies." 2.1 (Spring–Summer 1949): 24–33.

———. "Jean Giraudoux: Diplomacy and Dramaturgy." 3.1 or 5 (1950): 88–99.

———. "Valery Larbaud: Translator and Scholar." 6 (1950): 83–90.

———. "Marriage vs. Love in the World of Giraudoux." 11 (1953?): 106–15.

———. "Félicien Marceau: A Modern Romantic Novelist." 24 (Summer 1959): 80–86.

———. "Rousseau and France." 28 (Fall–Winter 1961–62): 122–35.

———. "The Eighteenth Century." 32 (October 1964): 29–39.

———. "Fiction Reader, Novel Writer." 35 (December 1965): 5–11.

———. "Corneille and the Classics." 38 (May 1967): 138–50.

Mazars, Pierre. "Giorgio de Chirico." 31 (May 1964): 112–67.

McCarthy, Patrick. "Sartre, Nizan and the Dilemmas of Political Commitment." 68 (1985): 191–205.

McCracken, Peggy. "The Poetics of Sacrifice: Allegory and Myth in the Grail Quest." 95 (1999): 152–68.

McKenna, Andrew J. "Allodidacticism: Flaubert 100 Years After." 63 (1982): 227–44.

McMahon, Joseph H. "What Rest for the Weary." 27 (Spring–Summer 1961): 131–39.

———. "Madame de Warens." 28 (Fall–Winter 1961–62): 97–105.

———. "Keeping Faith and Holding Firm." 29 (Spring–Summer 1962): 26–32.

———. "A Reader's Hesitations." 30 (1963): 96–107.

———. "City for Expatriates." 32 (October 1964): 144–58.

———. "Ducis: Unkindest Cutter?" 33 (December 1964): 14–25.

———. "From Things to Themes." 34 (June 1965): 5–17.

———. "Where Does Real Life Begin?" 35 (December 1965): 96–113.

———. "More Perfect Souls." 38 (May 1967): 27–46.

McNeece, Lucy Stone. "Decolonizing the Sign: Language and Identity in Abdelkebir Khatibi's *La mémoire tatouée.*" 83 (1993): 12–29.

McPherson, Karen, Brigitte Mahuzier, Charles A. Porter, and Ralph

Sarkonak. "Editors' Preface [*Same Sex / Different Text? Gay and Lesbian Writing in French*]." 90 (1996): 1–4.

Mead, William. "*La nouvelle Héloïse* and the Public of 1761." 28 (Fall–Winter 1961–62): 13–19.

Mehlman, Jeffrey. "French Freud . . . " 48 (1972): 5–9.

———. "The 'Floating Signifier': From Lévi-Strauss to Lacan." 48 (1972): 10–37.

———. "Jacques Lacan: Introductory Note." 48 (1972): 38.

———. "Jacques Derrida: Introductory Note." 48 (1972): 73–74.

———. "On Tear-Work: L'ar- de Valéry." 52 (1975): 152–73.

Mehrez, Samia. "Azouz Begag: Un di zafas di bidoufile (Azouz Begag: Un des enfants du bidonville) or The Beur Writer: A Question of Territory." 82 (1993): 25–42.

Meijer, Marianne S. "Guesswork or Facts: Connections between Montaigne's Last Three Chapters (III:11, 12 and 13)." 64 (1983): 167–79.

Méla, Charles. "Perceval." English adaptation by Catherine Lowe and Charles Méla. 55 & 56 (1977): 253–79.

Melançon, Joseph. "The Writing of Difference in Québec." Trans. Lisa Gosselin. 65 (1983): 21–29.

Mellon, Stanley. "The July Monarchy and the Napoleonic Myth." 26 (Fall–Winter 1960–1961): 70–78.

Mendel, Sydney. "From Solitude to Salvation: A Study in Development." 30 (1963): 45–55.

Mendelson, Edward. "Revision and Power: The Example of W.H. Auden." 89 (1996): 103–12.

Mendès-France, Pierre. "Economic Equilibrium and Social Progress." Trans. Imbrie Buffum and Pierre Barthelémy. 15 (Winter 1954–55): 68–88.

Menke, Anne M., and Alice A. Jardine. "Exploding the Issue: 'French' 'Women' 'Writers' and 'the Canon'? Fourteen Interviews." 75 (1988): 229–58.

Mercier, Louis-Sébastien, et al. "Plus ça change: An American in Paris." 32 (October 1964): 50–54.

Merlin, Hélène. "Fables of the 'Mystical Body' in Seventeenth-Century France." Trans. Allison Tait. 86 (1994): 126–42.

Messner, Charles. "The French Theatre: A Bibliography." 3.1 or 5 (1950): 113–17.

Metz, Christian. "Aural Objects." Trans. Georgia Gurrieri. 60 (1980): 24–32.

Michaux, Henri. "Selections ["Projection," "Nausea or Is It Death Coming," "The Nonays and the Oliabairians," "Magic"]." Trans. Richard Ellmann. 1.2 (Fall–Winter 1948): 53–58.

Michelman, Fredric. "The West African Novel Since 1911." 53 (1976): 29–44.

Miel, Jan. "Jacques Lacan and the Structure of the Unconscious." 36 & 37 (October 1966): 104–11.

———. "Ideas or Epistemes: Hazard versus Foucault." 49 (1974): 231–45.

Miller, Christopher L. "Nationalism as Resistance and Resistance to Nationalism in the Literature of Francophone Africa." 82 (1993): 62–100.

Miller, D. A. "Balzac's Illusions Lost and Found." 67 (1984): 164–81.

Miller, J. Hillis, Peter Brooks, and Shoshana Felman. "Foreword [*The Lesson of Paul de Man*]." 69 (1985): iii.

Miller, J. Hillis. "In Memoriam [Paul de Man]." 69 (1985): 3–4.

———. "Impossible Metaphor: Stevens's 'The Red Fern' as Example." 69 (1985): 150–62.

Miller, Nancy K., and Joan Dejean. "Editors' Preface [*The Politics of Tradition: Placing Women in French Literature*]." 75 (1988): 1–6.

Miller, Nancy K. "Men's Reading, Women's Writing: Gender and the Rise of the Novel." 75 (1988): 40–55.

———. "Libertinage and Feminism." 94 (1998): 17–28.

Minor, Anne. "Nathalie Sarraute: *Le Planétarium*." Trans. Barbara Brackenridge. 24 (Summer 1959): 96–100.

———. "The Short Stories of Albert Camus." Trans. Barbara Brackenridge. 25 (Spring 1960): 75–80.

Mitchell, Jeremy. "Swinburne—The Disappointed Protagonist." 35 (December 1965): 81–88.

Mitterand, Henri. "The Calvary of Catherine Maheu: The Description of a Page in *Germinal*." Trans. Julia Bloch Frey. 42 (1969): 115–25.

Mizumura, Minae. "Renunciation." 69 (1985): 81–97.

Modiano, Patrick. *Quartier perdu* [excerpts]. Trans. Sarah Barbour. Intro. Victoria Bridges. Special Issue (1988): 259–83.

Moger, Angela S. "That Obscure Object of Narrative." 63 (1982): 129–38.

Mohrt, Michel. "Ethic and Poetry in the work of Camus." 1.1 (Spring–Summer 1948): 113–18.

———. "Three Plays of the Current Paris Season." 3.1 or 5 (1950): 100–104.

———. "Jacques Copeau, Charles Dullin." 3.1 or 5 (1950): 105–7.

———. "Robert Penn Warren and the Myth of the Outlaw." 10 (1952): 70–84.

Montag, Warren. "'The Soul is the Prison of the Body': Althusser and Foucault, 1970–1975." 88 (1995): 53–77.

Moore, Gerald. "Colonial Portraits in a Changing Frame." 53 (1976): 45–63.

Moore, W. G. "The French Notion of the Comic." 23 (Summer 1959): 47–53.

———. "Lucretius and Montaigne." 38 (May 1967): 109–14.

Morel, Jean-Pierre. "A 'Revolutionary' Poetics?" 39 (1967): 160–79.

Morot-Sir, Edouard. "The 'New Novel.'" 31 (May 1964): 166–74.

Morris, Edward. "Intimacy." 1.1 (Spring–Summer 1948): 73–79.

Morrissette, Bruce. "Games and Game Structures in Robbe-Grillet." 41 (1968): 159–67.

Mortier, Roland. "The 'Philosophes' and Public Education." 40 (1968): 62–76.

Moscovici, Serge. "The Proper Use of Polemics." Trans. M[ichel] B[eaujour]. 58 (1979): 55–83.

Mudimbe-Boyi, Elisabeth. "The Poetics of Exile and Errancy: *Le baobab fou* by Ken Bugul and *Ti Jean l'horizon* by Simone Schwarz-Bart." 83 (1993): 196–212.

Munhall, Edgar. "Portraits of Napoleon." 26 (Fall–Winter 1960–1961): 3–20.

Murdoch, H. Adlai. "Rewriting Writing: Identity, Exile, and Renewal in Assia Djebar's *L'amour, la fantasia*." 83 (1993): 71–92.

Murray, Jack. "Ionesco and the Mechanics of Memory." 29 (Spring–Summer 1962): 82–87.

———. "Proust's Beloved Enemy." 32 (October 1964): 112–17.

———. "The Mystery of Others." 34 (June 1965): 65–72.

Murray, Timothy. "Philosophical Antibodies: Grotesque Fantasy in a French Stoic Fiction." 86 (1994): 143–63.

Nancy, Jean-Luc. "Exscription." Trans. Katherine Lydon. 78 (1990): 47–65.

———. "The Unsacrificeable." Trans. Richard Livingston. 79 (1991): 20–38.

———. "Les iris." Trans. Michael Syrotinski. 81 (1992): 46–63.

Neefs, Jacques. "Cyrano: 'Des Miracles de Rivière.'" Trans. Charles S. Fineman. 49 (1974): 185–98.

Neefs, Jacques, Michel Contat, and Denis Hollier. "Editors' Preface [*Drafts*]." Trans. Alyson Waters. 89 (1996): 1–5.

Neefs, Jacques. "A Select Bibliography of Genetic Criticism." 89 (1996): 265–67.

Nepveu, Pierre. "A (Hi)story that Refuses the Telling: Poetry and the Novel in Contemporary Québécois Literature." Trans. Karen McPherson. 65 (1983): 90–105.

Nesbit, Molly. "What Was an Author?" 73 (1987): 229–57.

Newels, Margarete. "From Narrative Style to Dramatic Style in *Les moralités*." Trans. Joe Breines. Special Issue (1991): 252–68.

Newmark, Kevin. "Editor's Preface [*Phantom Proxies: Symbolism and the Rhetoric of History*]." 74 (1988): iii–vii.

———. "The Forgotten Figures of Symbolism: Nerval's *Sylvie*." 74 (1988): 207–29.

———. "Beneath the Lace: Mallarmé, the State, and the Foundation of Letters." 77 (1990): 243–75.

———. "Ingesting the Mummy: Proust's Allegory of Memory." 79 (1991): 150–77.

Nichols, Stephen G., and Kevin Brownlee. "Editor's Preface [*Images of Power: Medieval History/Discourse/Literature*]." 70 (1986): 1–4.

Nichols, Stephen G. "Fission and Fusion: Mediations of Power in Medieval History and Literature." 70 (1986): 21–41.

———. "Medieval Women Writers: *Aisthesis* and the Powers of Marginality." 75 (1988): 77–94.

——. "Marie de France's Commonplaces." Special Issue (1991): 134–48.

——. "Poetic Places and Real Spaces: Anthropology of Space in Crusade Literature." 95 (1999): 111–33.

Niess, Robert L. "Julien Benda: The Poet's Function." 2.2 or 4 (1949): 67–78.

Nodelman, Sheldon. "Structural Analysis in Art and Anthropology." 36 & 37 (October 1966): 89–103.

Norman, Buford. "Thought and Language in Pascal." 49 (1974): 110–19.

Noth, Ernst Erich. "The Prophetism of Georges Bernanos." 2.2 or 4 (1949): 105–19.

——. "The Struggle for Gide's Soul." 7 (1951): 12–20.

Noulet, E. "Tone in the Poems of Paul Valéry." Trans. Georges Bernauer. 44 (1970): 39–50.

Nouvet, Claire. "Foreword [*Literature and the Ethical Question*]." 79 (1991): 1–2.

——. "An Impossible Response: The Disaster of Narcissus." 79 (1991): 103–34.

——. "Dangerous Resemblances: The *Romance of the Rose*." Special Issue (1991): 196–209.

O'Brien, Justin. "Gide's Fictional Technique." 7 (1951): 81–90.

O'Doherty, Brian. "Man Ray." 31 (May 1964): 119–22.

O'Donnell, Thomas. "Robbe-Grillet's Ghost Town." 57 (1979): 195–207.

Okam, Hilary H. "Introduction [*Traditional and Contemporary African Literature*]." 53 (1976): 3–4.

——. "Aspects of Imagery and Symbolism in the Poetry of Aimé Césaire." 53 (1976): 175–96.

Ollier, Marie-Louise. "The Author in the Text: The Prologues of Chrétien de Troyes." Trans. David Baker. 51 (1974): 26–41.

Orr, Linda. "A Sort of History: Michelet's *La sorcière*." 59 (1980): 119–36.

——. "The Blind Spot of History: Logography." 73 (1987): 190–214.

Ortali, Ray. "Ronsard: From *Chevelure* to *Rond Parfait*." Trans. Buford Norman. 47 (1972): 90–97.

Osmont, Robert. "J. J. Rousseau and the Idea of Love." Trans. E.R. Porter. 28 (Fall–Winter 1961–62): 43–47.

Owen, Stephen. "A Monologue of the Senses." 61 (1981): 244–60.

Oxenhandler, Neal. "'The Balcony' of Charles Baudelaire." 9 (1952): 56–62.

——. "Jacob's Struggle with the Angel." 12 (Fall–Winter 1953): 41–46.

——. "Jean Cocteau: Theatre as Parade." 14 (Winter 1954–55): 71–75.

——. "*Nekrassov* and the Critics." 16 (Winter 1955–56): 8–12.

——. "Poetry in Three Films of Jean Cocteau." 17 (Summer 1956): 14–20.

Pacifici, Sergio J. "Existentialism and Italian Literature." 16 (Winter 1955–56): 79–88.

——. "Notes Toward a Definition of Neo-Realism." 17 (Summer 1956): 44–53.

———. "Something Old and Something New: A View of Contemporary Italian Poetry." 21 (Spring–Summer 1958): 154–67.

Paganini, Maria. "Intertextuality and the Strategy of Desire: Proust's 'Mélancolique Villégiature de Mme de Breyves.'" Trans. Janet Beizer. 57 (1979): 136–63.

Pamplume, Louis. "Gabriel Marcel: Existence, Being, and Faith." Trans. Beth Brombert. 12 (Fall–Winter 1953): 88–100.

Pardee, W. Hearne. "The Images of Vision." 34 (June 1965): 19–23.

Parnell, Charles. "André Gide and his *Symphonie pastorale.*" 7 (1951): 60–71.

Parry, Adam. "Thucydides' Use of Abstract Language." 45 (1970): 3–20.

Pasinetti, P. M. "The 'Jeanne Duval' Poems in *Les fleurs du mal.*" 1.2 (Fall–Winter 1948): 112–17.

Pastoureau, Henri. "Sado-Masochism and the Philosophies of Ambivalence." 35 (December 1965): 48–60.

Paterson, Janet M. "Anne Hébert and the Discourse of the Unreal." 65 (1983): 172–86.

Patterson, Yolanda Astarita. "Simone de Beauvoir and the Demystification of Motherhood." 72 (1986): 87–105.

———. "Some Personal Reflections [In Memoriam: Simone de Beauvoir]." 72 (1986): 207–9.

Pavel, Thomas G. "Racine and Stendhal." 76 (1989): 265–83.

Payen, Jean-Charles. "A Semiological Study of Guillaume de Lorris." Trans. Margaret Ann Leff. 51 (1974): 170–84.

Pecora, Vincent P. "Ethics, Politics, and the Middle Voice." 79 (1991): 203–30.

Pepper, Thomas. "Kneel and You Will Believe." 88 (1995): 27–41.

———. "Editor's Preface: The Law—The Not Good Enough Father [*The Place of Maurice Blanchot*]." 93 (1998): 1–7.

Percheron, Daniel. "Sound in Cinema and its Relationship to Image and Diegesis." Trans. Marcia Butzel. 60 (1980): 16–23.

Perec, Georges. "Still Life/Style Leaf." Trans. Harry Mathews. 61 (1981): 299–305.

———. *W ou le souvenir d'enfance* [excerpt]. Intro. and Trans. Leonard R. Koos. Special Issue (1988): 185–208.

Perron, Paul. "On Language and Writing in Gérard Bessette's Fiction." Trans. Brian Massumi. 65 (1983): 227–45.

Peschel, Enid Rhodes. "Foreword [*Intoxication and Literature*]." 50 (1974): 5–7.

———. "Arthur Rimbaud: The Aesthetics of Intoxication." 50 (1974): 65–80.

Peyre, Henri. "Existentialism—A Literature of Despair?" 1.1 (Spring–Summer 1948): 21–32.

———. "The Significance of Surrealism." 1.2 (Fall–Winter 1948): 34–49.

———. "What Greece Means to Modern France." 6 (1950): 53–62.

————. "English Literature Seen through French Eyes." 6 (1950): 109–19.

————. "Friends and Foes of Pascal in France Today." 12 (Fall–Winter 1953): 8–18.

————. "Romantic Poetry and Rhetoric." 13 (Spring–Summer 1954): 30–41.

————. "Paul Claudel (1868–1955)." 14 (Winter 1954–55): 94–97.

————. "Painters and Sculptors of France Today." 19 & 20 (Spring 1957–Winter 1958): 50–74.

————. "French Poets of Today." 21 (Spring–Summer 1958): 118–34.

————. "Camus the Pagan." 25 (Spring 1960): 20–25.

————. "Napoleon: Devil, Poet, Saint." 26 (Fall–Winter 1960–1961): 21–31.

————. "Note on a Few Recent Publications on Napoleon." 26 (Fall–Winter 1960–1961): 128–30.

————. "Contemporary Feminine Literature in France." 27 (Spring–Summer 1961): 47–65.

————. "The Significance of Surrealism." 31 (May 1964): 23–36.

————. "Shakespeare's Women: A French View." 33 (December 1964): 107–19.

Pflaum-Vallin, Marie-Monique. "Elsa Triolet and Aragon: Back to Lilith." Trans. Joseph H. McMahon. 27 (Spring–Summer 1961): 86–89.

Philip, André. "France's Economic Situation." Trans. Raymond Giraud. 15 (Winter 1954–55): 89–98.

Philip, Michel. "Balzac's Heaven and Hell." 32 (October 1964): 77–81.

————. "The Hidden Onlooker." 34 (June 1965): 37–42.

Picard, Raymond. "Racine Among Us." Trans. John M. Guret. 3.1 or 5 (1950): 41–50.

Picon, Gaëtan. "Remarks on Gide's Ethics." 7 (1951): 3–11.

————. "Concerning Noël Devaulx." 8 (1951): 48–50.

————. "Man's Hope." Trans. Rima Drell Reck. 18 (Winter 1957): 3–6.

————. "Zola's Painters." Trans. J. L. Logan. 42 (1969): 126–42.

Pingaud, Bernard. "The School of Refusal." Trans. Kenneth Douglas. 24 (Summer 1959): 18–21.

Pinget, Robert. *Charrue* [excerpt]. Trans. Karen McPherson. Intro. Martine Reid. Trans. Brigitte Szymanek. Special Issue (1988): 97–114.

Pitou, Spire. "Evil, Grace, and Luc Estang." 12 (Fall–Winter 1953): 47–53.

Pizzorusso, Arnaldo. "Situations and Environment in *Margot la ravaudeuse*." 40 (1968): 142–55.

Plantinga, Leon B. "Berlioz' Use of Shakespearian Themes." 33 (December 1964): 72–79.

Pletsch, Carl. "The Self-Sufficient Text in Nietzsche and Kierkegaard." 66 (1984): 160–88.

Plottel, Jeanine Parisier. "Surrealist Archives of Anxiety." 66 (1984): 121–34.

Poggioli, Renato. "The Poetry of St.-J. Perse." 1.2 (Fall–Winter 1948): 5–33.

———. "The Avant-Garde and Politics." 39 (1967): 180–87.

Poirion, Daniel. "Afterword [*Contexts: Style and Values in Medieval Art and Literature*]." Trans. Sahar Amer. Special Issue (1991): 281–86.

———. "Mask and Allegorical Personifcation." 95 (1999): 13–32.

———. "Literature as Memory: 'Wo die Zeit wird Raum.'" 95 (1999): 33–46.

Poloniecka, Rysia. "Herring Story." Trans. Anna Lehmann. 85 (1994): 81–90.

Ponge, Francis. "The Goat." Trans. Henry B. Richardson. 21 (Spring–Summer 1958): 168–71.

Pontalis, J. B. "Michel Leiris, or Psychoanalysis without End." Trans. David Macey. 81 (1992): 128–44.

Pontalis, J. B., and Jean Laplanche. "Appendices ["Anaclisis," "Deferred Action," "Foreclosure," "Imaginary," "Mirror Stage," "Narcissism," "Phallus," "Symbolic"]." Selected articles from *Vocabulaire de la psychanalyse*. Trans. Peter Kussel and Jeffrey Mehlman. 48 (1972): 179–202.

Porter, Charles A. "Françoise d'Eaubonne's *Le temps d'apprendre à vivre*." 27 (Spring–Summer 1961): 142–43.

———. "Imperiled Pedestrian." 32 (October 1964): 55–67.

———. "Chateaubriand's Classicism." 38 (May 1967): 156–71.

———. "Life in Restif Country." 40 (1968): 103–17.

———. "Foreword [*Men/Women of Letters*]." 71 (1986): 1–14.

———. "Foreword [*After the Age of Suspicion: The French Novel Today*]." Special Issue (1988): 1–4.

Porter, Charles A., Brigitte Mahuzier, Karen McPherson, and Ralph Sarkonak. "Editors' Preface [*Same Sex / Different Text? Gay and Lesbian Writing in French*]." 90 (1996): 1–4.

Portuges, Catherine. "Attachment and Separation in *The Memoirs of a Dutiful Daughter*." 72 (1986): 107–18.

Poulet, Georges. "Maurice Blanchot as Novelist." 8 (1951): 77–81.

Prévert, Jacques. "Picasso Goes for a Stroll." Trans. Noelle Gillmor. 21 (Spring–Summer 1958): 14–15.

Price, Blanche. "Jean Grosjean—An Introduction." 21 (Spring–Summer 1958): 32–39.

Price, Jonathan B. "Montherlant's Exemplar." 33 (December 1964): 101–4.

Priebe, Richard. "Demonic Imagery and the Apocalyptic Vision in the Novels of Ayi Kwei Armah." 53 (1976): 102–36.

Prince, Gerald. "*La nausée* and the Question of Closure." 67 (1984): 182–90.

Pucci, Suzanne Rodin. "The Spectator Surfaces: Tableau and Tabloid in Marivaux's *Spectateur français*." 92 (1997): 149–70.

Pucciani, Oreste. "The Universal Language of Symbolism." 9 (1952): 27–35.

Putnam, Michael. "Simple Tibullus and the Ruse of Style." 45 (1970): 21–32.

Quinn, Patrick F. "The Profundities of Edgar Poe." 6 (1950): 3–13.

Rabaté, Dominique. "The Critical Turn: Blanchot Reads des Forêts." Trans. Thomas Pepper. 93 (1998): 69–80.

Raczymow, Henri. "*Tales of Exile and Forgetfulness* (Excerpt)." Trans. Alan Astro. 85 (1994): 91–97.

———. "Memory Shot Through with Holes." Trans. Alan Astro. 85 (1994): 98–105.

Radcliff-Umstead, Douglas. "Giulio Camillo's Emblems of Memory." 47 (1972): 47–56.

Radke, Judith J. "The Theatre of Samuel Beckett: 'Une durée à animer.'" 29 (Spring–Summer 1962): 57–64.

Ragon, Michel. "In Praise of Sculpture." Trans. Howard B. Garey. 19 & 20 (Spring 1957–Winter 1958): 15–26.

Ramsey, Warren. "Supervielle's 'L'escalier.'" 1.2 (Fall–Winter 1948): 65–66.

———. "Laforgue and the Ironic Equilibrium." 1.2 (Fall–Winter 1948): 125–39.

———. "'Words of Light' and 'Somber Leaves': The Poetry of Léon-Paul Fargue." 9 (1952): 112–22.

Ranum, Orest. "Encrustation and Power in Early Modern French Baroque Culture." 80 (1991): 202–26.

Raoul, Valerie. "Documents of Non-identity: The Diary Novel in Québec." 65 (1983): 187–200.

Rastier, François, and A. J. Greimas. "The Interaction of Semiotic Constraints." 41 (1968): 86–105.

Raybaud, Antoine. "Nomadism between the Archaic and the Modern." Trans. Ronnie Scharfman. 82 (1993): 146–57.

Reck, Rima Drell. "Françoise Mallet-Joris and the Anatomy of the Will." 24 (Summer 1959): 74–79.

———. "*Les mandarins*: Sensibility, Responsibility." 27 (Spring–Summer 1961): 33–40.

———. "Appearance and Reality in Genet's *Le balcon*." 29 (Spring–Summer 1962): 20–25.

———. "Mauriac's Inferno." 32 (October 1964): 118–23.

Reeder, Claudia, Colette Gaudin, Mary Jean Green, Lynn Anthony Higgins, Marianne Hirsch, Vivian Kogan, and Nancy Vickers. "Introduction [*Feminist Readings: French Texts/American Contexts*]." 62 (1981): 2–18.

Regalado, Antonio. "The Counterrevolutionary Image of the World." 39 (1967): 98–118.

Regalado, Nancy Freeman. "Poets of the Early City." 32 (October 1964): 12–21.

———. "Effet de réel, Effet du réel: Representation and Reference in Villon's *Testament*." 70 (1986): 63–77.

———. "Introduction [*Contexts: Style and Values in Medieval Art and Literature*]." Special Issue (1991): 1–7.

————. "The Medieval Construction of the Modern Reader: Solomon's Ship and the Birth of Jean de Meun." 95 (1999): 81–108.

Reichler, Claude. "Talma as Néron in *Britannicus*, or, Putting a Monster to Good Use." Trans. Deidre Dawson. 76 (1989): 127–45.

Reid, Martine. "Correspondences: *Stendhal en toutes lettres*." Trans. Mark Gross with Alan Stoekl. 71 (1986): 149–68.

————. "Editor's Preface: Legible/Visible [*Boundaries: Writing and Drawing*]." Trans. Nigel P. Turner. 84 (1994): 1–12.

————. "Bricolage: An Interview with Michel Butor." Trans. Noah Guynn. 84 (1994): 17–26.

Reiss, Timothy J. "The Dialectic of Language in the Theater: Corneille from *Mélite* to *Le Cid*." 45 (1970): 87–101.

————. "Psychical Distance and Theatrical Distancing in Sartre's Drama." 46 (1971): 5–16.

————. "Jodelle's *Cléopâtre* and the Enchanted Circle." 47 (1972): 199–210.

————. "Introduction: The Word/World Equation [*Science, Language, and the Perspective Mind: Studies in Literature and Thought from Campanella to Bayle*]." 49 (1974): 3–12.

————. "Structure and Mind in Two Seventeenth-Century Utopias: Campanella and Bacon." 49 (1974): 82–95.

————. "Descartes, the Palatinate, and the Thirty Years War: Political Theory and Political Practice." 80 (1991): 108–45.

Rendall, Steven. "Montaigne under the Sign of Fama." 66 (1984): 137–59.

Reverdy, Pierre. "Four Poems from *La lucarne ovale* ["Monotonous Day," "Motionless Reality," "For the Moment," "From Another Sky"]." Trans. Robert Cohn. 1.2 (Fall–Winter 1948): 59–62.

Rey, Jean-Michel. "Freud's Writing on Writing." Trans. G.W. Most and James Hulbert. 55 & 56 (1977): 301–28.

Riberette, Pierre. "On Editing Chateaubriand's Correspondence." Trans. Charles A. Porter. 71 (1986): 131–47.

Rice, Donald B. "In the Interval: Butor and Decor." 57 (1979): 208–27.

Richman, Michèle. "Bataille Moralist?: *Critique* and the Postwar Writings." 78 (1990): 143–68.

————. "Leiris's *L'âge d'homme*: Politics and the Sacred in Everyday Ethnography." 81 (1992): 91–110.

Ricoeur, Paul. "Sartre's *Lucifer and the Lord*." 14 (Winter 1954–55): 85–93.

Ridgely, Beverly S. "Racan and the Old and New Astronomies." 49 (1974): 154–69.

Riffaterre, Michael. "Describing Poetic Structures: Two Approaches to Baudelaire's *Les chats*." 36 & 37 (October 1966): 200–42.

————. "Descriptive Imagery." 61 (1981): 107–25.

————. "Prosopopeia." 69 (1985): 107–23.

Rifkin, Adrian. "Musical Moments." 73 (1987): 121–55.

Rigolot, François. "Montaigne's Purloined Letters." 64 (1983): 145–66.

Rippere, Victoria L. "Towards an Anthropology of Literature." 36 & 37 (October 1966): 243–51.

Robbins, Jill. "*Visage, Figure:* Reading Levinas's *Totality and Infinity*." 79 (1991): 135–49.

Robert, Marthe. "The Grimm Brothers." Trans. Wyley L. Powell. 43 (1969): 44–56.

Robichon, Suzanne, and Anne F. Garréta. "Select Bibliography of Works in French Related to Lesbian Issues and Problematics." 90 (1996): 242–52.

Robin, Régine. "Toward Fiction as Oblique Discourse." Trans. Marie-Rose Logan. 59 (1980): 230–42.

Robinson-Valéry, Judith. "Valéry's View of Mental Creativity." 44 (1970): 3–18.

———. "The 'Rough' and the 'Polished.'" 89 (1996): 59–66.

Rocheleau, Alain-Michel. "Gay Theater in Quebec: The Search for an Identity." Trans. Luke Sandford. 90 (1996): 115–36.

Roedig, Charles F. "Malraux on the Novel (1930–1945)." 18 (Winter 1957): 39–44.

———. "A Bibliographic Note on Malraux's Art Criticism." 18 (Winter 1957): 129–30.

Roger, Philippe. "The Distracted Womanizer." Trans. Bettina Lerner. 94 (1998): 163–78.

Romanowski, Sylvie. "Descartes: From Science to Discourse." 49 (1974): 96–109.

Ron, Moshe. "A Reading of 'The Real Thing.'" 58 (1979): 190–213.

———. "The Art of the Portrait According to James." 69 (1985): 222–37.

Rooney, Ellen. "Better Read Than Dead: Althusser and the Fetish of Ideology." 88 (1995): 183–200.

Ropars-Wuilleumier, Marie-Claire. "The Disembodied Voice: *India Song*." Trans. Kimberly Smith. 60 (1980): 241–68.

Roque, Georges. "Writing/Drawing/Color." Trans. Caroline Weber. 84 (1994): 43–62.

Rosello, Mireille. "'One More Sea to Cross': Exile and Intertextuality in Aimé Césaire's *Cahier d'un retour au pays natal*." Trans. Robert Postawsko. 83 (1993): 176–95.

Rosen, Philip. "Adorno and Film Music: Theoretical Notes on *Composing for the Films*." 60 (1980): 157–82.

Ross, Kristin, and Alice Kaplan. "Introduction [*Everyday Life*]." 73 (1987): 1–4.

Ross, Kristin. "Rimbaud and the Transformation of Social Space." 73 (1987): 104–20.

———. "Schoolteachers, Maids, and Other Paranoid Histories." 91 (1997): 7–27.

Roudiez, Leon S. "A Glance at the Vocabulary of Nathalie Sarraute." 27 (Spring–Summer 1961): 90–98.

Roussin, Philippe, and Alice Kaplan. "A Changing Idea of Literature: The Bibliothèque de la Pléiade." 89 (1996): 237–62.

Rubé, Pierre. "Who Was Albert Camus?" Trans. Kenneth Douglas. 25 (Spring 1960): 3–9.

Rubin, David Lee. "Consciousness and the External World in a Caprice by Saint-Amant." 49 (1974): 170–77.

Russell, Daniel. "Du Bellay's Emblematic Vision of Rome." 47 (1972): 98–109.

Russo, Elena. "Editor's Preface [Exploring the Conversible World: Text and Sociability from the Classical Age to the Enlightenment]." 92 (1997): 1–7.

———. "The Self, Real and Imaginary: Social Sentiment in Marivaux and Hume." 92 (1997): 126–48.

Ryan, Michael. "Deconstruction and Radical Teaching." 63 (1982): 45–58.

Sabbagh, Céline. "Calypso: A Theme of Ambiguity, a Theme of Fascination." 44 (1970): 106–18.

Sade, D. A. F. de. "Notes on the Novel." 35 (December 1965): 12–19.

Saint-Amand, Pierre. "The Secretive Body: Roland Barthes's Gay Erotics." Trans. Charles A. Porter and Noah Guynn. 90 (1996): 153–71.

———. "The Immortals." Trans. Jennifer Curtiss Gage. 94 (1998): 116–29.

Sallenave, Danièle. Les portes de Gubbio [excerpt]. Intro. and Trans. Deidre Dawson. Special Issue (1988): 237–57.

Sarkonak, Ralph. "Editor's Preface [The Language of Difference: Writing in QUEBEC(ois)]." 65 (1983): iii–vi.

———. "Accentuating the Differences." 65 (1983): 3–20.

———. "A Brief Chronology of French Canada, 1534–1982." 65 (1983): 275–82.

Sarkonak, Ralph, Brigitte Mahuzier, Karen McPherson, and Charles A. Porter. "Editors' Preface [Same Sex / Different Text? Gay and Lesbian Writing in French]." 90 (1996): 1–4.

———. "Traces and Shadows: Fragments of Hervé Guibert." 90 (1996): 172–202.

Sarraute, Nathalie. Disent les imbéciles [excerpt]. Trans. Maria Jolas. L'usage de la parole [excerpt]. Trans. Barbara Wright in consultation with the author. Elle est là [excerpt]. Trans. Marie-Anne Fleming. Enfance [excerpt]. Trans. Barbara Wright in consultation with the author. Intro. Eric Eigenmann. Special Issue (1988): 7–24.

Sartre, Jean-Paul. "Scenes from Les mains sales." 1.1 (Spring–Summer 1948): 3–20.

———. "William Faulkner's Sartoris." 10 (1952): 95–99.

———. "The Anti-Novel of Nathalie Sarraute." Trans. Beth Brombert. 16 (Winter 1955–56): 40–44.

———. "From *Being and Nothingness*: The Caress." Trans. Kenneth Douglas. 16 (Winter 1955–56): 96–99.

———. "Sartre's Notes for the Fourth Volume of *The Family Idiot*." Trans. Philippe Hunt and Philip Wood. 68 (1985): 165–88.

Sauvy, Alfred. "Estimates and Life." Trans. Kenneth Douglas. 15 (Winter 1954–55): 99–114.

Savigneau, Josyane, and Anne F. Garréta. "A Conversation." 90 (1996): 214–34.

Scaldini, Richard J. "*Les aventures de Télémaque*, or Alienated in Ogygia." 57 (1979): 164–79.

Scharfman, Ronnie. "Mirroring and Mothering in Simone Schwartz-Bart's *Pluie et vent sur Télumée Miracle* and Jean Rhys' *Wide Sargasso Sea*." 62 (1981): 88–106.

Scharfman, Ronnie, and Françoise Lionnet. "Editors' Preface [*Post/Colonial Conditions: Exiles, Migrations, and Nomadisms*. Vol. 2]." 82 (1993): 1–2.

Scharfman, Ronnie. "The Other's Other: The Moroccan-Jewish Trajectory of Edmond Amran El Maleh." 82 (1993): 135–45.

Schechner, Richard. "The Enactment of the 'Not' in Eugène Ionesco's *Les chaises*." 29 (Spring–Summer 1962): 65–72.

Scheffler, Harold W. "Structuralism in Anthropology." 36 & 37 (October 1966): 66–88.

Schehr, Lawrence R. "Defense and Illustration of Gay Liberation." 90 (1996): 139–52.

Schendel, Michel van. "*Refus global*, or the Formula and History." Trans. Ruth G. Koizim. 65 (1983): 53–73.

Schestag, Thomas. "Mantis, Relics." Trans. Georgia Albert. 93 (1990): 221–51.

Schivelbusch, Wolfgang. "The Policing of Street Lighting." 73 (1987): 61–74.

Schneider, Pierre. "A Note on the Exquisite Corpse." 1.2 (Fall–Winter 1948): 85–91.

———. "Jean-Paul Riopelle." Trans. Paul Mankin. 19 & 20 (Spring 1957–Winter 1958): 85–93.

Schor, Naomi. "Introduction [*Zola*]." 42 (1969): 5–7.

———. "Zola: From Window to Window." 42 (1969): 38–51.

———. "Female Paranoia: The Case for Psychoanalytic Feminist Criticism." 62 (1981): 204–19.

———. "Idealism in the Novel: Recanonizing Sand." 75 (1988): 56–73.

Schwab, Gabriele. "The Dialectic of Opening and Closing in Samuel Beckett's *Endgame*." Trans. D.L. Selden. 67 (1984): 191–202.

Schwartz, Jerome. "Gargantua's Device and the Abbey of Theleme: A Study in Rabelais' Iconography." 47 (1972): 232–42.

Scodel, Joshua. "The Affirmation of Paradox: A Reading of Montaigne's 'De la Phisionomie' (III:12)." 64 (1983): 209–37.

Scully, Vincent J., Jr. "The Nature of the Classical in Art." 19 & 20 (Spring 1957–Winter 1958): 107–24.

Seidel, Linda. "The Value of Verisimilitude in the Art of Jan van Eyck." Special Issue (1991): 25–43.

Seliwoniuk, Jadwiga. "Gérard Bessette and His Dream of 'Genarration.'" 65 (1983): 246–55.

Sellin, Eric. "The Unknown Voice of Yambo Ouologuem." 53 (1976): 137–62.

Semple, Benjamin, and Françoise Jaouën. "Editors' Preface: The Body into Text [*Corps Mystique, Corps Sacré: Textual Transfigurations of the Body from the Middle Ages to the Seventeenth Century*]." 86 (1994): 1–4.

Semple, Benjamin. "The Male Psyche and the Female Sacred Body in Marie de France and Christine de Pizan." 86 (1994): 164–86.

Senghor, Léopold Sedar. "Song (For Two Flutes and a Far-away Tom-Tom)" in "Two Love Poems from the French Colonies." Trans. Miriam Koshland. 11 (1953?): 4.

Serge, Victor. "Is a Proletarian Literature Possible?" Trans. Anna Aschenbach. 39 (1967): 137–45.

Serres, Michel. "Jules Verne's Strange Journeys." Trans. Maria Malanchuk. 52 (1975): 174–88.

Shank, Theodore. "The Theatre of the Cultural Revolution." Trans. Wyley L. Powell. 46 (1971): 167–85.

Sharrat, Peter. "Peter Ramus and Imitation: Image, Sign, and Sacrament." 47 (1972): 19–32.

Shattuck, Roger. "The Doubting of Fiction." 6 (1950): 101–8.

———. "Proust's Stilts." 34 (June 1965): 91–98.

Shiff, Richard. "The Original, the Imitation, the Copy, and the Spontaneous Classic: Theory and Painting in Nineteenth-Century France." 66 (1984): 27–54.

Showalter, English, Jr. "Money Matters and Early Novels." 40 (1968): 118–33.

———. "Authorial Self-Consciousness in the Familiar Letter: The Case of Madame de Graffigny." 71 (1986): 113–30.

———. "Writing off the Stage: Women Authors and Eighteenth-Century Theater." 75 (1988): 95–111.

Sibony, Daniel. "*Hamlet*: A Writing-Effect." Trans. James Hulbert with the assistance of Joshua Wilner. 55 & 56 (1977): 53–93.

Siegfried, André. "History of the Mendès-France Government." Trans. Bryant C. Freeman. 15 (Winter 1954–55): 61–67.

Simon, Alfred. "The Theatre in May." William F. Panici. 46 (1971): 139–48.

Simon, Claude. *Leçon de choses*. Trans. Daniel Weissbort. Intro. Barbara Vinken. Special Issue (1988): 45–60.

Simon, John F. "Hulot, or, The Common Man as Observer and Critic." 23 (Summer 1959): 18–25.

Simon, John K. "The Glance of Idiots: The Novel of the Absurd?" 25 (Spring 1960): 111–19.

———. "Madness in Sartre: Sequestration and the Room." 30 (1963): 63–67.

Simons, Margaret A. "Beauvoir and Sartre: The Philosophical Relationship." 72 (1986): 165–79.

———. ["In Memoriam: Simone de Beauvoir"]. 72 (1986): 203–5.

Simont, Juliette. "The *Critique of Dialectical Reason*: From Need to Need, Circularly." Trans. Thomas Trezise. 68 (1985): 108–23.

Sivert, Eileen Boyd. "*Lélia* and Feminism." 62 (1981): 45–66.

Slochower, Harry. "The Function of Myth in Existentialism." 1.1 (Spring–Summer 1948): 42–52.

———. "André Gide's *Theseus* and the French Myth." 2.2 or 4 (1949): 34–43.

Smith, John E. "Rousseau, Romanticism, and the Philosophy of Existence."13 (Spring–Summer 1954): 52–61.

Smith, Madeleine M. "The Making of a Leader." 1.1 (Spring–Summer 1948): 80–83.

———. "Mallarmé and the *Chimères*." 11 (1953?): 59–72.

Smith, Stephen. "Fragments of Landscape, Scraps of Décor: Maurice Roche's *Compact*." 57 (1979): 48–57.

Sobel, Eli. "The Earliest Allegories and Imagery of Hans Sachs: An Introductory Essay." 47 (1972): 211–17.

Sollers, Philippe. "Freud's Hand." Trans. Barbara Johnson. 55 & 56 (1977): 329–37.

———. *Femmes* [excerpt]. Intro. and Trans. Philip Barnard and Cheryl Lester. Special Issue (1988): 163–84.

———. "What Is Libertinage?" Interviewed by Catherine Cusset. Trans. Roger Celestin. 94 (1998): 199–212.

Solomon, Philip H. "Céline's *Death on the Installment Plan*: The Intoxications of Delirium." 50 (1974): 191–203.

———. "Foreword [*Locus: Space, Landscape, Decor in Modern French Fiction*]." 57 (1979): 3–4.

———. "The View from a Rump: America as Journey and Landscape of Desire in Céline's *Voyage au bout de la nuit*." 57 (1979): 5–22.

Sonnenfeld, Albert. "The Yellow Laugh of Tristan Corbière." 23 (Summer 1959): 39–46.

———. "Napoleon as Sun Myth." 26 (Fall–Winter 1960–1961): 32–36.

———. "Hamlet the German and Jules Laforgue." 33 (December 1964): 92–100.

———. "Mallarmé: The Poet as Actor as Reader." 54 (1977): 159–72.

Soriano, Marc. "From Tales of Warning to Formulettes: The Oral Tradition in French Children's Literature." Trans. Julia Bloch Frey. 43 (1969): 24–43.

Soupault, Philippe. "Traces Which Last." 31 (May 1964): 9–22.

Spackman, Barbara. "Machiavelli and Maxims." 77 (1990): 137–55.

Spear, Thomas. "Politics and Literature: An Interview with Tahar Ben Jelloun." Trans. Caren Litherland. 83 (1993): 30–43.

Spence, Jonathan. "On Chinese Revolutionary Literature." 39 (1967): 215–25.

Spivak, Gayatri Chakravorty. "The Letter as Cutting Edge." 55 & 56 (1977): 208–26.

———. "French Feminism in an International Frame." 62 (1981): 154–84.

Spoerri, Theophil. "Mérimée and the Short Story." Trans. Trude Douglas. 2.2 or 4 (1949): 3–11.

———. "The Smile of Molière." Trans. Kenneth Douglas. 3.1 or 5 (1950): 51–65.

Sprinker, Michael. "The Legacies of Althusser." 88 (1995): 201–25.

St. Aubyn, Frédéric. "The Social Consciousness of Rimbaud." 2.2 or 4 (1949): 26–33.

Stamelman, Richard. "The Strangeness of the Other and the Otherness of the Stranger: Edmond Jabès." 82 (1993): 118–34.

Stanton, Domna C. "The Fiction of Préciosité and the Fear of Women." 62 (1981): 107–34.

Starobinski, Jean. "The Illness of Rousseau." 28 (Fall–Winter 1961–62): 64–74.

———. "Reflections on Some Symbols of the Revolution." Trans. John D. Lyons. 40 (1968): 47–61.

———. "The Body's Moment." Trans. John A. Gallucci. 64 (1983): 273–305.

Stegmann, André. "Richness and Ambivalence of the Symbol in the Renaissance." Trans. Jean-Pierre Coursodon and Edward Miller. 47 (1972): 5–18.

Stein, Gertrude. "Jean Atlan: Abstract Painting." 31 (May 1964): 118.

Steiner, Herbert. "A Note on 'Symbolism.'" 9 (1952): 36–39.

Sternberg, Meir. "Ordering the Unordered: Time, Space, and Descriptive Coherence." 61 (1981): 60–88.

Stewart, Philip. "The Child Comes of Age." 40 (1968): 134–41.

Stierle, Karlheinz. "Position and Negation in Mallarmé's 'Prose pour des Esseintes.'" Trans. Sibylle Kisro. 54 (1977): 96–117.

Stock, Brian. "History, Literature, and Medieval Textuality." 70 (1986): 7–17.

Stock, Irvin. "A View of Les faux monnayeurs." 7 (1951): 72–80.

Stoekl, Allan. "Editor's Preface [On Bataille]." 78 (1990): 1–6.

———. "Truman's Apotheosis: Bataille, 'Planisme,' and Headlessness." 78 (1990): 181–205.

Strauss, Jonathan. "The Inverted Icarus." 78 (1990): 106–23.

Suchecky, Bernard. "The Carmelite Convent at Auschwitz: The Nature and Scope of a Failure." 85 (1994): 160–73.

Suleiman, Susan Rubin. "A Double Margin: Reflections on Women Writers and the Avant-garde in France." 75 (1988): 148–72.

Sungolowsky, Joseph. "Vigny's Unmythical Vision of Napoleon." 26 (Fall–Winter 1960–1961): 63–69.

———. "Criticism of *Anti-Semite and Jew*." 30 (1963): 68–72.

Supervielle, Jules. "'L'escalier.'" 1.2 (Fall–Winter 1948): 3–4.

———. "In Space and Time" and "Descent of Giants." Trans. Warren Ramsey. 1.2 (Fall–Winter 1948): 63–64.

Sutherland, Donald. "Time on our Hands." 10 (1952): 5–13.

Swados, Harvey. "*La Strada*: Realism and the Comedy of Poverty." 17 (Summer 1956): 38–43.

Swenson, James. "Revolutionary Sentences." 93 (1998): 11–29.

Syrotinski, Michael. "Noncoincidences: Blanchot Reading Paulhan." 93 (1998): 81–98.

Taine, Hippolyte. "The Brink of an Abyss." 33 (December 1964): 33–36.

Talarico, Kathryn Marie. "Fundare domum: Medieval Modes and the *Roman d'Eneas*." 61 (1981): 202–24.

Talon, Henri A. "Julian Green: The American-born French Novelist." 10 (1952): 29–42.

Taylor, Robert E. "The SEXpressive *S* in Sade and Sartre." 11 (1953?): 18–24.

Temmer, Mark J. "The Poetry of Geo Norge." 21 (Spring–Summer 1958): 49–59.

———. "Comedy in *The Charterhouse of Parma*." 23 (Summer 1959): 92–99.

———. "Rousseau and Thoreau." 28 (Fall–Winter 1961–62): 112–21.

———. "André Pieyre de Mandiargues." 31 (May 1964): 99–104.

———. "Style and Rhetoric." 35 (December 1965): 20–28.

Terdiman, Richard. "Structures of Initiation: On Semiotic Education and Its Contradictions in Balzac." 63 (1982): 198–226.

Thévoz, Michel. "Dubuffet: The Nutcracker." Trans. Laura Harwood Wittman. 84 (1994): 198–221.

Thibaudeau, Barbara. "Condemned to Lie." 34 (June 1965): 55–63.

Thibaudeau, Jean. "Novels, not Philosophy." Trans. Wayne Guymon. 52 (1975): 311–26.

Thiesse, Anne-Marie, and Hélène Mathieu. "The Decline of the Classical Age and the Birth of the Classics." Trans. Lauren Doyle-McCombs. 75 (1988): 208–28.

Thomas, Chantal. "The Role of Female Homosexuality in Casanova's *Memoirs*." Trans. Noah Guynn. 94 (1998): 179–83.

Thomas, Henri. *Le croc des chiffoniers* [excerpts]. Intro and Trans. Michael Syrotinski. Special Issue (1988): 25–44.

Thomasset, Claude. "Toward an Understanding of 'Truthfulness' in the French Version of the *Pratique* by Maître Bernard de Gordon." Trans. Sahar Amer. Special Issue (1991): 171–81.

Thompson, Kristin. "Early Sound Counterpoint." 60 (1980): 115–40.

Thorlby, Anthony. "Rilke and the Ideal World of Poetry." 9 (1952): 132–42.

Tilton, Elizabeth Meier. "Charles Sorel's Alternative Paradise: The Ideal of Unproblematic Love." 58 (1979): 165–81.

Tirolien, Guy. "The Soul of the Black Land" in "Two Love Poems from the French Colonies." Trans. Miriam Koshland. 11 (1953?): 3.

Tisseron, Serge. "All Writing is Drawing: The Spatial Development of the Manuscript." 84 (1994): 29–42.

Todorov, Tzvetan. "Structuralism and Literary Criticism [Annotated Bibliography]." 36 & 37 (October 1966): 269–70.

———. "Valéry's Poetics." Trans. Elizabeth Willis. 44 (1970): 65–71.

———. "The Discovery of Language: Les liaisons dangereuses and Adolphe." Trans. Frances Chew. 45 (1970): 113–26.

———. "On Literary Genesis." Trans. Ellen Burt. 58 (1979): 214–35.

———. "L'être et l'autre: Montaigne." Trans. Pierre Saint-Amand. 64 (1983): 113–44.

Tolmachev, M. V. "Impressionist-Classicist Tensions." Trans. Harold Beyerly. 34 (June 1965): 29–35.

Tournier, Michel. La goutte d'or [excerpt]. Trans. Barbara Wright. Intro. Christopher Rivers. Special Issue (1988): 115–32.

Tournon, André. "Self-Interpretation in Montaigne's Essais." Trans. Matthew Senior. 64 (1983): 51–72.

Turnell, Martin. "André Gide and the Disintegration of the Protestant Cell." 7 (1951): 21–31.

Ulmer, Gregory L. "'A Night at the Text': Roland Barthes's Marx Brothers." 73 (1987): 38–57.

Ungar, Steven. "Night Moves: Spatial Perception and the Place of Blanchot's Early Fiction." 57 (1979): 124–35.

———. "The Professor of Desire." 63 (1982): 80–97.

———. "Phantom Lascaux: Origin of the Work of Art." 78 (1990): 246–62.

Vaccaro, Jean-Michel. "Metrical Symbolism in Schütz' Historia der Geburt Jesu Christi." Trans. Charles S. Fineman. 47 (1972): 218–31.

Vance, Christie. "La nouvelle Héloïse: The Language of Paris." 45 (1970): 127–36.

Vance, Eugene. "The Word at Heart: Aucassin et Nicolette as a Medieval Comedy of Language." 45 (1970): 33–51.

———. "Chrétien's Yvain and the Ideologies of Change and Exchange." 70 (1986): 42–62.

———. "Style and Value: From Soldier to Pilgrim in the Song of Roland." Special Issue (1991): 75–96.

Vanpée, Janie, and E. S. Burt. "Editors' Preface [Reading the Archive: On Texts and Institutions]." 77 (1990): 1–4.

Vanpée, Janie. "Rousseau's *Emile ou de l'éducation:* A Resistance to Reading." 77 (1990): 156–76.

Vercier, Bruno. "An Interview with Renaud Camus." Trans. Charles A. Porter with Ralph Sarkonak. 90 (1996): 7–21.

Verdier, Philippe. "Delacroix and Shakespeare." 33 (December 1964): 37–45.

Verstraeten, Pierre. "The Negative Theology of Sartre's *Flaubert.*" Trans. Pierre Verstraeten, Philippe Hunt, and Philip Wood. 68 (1985): 152–64.

Véza, Lorette. "A Tentative Approach to Some Recent Novels." 27 (Spring–Summer 1961): 74–80.

Vial, Fernand. "François Mauriac as Dramatic Author." 3.1 or 5 (1950): 68–74.

———. "Symbols and Symbolism in Paul Claudel." 9 (1952): 93–102.

Viala, Alain. "*Les Signes Galants:* A Historical Reevaluation of *Galanterie.*" Trans. Daryl Lee. 92 (1997): 11–29.

Viatte, Françoise. "Weaving a Rope of Sand." Trans. Roland Racevskis. 89 (1996): 85–102.

Vickers, Nancy, Colette Gaudin, Mary Jean Green, Lynn Anthony Higgins, Marianne Hirsch, Vivian Kogan, and Claudia Reeder. "Introduction [*Feminist Readings: French Texts/American Contexts*]." 62 (1981): 2–18.

Vickers, Nancy J., and Ann R. Jones. "Canon, Rule and the Restoration Renaissance." 75 (1988): 9–25.

Vidal-Naquet, Pierre. "Interpreting Revolutionary Change: Political Divisions and Ideological Diversity in the Jewish World of the First Century A.D." Trans. Maria Jolas. 59 (1980): 86–105.

Vigée, Claude. "The Interplay of Love and the Universe in the Work of Lucien Becker." Trans. John Houston. 21 (Spring–Summer 1958): 23–29.

Viggiani, Carl A. "Camus and the Fall from Innocence." 25 (Spring 1960): 65–71.

———. "Camus and *Alger Républicain* 1938–1939." 25 (Spring 1960): 138–43.

Vila, Anne C. "Beyond Sympathy: Vapors, Melancholia, and the Pathologies of Sensibility in Tissot and Rousseau." 92 (1997): 88–101.

Vilar, Jean. "The Director and the Play." Trans. Richard R. Strawn. 3.1 or 5 (1950): 12–26.

Villiers de L'Isle-Adam, Philippe de. "Two Poems ["The Gifts," "The Avowal"]." Trans. Richard Wilbur. 1.2 (Fall–Winter 1948): 118.

Vitz, Evelyn Birge. "Inside/Outside: First-person Narrative in Guillaume de Lorris' *Roman de la Rose.*" 58 (1979): 148–64.

Voisine, Jacques. "Self-Ridicule in *Les confessions.*" 28 (Fall–Winter 1961–62): 55–63.

Voltaire. "A Shakespeare Journal." 33 (December 1964): 5–13.

Vouilloux, Bernard. "Drawing between the Eye and the Hand: (On Rousseau)." Trans. Christine Cano and Peter Hallward. 84 (1994): 175–97.

Vries, Hent de. "'Lapsus Absolu': Notes on Maurice Blanchot's *The Instant of My Death.*" 93 (1998): 30–59.

Vulliet, Armand. "Letters to Claude Lanzmann and to the *Grand Larousse.*" Trans. Madeleine Dobie. 85 (1994): 152–59.

Wadsworth, Philip A. "Ovid and La Fontaine." 38 (May 1967): 151–55.

Walker, Philip. "The Mirror, the Window, and the Eye in Zola's Fiction." 42 (1969): 52–67.

Walzer, P. O. "The Physiology of Sex." Trans. A.A. Littauer and J.L. Logan. 44 (1970): 215–30.

Wardropper, Bruce W. "The Dramatization of Figurative Language in the Spanish Theater." 47 (1972): 189–98.

Warminski, Andrzej. "In Memoriam [Paul de Man]." 69 (1985): 12–13.

———. "Dreadful Reading: Blanchot on Hegel." 69 (1985): 267–75.

———. "Reading Over Endless Histories: Henry James's *Altar of the Dead.*" 74 (1988): 261–84.

———. "Monstrous History: Heidegger Reading Hölderlin." 77 (1990): 193–209.

———. "Hegel/Marx: Consciousness and Life." 88 (1995): 118–41.

Warszawski, Oser. "A Contract (Monologue)." Trans. Alan Astro. 85 (1994): 106–12.

Weber, Eugen. "Psichari and God." 12 (Fall–Winter 1953): 19–33.

Weber, Samuel. "The Vaulted Eye: Remarks on Knowledge and Professionalism." 77 (1990): 44–60.

———. "Double Take: Acting and Writing in Genet's 'L'étrange mot de . . .'" 91 (1997): 28–48.

Weil, Eric. "French Complexes." Trans. Josephine Ott. 15 (Winter 1954–55): 24–29.

Weinberg, Kurt. "Heine and French Poetry." 6 (1950): 45–52.

———. "The Theme of Exile." 25 (Spring 1960): 33–40.

———. "Nietzsche's Paradox of Tragedy." 38 (May 1967): 251–66.

Wellek, René. "French 'Classical' Criticism in the Twentieth Century." 38 (May 1967): 47–71.

Wenzel, Hélène V. "Introduction [*Simone de Beauvoir: Witness to a Century*]." 72 (1986): v–xiv.

———. "Interview with Simone de Beauvoir." Trans. Hélène V. Wenzel. 72 (1986): 5–32.

Whiting, Charles G. "The Case for 'Engaged' Literature." 1.1 (Spring–Summer 1948): 84–89.

———. "Femininity in Valéry's Early Poetry." 9 (1952): 74–83.

———. "Préciosité in 'La jeune Parque' and *Charmes.*" 44 (1970): 119–27.

Wieviorka, Annette. "Jewish Identity in the First Accounts by Extermination

Camp Survivors from France." Trans. Françoise Rosset. 85 (1994): 135–51.

Wieviorka, Wolf. "Too Bad He's a Frenchman." Trans. Alan Astro. 85 (1994): 113–16.

Wilden, Anthony G. "Jacques Lacan: A Partial Bibliography [Annotated Bibliography]." 36 & 37 (October 1966): 263–68.

Williams, Alan. "Is Sound Recording Like a Language?" 60 (1980): 51–66.

Williams, James S. "All Her Sons: Marguerite Duras, Antiliterature, and the Outside." 90 (1996): 47–70.

Williams, L. Pearce. "Robert Aron's History of Vichy." 15 (Winter 1954–55): 115–19.

Wimsatt, William K. "Prufrock and Maud: From Plot to Symbol." 9 (1952): 84–92.

———. "How to Compose Chess Problems, and Why." 41 (1968): 68–85.

———. "In Search of Verbal Mimesis." 52 (1975): 229–48.

Wimsatt, William K., and Janet K. Gezari. "Vladimir Nabokov: More Chess Problems and the Novel." 58 (1979): 102–15.

Winandy, André. "The Twilight Zone: Imagination and Reality in Jules Verne's *Strange Journeys*." Trans. Rita Winandy. 43 (1969): 97–110.

———. "Foreword [*Image and Symbol in the Renaissance*]." 47 (1972): 3.

———. "Piety and Humanistic Symbolism in the Works of Marguerite d'Angoulême, Queen of Navarre." 47 (1972): 145–69.

———. "Rabelais' Barrel." 50 (1974): 8–25.

Wolitz, Seth L. "Imagining the Jew in France: From 1945 to the Present." 85 (1994): 119–34.

Wood, Philip. "Sartre, Anglo-American Marxism, and the Place of the Subject in History." 68 (1985): 15–54.

Woodhull, Winifred. "Exile." 82 (1993): 7–24.

Wright, Gordon. "The Resurgence of the Right in France." 15 (Winter 1954–55): 3–11.

Yelin, Louise. "'Buffoon Odyssey'? Christina Stead's *For Love Alone* and the Writing of Exile." 82 (1993): 183–203.

Zamparelli, Thomas. "Zola and the Quest for the Absolute in Art." 42 (1969): 143–58.

Zanger, Abby. "Making Sweat: Sex and the Gender of National Reproduction in the Marriage of Louis XIII." 86 (1994): 187–205.

Zardoya, Concha. "Present-Day Spanish Poetry." 21 (Spring–Summer 1958): 145–53.

Zéraffa, Michel. "The Young Novelists: Problems of Style and Technique." 8 (1951): 3–8.

Zimra, Clarisse. "Disorienting the Subject in Djebar's *L'amour, la fantasia*." 87 (1995): 149–70.

Zink, Michel. "The Allegorical Poem as Interior Memoir." Trans. Margaret Miner and Kevin Brownlee. 70 (1986): 100–26.

———. "The Time of the Plague and the Order of Writing: Jean le Bel, Froissart, Machaut." Trans. Katherine Lydon. Special Issue (1991): 269–80.

Ziolkowski, Theodore. "Camus in Germany, or the Return of the Prodigal." 25 (Spring 1960): 132–37.

———. "Napoleon's Impact on Germany: A Rapid Survey." 26 (Fall–Winter 1960–1961): 94–105.

———. "Max Frisch: Moralist without a Moral." 29 (Spring–Summer 1962): 132–41.

Zumthor, Paul. "Narrative and Anti-Narrative: *Le Roman de la Rose*." Trans. Frank Yeomans. 51 (1974): 185–204.

———. "The Impossible Closure of the Oral Text." Trans. Jean McGarry. 67 (1984): 25–42.

Contributors

JAMES AUSTIN is a doctoral candidate in French at Yale University. He is currently preparing a dissertation on Proust and pastiche.

R. HOWARD BLOCH is Augustus R. Street Professor of French at Yale University and author of *Medieval French Literature and Law, Etymologies and Genealogies: A Literary Anthropology of the French Middle Ages, The Scandal of the Fabliaux, Medieval Misogyny and the Invention of Western Romantic Love,* and *God's Plagiarist: Being an Account of the Fabulous Industry and Irregular Commerce of the Abbé Jacques-Paul Migne.*

MARYSE CONDÉ is currently the Director of the Center for French and Francophone Studies at Columbia University. Her novels include *I, Tituba, Black Witch of Salem, Crossing the Mangrove,* and, most recently in English, *Windward Heights.* In December 1999 she was awarded the Marguerite Yourcenar Prize for *Le coeur à rire et à pleurer.*

JOAN DEJEAN teaches seventeenth and eighteenth century French literature at the University of Pennsylvania and is the author, most recently, of *Ancients against Moderns: Culture Wars and the Making of a fin de Siècle.*

PAUL DEMAN (1919–1983) was Sterling Professor of Comparative Literature at Yale University. His major works include *Blindness and Insight: Essays in the Rhetoric of Contemporary Criticism, The Resistance to Theory,* and *Allegories of Reading: Figural Language in Rousseau, Nietzsche, Rilke, and Proust.*

CHRISTINE DELPHY is the cofounder (with Simone de Beauvoir) of *Questions Féministes* and of *Nouvelles Questions Féministes,* women's studies journals published in France.

YFS 97, *50 Years of Yale French Studies, Part 2,* ed. Porter and Waters, © 2000 by Yale University.

SHOSHANA FELMAN is the Thomas E. Donnelley Professor of French and Comparative Literature at Yale University. She is the author of *The Literary Speech Act: Don Juan with Austin, or Seduction in Two Languages* (Cornell University Press, 1984), *Writing and Madness: Literature/Philosophy/Psychoanalysis* (Cornell University Press, 1985), *Jacques Lacan and the Adventure of Insight* (Harvard University Press, 1987), and *What does a Woman Want? Reading and Sexual Difference* (Johns Hopkins University Press, 1993). She is also the editor of *Literature and Psychoanalysis: The Question of Reading—Otherwise* (Johns Hopkins University Press, 1982) and co-author, with Dori Laub, or *Testimony: Crises of Witnessing in Literature, Psychoanalysis, and History* (Routledge, 1992).

LAURENT JENNY is Professor of French Literature at the Université de Genève. He is the author of numerous articles and books, including *La terreur et les signes* (Gallimard, 1982) and *La parole singulière* (Berlin, 1990).

RICHARD KLEIN is Professor of French at Cornell University. "Nuclear Criticism," inspired by the work of Jacques Derrida, was an attempt to draw the implications for contemporary culture of the possibility of total nuclear war. The threat having diminished, Klein has authored in the meantime *Cigarettes are Sublime* (Duke University Press), *Eat Fat* (Pantheon), and the forthcoming, *Jewelry Talks (a novel theory)* (Pantheon).

DARYL LEE received his PhD in French Literature from Yale University.

CHARLES A. PORTER, Professor of French at Yale University, has written on Restif de la Bretonne, Chateaubriand, and Renaud Camus, among others.

KRISTIN ROSS is Professor of Comparative Literature at New York University. She is the author of *The Emergence of Social Space: Rimbaud and the Paris Commune* (Minnesota, 1988), *Fast Cars, Clean Bodies: Decolonization and the Reordering of French Culture* (MIT, 1995), and co-editor, with Alice Kaplan, of *Yale French Studies 73: Everyday Life.* She is at work on a book about French cultural memory and the political upheavals of the 1960s.

ALYSON WATERS is the Managing Editor of *Yale French Studies* and a translator. She teaches translation and translation theory in the Yale French Department and has translated Louis Aragon, Eric

Chevillard, Assia Djebar, Margot Kerlidou, and Henri Michaux, among others.

SUSAN WEINER is Assistant Professor of French at Yale University and author of the forthcoming *Enfants Terribles: Femininity, Youth, and the Mass Media in France, 1945–1968* (Johns Hopkins University Press, 2000).

The following issues are available through **Yale University Press**, Customer Service Department, P.O. Box 209040, New Haven, CT 06520-9040.

69 The Lesson of Paul de Man (1985) $17.00
73 Everyday Life (1987) $17.00
75 The Politics of Tradition: Placing Women in French Literature (1988) $17.00
Special Issue: After the Age of Suspicion: The French Novel Today (1989) $17.00
76 Autour de Racine: Studies in Intertextuality (1989) $17.00
77 Reading the Archive: On Texts and Institutions (1990) $17.00
78 On Bataille (1990) $17.00
79 Literature and the Ethical Question (1991) $17.00
Special Issue: Contexts: Style and Value in Medieval Art and Literature (1991) $17.00
80 Baroque Topographies: Literature/History/ Philosophy (1992) $17.00
81 On Leiris (1992) $17.00
82 Post/Colonial Conditions Vol. 1 (1993) $17.00
83 Post/Colonial Conditions Vol. 2 (1993) $17.00
84 Boundaries: Writing and Drawing (1993) $17.00
85 Discourses of Jewish Identity in 20th-Century France (1994) $17.00
86 Corps Mystique, Corps Sacré (1994) $17.00
87 Another Look, Another Woman (1995) $17.00
88 Depositions: Althusser, Balibar, Macherey (1995) $17.00
89 Drafts (1996) $17.00
90 Same Sex / Different Text? Gay and Lesbian Writing in French (1996) $17.00
91 Genet: In the Language of the Enemy (1997) $17.00
92 Exploring the Conversible World (1997) $17.00
93 The Place of Maurice Blanchot (1998) $17.00
94 Libertinage and Modernity (1999) $17.00
95 Rereading Allegory: Essays in Memory of Daniel Poirion (1999) $17.00
96 50 Years of *Yale French Studies*, Part I: 1948-1979 (1999) $17.00

Special subscription rates are available on a calendar-year basis (2 issues per year):
Individual subscriptions $26.00
Institutional subscriptions $30.00

ORDER FORM   **Yale University Press**, P.O. Box 209040, New Haven, CT 06520-9040
I would like to purchase the following individual issues:

_____
_____

For individual issues, please add postage and handling:
Single issue, United States $2.75   Each additional issue $.50
Single issue, foreign countries $5.00   Each additional issue $1.00
Connecticut residents please add sales tax of 6%.

Payment of $_____ is enclosed (including sales tax if applicable).

MasterCard no. _____ Expiration date _____

VISA no. _____ Expiration date _____

Signature _____

SHIP TO _____
_____
_____

See the next page for ordering other back issues. Yale French Studies is also available through Xerox University Microfilms, 300 North Zeeb Road, Ann Arbor, MI 48106.

The following issues are still available through the **Yale French Studies Office**, P.O. Box 208251, New Haven, CT 06520-8251.

19/20 Contemporary Art $3.50	42 Zola $5.00	54 Mallarmé $5.00
33 Shakespeare $3.50	43 The Child's Part $5.00	61 Toward a Theory of Description $6.00
35 Sade $3.50	45 Language as Action $5.00	
39 Literature and Revolution $3.50	46 From Stage to Street $3.50	
	52 Graphesis $5.00	

Add for postage & handling

Single issue, United States $3.00 (Priority Mail)   Each additional issue $1.25
Single issue, United States $1.80 (Third Class)   Each additional issue $ .50
Single issue, foreign countries $2.50 (Book Rate)   Each additional issue $1.50

YALE FRENCH STUDIES, P.O. Box 208251, New Haven, Connecticut 06520-8251
A check made payable to YFS is enclosed. Please send me the following issue(s):

Issue no.   Title   Price

_____ _____

_____ _____

                                                  Postage & handling _____

                                                              Total _____

Name _____

Number/Street _____

City _____ State _____ Zip _____

- -

The following issues are now available through Periodicals Service Company, 11 Main Street, Germantown, N.Y. 12526, Phone: (518) 537-4700. Fax: (518) 537-5899.

1 Critical Bibliography of Existentialism	19/20 Contempoary Art
2 Modern Poets	21 Poetry Since the Liberation
3 Criticism & Creation	22 French Education
4 Literature & Ideas	23 Humor
5 The Modern Theatre	24 Midnight Novelists
6 France and World Literature	25 Albert Camus
7 André Gide	26 The Myth of Napoleon
8 What's Novel in the Novel	27 Women Writers
9 Symbolism	28 Rousseau
10 French-American Literature Relationships	29 The New Dramatists
11 Eros, Variations...	30 Sartre
12 God & the Writer	31 Surrealism
13 Romanticism Revisited	32 Paris in Literature
14 Motley: Today's French Theater	33 Shakespeare in France
15 Social & Political France	34 Proust
16 Foray through Existentialism	48 French Freud
17 The Art of the Cinema	51 Approaches to Medieval Romance
18 Passion & the Intellect, or Malraux	

36/37 Structuralism has been reprinted by Doubleday as an Anchor Book.
55/56 Literature and Psychoanalysis has been reprinted by Johns Hopkins University Press, and can be ordered through Customer Service, Johns Hopkins University Press, Baltimore, MD 21218.